ART WILLIAMS

WITH KAREN KASSEL HUTTO

First Edition, June 2006

Digital Edition, September 2013

Copyright © 2013 by Art Williams

ISBN: 1492989932 , ISBN 13: 9781492989936

All rights reserved under International and Pan-American Copyright Conventions.

Published in the United States, Atlanta, Georgia, 2006.

Published by NightGlass Group.

Visit our Web site at www.ArtWilliamsBest.com

Dedication

"If you want to win, you have to pay the price."

I've said this phrase a million times, but I didn't make it up. I learned it from the man who, outside of my parents, influenced my life the most: Coach Tommy Taylor.

Coach Taylor taught me how to compete and win and to never give up. Because of him, I've achieved more in my life than I ever dreamed possible. But even more special, he taught me how to look inside a human heart and unlock the hidden potential.

What a gift.

Coach Taylor, for 43 years you were a part of my life. You were a second father and a committed friend. In loving memory, I dedicate this book to you...

My coach. My friend.

My hero.

COACH TAYLOR

"A COMPANY OF DESTINY"

In 1963, Norman F. Dacey published the first edition of his book, *What's Wrong with Your Life Insurance*, a powerful best seller that exposed the scams and deceptions of the life insurance industry. In his epilogue, he wrote:

> *Where, now, will the American people find a champion willing and able to harness the strength of this financial giant? Who will lay the present sorry mess open to the light of day? Where will we find a man with the temerity to face these latter-day "untouchables," to stand in the path of this juggernaut and cry "Halt"? When he is found and takes the job and does it, he will never be forgotten, for he will have brought the American people more financial independence and self-respect than a hundred years of Social Security.*

In 1967, a series of remarkable circumstances led Art Williams to read this book. One day he would fulfill this prophecy.

Published by NightGlass Group

All Rights Reserved

Atlanta, Georgia

August 2013

© Art Williams

Table of Contents

CONTENTS

Prologue	**6**
Part I: The Early Years	**7**
1 Cairo U.S.A.	8
2 Greatest Family	10
3 Coach Taylor	14
4 Dream Life	18
Part II: Coaching	**23**
5 Thomasville	24
6 Baxley	26
7 Kendrick	34
8 Toughest Decision	42
Part III: Ten Hard Years	**52**
9 ITT Financial Services	53
10 Waddell & Reed	64
11 Financial Assurance	80
Part IV: Launching the Dream	**95**
12 No Name, Just Cause	96
13 The War Begins 111	108
14 Boe	118
15 National Home Life	122
16 PennCorp	135
Part V: The Glory Years	**146**

17 Greatest Growth Year	147
18 Crossroads	163
19 Going Public	183
20 Big Time	198
21 National Champs	209

Part VI: Golden Era — 224

22 Momentum	225
23 Common Sense	241
24 New Era	257
25 Dynasty	271
26 A Hard Good-bye	292
27 Legacy	296
Epilogue: Looking Back	303

Notes

Co-Author's Note	308
Company Timeline	311
Glossary	317
1989 Top Earners	319
Author's Note	328

Prologue

MARCH 9, 1990.

Opening night of the A.L. Williams convention.

Forty thousand leaders and managers from all over North America pack the seats of the New Orleans Superdome. Stomps, cheers and chants rattle the rafters.

A short, stocky, balding man in a black tuxedo steps to the podium. He shouts into the microphone. "You know what?"

"What?" the audience roars.

"This is mind-boggling!" Cheers and applause explode from the crowd.

The man grips the podium with the same fierce intensity he brings to his work. "Every now and then, if you're lucky, you get to do something really special. Tonight, you are participating in an event that is monumental. *Historic*.

"People ask me all the time – Did you ever dream A.L. Williams would become the magnificent success it is today? No way. I think back to 1977, to those 85 scared but proud people who started this company. There was no reason to suspect we would survive... much less become a great American success story. The number one company in our industry... the largest industry in the world.

The man pauses. He looks hard at the crowd. "I believe the difference between winning and losing is... *this much*.

"To win, you have to do what's right. Tell the truth. Be positive. Never give up. Life will give you what you're willing to fight for.

"This company was built for you to win... Are you willing to fight to make that happen?"

The speech ends with thunderous applause. In years to come, this night will shine, a pinnacle for A.L. Williams, the 13-year-old company that changed an industry and a million lives.

For Art Williams, it marks the beginning... and the end... of an era.

PART I - The Early Years

"A cowboy must never shoot first, hit a smaller man, or take unfair advantage. He must never go back on his word, or a trust confided in him. He must always tell the truth. He must be gentle with children, the elderly and animals. He must be free from racial and religious prejudices. He must help people in distress.

He must be a good worker. He must keep himself clean in thought, speech, action and personal habits. He must respect women, parents and his nation's laws.

The Cowboy is a patriot."

– GENE AUTRY'S "COWBOY CODE"

1 Cairo U.S.A.

Some people grow up, move away and forget all about where they came from. They become different people in different places. Not me. I've traveled all over the world, but I'm pretty much the same Art Williams who grew up in Cairo, Georgia. From the

very beginning, my small-town southern roots defined me. Without them, I doubt my life would've turned out the way it has.

My childhood years came at an extraordinary time in American history, a golden era that no longer exists. I was blessed to be part of an extraordinary family, full of strong people who loved me and believed in me. I lived in a community totally dedicated to helping its young people grow up and become good, solid citizens. I played with champion athletes and worked for world-class coaches. I wasn't a "brain" or the greatest athlete, yet somehow I was given remarkable opportunities to excel in both school and sports. Every day of my youth, special people loved and encouraged me, taught me how to work hard and do right.

All that positive influence pointed me in one direction. More than anything, I wanted to grow up and be a high school football coach, just like my daddy and just like my coach.

THE ORIGINAL "MAYBERRY"

On April 26, 1942, I was born in Waycross, Georgia, and named Arthur Lynch Williams, Jr., after my father. When I was two, we moved 125 miles southwest to the town of Cairo (KAY-roe), population 10,000. Cairo, county seat of Grady County on the state line, is 35 miles north of Tallahassee, Florida. That's where my two brothers, Bill and Don, were born.

Grady County, blessed with rich soil and good weather, back then was one of Georgia's most productive farming areas. In addition to prize-winning livestock, local farmers grew thousands of acres of commercial crops – corn, sorghum, peanuts, sugar cane and cucumbers – on the lush, rolling farmland. The whole county called itself "the nation's Okra Capital."

Cairo sat in the middle of all that and the heart of its industry came from the W.B. Roddenbery Company, a business started by a local man, Dr. Seaborn Anderson Roddenbery. He put Cairo on the map when he opened a general store and started selling his homemade cane syrup out of cypress barrels in 1862. By 1889, he was selling it under his own Roddenbery label. By the time the high school opened in 1910, syrup production was such a vital part of the community's economy that the athletic teams proudly called themselves the Cairo High School Syrupmakers and Syrupmaids.

In 1944, when we moved to Cairo, we found a thriving, middle-class community with all the perks a small southern town could offer. Television didn't exist then, but Andy Griffith could've modeled his "Mayberry" show after Cairo – neat, clean neighborhoods, a busy downtown with a big brick courthouse, department stores and sidewalks, a train depot, fire and police stations, a movie theater, two elementary schools, a middle school, a high school, a hospital, lots of playing fields, a swimming pool and a recreation department. We lived in a real "apple pie" slice of Americana.

THE BEST LIFE

In Cairo, many citizens had lived through the Depression and World War II and they knew what it was like to do without. Yet those hardships somehow united them. They worked to give their children the best life possible. People went out of their way to be friendly. As kids, we played outside all over town until after dark. By the time I got to first grade, Mother would give me money and let me walk the mile into town by myself to get a haircut. Safety? Somebody's mama or daddy was always looking out the window, making sure we were okay.

As kids, we provided "the entertainment." The whole town kept a calendar brimming with Sunday School parties, Boy Scouts and Bible Club at school. Cairo was a sports factory in those years too, and Cairo people supported the teams like you couldn't believe. Our recreation department offered a year-round sports program from age six and up, with football, baseball, basketball, track and swimming. Our "midget" baseball and football teams played in tournaments all over South Georgia. Wherever a Cairo team played, you could always find a loyal fan club, cheering them on. The whole town literally closed down on Friday nights so everyone (and I do mean everyone) could go to the high school football games.

SMALL-TOWN RULES

I have so many good memories of Cairo – Saturday afternoon matinees, ice cream after church, fireworks on Christmas Eve, Sunday drives in Daddy's new car. What a special time and place.

Kids heard the same message everywhere we went – school, church, community and, of course, at home – with no confusion about expectations. If you wanted something, you had to work for it. You didn't lie, steal or cheat. You didn't drink or do drugs. (And if you did, heaven help you; your parents would know before you made it through the front door.) If you got married, you stayed married. You took care of your family, went to church, worked hard at your job.

The entire Cairo community was built on the strong values of strong people, determined to pass that moral code on to their children. Nobody more so than two of the strongest people I've ever known. My parents.

2 The Greatest Family

My father, Arthur Lynch Williams, was born November 18, 1914, and raised in Blakely, Georgia, a small town near the Alabama border. He spent his youth helping his father on their family farm, but he didn't want to be a farmer. Daddy had academic and athletic gifts. He first wanted to attend medical school and become a doctor, but his parents couldn't afford it. Instead, he went to Vanderbilt University on a football and baseball scholarship, playing in the mid-1930s when Vanderbilt fielded teams that made it a national sports powerhouse.

As the first person from his family to earn a scholarship and attend college, Daddy's achievement made him a bit of a hero. His athletic ability and chemistry degree didn't qualify him to be a doctor, but it did make him the next best thing: a teacher and a coach.

Fresh out of college, he landed at the high school in Tifton, Georgia, where he chalked formulas on a blackboard and plays on a clipboard, as physics instructor and assistant football coach. He caught the eye of my mother, Betty Henderson, a high school junior. They married after she graduated in 1940.

The next year, Daddy took a better assistant coaching job at Waycross, where I was born. My parents moved to Cairo when Daddy received his first head coaching position at Cairo High School in 1944.

There's nothing like being the head football coach. Arthur Williams and the mighty Cairo Syrupmakers "clicked" from the first practice. They had a good first season, and an even better second one. So good, in fact, that Daddy's 1945 team went all the way to the South Georgia Championship before the Thomasville Bulldogs, Cairo's arch rival, beat them, 7-6.

Even in this tough loss, Daddy's coaching skills made a big impression. The next week, when Thomasville's Coach Gardner unexpectedly became so ill he was unable to coach his team, he asked my father to take his place – a remarkable opportunity. Can you imagine asking your arch rival to coach your team for the state championship? Amazing! But Coach Gardner had seen what my dad could do. And Thomasville won, of course.

Not long after that, Jordan High School in Columbus, a big AAA school, came calling with a head coaching job. A big step up the coaching ladder, but it also meant our family had to move to Columbus. Before that happened, however, Mr. Julian Roddenbery made a fateful intercession.

THE MIGHTY PICKLE

"Mr. Julian," as everyone in town called him, was the grandson of the original Dr. Roddenbery and the man responsible for changing the W.B. Roddenbery Company from a small-town syrup maker into a national food manufacturer and distributor. He added new product lines – pickles in 1936 and peanut butter in 1937– and created a national image for his company. Along with farming, the Roddenbery syrup and pickle factories provided most of the industry – and jobs – in Cairo.

Mr. Julian was a good businessman and an excellent people person. He loved Cairo and passionately followed all the athletic teams. He rarely missed a game – football, baseball or basketball. If Cairo played, he was there. And if they won, he often treated the players to dinner at a downtown café. Roddenbery office walls gleamed with decades of pictures of Cairo Syrupmakers in red and black uniforms. More than a devoted fan, people joked that when Mr. Julian cut his finger, it bled red and black.

No doubt about it, Mr. Julian was an important man in our town. He liked what Daddy had done for the Cairo football team. And he had a plan that did not include us relocating to Columbus.

Mr. Julian wanted Daddy to stay in Cairo and run his pickle factory.

HOME TO STAY

The offer paid better than coaching and would let our family settle down in Cairo. No more moving from school to school. It also gave Daddy the opportunity to go back to college, an idea he liked. The factory manager job required a master's degree in food chemistry. Mr. Julian would pay Daddy to manage the factory and get his master's degree.

Michigan State University offered the best food chemistry graduate program, so that fall, Daddy happily went off to school – not to Cairo or Columbus as a teacher and coach, but to East Lansing as a graduate student. Mother, my new baby brother Bill, and I stayed in Cairo while Daddy commuted to Michigan. His Cairo football team beat Thomasville and went on to win the 1946 state championship that fall. Though out of coaching, Daddy got credit from most folks for the victory, since he had built the team and most of his players returned from the previous season. It was always a big deal to beat Thomasville. And then to win the state championship... It might as well have been the Super Bowl.

With his master's, Daddy returned to Cairo and worked as head chemist and manager of the Roddenbery Pickle Company until the day he died. He made good use of all those thousands of acres of vegetables in Grady County and invented dozens of new pickle recipes, including his most famous, the okra pickle. His recipes were produced at the plant and sold all over the United States. In fact, under Daddy's management, the Roddenbery factory became the number one producer of pickles in the United States. Old Mr. Julian sure knew what he was doing when he picked my father to run his factory.

Beyond his work, Daddy emerged as a respected member of our church and community and a gifted speaker. If dignitaries visited Cairo, my father often introduced them at public events. He had a knack for getting away with saying outrageous things – not making people mad, but making them laugh.

TED HARRISON, COUSIN:

The best way to describe Arthur Williams was that he was a man's man. Men really liked him. He had a good sense of humor. He was quiet but very strong, under control, a thinker. He was a good fit with Betty because she was an exceptionally strong woman. She was tough – as tough as any man I knew. She would've run over most men. She didn't run over Arthur.

I don't remember watching Daddy coach, but adults in Cairo talked about my father as a great coach and man. It made me want to be a coach, just like him.

In June 2001, nearly 40 years after my father's death, I received a call from Lewis Carr, a former quarterback for Cairo High. He reminisced about the great teams, and closed our conversation by saying, "Coach Williams was like a second dad to me."

Even now, that comment means the world to me.

FAMILY LIFE

Like most women in the 1940s and 50s, my mother, Betty Henderson Williams, was a traditional homemaker. In many ways, she and Daddy were a classic case of "opposites attract" – my father quiet and reserved, my mother outgoing, vocal, a little hot-tempered. With strong beliefs and principles, Mother taught us right from wrong and the value of hard work. She loved each one of us with her whole heart… but she didn't put up with any nonsense. Tough and demanding, she still made it clear we were her number one priority. We might squabble or disagree at home, but if something negative came in from "the outside," Mother stood up for us like a mama bear with cubs. Our staunchest, fiercest ally, Mother was absolutely the glue that held our family together.

Mother always encouraged responsibility, and as we grew up we did lots of odd jobs to earn a little extra money – selling peanuts, shelling peas, taking care of horses. At home, I often babysat my younger brothers so my parents could have a Friday night date. I changed diapers, warmed bottles and got brothers to bed on time. I was just a kid myself, but all that stuff didn't bother me. My parents trusted me to take care of Bill and Don while they were gone, and I didn't let them down.

I admired him greatly, but Daddy and I differed in many ways. With great taste in clothes, he always wore suits and ties to work. And he was a "brain," the studious type.

I hated to dress up, and I could've cared less about school. Daddy was laid back most of the time, but when I brought home report cards covered in Cs, he would stalk out of the room mad. Mother would wink at me and say, "Now Arthur, calm down." Later, she'd put her arms around me and tell me I would do something special one day. She believed in me intensely, holding to the notion I would become successful… even if my grades didn't give a hint of it at the time.

ATTITUDE IS EVERYTHING

Mother often told us, "I don't care what you do, I will always be here for you." But she did have her limits. Her biggest issue? Attitude. She would not tolerate a negative attitude, pouting or quitting. She did not put up with it. No matter what happened, she expected us to stay positive, "look happy" (even if we weren't), and to never, ever quit.

Mother gave us another gift – a strong sense of responsibility to be successful. She had a reason.

My mother grew up in the shadow of very successful grandparents. Her grandfather, known to everyone as Papa Henderson, pretty much built the town of Ocilla, Georgia, (about twenty miles northeast of Tifton) in the early 1900s. Papa Henderson was the local baron – he owned the bank, a large dairy, and lots of land. Mother's parents owned a turpentine business in tiny, rural Alapaha. For schooling, she lived with her grandparents in Ocilla, where she enjoyed a more luxurious lifestyle than her parents could offer.

Until my great-grandfather died, Mother would take us to Ocilla once a month for a big Sunday dinner with Papa Henderson and tell us endless stories about his many accomplishments. Those Sunday dinners with Papa made great memories. Mother's relatives came – her brother, Bob Henderson and his family from Cairo, and her sister, Ann Harrison, and her family from Tallahassee, including her son Ted, who became as close as a brother and would one day play a key role in my future.

Everyone brought food like you couldn't believe. They'd fill up a long table with chicken, ham, roast beef, creamed potatoes, gravy, biscuits, rolls, a dozen vegetable dishes, casseroles, homemade pies and cakes. Plenty of sweet tea sweated the pitchers and Daddy always brought his latest pickle recipes. We'd sit down and eat like crazy. After dessert, the women would throw a sheet over the table, and we kids would go off and play while the adults caught up on the news. At suppertime, the sheet came off and we ate all over again. Hog heaven!

Mother's father inherited Papa's fortune, but sadly lost it all in bad business decisions, a source of deep disappointment for my mother. Her positive and exuberant spirit overcame that hurt though. She looked to us, her children, to do our best in future professions, whatever they might be. Responsibility to family, to her, was everything.

3 Coach Taylor

Coach Tommy Taylor, hired as Cairo's first full-time Recreation Director, moved to town in 1953. He brought a vision and a work ethic that would change the lives of hundreds of kids in the next 20 years.

Born in California, Coach Taylor graduated from San Diego High School in 1943, then served two years in the Air Force as a flight officer, bombardier and navigator in World War II. After the war, he attended two years of junior college in Fort Myers, Florida, before transferring in 1946 to the University of Florida in Gainesville. He earned his bachelor's degree there, with a double major – Physical Education and Health, and Recreation and Athletics, plus a Speech minor. He lettered in varsity track three years as one of the country's top pole vaulters, matched wits with peers as a member of the debate team, and graduated with honors in 1949. Coach Taylor stayed one more year as a graduate assistant, pursuing a master's degree in Administration and Supervision of Secondary Schools. An excellent tennis player, he coached the Junior Davis Cup for the state of Florida that year. On the way to achieving his master's degree, once again with honors, at Florida State University, he pitched in the 1949 fastpitch softball World Tourney and was voted Most Valuable Player.

When he arrived in Cairo, Coach Taylor was not quite 30 years old, married with children, and wise beyond his years. He had played, coached and excelled in just about every sport known to man… and he had a gift and a passion for transferring that knowledge to kids.

Most people wanted to coach high school, but Coach Taylor loved youngsters. He understood instinctively that every child, even as young as six or seven years old, wanted to "be somebody," and he found all kinds of ways to get kids involved in athletics.

Coach Taylor made it clear he took his job seriously. He wasn't somebody's dad volunteering in his off-hours. He was professional, full-time, serious about winning. He immediately set up a year-round sports program that knocked the socks off of anything Cairo had seen before. He started fall football leagues, winter basketball, spring track and field programs, summer baseball and swim teams. He organized huge county field days with track meets and basketball tournaments.

Coach Taylor gave away hundreds of ribbons at every organized sports event. If a kid showed up and did something, he went home with a ribbon. At every elementary, middle school and high school in Grady County, Coach Taylor posted record boards: most sit-ups, most push-ups, fastest 100-yard dash, and so on. I stenciled in hundreds of names on those record boards. It was a big deal to be a "record holder," let me tell you, and Coach Taylor knew it. He used those boards to motivate kids to the next level – run faster, jump higher, throw farther. And it worked.

Coach Taylor's efforts created a first-rate "feeder" program that started in the lowest elementary grades. Over time, that program transformed Cairo from an average competitor into a high school sports powerhouse. The "mighty Syrupmakers" lived up to their name under his watch.

No doubt about it, Coach Taylor was a world-class coach. And I was lucky enough to grow close to him.

"Coach Taylor was the Pied Piper of Hamlin for all the young boys in Cairo. They followed him everywhere and they did whatever he said. He could get them to do anything."

– ANGELA WILLIAMS

FIRST JOB

In all my 11 years, I'd never met a tougher, more competitive, more positive person than Coach Taylor. I couldn't get enough of him. Neither could the other kids in Cairo.

Like my parents, Coach Taylor believed in giving kids responsibility and teaching them the value of hard work. He took one look at me and put me to work. Electronics lay years in the future at the baseball park in 1953, so for 25 cents a night, I would sit in centerfield and hang wooden score cards on nails during games. Then I cleaned up the ballpark after everybody went home.

My first job gave me a new level of maturity. I had spending money. I could pay my own way when I wanted something extra – a hamburger or ice cream or a movie. I liked it so much, I worked for Coach Taylor the next 11 years. I never asked my parents for money, even after I graduated and went off to college.

WINNER

Coach Taylor caused quite a sensation in town, and just as Mr. Julian saw something special in my father, the school administrators at Cairo High School recognized Coach Taylor's talents and hired him as their full-time track coach in 1955.

What a great decision. For the next 18 years, Cairo never lost a regional track championship – 118 wins and zero losses. Even more impressive, they won the state championship 12 of those 18 years. A couple of years later, Coach Taylor became Cairo High's head basketball coach, and he built a tremendous program there, too – 361 wins and 73 losses, nine regional championships and two back-to-back state championships. He also became the assistant football coach. From 1953 to 1973, working two full-time jobs, Coach Taylor racked up a winning record that was just unbelievable.

Folks in Cairo weren't the only ones with this opinion. Coach Taylor's brilliance earned him 32 "Coach of the Year" awards. Perhaps his greatest honor was being named "Southeast United States Coach of the Year" in track. Twice.

AS REC DIRECTOR:

- 6 fastpitch softball state championships
- 4 midget football state championships
- 3 midget track state championships
- 2 swimming state championships
- 1 midget basketball state championship

TOTAL: 16 STATE CHAMPIONSHIPS

AT CAIRO HIGH:

- 12 track state championships, 5 years consecutive
- 2 basketball state championships, back-to-back years

TOTAL: 14 STATE CHAMPIONSHIPS

FANATIC

Coach Taylor's real gift came in strategizing, a discipline that eventually earned him the nickname "the old gray fox." To him, there was no excuse for being disorganized, even if it meant staying up all night planning! He approached every event he coached with the same intensity. Whether it was a midget football game or a high school state basketball championship – he wanted to win.

Coach Taylor held all of us to the same high standards. He drew unprecedented performances from his players. Want to know the reason I ended up attending college on a full football scholarship? Coach Taylor… and he did that for dozens of other players. He just had a knack for seeing the potential in kids, and over and over, he coached average, ordinary athletes to do extraordinary things.

Richard Crane is a good example. Coach Taylor took one look at Richard and recruited him for the track team. I don't think Richard even knew what track was… but he learned. He became a discus thrower and shot putter. It wasn't easy. Coach Taylor often had to go by Richard's house and make him come to practice. He simply refused to let Richard quit. In the end, Richard earned a full track scholarship to Auburn University and broke the all-time Southeastern Conference discus record.

GYM RAT

Once in high school, I never went on vacation with my family again. I was practicing, playing or working for Coach Taylor. For Coach, Christmas holidays were an opportunity – to practice basketball, not once, but twice a day. I loved it.

I spent thousands of hours with Coach Taylor. I'd go to school until three, practice whatever sport was in season until 5:30, and then I'd go to work, coaching midget football, basketball or swimming. After that, I'd head to Coach Taylor's office at the Rec Department, and we'd talk until dark.

Night after night, I drilled him with questions about coaching. I wanted to know everything, and he would patiently answer every question. I'd become a gym rat, a kid who couldn't get enough of sports. For some reason, Coach Taylor took the time with me. I yearned for the day when I could be a coach like him. He held an awe-inspiring respect among so many Cairo athletes and I longed to motivate kids the same way.

RULES FOR LIFE

Many years later, in 1993, we honored Coach Taylor with a special reunion. Many of his players came back to Cairo from all over the United States. The town declared it "Tommy Taylor Day," and officials in a special dedication service named the Cairo High School track in his honor.

A grand celebration and well deserved. At the reunion banquet, Coach Taylor handed out a business card printed with a few "rules to his boys." They summed up his coaching philosophy, but even more importantly, they captured the simple but powerful philosophy he lived by.

I still have that card. Those three basic principles formed the bedrock of my management philosophy in both coaching and business. They are the "keys to success" in any organization – business, school, church, club, you name it.

I realized one other thing that night, too – how deeply Coach Taylor's recognition and motivation principles had sunk into my thinking. Watching Coach Taylor all those years, it became crystal clear that recognition is a powerful force in building a team. Everyone wants praise for a job well done, whether you are a kid running a relay race or an adult building a business. If you praise and recognize successful behavior, chances are a person will repeat the performance.

Years after those days with Coach Taylor, A.L. Williams became world famous for recognition. Door-sized plaques, six-foot high trophies, Super Bowl rings, Rolex watches, trips to Europe and Hawaii, and of course, our famous T-shirts – we found inventive and memorable ways to praise our leaders for top performances.

I owe that to Coach Taylor, the master motivator. I owe that much and more. He was like my second dad, and he will always be the greatest coach in the world to me.

I didn't know it at the time, but the lessons I learned from him in Cairo would shape my future in profound ways.

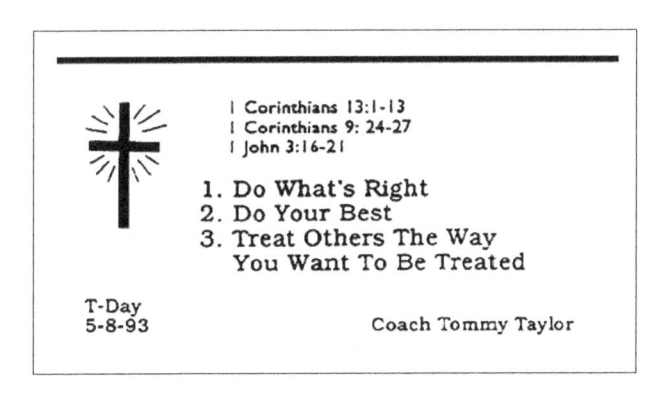

I Corinthians 13:1-13
I Corinthians 9: 24-27
I John 3:16-21

1. **Do What's Right**
2. **Do Your Best**
3. **Treat Others The Way You Want To Be Treated**

T-Day
5-8-93

Coach Tommy Taylor

4 Dream Life

By the time I was 15 and in the tenth grade, I was pretty self-sufficient. I played sports in the school year and managed the city swimming pool and the ballpark during summers and holidays. My parents bought me my first car, a 1952 red Studebaker. I didn't have a learner's license but I could still drive, one of the benefits of living in a small town in 1957. Mother and Daddy trusted my ability to be a responsible driver and to take care of the car. Daddy made it clear it was up to me to keep it repaired, gassed up and clean. And buddy, I did. You saw never anyone take better care of a car. I wouldn't let my friends get in and spill milkshakes on the seats or leave trash on the floor. I certainly didn't burn rubber – I was paying for those dadgum tires!

About that time, Coach Taylor put me in charge of coaching a midget football team. I ate it up. I didn't like coaching, I loved it. I loved working with those 12-year olds. Everything I learned from Coach Taylor I tried out on them, along with some of my own "fundamentals." Our team did well – we earned the huge honor of a spot at the Midget Bowl, held in Waycross for teams all over Georgia. Parents helped out, of course, but it was up to me to plan every detail of the two-night trip, to get the boys there and coach the games. I loved strategizing and calling the plays. What a great experience for all of us.

WINNING

Along this time, I began dating my sweetheart, Angela Hancock. I fell in love with Angela in the second grade. I know that sounds corny, but it's true. She sat in front of me in school, and I fell in love with her ponytail.

Angela was oldest of three girls and her father held the important job of being a family doctor in town. As we grew up together, I always had a sense that Angela was "the one."

By the time we reached the fifth grade, we would walk downtown to the Saturday afternoon show with all our friends. Our parents never worried about safety or if the movie was fit to watch. The price was right, too. I paid for both of us with my hard-earned money – 15 cents a ticket, a nickel each for popcorn and a Coke.

Westerns drew the crowds back then, and the Cairo theater showed dozens of them at the Saturday matinee, both new and old releases. Adventures of big-screen cowboys like Roy Rogers, Gene Autry, Hopalong Cassidy and Tom Mix simply took our breath away. The stories rarely varied – lots of bad guys and plenty of shoot-outs. In the end, the good guys always won. After such pure inspiration, I would swagger out of the theater on top of the world. Sometimes I wore my gun and holster set from Christmas.

In my 11-year-old mind, I was just like Roy and Gene – bring on the bad guys, I'd take all comers! I had the fastest gun and the prettiest girl.

By eighth and ninth grade though, my attention turned completely to sports. Then, in high school, I just "took off." As a freshman, I played three sports, football, basketball and baseball, lettering in all. I think it's a shame that high schools today have grown so big that kids have to choose one sport. Most only get to play varsity just their junior and senior years. I lettered in three sports all four years of high school and loved every minute of it.

As the starting quarterback my sophomore, junior and senior years, football ruled! Coach West Thomas, my football coach and another very influential man in my life, even let me call the plays – something I didn't have the guts to let my own quarterbacks do later on.

LOSING

I knew disappointment, too. My junior year in high school, our football team ranked number one in the state all season long. What a big deal, let me tell you! Our school was pumped, and so was the entire town. The last game of the year, we played – who else – Thomasville.

In the two previous football seasons combined, we won 18 and lost only two… with both losses to Thomasville. Talk about tough games. The first loss? 7-0. The second loss, 2-0. We missed a field goal on the last play of the game. The Bulldogs always played tough, but this season we had everything in our favor – our whole team back, a number one state ranking, a season full of wins. In my mind, there was already a big check mark in the Win column for the mighty Syrupmakers. On the bus ride to Thomasville, I told Coach Thomas, "There is no way we'll lose."

We lost, 14-7.

We were *devastated*. The whole town went into mourning. I will never forget that game. It gave me nightmares for the next 40 years. But it taught me a lesson. You can never let down. You can never think you've won until you actually have. Complacency and overconfidence pave the road to losing.

Years later, a company called Prudential would pay the price for that loss.

DECISIONS

Going into my senior year, I hoped for a repeat of my junior year – only with a better ending. But in the fifth game of the season, I got tackled running the ball and broke my arm. Just like that, my high school football career ended.

Until then, big colleges scouted me regularly. They stopped looking after I broke my arm. I watched my team finish the season without me, wondering what the future would hold.

Even with this setback, life was good. I made the South Georgia All-Star team as a quarterback, a huge honor. We won the regional championship in basketball and lost a tough game in the semi-finals of the state tournament. In school, classmates elected me president of our senior class and "Mr. Cairo High School" – really special honors.

Angela Hancock, my wife-to-be, knew these honors wouldn't affect the person inside me: "Art's mother, as well as Tommy Taylor, taught Art to be aggressive and competitive on the ball field. But socially he was quiet. If there was a sock hop after the game, he almost never stayed, and if he did he sat along the wall. He usually went home and went to bed. He had no interest in tearing around town in his car. He was voted 'Mr. CHS' not because he was flashy, but because he was a hard worker and led by example, even at that age."

Spring baseball went well. In fact, the St. Louis Cardinals called me about a minor league contract. I'd always had my heart set on playing college football, but now the possibility of playing professional baseball really turned my head.

Daddy had other ideas. Determined to see me get a college education, he immediately killed all talks with the Cardinals and enrolled me at The Citadel in Charleston. He even secured a football scholarship for me. To please him, I spent a weekend there but hated it. I had no interest in military discipline and I sure didn't like the idea of wearing a formal uniform and tie to class every day. Even then, I hated ties.

Then Presbyterian College, an all-boys school in Clinton, South Carolina, offered me a football scholarship. I told Daddy I wanted to go there. He agreed, but he wasn't happy about it. He'd set his heart on seeing his oldest son play football for The Citadel.

ANGELA

That fall, Angela and I went separate ways for the first time in our lives. She enrolled at Wesleyan College, a small all-girls school in Macon, Georgia. As a quarterback for Presbyterian, I had to report to practice two weeks earlier than other teammates. The South Georgia All-Star game meant I had to leave home a week before that.

So, one Sunday afternoon in early August, I packed the car and headed off to Georgia Tech in Atlanta. That Friday night, we played our North vs. South game at Grant Field, Georgia Tech's stadium, in front of 28,000 people. My South team won, 28-0 – a great way to end my high school football career.

I drove to Clinton and immediately began football workouts at PC. Once the season started, football players were required to stay at school. We practiced all week and played every Saturday – nobody went home.

Boy, that was different. I had never been away from home. In high school I didn't even go away on vacations with my family. Adjusting to schoolwork and the PC football program was tougher than I expected. I felt lonesome and homesick. Angela came to visit a few weekends, and that helped me survive.

On Thanksgiving Day, PC played Newbury. When the game ended, I got in my car and drove home like a maniac. After four months, it was great to be home, and an even greater relief to be with Angela. We'd been absolutely miserable apart.

We made a decision then, and did something that every young couple thinks about at least once when they're madly in love: We ran off and got married.

DADDY

At the end of my sophomore year, PC's head football coach, Frank Jones, took a head offensive coordinator position at Mississippi State University. Coach Jones asked me to go with him and arranged for a full football scholarship. The move to Mississippi State improved life in every way. Starting off our junior year, Angela and I moved into married housing with our first baby, Arthur Lynch Williams III. MSU offered us far better options for completing our degrees – English for Angela and physical education for me. Both of us attended with full scholarships, so financially we were fine, even on our limited budget. We "settled" as a family for the first time since leaving home, and finally enjoyed college life.

Our junior year, busy with football, classes and our baby, we absolutely had a ball at MSU. We enjoyed being together as a couple, loved being parents, loved our classes, made terrific new friends. Still, by the time we pulled into Cairo for Easter break in April 1963, we were tired and anxious to wrap up the school year.

That Thursday night, Angela and I went out to dinner in Tallahassee with her parents, Dr. and Mrs. Hancock. Mother was at a card party, while Daddy stayed home with Don. Driving back from the restaurant, a feeling of sickness hit me unexpectedly. All of a sudden, I just felt *terrible*. Looking back, it was probably some kind of premonition.

As we pulled into the Hancocks' driveway, J.B. Davis, a family friend and neighbor, waited at the back door. Mrs. Hancock got out of the car first. Mr. Davis told her something and and she began to cry. Angela flew over the backseat, frantic that something had happened to our baby. But it wasn't Art. It was my father. Daddy had suffered a heart attack while we were gone. He'd been rushed to the hospital. Dr. Hancock immediately took off to the hospital to help. Another family friend, Mary Thomas, drove up and took Angela and me to my parents' house, one block away.

I was wondering how long it took to recover from a heart attack when Mary turned and said, "Art, I'm so sorry your dad didn't make it."

In that moment, the bubble popped on my perfect little "Mayberry" world. I never imagined this. Daddy was only 48 years old, young and strong. He *couldn't* be dead. I just couldn't take it in.

Our house was already full of people when we got there. I took one look at my devastated mother and burst into tears. Somebody told me the story: Daddy went to check on something at the pickle factory and had a massive heart attack on the way home. Someone found him in his car at a filling station, where he'd apparently eased it into the parking lot as the attack came on. The ambulance came, but Daddy was dead before they got him to the hospital.

It was more awful than I could stand. I think every person in Cairo came over that day. People brought food, comforted Mother, talked, ate, cleaned up. They meant well, of course. In normal times, I loved being surrounded by a houseful of friends and relatives in a warm hubbub of food and conversation. Not now. The next few days passed in slow motion. I just wished they would all go home. I didn't want to talk or eat. I just wanted to be alone with my family. I wanted to make the ache in my heart go away.

GOOD-BYE, CAIRO

My years in Cairo had prepared me well.

My mother's driving spirit had instilled a strong desire to do something important, to "be somebody." My father had taught me money management, Coach Taylor toughness.

Outstanding high school teams taught me how to "win big." Life did not scare or intimidate me. I knew I was meant to do something special with my life.

Funny thing, though – I was a regular kid. An average student. Never studied. Never took home a book. A good athlete, but not a great one. Certainly not a superstar like Bill Stanfill or Bobby Walden, two Cairo athletes who went on to play pro football.

Yet for some reason, the good Lord saw fit to put me in a world that offered so much opportunity and success. I was given loving parents who made me feel special. I grew up in a tight-knit community that loved kids and sports. From the fifth grade on I had a paying job. Coaching by 15, I took a team to the Midget Bowl in Waycross, and lettered in three sports through high school.

I had the gift of hundreds of hours with Coach Taylor, my hero, working for him, learning to coach. I earned a football scholarship and even got a college degree. To top it off, I married the girl I'd loved all my life.

No doubt about it – my early years were a "dream life." Idealistic. Inspirational.

Self-assured. Just like in those cowboy movies, things got a little hard now and then. But in the end, they always just seemed to go my way.

With Daddy gone, that era in my life ended. Looking at Mother, Bill and Don, I knew nothing would ever be the same again. Already Mother leaned on me for support and advice.

None of us had the power, of course, to imagine how profoundly the loss of my father would affect us. His passing marked one of those turning points in every life. It forever changed our family. One day, it would ignite in me a new passion and a cause that would affect the lives of millions.

But for now, there was only grief. It was simply beyond my ability to see how anything good could come out of something so sad.

PART II - Coaching

COACHING

"You must learn how to hold a team together. You lift some men up… calm others down…until finally, they've got one heartbeat. Then, you've got yourself a team."

– COACH "BEAR" BRYANT

5 Thomasville

Mother always told me, "Art, you were born an old man." With my father's untimely passing, that statement never seemed truer. It brought a new level of seriousness to my life.

I looked at my mother and saw how scared she was. Daddy had left her with no will, not much savings, and too little life insurance. She had no formal education. She had never worked outside the home. For my father's 17 years of hard work at the pickle company – dozens of original recipes, product line development, number one pickle company in the country and so on – Julian Roddenbery awarded my mother one year's salary, about $10,000. How would that keep the family running from day to day for very long?

As a family we had always been extraordinarily close, so seeing Mother in this situation troubled me. A lot. With my jobs and college scholarship, I didn't depend on my parents to pay my bills and never worried whether they could pay theirs. Suddenly I felt responsible for Mother and my younger brothers, both of whom were still in school – Bill, a junior in high school and Don, a sixth grader. In a sense, I became head of two families the day my father died – my own and my mother's. A new leadership position… and it changed me.

MOVING ON

For starters, college took on a whole new meaning. Until now, content to just get by, I'd been an average "C" student. Not any more. People depended on me. School had a purpose. Instead of B's and C's, I started making A's. I took more classes each semester and pushed through a year-and-a-half of school in one year. The transfer from PC to MSU extended my football scholarship from two to three years, but I couldn't justify staying in college another year just to play football. My football career would end here, with no professional contracts in my future. The time had come to get my degree and start earning a living.

When Angela and I finished Mississippi State in spring 1964, we didn't even stay for the graduation ceremonies. Somehow, putting on a cap and gown and walking down the aisle seemed like a waste of time. Instead, we packed up a U-Haul and our children (our daughter, April, came three weeks before graduation), and headed back to Cairo. I worked at the Recreation Department that summer, and we lived at home with both my mother and Angela's parents.

Years later in A.L. Williams, I often talked about how we are "only here for a flicker." A burning sense of urgency to "do something big" and take life seriously came alive when my father died. For the first time, I understood how brief life is. There would be many funerals to come, but none of them, not even Mother's, ever hit me as hard as Daddy's. He was simply too young and too strong to be gone.

It only made things worse to realize that he had died without us ever exchanging a father-son "I love you." That type of affection just wasn't done in those days.

COACH AT LAST

In the final months of college, I applied for every coaching job I could find in South Georgia. Angela and I wanted to stay as close to Cairo as possible to be near our families.

An unbelievable blessing came to us – my first coaching job, as offensive and defensive backfield coach at Thomasville High School, just 12 miles from Cairo. Angela got a position there, too, as an English teacher. We were pleased; our parents were pleased. We moved in August and dug right in.

For the first time in our married lives, Angela and I experienced a little financial "breathing room." Together, our salaries added up to about $9,000 (before taxes) – to us, a fortune. For years, we had lived off $1,200 a year – my annual income from working summers and holidays at the Rec Department. We rented an apartment in Thomasville for $75 a month and lived off my salary, putting all of Angela's income in a savings account, about $2,700. We'd never had that much money in our life!

We spent two very enjoyable years in Thomasville. Just 12 miles from home, we saw our families any time we wanted. Mother, Bill and Don visited often. We had two great kids, lots of friends, money in the bank, and I was doing what I'd dreamed of all my life: coaching football.

BULLDOG FEVER

As fanatical as Cairo was about football, Thomasville took it a notch higher. I couldn't help but remember all those hard-fought football games against them in high school, especially that extra bitter loss my junior year. But I worked as a Thomasville coach now. Friday nights were electric and, just like in Cairo, every person in Thomasville came to the games. The townspeople raved about their Bulldogs, and I enjoyed the team spirit, even when we played Cairo. In fact, Cairo beat Thomasville my first year, thanks in large part to Bill Stanfill, who went on to play for the University of Georgia and win the Outland trophy as the nation's number one college defensive lineman. Later, he made All-Pro four times with the Miami Dolphins – a real superstar.

Thomasville's head coach, Joe Sumrall, proved to be an excellent coach and teacher. My strength was offense and Coach Sumrall gave me a lot of freedom and responsibility, letting me call the plays my second year. I introduced a passing offense different from the ball-control style he had run for years. On defense, I had much to learn and he took the time to teach key principles that made me a "total" football coach.

Just for fun, I started a weekly recognition program called the "Mad Dog" Award. I had Angela paint a giant picture of a fierce-looking bulldog, which I posted in the lunchroom. Every Friday, I got the team together in front of that picture and honored the "Mad Dog" players of the week. This little thing made a big difference on the field. Everybody wanted to be a "Mad Dog." It confirmed all I had learned during my years with Coach Taylor.

Giving praise in private is valuable, but it doesn't compare to giving it in front of a group. Something really powerful comes with public praise for a person after a job done well. It motivates the whole group to improve.

We fielded two great teams during my stay in Thomasville; both were ranked top 10 in the state. The second year, we should've won the state championship… but we got beat by an Atlanta school 7-6 in the semi-finals. We had the better team. We won every statistic. But we lost on the scoreboard – the only number that counts.

Yes, life was good in Thomasville. Except for one little problem…

I was miserable.

6 Baxley

In 1966, near the end of my second year at Thomasville, I began applying for every head football coaching position I could find in Georgia. More than anything I wanted to be the head coach, not an assistant.

Everything in my background prepared me for that position. My coaching experience stretched back to the fifth grade. I was ready, but convincing a school to hire me? Even high schools looked for experienced guys, usually with 10 or more years as a head coach.

Then the break came. The head football coach position opened at Appling County High School in Baxley, Georgia, a town of about 12,000 people. I think Baxley offered me that job because my Cairo football coach, West Thomas, coached winning teams at Baxley 20 years earlier. Baxley's current teams were not exactly what you call "winning." In fact, they had won just one game in two years and hadn't seen a winning season since Coach Thomas. They could afford to take a chance on me. What did they have to lose?

Before signing the contract, I went to see Charles McDaniel, the superintendent of Thomas County schools, where I currently coached at Thomasville. What he told me almost made my teeth fall out: Coach Sumrall might be leaving. Mr. McDaniel knew I had been looking for a head coach position and he wanted to offer me the job… if Coach Sumrall left. I was flattered beyond belief. Thomasville, one of the best football schools in the state of Georgia, had everything – winning tradition, great players, total community support, an established program. You were practically guaranteed to win nine or 10 games a season. Head coach in Thomasville? A dream come true, the best of all worlds.

I went to see Coach Sumrall. I told him about my situation and the conversation with Mr. McDaniel. He confided that he had considered a coaching position in Mississippi, but decided not to take it. He would stay in Thomasville. So, with Coach Sumrall securely in his position at Thomasville, I accepted my first head coaching job at Baxley.

SPRING

Our new community tested Angela and me at first. We had felt so at home in Thomasville and Baxley was all new. But with our usual enthusiasm, we poured our energy into fixing up our first house and getting involved at school. We felt "rich" financially, too – my salary took a big jump to $6,300.

As the new football coach, I knew my first job – to rally the community around my cause. I set out to visit all the social clubs in town, introduce myself, explain my philosophy for a winning football team. At school, I told students that the Appling County Pirates were done losing. Count on it, I said – our football team is going to be great.

My PR campaign worked. The whole town buzzed about football and 75 boys came out for spring practice. I was so excited!

With my Cairo-Thomasville football heritage, I started right in with tough practices. What a shock. I expected the boys to need a lot of work… but these players knew almost nothing about football. After two weeks of practice, my two "experienced" quarterbacks quit. The "team" withered down to a mere 19 players, and a couple of these had never played football before. What a mess.

In the middle of this ordeal, an interesting bit of news came my way: Coach Sumrall had decided to leave Thomasville after all! He'd accepted the head coach position at Warner Robins High School in Warner Robins, Georgia.

I felt sick. Here was my dream job, suddenly available… and I couldn't take it. I was already under contract at Baxley, and I'd made a personal commitment to my 19 players. I couldn't leave.

LOU MILLER, BAXLEY DEFENSIVE COACH:

That fact that Art stayed in Baxley shows a lot about his character. He was offered the Thomasville job after he took the position at Baxley. Most people would've gone back on their promise and taken the Thomasville job – it was one of the best football coaching jobs in Georgia. But he had made the commitment to Baxley and he stayed.

Brushing it off, I set up a scrimmage game against last year's seniors – the team that won just one game in two years.

The whole town showed up on a spring Friday night to watch. The boys on the other team, the "old" seniors, straggled in minutes before game time. I handed out their pads, realizing they didn't have a coach and hadn't bothered to practice. Well, this ought to be interesting, I thought. I expected to beat them 100 to nothing.

Boy, was I wrong.

We lost, and I mean we lost bad. After four weeks of grueling practice, a bunch of guys who could've cared less just totally put us to shame.

Watching that ragtag team slink off the field, I saw my whole coaching career go up in flames.

That weekend, I sunk to a new low. I moped, I cried, I pouted. I second-guessed every part of my decision to leave Thomasville and come to Baxley. Back in Thomasville, I would've been coaching one of the best football teams in Georgia. Instead, I was stuck in Baxley, the same tough league as Thomasville, with no players, no program, no traditions. I didn't see any way in the world to win.

TURNING POINT

It called for a hard personal decision. I could drag into school looking the way I felt – defeated and depressed – or I could live the lesson Mother taught me and act happy anyway. I thought about Coach Taylor, too. What would he do? Well, that made it easy.

Monday morning came. I marched into the principal's office, grabbed the PA microphone and called the football players down to the locker room, all 19 of them.

I looked at those boys, heads down, staring at the floor. They had been humiliated in front of the whole town, beaten by last year's losers. I knew I sat on a powder keg, and my attitude could either set off an explosion or power us to a whole new level. It was up to me. I don't know what these boys expected me to say, but I gave it to them straight:

"Fellas, I want to tell you something. When I came to Baxley, I told you I was a stud and we were going to do something big and special with this team. You all came out here and believed me. We started with 75, now we have 19. Before last Friday night, three groups of people thought we were going to win: us, the school and the town. Only one group thinks we're going to win now and that's us.

"The school doesn't think we can do it. The town thinks we are going to be a joke around here, just like always.

"But I can flat tell you this – I ain't nothin' but a double stud, and we *are* going to win! As good as I thought the opportunity was four weeks ago, it's 10 times better today... because nobody expects us to win. But we *are* going to win! No doubt in my mind. And we're going to look like heroes to everybody."

When I stopped talking, those boys weren't looking at the floor anymore. They stared at me, the light back in their eyes. They saw I was serious, I believed what I was saying. That moment was a turning point in my life – and theirs. We chose to face that first test with strength instead of defeat. It made all the difference. Nothing had changed from Friday night to Monday morning – nothing but our perspective.

I still had a mountain to climb, but now I had something to fight for – my promise to those boys that we would win.

In Thomasville, I probably would've coached that team to the state championship. Thomasville had been a winning team for 40 years. But in truth, I would've just been carrying on someone else's tradition, just executing a long established program.

At Baxley, I had an opportunity. I could build a program from scratch. I could create the traditions myself. I could teach those boys, all 19 of them, how to play real football.

I had a chance to really make a difference.

SUMMER

From that day on, I did everything I could to give those kids a little pride. I brought in weights, something they'd never had, and started them on a summer weight-lifting program. I painted the locker room and hung up motivational signs like "The Difference between Champ and Chump is U," and "The Harder You Work the Luckier You Get." I got permission from the school to buy new uniforms and rent an air-conditioned Greyhound bus for our away games, another first. I wanted those kids to know they were "somebody," a team worth fighting for.

I needed a good assistant, so I called up Lou Miller, a fellow football player and fraternity buddy from Presbyterian College. He agreed to be my defensive coach. That summer, we sat down and put together a football program from scratch.

How? First, we threw out the two-inch thick playbook I'd built since Thomasville. These boys didn't understand the game and didn't know how to win. We didn't need anything "fancy" or "pretty;" we needed simplicity. Lou and I drew up a seven-page playbook. Our only chance to win was to be tougher – mentally and physically – than our competition.

Late in July, we packed up and went to a football camp in South Carolina with five other teams. The first morning, Lou and I had the whole team out for a three-mile run at 6 a.m. Our boys didn't know what to think. They had never been asked to do such a "crazy" thing before and they took a lot of ribbing from the other players.

"Coach Williams and Coach Miller had us convinced we were going to this camp in the mountains where it was cool," remembers our quarterback, George Thomas. "Actually it was somewhere in South Carolina by a swamp, about 110 degrees in the shade. But we got up early and ran hard. We beat all the other teams in camp. We were just in better shape than everyone else."

The teams paired up to scrimmage every day. We won the first two games we played. After that, two teams quietly joined us for our 6 a.m. run. For the first time ever, my players got a taste of winning. Other teams copying what we did? That had never happened to Baxley boys before. What a turnaround. It was exciting… but boy, did we still have a long way to go.

- - - - - - - - - - -

"Coach Williams came my senior year. I'd never played quarterback. He called me "Little Man" because I was – 135 pounds. Coach Williams made us believe we were winners and demanded that we never accept losing. We were just plain tougher than anybody else!"

– GEORGE THOMAS,

BAXLEY QUARTERBACK

- - - - - - - - - - -

FALL

Football officially started in August. The guys couldn't believe how hard we expected them to work. I had one rule: You had to come to practice – everybody – or you were kicked off the team.

One day Johnny Campbell, an offensive guard, strolled out to practice wearing his blue jeans. I said, "Johnny, what's wrong with you? Why aren't you suited up?" He said, "Coach, a bee stung my eye. See? It's closed up. And my face is swollen. I can't get my helmet on."

Now, I could see that his eye was shut and face swollen. But I wasn't about to let him off the hook.

"What does that mean?" I asked, folding my arms.

He looked a little confused. "Well, Coach, I can't hardly see out of that eye," he said, waving his hand around his face.

I cut to the chase. "Johnny, if you want to play on this football team, you practice. Everybody practices. So either go put your uniform on and practice, or get on out of here.

"Besides," I added, "if you can play with one eye, just think how good you'll play with two."

He kind of blinked at me, with his one good eye, then trudged off to the locker room to suit up.

Excuses were the worst thing in the world to me. We lacked the size, talent and speed of other football teams in our league. Soon we would be knocking heads with some of the best high school football teams in the state – Jesup, Waycross, Dublin. We couldn't change our schedule. But we could change two things: mentally, we could be tougher than anybody else. And physically, we could work harder.

Vince Lombardi said, "Fatigue makes cowards of us all." The Baxley boys couldn't win with tricks or gimmicks. They sure couldn't win with excuses. Our only chance of being competitive – outwork the other teams.

FIRST GAME

The first game of the season we faced Jefferson Davis High School in Hazelhurst. Lou and I had an extra incentive to win. Their head coach was Frank King, a fraternity buddy from our PC days. Frank often came over to my house for dinner, so of course this game carried more than a little friendly rivalry.

Little did Frank know that Lou and I had him all figured out. Well, sort of.

A couple of weeks before school, Lou and I took a little scouting expedition to Hazelhurst. We snuck through a swamp to watch Frank's team practice. There we sat in dawn's early light, spying and snickering to ourselves – we really had one up on old Frank! We kept it a secret for years... but he still enjoys the last laugh.

As the sun rose, we began slapping ourselves silly, covered up with mosquitoes. We were nearly eaten alive before we got out of that swamp! So much for that covert operation.

Friday afternoon before the game, over our usual pre-game meal at my house, Lou and I planned strategy. All of a sudden, a neighbor burst through the door.

My little son, Art, had been in a bike accident. I rushed out and there he lay on the highway, unconscious. He'd somehow gone over his handlebars and hit his head.

Lou ran to get his car and he and I rushed Art to the hospital. Angela followed in our car. Two hours later, tests showed us Art would be fine... but he was still in a coma. Dr. Beddingfield, a close family friend, assured Angela and I he would be fine. Still, we were sick with worry.

Angela encouraged me to go on to the game. I knew I needed to – it was my first game as head coach, but the thought of leaving my little son lying unconscious in the hospital was almost more than I could bear. Walking out the hospital door that afternoon was one of the toughest things I've ever had to do.

PEP TALK

Before we boarded the bus, I called the team into the locker room.

"Look," I said, choking up a bit, "nothing is more important to me in my life than my family. I just left our son, Art, in the hospital. I didn't want to leave him. He's hurting and I'm hurting.

"Tonight, I better not see anybody feeling sorry for themselves. I better not see anybody not giving 100 percent. I expect the best effort of your lives tonight, understand?"

The boys nodded, catching my emotion. The bus rode to Hazelhurst, silent and somber. Nobody said a word.

The game was supposed to be an even match, but our Baxley boys played like lights out that night. We absolutely killed Jefferson Davis. Frank told me how impressed he felt as we shook hands after the game.

What a thrill for the team. It was the beginning of great things for all of us.

A friend raced me back to the hospital in his car, where I joined Angela at Art's bedside. The adrenaline of victory quickly drained away in the face of a contest that really mattered. We sat up all night, praying and worrying. At 10 o'clock the next morning, 18 hours later, our son opened his eyes. Just like Dr. Beddingfield said, he was fine.

What a way to start the season.

WAYCROSS

By the time we played number-one-ranked Waycross that fall, we had won four games lost just one. The whole town buzzed with school spirit. Every Friday night, Baxley people packed out the stands. I felt pleased with our progress, but playing Waycross was a different story. We just weren't in the same league as the Gators. They had a long history of winning, with lots of players going on to major football schools like Georgia, Florida State and Nebraska. They were awesome.

Baxley had not beaten Waycross in 12 years. I honestly felt a 28-point loss would be a great effort by our team. But of course, I told them how confident I was that we'd "shock the whole state and beat the number one team!"

Friday night, we welcomed two Trailway buses from Waycross. As it turned out, it wasn't the team – it was the band. Just the band took two Trailway buses.

Our high school didn't even have a band.

Two more Trailway buses pulled in. The doors opened and football players started piling out. They just kept coming and coming – 60 players and eight varsity coaches. Our school had 19 players and two coaches: Lou and me. We were scared to death.

But as the game got underway, I stopped being scared. Our boys were playing like their lives depended on it. They were holding their own against a far superior team. More incredibly, they were winning.

Near the end of the third quarter, the score stood 7-6 in our favor. All the hard work and extra conditioning was paying off, but a grueling fourth quarter lay ahead – the ultimate test.

Near the end of the third quarter, we found ourselves in a gut-check situation – the ball sat on our own 25-yard line with 4th down and one skinny yard to go.

I called time out, but the boys knew what I was going to say. We'd gone over this play a hundred times. We never punted on fourth-and-one – it was one of my principles. If we couldn't get one yard for a first down, we didn't deserve to win.

The boys charged out. Waycross' defensive line stopped us cold, then turned the offense around for a quick, short touchdown. We moved into the fourth quarter with the Gators leading, 13-7. The fans howled. They thought I had just made the dumbest call in the history of high school football.

But the game wasn't over.

In the middle of the fourth quarter, we scored another touchdown and kicked the extra point, putting us back on top, 14-13. Now, could our defense hold the tough Gator offense until the clock ran out? This was it – we were looking at making history, if we could tough it out for a few more minutes.

At this moment I spotted one of my linebackers, Roy Skinner, limping around all over the field. A very bad move on his part. I was *furious*. Here we were, about to beat the number one team in the state and Roy decided to get hurt.

I called time out…and boy, I let Roy have it. "If you get hurt, I'm not going out there to pick you up," I yelled. "And I'm not going to call time out again either. If you get hurt, or anybody else…" I waved my arm at the whole team. "It's your job to get yourself off the field. We're not stopping the whole game because of you. Got it?"

He got it.

Roy ran back out on the field. Our defense held. We won the game.

We won. We upset the number one team in Georgia! Those ragtag boys, the same ones who couldn't beat last year's losers in spring scrimmage, pulled off the impossible. That game tested us all and we passed with flying colors. It changed Baxley's attitude for good. We learned that you don't outsmart people in the big leagues – you outwork them.

If your players are tougher, believe in each other and are motivated to win *so bad*, then they have a chance to beat anybody. They can beat bigger and more talented teams. They can even beat teams with bands, Trailway buses and eight dadgum coaches.

- - - - - - - - - - - -

"Coach Williams had us believing we were not supposed to get hurt. And if you did get hurt, nobody better know it. I broke my leg in the fifth game of my sophomore year. I ran off the field myself. There was no way anybody was going to know I was hurt, until after the game."

– ALEX JOHNSON, LINEBACKER

- - - - - - - - - - - -

REWARDS

It was all over the papers how little old Appling County beat the mighty Waycross Gators. I was so proud of those guys I couldn't stand it!

Over and over I told them, "Football is not a team game. Football is a game between you and that guy in the wrong-colored jersey on the other side of the line. Somebody's going to win – you or him. The guy who wins is the guy who wants it most."

This philosophy became an "unwritten law" later on at A.L. Williams: You can never show hurt… Never show doubt… Never show quit. The difference between great and average is "this much" – and that extra edge is always mental toughness.

We went 7 and 3 that first season – Baxley's best record in 20 years. I'd given out small awards every week all season long, but I really poured on the praise at our end-of-season banquet. Recognition didn't exist before I came, and I couldn't wait to give out awards. All the players got letter jackets, trophies and T-shirts. Lou and I made speeches about each one of them. When those kids walked out that night, they knew they had done something they could be proud of the rest of their lives.

In turn, the town showered Angela and me and Lou with gifts – a shotgun and a case of shells, a new freezer filled with beef, a stereo, a year's membership to the Appling County Country Club. It felt like Christmas.

At the Georgia Sportswriters banquet that winter, I was honored with my first Georgia "Coach of the Year" award.

How amazing to look back on that year, 1967. What looked like the worst disaster of my life had turned into a triumph. Not just for me, but for the whole town.

Beating Waycross (the number one team in the state) became a defining moment in my life. Our Baxley team had pulled off the impossible. It taught me a valuable lesson: *You win with your heart.*

My players wanted to prove to everybody that they were special. And they were willing to do whatever I asked of them to win. I asked a lot... and they gave a lot. They taught me that "heartpower" could beat talent!

I never forgot that. In fact, that "lesson learned" would play out over and over again in the years ahead. Some of the best things in life come out of the deepest disappointments... if you are tough enough to fight through the obstacles.

7 Kendrick

Our second season at Baxley we went 7-3 again and unbelievably, we beat the state's top-ranked team that year, too – Dodge County – oddly enough by the same score as Waycross, 14-13.

News of my coaching success began to get around. Two years before, nobody wanted a young, inexperienced coach. Now, I was a hot commodity. Head coaching offers came in from all over the state, and it got me itching to move up. I relished the idea of taking on a bigger football program. When I received an offer to be head football coach and athletic director at Kendrick High School in Columbus, Georgia, I accepted and our family relocated there in the summer of 1968.

Baxley to Kendrick was a big step up in school size, job responsibility and salary. Appling County High School ranked AA with about 600 students. Kendrick High School ranked AAA, the highest classification in Georgia at the time, with more than 2,000 students. A brand new school, Kendrick opened as the seventh high school in Columbus.

My salary jumped to $10,700.

Newly built, Kendrick had no football program at all. Once again I would be starting from scratch. Kendrick presented me with a new challenge – a chance to prove that I could build a successful football program – and an entire athletic department – from the ground up. I saw only positives. And unlike the Baxley situation, I had time on my side.

FIRST YEAR

As the school year began, three things stood in my favor. First was Ralph Toole, Kendrick's principal. When he hired me, Mr. Toole explained his vision. To him, building a good football team offered the quickest way to get free local publicity and establish Kendrick as a prominent school. Completely committed to that "cause," he put me totally in charge from day one. Whatever I needed, I got, including the freedom to choose my own assistant coaches. He believed in me and I worked hard not to let him down.

The second thing was Lou Miller. Lou agreed to join me again as assistant coach, and together we organized every aspect of Kendrick's football program – uniforms, weight room, weekly practice schedules and goals, a playbook, even "new" traditions. In fact, we were so new we didn't even have upperclassmen. Our teams would be made up of freshmen and sophomores only. What a blast! I couldn't wait to see what we could do.

The third thing was my brother, Don. When Angela and I moved to Columbus, Mother decided to relocate there as well. Don was a sophomore by then, and Mother wanted him to play football for me. I showed him the playbook and in 30 minutes he understood our offense. Everything shot off to a great start.

FAMILY REUNION

Angela and I both taught that first year in Columbus. Our daughter, April, entered kindergarten in the fall, freeing up Angela to go back into the classroom. She taught English; I coached football.

We also made another big decision. That summer, Angela and I began studying for our masters' degrees at Auburn University. We'd planned to for a long time, and now the time was right. For two and a half years, we spent summers attending classes at Auburn, and during the school year we each took a class one night a week.

I wanted eventually to be a high school principal, a typical career track for many coaches. A master's degree in School Administration would give me the credentials for that position down the line. Angela pursued a master's degree in English; she'd be qualified for college level teaching.

What a hectic time in our lives! Both of us working, raising two small children. Beyond studying, we continually drove back and forth to Auburn, a 90-minute drive each way. Still, we were investing in our future, doing it the best way we knew how.

At Thanksgiving that year, my mother held a family reunion at her home in Cairo. (She was able to keep our old family home, even after moving to Columbus.) Angela and I and the kids drove down for the holiday get-together. I had no idea how important that trip would turn out to be.

It had been almost five years since my father had died. The reunion gave us a needed opportunity to spend some time with beloved relatives. Since Daddy's death, my brother, Bill, had graduated from high school, spent two years in the service, then gone on to college. We'd see him again over turkey and dressing.

Mother had taken on various odd jobs to pay the bills. She finally settled on buying and selling antiques as a trade of choice. She even opened her own antique shop in her new home in Columbus. My little brother, Don, recalls, "The first house we had in Columbus had no heat. It had hot water upstairs but none downstairs, where Mother had her antique shop. She worked seven days a week, long hours, hard work. She was always buying and selling pieces and trying to move all that furniture around by herself. I came home from school more than once to find my mattress on the floor – she'd sold my bed frame while I was at school! She gave and gave, worked all the time. And she never missed one of my games."

Angela and I had been as supportive of Mother as possible. So had many others. But the years without Daddy had been rough for her, no two ways about it.

Raising Don alone proved trying at times. Of the three sons, Don had been the "Daddy's boy." Losing his father sent Don into a shell for months. His schoolwork took a nosedive. Playing ball seemed to be the only thing he cared about. I took on the father role with Don, and tried my best to help him through those years.

Bill tested Mother, too, in other ways. Headstrong, smart and a bit of troublemaker, Bill gave both my parents gray hair in his teen years. His decision to go into the service after high school gave Mother a little relief at home… and a chance to focus on Don.

In spite of it all, Mother's indomitable spirit and drive kept her going. She'd taught us the value of a positive attitude. To never give up. I was proud to see her live out her own philosophy, facing some of the hardest challenges in life.

A DISTURBING CONVERSATION

After a wonderful Thanksgiving lunch, my cousin, Ted Harrison, nudged me toward the living room, saying he wanted to show me something. Ted was a CPA, but recently he had started selling term insurance and investments with a company called ITT Financial Services.

We sat down, and he produced some company literature to show me a financial concept called "Buy Term and Invest the Difference." It turned out to be a moment of destiny.

Ted explained how I could buy $150,000 of "decreasing term" for about the same amount I paid for my $15,000 whole life, or "cash surrender value," policy. I could take the $100 a month I was saving in my teacher's credit union (at 5 percent interest) and earn maybe 12 or 15 percent interest. How? By investing it directly into the American economy with a mutual fund. Purchasing a low-cost term insurance policy, he explained, would assure Angela and the kids of a lot more protection if I died unexpectedly. They would also be the benefactors of cash accumulating in a mutual fund at a far greater interest rate than a passbook savings account… or in my current whole life policy.

I looked at Ted. What he told me didn't sink in. "Ted," I said, "I've never heard of term insurance."

"It's the oldest form of life insurance," he explained. "It's been around for more than 100 years. In fact, term is the basis for all other forms of insurance. It's nothing more than pure death protection. Everyone in the financial services industry knows about it, but most companies don't sell it."

"Why?" I asked.

"Because it's so cheap," Ted continued. "Companies can't really make a profit selling term, and agents can't make a living on the low commissions. Even though most life insurance agents own term insurance for their own families, they are taught to sell the more expensive whole life-cash value products to their clients."

"That doesn't make sense," I said.

"Right!" said Ted. "The cash surrender value life insurance concept is flawed. It's designed as a 'bundled' product – the consumer has to buy term life insurance and the savings account in one policy. That means higher premiums – substantially higher – for the consumer. Of course, the life insurance agent gets a high commission. That's how he makes a living."

"Wait a second," I said, thinking hard. "I want to be sure I understand this. For the same price I'm paying a month now for this $15,000 whole life policy, you say I could get $150,000 of term? One hundred and thirty-five thousand dollars more?"

"That's right," Ted nodded. "You've got it." It hit me like a flash of lightning, sitting there in my parents' home. I thought back to my childhood. We never had any money; nobody in Cairo did. Somehow, we all just worked hard and got by. I'd never really thought about insurance or investments.

But since Daddy's death, I'd learned that a family acquaintance sold him several small whole life policies, and he'd paid huge amounts in premiums over the years. I just thought that was the way things were done with life insurance. You didn't have choices. You bought a little whole life policy and then when someone died, you used it to pay the funeral expenses.

If what Ted told me was true, Daddy never knew any better. And here I was, five years later, putting my family in the same bad situation. If I died, I would leave Angela and the children with not even enough money to live on for a year – a little savings in a teacher's credit union account and a $15,000 burial policy. Angela would walk away from my graveside in the same painful condition my mother faced now.

I never knew a different option existed for life insurance. And this was not just a little different. According to Ted, for the same price as my $15,000 whole life policy, I could buy term and have ten times more coverage.

I started to get mad. When I bought the whole life policy, I was an assistant football coach in Thomasville, making $4,500, with a wife and two little kids to support. A life insurance agent had sold me that little policy when he could've given me $150,000 for the same price. Why didn't he mention there was another, better, option? And term was most likely the option my agent used to insure his own family.

"There's something else you should understand about your whole life policy," Ted continued. "It's either-or. You either get your cash value at the end of the policy or you get the death benefit. You don't get both."

"What does that mean?" I asked, feeling my blood rise.

"With your $15,000 policy," Ted explained, "if you built up $10,000 in the cash value and then died, Angela would get just the $15,000. The $10,000 you'd accumulated would go back to the company."

"How can that be?" I asked, really disturbed now.

"It's how cash value policies work," Ted responded. "Most people don't understand that. Whole life policies are complicated. But it's true – you either get one or the other, but not both. I think a better way to handle your money is to keep your investments separate from your life insurance. That way, you get full benefits from both. You get your death benefit from your term policy, and you get a much better return on your investment by saving your money separately in a mutual fund. That's what 'Buy Term and Invest the Difference' is all about, Art."

- - - - - - - - - - - - - - -

"BUY TERM & INVEST THE DIFFERENCE"

$100,000 policy

Whole Life - $1,200

Term - $200

Savings – $1,000

- - - - - - - - - - - - - - -

"I see," I mumbled. By now, I was so mad I could barely see. Ted gave me a brochure and the conversation turned to other subjects. But my mind kept thinking over and over about Daddy's premature death and how much better off Mother would be right now if he'd known about term. A $150,000 death benefit would make quite a difference in her quality of life right now.

And here I was, Coach Williams, heading down the same awful path with my family.

DISCOVERING THE TRUTH

As we drove home the next day, I thought about our talk. It was plain as day to me that Ted didn't know what he was talking about. My cousin was a good guy and a good accountant, but new at this insurance thing. Obviously he got something wrong. I grew up hearing that if a thing sounded too good to be true, then it probably was.

Time to check it out for myself.

Back in Columbus, I dropped Angela and the kids at home and raced over to the Bradley Memorial Library. Under "term insurance," I found a large selection of information. Ted mentioned that *Consumer Reports* had a series of articles on term insurance, so I pulled them out. I also found articles in *Changing Times*, *Moneysworth*, and a book by Norman Dacey called *What's Wrong With Your Life Insurance*.

I read it all. As I did, I felt my face get hotter and hotter. I could barely keep my seat. All of it said the same thing as Ted: Whole life was a rip-off, and term insurance was the better product for consumers.

PROVIDENCE

The truth about life insurance impacted me instantly. It seemed to me that most insurance companies deliberately sold a product that left people poor in their wallets and desperately underinsured. I understood this information could be very powerful. If I didn't know the difference between whole life and term, then lots of other people probably didn't know it either. And what we didn't know could really hurt us.

That I knew first hand.

I started talking about life insurance. I couldn't stop. I brought it up in the teachers' lounge. I talked to all my coaches. I told people at church. I told them how my daddy got ripped off, and how I had the same kind of insurance.

It turned out that every single person had the same "mess" I had... and no one had ever heard of term insurance. Like me, they weren't aware they even had a choice when it came to life insurance.

- - - - - - - - - - - -

THE GULF LIFE POLICY

"We bought that Gulf Life policy in Thomasville from the father of one of Art's football players, a good man in the community. He came over and asked us a question: What could we afford to pay each month for life insurance? He didn't ask how much coverage we needed. Looking at our budget, we said $20-$25 a month. He flipped through his book, and sold us the $15,000 whole life policy. We thought we were buying the best policy for our family that we could afford."

– ANGELA WILLIAM

- - - - - - - - - - - -

I knew I was on to something big.

Three weeks after my talk with Ted, I attended a PTA meeting at Kendrick. I never went to PTA meetings, but for some unknown reason I went to that one. At the break, I met a guy named Forest Smith. His son went to Kendrick, but he didn't play football and I didn't know him. I asked Forest what he did for a living, and he said, "I'm the division manager for ITT Financial Services. We sell term insurance and mutual funds."

I almost dropped my Coke. I said, "You've got to be kidding!" I told him about my dad and my cousin, and what I'd learned at the library. I told him how I had talked to my friends, how they all had whole life, too. What a connection. We were both excited.

I didn't know it yet, but the door to my future had just appeared… and it wasn't a set of goal posts. Something was about to happen to fling that door wide open.

"I HATE SALES"

Forest and I talked several times in the next few weeks. He wanted to hire me to sell life insurance. My initial reaction? Well, *throw up*. Good people don't sell life insurance. People who can't do anything else for a living sell life insurance. I was a coach – Coach of the Year, in fact. I had a good job and a good reputation. I didn't see myself selling life insurance.

There was a reason I hated sales. Schoolteachers often take side jobs to earn extra money, and I'd done my share of moonlighting. When we lived in Thomasville, I often drove to Albany, an hour away, to referee boys and girls basketball games. I'd run up and down the basketball court for three hours and make $12. I umpired baseball games for $5 a night. One year, the coaches got together and sold Christmas trees. Every solid night for two weeks before Christmas, we sat out in the freezing cold, selling trees – and each made $50. The kids had a decent Christmas that year, but the trees were such a hassle we never sold them again.

The next summer I answered an ad in the paper on selling encyclopedias. I went to school for an entire week to learn how sell those durn things. I sold two sets – one to myself and one to Angela's parents. I hated that job so bad I even tried to make Angela go sell a few sets. She refused, rather loudly. The last thing I ever wanted to be was a salesman.

So here came Forest, all over me about "selling life insurance" when I hated even hearing those three little words in the same sentence.

Still, I couldn't stop thinking about the positives. The concept of "Buy Term and Invest the Difference" was so intriguing to me, and I couldn't get over the rip-off of whole life insurance. So many families would come out poorer than they had to, just like my family had.

Summer grew near, and I would have some extra time. So between Forest and the fire in my heart, I decided to give selling life insurance one try. I studied, took exams and earned my securities and insurance licenses. (In Georgia at that time, in 1968, you could get a six-month temporary insurance license.) The whole process took three months and cost me $115.

Four months after I saw "Buy Term and Invest the Difference" for the first time at my family reunion, I set up my first appointment, with one of my assistant football coaches, Robert Kelley, and his wife. An ITT District Manager, John Crawford, came along to "field train" me. We sat down at their kitchen table.

It felt comfortable. I knew the Kelleys well, and they knew me. I had already talked so much about life insurance at school that Robert knew my story by heart.

I learned that Robert and his wife had a $10,000 whole life policy. For the same money, I could offer them a $100,000 term policy. They socked away $100 a month in some kind of guaranteed savings program that earned 4 percent. I could offer better than that too, with a mutual fund returning a possible 12 to 15 percent growth rate. They wouldn't spend any additional money; they could take the same money they were already spending and get about 10 times more value on it.

When I left their house, they were hugging me and kissing me. I felt happy, too. On my first try, I made my first sale. What a thrill!

PART-TIME

John and I got back in the car, and he suggested we get a cup of coffee and figure out how much I'd earned. Suddenly it hit me. Four months of being excited about this thing, then going into business, and I didn't even know how much money I would make. I'd been so excited about the concept I really hadn't thought about the money yet. I'd just spent 45 minutes talking to this couple. All I could think of was running up and down a basketball court for three hours and earning $12. I didn't have any dollar amount in my head other than $12.

Then John looked up and said, "Art, you just made $325."

My vocabulary isn't big enough to tell you how I felt at that moment. I'd never been so stunned in my life. My first reaction? "I can't believe any company is stupid enough to pay me $325 for saving these people all that money in 45 minutes. You've got to be kidding!"

"No kidding, Art," John grinned.

I couldn't wait to tell Angela. From that point on, I started selling like a crazy man.

CRUSADER FIRST

It took two months to get a policy issued. Then the agent got paid 50 percent of the client's monthly premium payment. For example, if the client paid $20 a month on a policy, the agent earned $10 a month for the next 12 months – $120. Since ITT Financial Services paid agents once a month, it took three months to get my first check.

I understood that, but Angela didn't. I would come home at night all excited and say, "Hey, Angela, I just made $200!" I was out making two or three sales a week. But since checks were so slow to come in, Angela at first thought it was all just talk.

Then I finally got my first check – for $9.63. Angela? Not impressed. Only a few months later, though, I started getting checks for $500, $600 and $1,000 a month. My first year with ITT, I managed to earn $15,000 working part-time – more than my $10,700 salary as coach and AD. I sold part-time for ITT in Columbus for two and a half years; Angela and I saved $42,000 – just from my part-time earnings. That was like a million dollars to us then.

I still hated sales. The last thing I wanted to be called was a salesman. But something mattered to me more than that label – telling people about term insurance and giving them a choice in death protection. I just knew if they heard my personal story and the truth about life insurance, they would choose something better. Who wouldn't want to switch to a policy that offered more protection for less money? To me, it was a no-brainer.

My passion made me immediately successful in selling "Buy Term and Invest the Difference." I believed in it with my whole heart. I knew it was right for consumers. I was a living example of how the wrong kind of life insurance can affect your family.

So I was not a salesman – I was an educator. I took an educational approach with people. I never wore a suit and tie. I dressed like a coach, because I was a coach. Coach Williams. I never wanted to be anyone else – just a real guy with a story and a solution that could improve a family's life.

When I went into someone's home, I was strictly "anti-sales." I never made a sale on the first interview. I'd tell the couple to "get your hands off your pocketbook!" Then I would ask them to show me what they currently owned and compare it with what I could offer them. On a yellow legal pad, we listed out their own policy, point by point, year by year, benefit by benefit. We compared it with an ITT term policy and a separate mutual fund investment. We took our time. I wanted them to understand life insurance. I wanted them to see for themselves what a rip-off whole life was for their family.

I didn't have sales brochures or computer print-outs, just a yellow legal pad and a pencil. Sometimes, I would show clients a research paper I'd written for my master's degree – on the evils of cash value life insurance. My first sales piece was a term paper!

I ended every interview with a proposal. "Look," I'd say, "if I can't give you eight to 10 times more value, or cut your costs by 50 to 75 percent, then I don't deserve your business." It worked. People could see for themselves that term insurance was better. I started selling so many policies it was unbelievable.

When I "sold" encyclopedias, I just did it for the extra money. No wonder it didn't work.

This was different. I believed in term insurance so much that not even my total distaste for sales got in the way.

That's the bottom line: The Crusade must come first. If you don't believe in what you're doing… That it's absolutely right for the people you serve… If you're in it only for the money… Then you might just as well go home.

8 Toughest Decision

Fall 1968, our second football season at Kendrick, we added juniors to our mix of freshmen and sophomores. Three new sophomores showed all-star potential. Jim Baker, tight-end; Donald Bird, running back; and Rudy Allen, quarterback.

Tall and skinny, Rudy played football in junior high and at the city recreation league. Kendrick would be his first year playing high school football. At first glance, he didn't look like a great football player. But it didn't take me long to see his natural ability. Physically and mentally, Rudy had everything he needed. He just needed to grow into it.

The best thing about Rudy? A ton of "want to." He loved to play football and I spent hours with him on fundamentals. Day after day, we worked on passing. Drill after drill, practice after practice, I had Rudy throwing that football. He learned fast.

By the last pre-season practice, I knew I had a star quarterback on my hands. But it created a dilemma. The starting quarterback the previous season, my brother Don, had done a great job. But facing this season and the next, when we would finally be competing against big AAA teams, I knew Rudy had that "something extra" a coach dreams of finding in a player. I put Rudy in as quarterback and played Don at wide receiver, which turned out to be a good position for him.

Breaking the news of this change to Don, and even worse, to our mother, put me on the hot seat for a while. Mother thought I had done Don a real disservice. But a leader is often called on to make hard decisions that affect a small number of people negatively and a large number positively. This was one of those times.

Rudy led us to a victorious 9-1 season. We beat the same teams that defeated us the previous year. And we came unbelievably close to an undefeated season. Our only loss was 7-6. We scored one touchdown in the fourth quarter, then went for the two-point conversion, but didn't get it done. We came up one yard short of a perfect season. Like I used to tell my Baxley players – we didn't lose that game, we just ran out of time.

"BIG TIME"

Kendrick quickly established its presence in the Columbus school system, and that made Mr. Toole happy. None of us knew it then, but heading into the next season, our football team was about to make Mr. Toole *very* happy.

In 1969, for the first time since Kendrick High opened its doors, our football team would play a regular regional AAA schedule and go up against powerful teams like Warner Robins, Macon Central and all six Columbus high schools. It would be tough, but we were ready. Our freshmen and sophomores had hardened into seasoned juniors and seniors. And we had the element of surprise on our side – opposing teams had no idea we could play football. Ranked last in our region, we would be "easy" wins, our competition expected.

They were in for a shock.

Coaching changes had taken place. Lou Miller, who had worked with me faithfully for four years, left Columbus to pursue his dream of professional golf. But I'd recruited a great coaching staff – Walt Landing, David Kirk, Charles Dowdell and Philip Marion.

We played well at the start, then better as the season progressed. Near the season's end, our record stood at 8 and 1, and we had won our Columbus-area championship. Macon Central had done the same in its region. Central fielded an exceptional team – big, tough veterans. Not surprisingly, they were number two in the state, behind Valdosta. We clung to the number eight spot.

"I WANT CENTRAL BAD!"

The week before the regional championship game with Macon, I called a Sunday practice, something I never did. We worked out hard in full pads. And I mean *hard*.

Monday morning, I called a team meeting. To every player and coach I tossed T-shirts with "I Want Central Bad!" splashed in red on the front. I told the team to put them on and wear them all week – even to bed! Then I gave a pep talk that made it all clear: We were going to beat Macon Central and win the regional championship. I didn't care what the papers said. I didn't care that we were the underdogs. No school had ever won the AAA regional championship their first year of competition. Winning that game would put us in the history books – if we wanted it bad enough.

We worked out hard again Monday, Tuesday and Wednesday. I did everything I could think of to prepare them mentally and physically for that game.

I love being the underdog. I love doing the impossible. I love winning when nobody thinks you can. We went to Macon and won that game. We put our name in the history books of Georgia high school football – the first school to ever win a AAA regional championship its first year of competition. More than 30 years later, that record still stands.

BLAZE OF GLORY

The Macon game was our best performance ever. But now we eyed an even bigger challenge the next Friday night… The number one-ranked, well-rested, incredibly powerful Valdosta team in the semi-finals of the state championship.

To grasp the magnitude of this game, you have to understand the Valdosta Wildcats. Coached by the legendary Wright Bazemore, the "Bear Bryant" of Georgia high school football, Valdosta had won 14 state championships and three national championships. Coach Bazemore turned Valdosta into the nation's winningest high school football program with 768 wins. His unbelievable records established Valdosta as the most recognized football prep school in the country.

Playing against Coach Bazemore presented the thrill of a lifetime… but boy, did we have our work cut out for us. Our no-name studs from Kendrick High would line up against *Valdosta*, the nation's capital of high school football.

Unforgettable memories would mark that special night.

I had no idea it would be the last high school game I ever coached.

We played on our own field at Columbus Memorial Stadium. The place swelled to the rafters with a sell-out crowd of 25,000 people. Local media worked all week on the build-up. Kendrick stepped onto the stage of "big time" high school football, and we enjoyed every minute of the attention and "circus" atmosphere that came along with it. We knew the odds, but we came to play and win. My pre-game speech fired up the guys so much they almost broke down the door to get on the field.

Their previous eight games, Valdosta held the opposing teams scoreless. We broke that streak in the first quarter with a touchdown. Our lead held for a quarter. At the end of the first half, we went to the locker room tied 14-14 – just unbelievable! The second half, Valdosta came on strong and beat us 28-14. They had so many players, they finally just wore us out.

Valdosta went on to win the national championship that year, 1969, and again in 1971. The next year, 1970, Coach Bazemore was awarded National Coach of the Year.

What a football powerhouse.

Playing against the best high school team in the country, coached by high school football's most famous coach… What a great way for Coach Williams to go out.

COACH OF THE YEAR

For the second time in five years of head coaching, I received the "Georgia Coach of the Year" award, this time for the AAA division. In my three years at Kendrick, our football team had climbed a mountain. We'd done so well and I knew we'd be even better the next year. All my best players returned – Rudy, Jim, Donald. We had good younger players coming up through the ranks, too. We stood a shot at winning big – the regional championship again, maybe even state. That's where we aimed. It was always our plan to win it all.

Still, change hung in the air. As the school year wore on, it became more and more obvious.

BEST OF ALL WORLDS

By now, I had advanced well into my second year working part-time for ITT Financial Services. I say part-time because that's an important part of the story. ITT had allowed me to work part-time, but that's not how companies usually operated. In fact, ITT didn't believe in hiring part-time people. They hired full-time salesmen, period. They made an exception with me.

My sales record made its way to ITT headquarters in Denver and attracted the attention of ITT president Frank Pierson. He nicknamed me his "All-American" and made it very clear he didn't like me working part-time. He called often, praising my "gift for the business," but mostly trying to convince me to work full-time.

I didn't take it too seriously. Truthfully, I had no intention of working for ITT full-time. Here I was, making $10,700 as head coach and AD and making $15,000 part-time selling term insurance and investments. I had the best of all possible worlds. I made more money part-time than most of ITT's Columbus agents earned full-time… and I packed away all of it in savings. At the same time, I did what I loved most: coach football. I saw no reason in the world to change things.

Coaching had one down side – financially I couldn't do some things for my family that I really wanted to do. We had a great life, but no big income. That's why I always tried to earn extra money. Working part-time for ITT solved that problem. At the end of two and half years, we had saved $42,000. In two or three more years, I figured we would have $100,000 in savings – *huge*. We'd soon have solid, long-term security and a big leg up on financial independence, our ultimate financial goal.

AN UNLIMITED MARKET

Over the next few months, several things happened that began to change my point of view.

First, I noticed a trend as I met with people at the kitchen table. For one thing, the size of the opportunity grew glaringly obvious. Everybody I talked to had the same type of policy I used to own – whole life. When I told them my story about my dad dying and the truth about whole life and term insurance, their reactions proved universally the same: They knew nothing about term insurance, and what they learned just thrilled them.

My educational approach, by this time, reached people in a whole new way. I used no pressure. I didn't sell on the first appointment. Instead, I asked to take their whole life policy and return it in a couple of days with a policy comparison. The second visit, I showed the comparison and what a term policy could offer. I explained investments, and the advantage of investing in a separate vehicle, like a mutual fund, instead of using a cash value life policy to save.

People listened to what I said. They related to my personal story. They understood that term insurance made sense.

Most happily made the change to "Buy Term and Invest the Difference." Delighted, they told their friends about me. Then I would go talk to their friends. Those friends would tell their friends. And on it went.

I never, *ever* felt like a salesman. I never talked to strangers. I never made a cold call. I went from one group of friends to another. Soon, I had contacts with families all over the state. They threw open their doors for Coach Williams. The market really seemed limitless.

A BUSINESS OF POLITICS

One day, things changed. I got a letter from the Georgia State Insurance Department. It required me to appear on a certain day and time at their office in Atlanta. I didn't know why, and the letter didn't explain it. The whole thing gave me a funny feeling. This mysterious appointment meant I had to take a day off from school and drive to Atlanta.

I showed up at the office of Richard Cain, the state's deputy insurance commissioner. He'd issued my summons after receiving a letter from a competing insurance agent stating that I had replaced a $10,000 whole life insurance policy with a $100,000 term policy on one of his clients.

Cain held up the letter. Staring at me hard, he asked in a low voice, "Mr. Williams, is this letter correct? Did you replace this agent's client's whole life policy with a term policy?"

"Yes, I did," I said, surprised by his tone.

Now it was his turn to be surprised. "Do you understand what you are doing is illegal? You can't replace cash value with term. It's called 'twisting.'"

State legislation at that time prohibited twisting – replacing a whole life policy with term *if* the replacement was not in the best interest of the client. The penalty for twisting? Ultimately, losing your license.

But there was another "twist" to this scenario. If you did the opposite procedure – replaced a term policy with whole life – *that* was called conversion and the Georgia State Insurance Department *endorsed* it!

I told Cain I didn't know what it was called, but yes, I had done it. I also told him, remembering my family and others I had helped, that I would continue to do it.

Cain's jaw dropped again. He couldn't believe my response. He held a complaint in writing; he thought he had me! He never dreamed I would admit to "twisting," because of the lose your- license penalty. But I then reminded him of something he seemed to have forgotten, ignored, or never known.

"Look," I said, "it's only twisting if I replace the policy with something that's not as good. The policy I replaced was a $10,000 whole life policy. I gave that family a $100,000 term policy for the same monthly premium. Is that not better for the client?"

Visibly uncomfortable, Cain looked at the paperwork.

"Well, yes, I guess you're right," he mumbled.

I smelled a win. "So if what I did is better for the client, then somehow I don't think that's illegal. Do you?" I asked pointedly. He didn't answer.

This troubling incident gave me my first glimpse into the biased world of life insurance – a world, I slowly learned, that seemed run entirely by "insider" politicians funded by big insurance corporations.

I found that most insurance commissioners (and their staff) didn't know a thing about the life insurance industry – the industry they supposedly represented on behalf of the public. What's more, most commissioners didn't care. Typically, an appointment to the position of State Insurance Commissioner gave these politicians a stepping stone in the advancement of their own careers. Some commissioners harbored grand plans to move up to more lofty political titles – lieutenant governor, or even governor. Dealing with day-to-day issues of insurance, the commissioners often showed themselves unfamiliar and uneducated. Their game? Politics, not insurance.

Such was the case with Richard Cain, in my opinion. As a deputy commissioner, he seemed uninformed. Since I was already in his office, I took the opportunity to educate him on "Buy Term and Invest the Difference." It blew him away. He had no idea such options even existed, never mind how much better they were for people. Here he was, threatening to take away my license… and he didn't even know the marketplace. By the end of our meeting, he dropped the "twisting" issue altogether. In fact, he didn't even give me a warning to stop replacing poor policies with good. The matter ended there. We shook hands, and I drove back to Columbus.

My experience with Mr. Cain marked the first of many "run-ins" I would experience with state insurance commissioners. This minor league example previewed showdowns on many fronts against a deeply corrupt and powerful industry.

ON TO SOMETHING BIG

I noticed another trend with people I met – a desperate need for extra money.

In the 1950s, most women, like my mother, worked in the home and didn't have an outside job. But in the '60s, either the husband had a second job or the wife worked part-time or even full-time to bring in extra income. Folks struggled for a decent standard of living, a nice home in a nice neighborhood, a decent car to drive.

It was like that for Angela and me. She would teach for a year, then feel guilty and stay home with the kids. Our car would wear out, so she'd go back and teach another year. I always kept a second job. We always needed extra income, plain and simple, and I saw clearly that other families did, too. Stuff like refereeing ball games or selling various products door-to-door paid little and offered even less professionally.

It struck me that I had the greatest part-time job in the world. I helped people, taught them how to improve their financial well-being, got paid well for my time. I worked in a legitimate profession that required a license. It dealt with $50,000, $100,000 or $200,000 policies, and investing money in mutual funds. That's an impressive kind of part-time business! A real second career, not some gimmicky sales scheme.

I started thinking about the idea of hiring people on a part-time basis. It came as just a glimmer at first. I knew I could recruit people to do what I was doing. They needed the extra income, just like we did. And they needed something else – a chance to be their own boss, in control of their careers.

I began to talk to Frank Pierson about this concept. To my way of thinking, ITT Financial Services recruited the wrong kind of people.

"People make a company, Frank," I said. "When people talk to me, they see Coach Williams come into their home, not an insurance salesman. I meet friends, or friends of friends. They know me. They know I have a family. They know I won't rip them off. I just know people I'm talking to would be interested in doing what I'm doing, part-time. It's the greatest part-time opportunity out there!"

Frank couldn't understand it, bless his heart. Here I was, working one or two days a week just six months a year, never during football season, making more money in six months than most salespeople did full time. Now I was talking about bringing in a whole sales force of part-timers. He didn't even like *me* working part-time!

He didn't buy it.

But I kept talking. My mind raced with possibilities. I just knew in my gut I was on to something big.

Why not recruit other people like me to work part-time? Other teachers and coaches and police officers and firemen and business men and women. The influential people in the community. I believed I could bring in unlimited numbers of people to work part-time and sell policies that made life better for others.

In two-and-a-half years of selling term insurance all over Georgia, I discovered universal similarities in the families I helped. In my mind, these observations were monumental. They sent a message – a big message.

1. "Buy Term And Invest The Difference" made other insurance concepts obsolete. A couple could buy $100,000 of term insurance for just $200 instead of $1,200 for cash value – a difference of $1,000 every year. A huge savings for any family.

2. "Buy Term And Invest The Difference" had nowhere to go but up. Everyone – everyone – had flawed cash value life insurance. Once people understood the difference between cash value and term, they all wanted term. Still, nobody was selling term. The market looked unlimited.

3. Almost everyone needed more insurance. The industry's average death benefit of under $6,000 paid for little more than a funeral. My old whole life policy of $15,000 would bury me and replace my salary for one measly year. With cash value policies, families like mine couldn't afford to buy enough coverage to help them financially survive a tragedy.

They needed coverage.

4. Full-timers couldn't get into homes to sell insurance. Their public image? Negative. Even below negative. Nobody wanted to let an insurance agent through the door.

5. People needed extra income. Selling term could mean a windfall. My part-time job paid $200 to $300 for an hour's work.

THE PART-TIME SOLUTION

How do you accomplish all that? Part-timers! Hire people like me to sell term insurance and investments on a part-time basis. Give them the same opportunity I had with ITT. *Why not?*

I kept giving Frank Pierson more and more reasons to build a sales force with part-timers. Finally, worn down by my calls, he flew me up to Denver (my first plane ride at age 27!). In a personal meeting, I spewed out all my ideas as fast I could talk.

1. **No pressure to sell** – A part-timer doesn't have to give up a guaranteed income. He/she isn't making sales to survive financially; it's extra income.

2. **Easy to get into homes** – People will talk to their friends because they know and trust them. Nobody wants a stranger in the home... especially talking about what happens if a family member dies.

3. **Warm market** – By talking to friends and friends of friends, all sales take place in a "warm" market. No cold calls.

4. **Better quality of business** – If a client buys a policy from someone he trusts, he tends keep it.

5. **Better quality of people** – Recruit the "centers of influence" in the community – coaches, teachers, pastors, policemen, housewives, business men/women, etc. Partner with people who are respected and known around town.

6. **Great way to make extra money** – Everyone needs extra income. Here is a way to do something good for a friend and earn $200 or $300 a sale, for about an hour's work.

7. **A professional business** – Financial services require licenses. It is a real profession... Not some gimmicky door-to-door scheme (like selling encyclopedias!).

8. **More efficient** – Part-timers don't need salaries, offices, secretaries, phones, desks, etc. Cut overhead expenses with part-timers and give huge savings to the company.

9. **Great way to have fun** – Enjoy helping friends and neighbors with valuable, life-changing financial information.

10. **Good Crusaders** – People who replace whole life policies with term work passionately for the cause of "Buy Term and Invest the Difference." They love to replace whole life policies with term. It's "payback" to the companies that "ripped them off."

11. **Great ways to prospect** – Nobody wants to buy anything, but almost everybody needs extra income. We offered the best extra income opportunity in the market. We would recruit first, and sell second.

"This is the way to build the ITT sales force," I said, wrapping it up. "There is no reason why we couldn't go out and 'recruit the world' like this!"

Finally, for the first time, Frank caught the vision, saw the possibility. Then he handed me an unexpected challenge.

"All right, All-American," he said, with a grin. "I want to see if you can build a different kind of company with this part-time opportunity concept. I'll give you one year to prove yourself. I'll pay you $25,000 a year, plus expenses, and give you access to all our resources at headquarters in Denver. I'll even let you stay in Columbus. We'll see what you can build... but you are going to have to go full-time with ITT to do it."

Frank Pierson was shrewd. His challenge hit my hot button. He offered an open door to my whole way of life – my need to lead, desire to "be somebody," to do something really important with my life.

When I went to Baxley, nobody would've taken that job but me. When I went to Columbus, everyone thought I was crazy to take a football program at a brand new school. But both jobs gave me an irresistible chance – to build a program from scratch.

Now here stood Frank Pierson, president of ITT Financial Services, offering me that same alluring opportunity. A chance to build a new kind of company with my own concepts. I could even stay in Columbus.

There was just one little problem.

I would have to leave coaching to do it.

ANOTHER LOOK AT THE INDUSTRY

Tough decisions rarely come at the "right" time.

Frank's special opportunity came when Angela and I were set, our family was doing great, we had $42,000 in the bank. My best football team yet would line up in the fall. We'd finally "settled." But this offer was now on the table, and I had to make a decision.

Then, another incident. I took a phone call from Dr. Shaw, the superintendent of Columbus schools. Like the letter I received from the Georgia State Insurance Department, this call gave me an eerie feeling. Dr. Shaw said a friend of his, a life insurance agent who worked for a competing company, had told him I sold life insurance on the side. Dr. Shaw scolded me for violating my teacher's contract, which stated that I was not to have any other form of income during the school year.

Well, that clause *was* in my contract. But nearly every teacher in the state of Georgia did something to earn extra income – you had to, to survive. Until now, moonlighting had never been a problem – I never knew a teacher or coach called down for scratching up extra income on the side. Plus, I worked for ITT just six months out of the year... never during football season.

Dr. Shaw went on and on. He told me I had caused a real stink around Columbus. He said several insurance agents were mad at me because I sold life insurance when I was supposed to be coaching football. Finally, he threatened to take away my coaching position if I didn't quit selling.

It didn't take an Einstein to figure out what was going on. Dr. Shaw didn't know anything about insurance. He did know his buddy, a political supporter, had a complaint, and he was taking up for him. The competing agents were playing dirty now. They didn't like it one bit that I was out there replacing their whole life policies. Instead of viewing me as healthy competition and trying to change or improve their own sales approach and products, they went behind my back to Dr. Shaw. They reasoned, cleverly, that if I got in trouble with the school system, I'd quit selling term.

Their sneaky approach appalled me. I hadn't grown up in that kind of world. I lived in a competitive one where people looked for a better way to win and worked hard to improve. But, I would learn over and over that the insurance industry played by different rules. Bad ones. They had no intention of changing faulty philosophies or products. They hated competition. They just wanted someone like me out of the way, and they had no qualms about using dirty, underhanded tactics to take me out.

So… I got my second glimpse into the corrupt, political world of the insurance industry. It upset me, but ultimately played only a minor role in my final decision.

TOUGH CALL

I spent the next four months agonizing. On the one hand, I looked at all the security in Columbus. We lived a great life and had so much going for us. Coaching was my dream job. How could I walk away from that?

Angela and I talked about Frank's offer. She offered her total support. But she was scared, too. We would be giving up the security of teaching and coaching, and Angela saw me first and foremost as a coach. That was who she married.

Days and weeks went by. Frank kept making the offer more and more attractive. He made my financial package practically risk-free. He put the ITT home office in Denver at my disposal. He wanted me to work five weeks experimenting in the field in Columbus, then spend one week in Denver, working with the "brains" there to analyze the work. If I became a success, he said, ITT would use my concepts as a model for other sales regions around the country.

The pressure intensified. Full-time with ITT, I would have an opportunity for the first time to recruit new people into the company – my people. I planned to recruit 10 to 20 people per month out of the Columbus office. Right now, that office recruited just three or four people a year. My concepts were risky and untried, totally new to ITT, totally groundbreaking in the industry. I could fail miserably.

But something inside of me said, this is right. Coach Williams – make that Art Williams – stood in the right place at the right time. I saw the opportunity to build something monumental.

BACK TO CAIRO

Finally, I decided to call a time out. Why not talk over the next play with a coach who knew the game better than anyone?

I got in the car and drove to Cairo.

Coach Taylor waited for me in his office. We remained as close as ever. The years passed but we still talked about everything. He was like a second father to me, and I knew I could trust him for sound advice.

Back on the familiar ground of my old hometown, Coach Taylor told me, "Art, if you feel like this could be big in business, then you really ought to do it."

"What about my coaching career?" I asked. "I've worked so hard."

"You've been a success in coaching," he smiled. "Nobody can take that away from you. Ever. All kinds of schools would give their right arm to have you come coach… and that will still be true if you decide to come back to coaching. And, you have your master's degree. You can teach or be a principal. If this doesn't work out, you haven't lost a thing. Go for it!"

Coach Taylor's reasoning hit home – and sealed the deal. Time to leave coaching and begin a career in financial services.

LEAVING KENDRICK

I left school almost immediately. I needed to get out of the way, let the new coach take over. They appointed one of my assistant coaches, David Kirk, as the new head coach. Angela finished out the school year teaching English.

After it was all finally settled, after four months of sleepless nights and stomach aches, I made up my mind never to struggle over a decision like that again.

I was a football coach, after all. I was used to calling the right play in 25 seconds or less. From now on, I would look at the facts, make the call and just get on with things. I would never punish myself like that again.

The decision to leave coaching was the toughest of my life. With that hard call behind me now, a bright new road of opportunity stretched ahead.

Looking back, never in my wildest dreams could I have predicted such a career change – and even less, where it all would lead.

Coaching demanded my very best. I was tough… or so I thought. But nothing compared to what I was about to take on.

At the start of 1970, I was 27 years old.

As the A.L. Williams story entered a new era, "toughness" took on a whole new meaning.

PART III - Ten Hard Years

"You've got to be smart to be number one in any business. But more importantly, you've got to play with your heart, with every fiber of your body. If you're lucky enough to find a guy with a lot of head and a lot of heart, he's never going to come off the field second."

– VINCE LOMBARDI,

"NUMBER ONE" SPEECH

9 - ITT Financial Services

I hit the ground running. Now full-time with ITT, I was out on appointments every night, talking to a book full of clients collected in the past two and a half years. The response? Mind-boggling! A recruitment goal of 5 to 10 people a month out of our Columbus office quickly shattered – I did double and triple that. I discovered people were for a good opportunity.

One new recruit stood above the rest – Randy Phelps. A National Guard pilot, Randy flew out of Fort Benning, a huge United States Army base near Columbus. From Day One, Randy showed a passion for term insurance… and my crusade. He drew from his military market and just sold and recruited like crazy. He got licensed in Alabama too, so he could sell there in his hometown, just an hour away. After our first year, he was doing so well he made the decision to leave his military career and come full-time with ITT. What a thrill for me! It really validated our opportunity, and his testimony gave a strong incentive for prospects to consider going part-time and for part-timers to go full-time.

The flurry of business activity prompted many changes. It became clear to me that instead of setting up appointments to make life insurance sales, we should "lead" with our business opportunity.

A starting conversation went like this: "I have got to tell you about my new part-time job. You won't believe this opportunity. It's changed my whole life. I think it could help you, too!"

Not surprisingly, people warmed quicker to talking about a great way to earn extra income than to talking about life insurance. Explaining the opportunity first got us in the door. About 50 percent of the time we got a recruit and a sale. About 95 percent of the time we made a sale. The market? Wide open.

Our sales team exploded in growth – both recruits and sales shot off the charts. We broke too many sales records to count. Just three months after I went full-time, my gutsy group of "term-ites" had shot to the top – the largest sales organization in ITT.

THE REASON WHY

Every policy I picked up convinced me more that "Buy Term and Invest the Difference" was incredibly right and good. Out in the field, working with families, it alarmed me that everybody had cash value policies and nobody had term. They didn't know it even existed. When presented with the term versus cash value numbers, they picked term coverage every time. It just made common sense.

Yet, as strongly as I believed in the crusade, nothing prepared me for paying death claims.

Term versus cash value was academic, just numbers… until I walked into a home, death claim check in hand. Seeing the widow and the children, the looks on their faces, the shock and the fear – tough every time.

My first death claim was the hardest. In that little house, I relived the loss of my own father and the pain of watching my mother try to recover, emotionally and financially. Death can wipe out a family. To go into a home, hug good people and hand them that check for $100,000 or $200,000… well, I felt I delivered a comfort my own family never saw. What a privilege to tell the grieving widow she wouldn't be forced to sell her home or make other huge sacrifices just to eat. Because she and her husband chose term insurance, she would be well cared for.

For years, I hand-delivered my death claim checks and went to many funerals. As years went by and we got bigger, attending every funeral became increasingly hard. But I always made an effort to talk to the widow or widower on the phone. I put myself in the place of every family who faced that devastating loss. I knew what it felt like. Now I had a way to offer them hope. It kept me driving on, working harder than ever.

PROVE IT AGAIN

Just as Frank Pierson had promised, I had the support of the Denver ITT home office right from the start. I shuttled between my office and theirs every six weeks. I'd spend an entire week in Denver, reviewing activities with the top executives. Home office staff came to Columbus too, nearly every week, observing our methods and activities.

With so many new recruits flooding into our system, we faced several problems right away. I took full advantage of my home office support to tackle them head on.

For example, commission structure. ITT offered three levels (or titles) on their computer system: Division Manager, District Manager and Representative. All new recruits started out at the Representative level, just as I had, and received 50 percent commission on their insurance and investment sales. At District, sales agents made 60 percent commission plus 10 percent in overrides. At Division, commissions went up to 70 percent plus 20 percent in overrides. The generous override commissions provided a terrific incentive for agents to bring new people into their organization. So it gave them a way to earn additional income from their sales team, instead of just being a personal producer.

Insurance Commissions –

Percentage of first-year premium, paid to the selling agent as income.

Override –

Percentage of commission collected on a sale, in addition to the commission received by a lower-level salesperson.

We ran into a huge problem with compensation. ITT paid all office expenses – rent, secretary, phone, utilities, etc. Every office got paid expenses whether it made money or not. The company would budget for a certain number of new offices each year, like 50 offices at $75,000 each, for a total of $3.75 million. If half of those offices produced, and half of them didn't, it meant a loss of $1.8 million in office expenses to the company.

To cover the loss, the company had to either cut commissions or raise product prices.

Rather than pass the cost on to the consumer and become less competitive, the shortfall usually came out of the field commissions budget. That meant, of course, good producers took the hit for the non-producers by having their compensation reduced. This system was grossly unfair. The company, in effect, punished producers and rewarded non-producers.

I worked relentlessly to figure out ways to increase commissions to our salespeople. I wanted a system that gave everyone an opportunity to earn more – but only on what they produced. To me, it became a personal responsibility issue. If you produced big numbers, you could afford to pay for a large office and administrative help. If you weren't doing much, then you'd better run a small office and answer the phone yourself… or maybe even work out of your home.

This simplified system would create tremendous growth incentive for productive agents and, at the same time, keep costs low. But it wasn't in place at ITT. Not even close.

CORPORATE LIMITATIONS

Another troublesome issue soon cropped up. Despite all kinds of good things happening to our growing organization, our explosive productivity did not produce higher incomes, either for me or my sales leaders.

Our sales and recruits multiplied like mad, but our incomes stayed about the same. This "holding pattern" frustrated me, and at first I couldn't understand it. How could sales grow so fast, but compensation stay the same?

It didn't take long to figure out. ITT simply had no plan in place for compensating a growing sales force. Cash revenues went to rewards for a few top sales producers, and that was it. In truth, ITT didn't really know how to deal with a growing sales force. For years, the company had plugged along with flat-line sales and no recruiting growth. Now, all of a sudden, both categories spiked clear off the charts – they had no idea what to do. Figuring out ways to address the issue and reward us with higher commissions didn't seem to even be part of their game plan.

The soaring numbers also rattled ITT's licensing and training. Again, there was no plan in place to assist people in these areas. To me, it violated the whole idea behind the free enterprise system – to reward people who really performed. My idea? *Help* them get trained and licensed. If they worked extra hard and made more sales, then dadgum it, set up a system to pay them more! That was the American way. Forget the politics. The bottom line to me was plain: If you do more, then you ought to get more.

Much to their detriment, ITT Financial Services didn't seem to understand these basic concepts. I did all I could to explain it to them, then took action on my own.

Their shortsighted approach would soon come back to haunt them.

A CHANGE IN LICENSING

Licensing issues developed with our fast-growing sales team. Because ITT emphasized investment sales more than insurance sales, it required its agents to become securities licensed first – a process that took about three months.

Three months? Forget that. New people joined our sales team every day. I couldn't have them waiting around, taking tests for three months before they could make sales. I needed them out in the field with their managers on appointments as soon as possible – within 48 hours after joining, if possible.

With Frank's blessing, I altered that rule and allowed my new recruits to get their insurance licenses first. The licensing change, though controversial at the time, proved to be a highly potent catalyst for growth. In Georgia then, a six-month temporary license cost $10. By getting the insurance license first, my new Reps could make sales and get paid right away. They didn't have to wait to make appointments and insurance sales (the easier sales to make). They could follow up with those new clients on investment needs in a few months, after they had their securities license. Or the field trainer could sell the securities with the insurance sale. Either way, it worked.

PHOENIX

The licensing change made for fast growth those first six months. We blew away all of ITT's sales records. Then I got called back to Denver. The executives had a new challenge for me.

"Okay, Art," they said, "you're a superstar in Columbus, let's see if you can teach this to a sales region that's not growing. We're sending you to Phoenix."

I spent one month in Phoenix, teaching the same concepts to ITT salespeople there. Just like in Columbus, they began to make huge leaps in sales and recruits in a matter of weeks.

That convinced Frank Pierson and the ITT execs that my concepts worked. They knew we'd hit on something big, something special.

That's when they gave me my next assignment. I had the choice of relocating to either Atlanta or Dallas, two major markets where ITT had experienced very little success. A Georgia boy, I chose Atlanta. Our family moved there in the fall of 1970, and I took over the ITT Financial Services office in the quaint suburb of Decatur.

ATLANTA

The move to Atlanta was a big one for Angela and me on several levels. Being small town folks, Atlanta looked enormous and presented some decision-making challenges. The ITT office sat off Memorial Drive, near Atlanta's "perimeter" interstate, I-285 – a perfect location for an office, but not for a family. We decided to settle in Snellville, a northern suburb with just 2,500 people. A good move for the kids, although it added a 60-minute commute to my workday.

For the first time in our lives, we didn't know a soul. We'd moved three times in seven years of coaching, but we'd always had friends and family nearby. In Atlanta, we had neither. We all went through adjustments, especially Art and April, who both had to start over in new schools and make new friends.

After some gentle persuasion on my part (and some kicking and screaming on hers), Angela decided to leave teaching to help me in the office as my secretary. With me working full-time on commission, it had been a comfort for us to have her steady teaching salary coming in the door. Now the time had come to step up and face the challenge, which we did with flying colors.

FRIDAY NIGHT FEELING

From my earliest days playing football, I cherished something I called the "Friday night feeling."

As a player and especially as a coach, I loved those butterflies in the stomach before a big game – that swirling mixture of anticipation, anxiety and excitement. After the decision to go full-time with ITT, I carried the "Friday night feeling" with me all the time. The change was so risky that I woke up every day scared to death… and excited beyond belief.

My main fear? *Failing*. I had never failed at anything, and now I wanted to succeed in this business *so much* I couldn't stand it. Just like football, I became obsessed with winning. So I did what I always did – I got up early and worked late. I did everything I knew how to do… and a little bit more. I worked harder than I ever had in my life… and I was used to working hard.

In football, you enjoy a win for about a day. Then you start preparing for the next game. When we moved to Atlanta, the need to prepare intensified. Atlanta was my next "game," and I meant to win it. I had "won" in Columbus and Phoenix; now I had to prove myself all over again in Atlanta.

I brought several important assets with me to Atlanta. One was Randy Phelps, my first full-timer. When he found out I was moving to Atlanta, he packed up his family and came too. He really proved his loyalty and commitment with that move.

I brought along my confidence too. The situation reminded me of attending my first "Coach of the Year" clinic in Atlanta. The program roster boasted several big-name coaches, including legendary Bear Bryant. Sessions started at 8:00 a.m. By 7:30, I'd parked myself in the front row. I wasn't about to miss one word of those coaching seminars – to learn new offenses and defenses from "the best." Other coaches didn't feel the same. They drug in at 10:30, 11 o'clock – a shocking lack of intensity, to me.

Noting that disparity filled me with confidence. I realized I could beat 90 percent of the competition just by showing up early! Why relax? Get after the competition. Outwork them. That's the way to win.

With that same level of intensity, I tackled the Atlanta ITT office. Its lackluster record didn't bother me. It felt just like starting over at Baxley or Kendrick. I sat atop a poorly performing program in desperate need of leadership, new ideas and a fresh start – a challenge I loved.

An interesting story. One year into going full time at ITT, Frank promoted me to Division Manager. Our office had gone from worst to first in just six months. An ITT lawyer named Ernie came to our office once a month and took a report back to the Denver execs. One thing he wrote hit me like a ton of bricks: "Art works like a professional athlete. It is incredible how much effort he puts into building his team. I think it's important we understand that, like a professional athlete, he's going to have a short business life. After ten or fifteen years, he and his guys are going to burn out." I didn't understand his point at the time. I really thought he was out in left field. But I never forgot it. Looking back, maybe old Ernie was right. The urgency of the day-to-day crises that began at ITT only intensified as the years passed. I didn't take time off for hobbies, never played golf. Found it hard to relax.

My goal? Every minute, every day, do what I could to improve, advance and enhance the sales force. Anything else, to me, was nothing more than a distraction from winning.

FULL TIMERS

By now I knew for dead certain that the part-time concept worked. We recruited an army of part-timers in Columbus. I was swamped with people. What a challenge, trying to help them all get trained and licensed. Clearly, ITT needed a system to manage a large influx of new reps. They didn't have one – why would they? Such growth was unknown in their 40 year history.

I discovered something else, too. People were looking for new careers. They didn't necessarily want a part-time solution; they wanted to change their lives. They hated their jobs, their bosses, their lifestyles. They wanted more. My part-time, extra-income opportunity appealed to them as full-time employment.

This startled me, and I struggled to fully understand it. I loved coaching, heart and soul. Leaving it behind had been the hardest decision of my life. Now I began to see my experience as unusual. Most people I talked to felt miserable in their jobs and wanted a way out of "the trap."

Right before my eyes, a whole new market opened up. Instead of just part-timers, why not build an army of full-timers, as well?

I saw a solution to my people management crisis. My "Friday night feeling" told me my move to Atlanta, untapped and unlimited, came at the perfect time.

All I needed was a little help from ITT.

GOLD MINE

My philosophy: Always, *always* work within your warm market. Cold calls? Don't waste your time. It's much easier to sell when a friend opens the door.

But I didn't know anybody in Atlanta. Our office was located in DeKalb County, with 21 high schools – triple the number of high schools in all of metro Columbus. And DeKalb was just one of four counties that made up the huge metropolitan Atlanta area. Millions of people lived here and, if experience held true, only a few knew the first thing about "Buy Term and Invest the Difference." That was the good news – the market was unlimited. Our office sat in the middle of a gold mine. Now… how to "make friends" with all those strangers?

Common sense kicked in. I hand-wrote letters to all 21 high school head football coaches in DeKalb County, plus a few in Gwinnett County, where I lived. The simple letter introduced me as Coach Art Williams, explained a little bit of my personal story and mentioned the part-time opportunity. I ended the letter by asking for a meeting in the next few days to tell them more.

I didn't know any of these coaches personally, but I did know some of their names. After seven years of coaching, I'm sure my name rang a bell with some of them, too. Coaching was my connection – I used it to my advantage. I talked their language. I knew their financial situations, how they always needed extra money to pay the bills.

I sent out the letters, waited three days, then started making phone calls.

Coaches typically have down time during the day, so I asked if I could see them during an off period or lunch period. I couldn't wait to talk to those guys. I couldn't wait to tell them my story, how much money I was making, and how much I'd saved.

In the late 1960s, having $42,000 in savings was practically unheard of. Here I was, a little old football coach from South Georgia, on my way to having $100,000 in savings if I kept it up. To think that I could offer the same opportunity to other people just like me – *unbelievable*. Every other part-time opportunity out there offered mere pennies compared to the money they could make selling insurance and investments part-time.

I met with 12 coaches. That was all it took. I recruited one coach and he led me to his friends. I recruited a couple more coaches and they led me to their friends. The system worked, just like it had in Columbus and Phoenix. I found a warm market, just by reaching out to a few fellow coaches.

Pretty soon we could barely keep up with all the new recruits coming into the office. In fact, I never did get through that list of 21 coaches. I never had time. All it takes is one recruit. Bring in one good person and you can build a business empire.

One of the coaches I wrote to was Bobby Johnson, South Gwinnett High School's head football coach. Bobby threw away my letter. But South Gwinnett's basketball coach, a guy named Tee Faircloth, picked the letter out of the trashcan, read it and called me. Over lunch one day, I explained the deal. He quickly grasped the concepts and the crusade and signed right up. As fast as he could, Tee hit the field part-time, making sales and telling friends about this great new opportunity.

Tee played four years on the Auburn University basketball team and that connection led us to recruit three of his fellow teammates – Bobby Buisson in Snellville, Randall Walker in nearby Carrollton, and later on, Bob Miller in Fort Lauderdale.

All these good men played big roles in the boom years that lay ahead.

LAST TO FIRST

By the end of 1973, our Atlanta office solidly sat in the number one spot in ITT. Talk about exciting – we were the big heroes in the company. My personal income hit $35,000, and I ran a thriving office with five full-time managers and 100 part-time agents. With Randy Phelps, I now had Tee Faircloth, Bobby Buisson, Rusty Crossland, Jim Martin, Ron Wright and my brother, Bill Williams, all working full-time.

Business soared in that little office on Memorial Drive. What could possibly go wrong?

A TRIP THAT SOLD THE DREAM

ITT did one thing right – contests and incentive trips. A real highlight for me turned out to be the ITT Financial Services annual convention in Las Vegas and Acapulco. Until that time, Angela and I had never traveled outside Georgia, Alabama, Florida or North Carolina.

For the first time in our lives, we found ourselves flying across the country, living it up in five-star hotels and being exposed to a whole new level of success. The 10-day meeting had productivity requirements. As Division Manager over the top sales organization in the company, I qualified to attend. So did the number one producer in my office, Tee Faircloth.

Angela and I, with Tee and his wife, Gay, flew first to ITT Financial Services' beautiful headquarters in Denver. We visited with Frank Pierson and other home office executives for three days. Then we spent five days at Caesar's Palace in Las Vegas. Then, incredibly, we spent *another* five days at the Acapulco Princess in Mexico, one of the world's top resorts. What an eye-opener! We'd never seen such luxury. The company did a super job of "selling the dream" to its top salespeople. We felt like royalty. What a welcoming reward, considering how hard we'd worked.

When I returned to the office after that trip, I noticed something about my attitude: I wanted to dream even bigger, work even harder. I wanted to recruit more people and make more sales. I set a new goal – a $100,000 income. That "dream trip" exposed me to a standard of living I'd never imagined. Art Williams, an ordinary guy, a football coach, had a shot at living a dream lifestyle.

I realized that if I worked harder, and if I motivated my team to work harder, we could all qualify to attend the next trip. At every meeting, I told my people about the trip, how incredible it felt, what they had to do to qualify. I told them to "go for it." Las Vegas and Mexico had been wonderful, but I knew the next trip would be even better if I could take a bunch of teammates along. They would come home just as fired up as I was.

From that point on, I knew the importance of incentive trips. What a boost to fly to a luxurious resort and receive the "red carpet treatment" for a few days. You feel important and appreciated. You remember why you work so hard. You have a great time with your spouse. You just never forget it. It sells the dream like nothing else.

BEGINNING OF THE END

Things clicked along for our team, but not for our company. In the 1960s, ITT Financial Services' parent company, International Telephone and Telegraph Corporation, had grown (under the management of CEO Harold Geneen) into one of the largest multinational conglomerates in the world. Headquartered in New York City, ITT Corporation managed 250 companies in about 60 countries and owned, among others, Sheraton Hotels, Continental Baking and Avis Rent-A-Car. In 1969, ITT negotiated to buy the Hartford Fire Insurance Corporation, a $1.4 billion purchase – the largest financial services takeover in U.S. history at that time.

Before the deal could go through, however, the United States Justice Department accused ITT of becoming a monopoly and slapped it with an antitrust lawsuit. The case attempted to block ITT's acquisition of three companies, including Hartford.

ITT did eventually buy Hartford, but the antitrust case dragged on for two years and generated lots of negative publicity, even after the case settled. In fact, that next year Senate hearings revealed that ITT made a $400,000 contribution to President Nixon's re-election campaign in an effort to sway him to stop antitrust prosecution against ITT. The case settled out of court in July 1971 in a firestorm of public controversy. The settlement required ITT to "voluntarily" sell off some smaller companies in exchange for purchasing Hartford. Two of the "sell-off" companies? ITT Mutual Funds and ITT Hamilton Life – our companies!

At the same time, rumors flew that ITT had hired an assassin to kill a dictator in Chile. ITT did have huge investment holdings in Chile, and CEO Geneen worried over a possible communist takeover by Chilean radical Salvadore Allende. To stymie Allende's presidential election campaign, Ganeen reportedly funneled $1 million of ITT funds through the CIA to support Allende's election opponent. The details of this outrageous story put ITT back in the daily news and kept it there for months.

The turmoil immediately impacted my sales force. The negative publicity from the Chile story certainly made it tough to stay positive about ITT. But fallout from the antitrust suit settlement damaged us even more. ITT Life Insurance Company went on the block, then sold to California Life. Hartford, the company ITT had sacrificed so much to keep, was brought in to underwrite the new life insurance business.

All these changes quickly produced an administrative nightmare. California Life handled old business and Hartford handled new business. With companies coming and going, files got lost, policies got misplaced – thousands of policies. It didn't take long for policyowners to start screaming, and I didn't blame them. We had a mess, and our heads were spinning trying to keep up with all the phone calls and paperwork.

Want a challenge? Try to motivate a team and keep writing business when you can't be sure which company handles your business from one day to the next… or whether they would even take care of your clients after policies get issued.

In all the confusion, I lost Randy Phelps. I wasn't totally surprised. He decided to return to being a full-time pilot. He loved the crusade, but he loved flying just a little bit more. I understood his decision, but it was a shame. I really believe if he'd stayed on, he would now be a millionaire many times over.

COMMISSION CRISIS

As if the situation wasn't chaotic enough, our commissions now began to disappear. Of all the problems we'd endured, this was by far the worst. As ITT Financial Services' number one producing office, we full-timers had built up a full year's worth of commission income.

Personally, I planned on a year of $1,500 a month in commissions from hundreds of sales. We never got any of it. Not a nickel. For me, it spelled a loss of $18,000. Losses to the sales force totaled hundreds of thousands. I felt sick. Our commissions simply vanished without a trace. California Life lost the files, or at least that's what we were told. Unbelievable.

With no way to get those commissions back, we had one option – go out and write new business to replace it. But that brought problems as well.

Selling for ITT Life Insurance presented no conflict of interest with our "Buy Term and Invest the Difference" philosophy. ITT believed in and promoted the concept. But Hartford? Totally different animal.

Like all big, traditional insurance companies, Hartford offered a couple of term products, but sold mostly cash-value products. It put us in the position of having to sell products from a company that didn't support "Buy Term and Invest the Difference."

What a nightmare. We were anti-traditionalists to the core. Hartford? As old-line as they came. We sold their term products and left the cash-value products alone, but they didn't like us, and we didn't like them. Somehow, that didn't matter to the executives. We were just supposed to close our eyes and make the best of it.

Talk about strange. In months, ITT Financial Services went from running like a well-oiled machine to almost total wipeout. Yesterday, the meteoric growth of our organization set new company records. Today, we struggled to survive. We weren't suffering because of anything we had done professionally. In fact, we had done everything in our power to make things better. But, as a tiny cog in the giant wheel of ITT Corporation, it trickled down to our little 'ol hard-working sales force to pay for extravagant mistakes higher up.

Frustrated beyond belief, I took the only action I could. I wrote Frank Pierson a long letter, and I did not mince words. I clearly outlined all the problems we faced because of the company sell-offs, the paperwork fiascoes and the lost commissions. It was harsh, but I wanted Frank to know the situation. After all, you don't "lose" paychecks and not expect to hear about it. As far as I was concerned, ITT had messed up a very good thing, and they had some answering to do.

I sent off my letter in a satisfied huff, completely confident I'd get the answers I wanted.

FIRED

A couple of weeks later, Frank Pierson flew to the Atlanta airport, set up a temporary office there and began to meet separately with all the Division Managers from the eastern United States. I was the last one on his list. I soon discovered why.

As I walked into the room, I saw Frank and several other ITT executives from New

York. Before I could even open my mouth, Frank dropped the bomb.

"Art, it looks to me like you need to go back and coach. As far as I'm concerned, you're gone."

My jaw dropped. I had never been fired before. I didn't know whether to walk out the door or walk over and slug him. Humiliating, especially with other people looking on.

But Frank wasn't done. He said, "Art, I don't think you want to stay in this business. I think you want to coach. You go think about it this weekend, but I don't really care about ever seeing you again. If you're serious about staying in this company, you'll be in my office in Denver, Monday morning at 8 o'clock."

Here I was, the number one guy at ITT Financial Services, and I'd just gotten the axe. Fired by a man I looked up to greatly, who called me his "All American," who believed in me enough to take huge risks with my ideas. Looking back, I can see my naiveté in having kept Frank Pierson on such a pedestal. After all, he was a human being – he put his pants on one leg at a time, like the rest of us.

In reality, ITT Corporation had forced Frank into a very uncomfortable position with tough decisions to make. But at the time I could see none of that. All I knew was that Frank Pierson was *the guy* who had believed in me, enticed me to come full-time, given me a chance to prove myself and my ideas, and cheered me on to victory. With Frank's encouragement I'd gone from part-time to full-time, and from there we had achieved amazing results – built a huge sales force, the likes of which ITT had never seen before, brought in hundreds of new recruits, sent sales skyrocketing and shattered all the company records.

Now... he'd fired me.

I was crushed. I went home sick as a dog for the entire weekend. I felt so upset I didn't know what to do. It reminded me of that weekend at Baxley after we lost the spring game. *Horrible.*

Frank left one of his vice presidents to babysit me. That weekend, the guy called me several times, encouraging me to go to Denver on Monday. At first I said *no way.* Frank's words and attitude cut me to the bone. I never wanted to speak to him again. To be fired *at all* was devastating, but to be fired so coldly, in front of big leaders from New York, well... that was really inexcusable.

But the closer Monday came, the more I got to thinking. This was my business. I had poured my life into it for three years. I loved my sales team and what we had accomplished. I wasn't ready to give up.

Angela and I flew to Denver Sunday night. Frank found me sitting in his office at 8 o'clock the next morning.

He seemed like the "old" Frank I knew so well. We talked through some of the issues in my letter. He said my letter had shocked him, and he apologized – a little bit – for the airport episode. We worked it out, and I wasn't fired anymore.

I was glad to be back. One thing hadn't changed, however. ITT Financial Services still reeled in a state of complete disarray.

A CALL FROM THE COMPETITION

A few weeks later, out of the blue, I got call from John Kostmeyer. I only knew John by reputation. He had been a top executive for ITT's corporate headquarters in New York and Frank Pierson's boss, in charge of the entire Denver operation. Now he served as chairman of the board for Waddell & Reed, another "Buy Term and Invest the Difference" company.

John invited me to his company headquarters in Kansas City to take a look at the Waddell & Reed operation. With ITT's shaky condition, the timing certainly felt right for checking out other options.

Meeting with John at their headquarters, I saw two important things. Waddell & Reed sold an improved product – Annual Renewable Term (ART). This "level" term product cost 25-50 percent less than the decreasing term product we sold at ITT. For the first time I'd found a "complete" term product, priced super competitively and also a perfect fit with our "Theory of Decreasing Responsibility." This theory proposes that people need more "death" protection when they're younger and have more responsibility – raising children, paying lots of bills and a mortgage. That's when they are most vulnerable financially. When children grow up and leave, the mortgage is paid, and other routine bills disappear, the couple's need for insurance drops significantly. Now, they need cash for retirement.

The theory illustrates the wisdom of purchasing low-cost, high-protection term, and investing "the difference" (between buying whole life and term) in a solid investment program.

With this plan, accumulated savings increase as you grow older, while your insurance needs decrease until eliminated altogether. You become, in effect, "self-insured." Looking at the Waddell & Reed ART product, I immediately saw how we could offer clients a term product with a "level" price for one year, five years, 10 years, or even 15 years. Families could "lock in" their premium price and free up more money to invest for the future. ART offered huge advantages over what we sold at ITT.

Something else John showed me, though, really got my blood pumping. ITT offered just three levels for growth: Representative, District Manager and Division Manager. Waddell & Reed offered four: Representative, District Manager, Division Manager and *Regional Vice President*. That fourth level opened the door to phenomenal growth – you could move your sales force 25 percent bigger and faster.

With Waddell & Reed, I could cover six states in the Southeast, with offices in all major cities. I could expand from one office in Atlanta to an entire region of the country. What an opportunity.

I didn't return home from Kansas City that night as planned. Instead I called Angela and told her what I thought this could mean for our future. I ended up staying two more days, carefully studying Waddell & Reed's system and analyzing what it could offer a sales force.

The end result? Sold. I decided to leave ITT and go with Waddell & Reed.

10 Waddell & Reed

In June 1973, I made the leap from ITT Financial Services to Waddell & Reed. I disappointed Frank Pierson, of course, but I think he understood. At ITT, the handwriting was on the wall in red ink and capital letters.

Just six months after we left, ITT Financial Services disbanded its sales force and went out of business altogether. Amazing – a company with a 40-year history and 3,000 sales agents across the United States totally disappeared. Our decision to leave before the ship went down could not have been better timed.

The move to Waddell & Reed caused a commotion in our office. All my full-time managers made the jump with me – Tee Faircloth, Bobby Buisson, Ron Wright, Jim Martin, Rusty Crossland and Randall Walker. Many part-timers did, too. One by one they joined me at Waddell & Reed's regional office, oddly enough located just one mile down the road.

NUMBER ONE AGAIN

Waddell & Reed offered 13 sales regions. I came in as Regional Vice President over the six-state Southeast Region, dead last in production. *Of course*. Well, we'd soon fix *that*.

That fourth level promotion meant I could promote people faster, recruit faster and make more sales. Once again, we took off like gangbusters. We broke records right and left. Everything I had done at ITT continued at Waddell & Reed, but on a much higher level.

One special program addition really threw fuel on the fire.

WHAT WADDELL & REED OFFERED

1. Fourth promotion level – The Regional Vice President position offered bigger growth incentive for sales reps to "move up."

2. Advance pay – 75% advance commissions offered 9 months' commission when you made the sale upfront.

3. Fast pay – Agents paid twice a month instead of once.

4. Larger territory – Sales region covered six states versus one city.

5. Annual Renewable Term (ART) – .The first permanent term product.to age 100, competitively priced.

THE FAST START SCHOOL

Even in the earliest days of my Columbus office, new recruits streamed in so fast I needed an effective way to communicate with them on a regular basis. Don't get me wrong – I enjoyed the steady influx of new people. But I worried about them understanding our mission and purpose. With my Waddell & Reed team just getting off the ground, I didn't have many experienced people to share training responsibilities. My growing numbers made it impossible to train people individually. We needed a way to systematically train large numbers of new recruits.

So, I came up with one: The "Fast Start School" – a weekend training and communications event for 50 or more people.

It worked very simply. Every sixth weekend, we met at the office or in a local hotel. We talked "Buy Term and Invest the Difference" from 6 p.m. Friday night till 12 noon Sunday – two and a half days. I invited other leaders to speak, too, but I "preached" about 16 hours myself. These sessions proved key to building overall integrity in our agents, instilling our unique business philosophy.

I wanted new recruits to comprehend our crusade. We were on a mission to right the wrongs of the life insurance industry. Our battle cry? "Buy Term and Invest the Difference." We were different from the rest of the industry – I wanted that clear in everyone's mind.

Absorbing our educational sales approach became critical:

• Never sell on the first visit. Ask to evaluate a family's current whole life policy.

• Return with a policy comparison on the second visit. Show families on paper the differences between what they already had and what could be had with our products.

• Educate the family on "Buy Term and Invest the Difference."

• Let the family decide what's better: term or whole life.

I always made two promises at the kitchen table. I'd say, "Mr. and Mrs. Consumer, if you need more insurance, I will give you eight to 10 times more protection for the same money. Or, I'll give you the same protection and cut your costs by 75 to 80 percent. If I can't do one of those two things for you, then I don't deserve your business."

I wanted our sales team to know how to tell their clients the same thing. The goal? Educate people with *facts*. Then let them see for themselves the options we could offer.

I pounded the podium on warm market referrals. *No* cold calls, soliciting, or talking to strangers. *No* passing out balloons to kids at the county fair, hoping to rope in their parents. I despised those kinds of gimmicks. Appointments came only through friends, then *their* friends, and so on.

I carefully explained the "one friend" method: You meet a friend. You ask him or her to write down the names of 10 other friends who might be interested in a good part-time business opportunity. (As a side comment, I always said that if you talk to someone who doesn't have 10 friends, he's probably not a good recruit!) Out of those 10 friends, let's say you recruit five. Each of those five recruits has 10 friends. That gives you 50 more people to talk to. Of those 50 people, you get 25 recruits… and 250 new people to talk to. Of those 250, you get 125 recruits… and 1,250 new friends to talk to.

This method could keep an agent recruiting in a warm market for a hundred years, never once talking to a stranger. For the first time in Waddell & Reed's history, agents had a way to recruit by multiplication, instead of straight-line addition. We'd found a way to build a big, quality sales force fast.

The Fast Start School gave us a terrific forum to systematically, but warmly, welcome large numbers of new people into the business. It helped us compress time frames and grow fast – first into a regional and then later on a national sales force. It really worked!

Yes, that first year at Waddell & Reed zipped along great, except for one little thing: A major crisis that almost killed our organization... and put Waddell & Reed on the brink of extinction.

THE SEC BOMBSHELL

Go back with me a moment to my family reunion in 1967. My cousin Ted Harrison tells me about an insurance product I didn't know existed.

"All the traditional agents own term policies, but they don't sell it to their clients because it's inexpensive and they can't make a living selling it," he says.

That was the problem with term insurance. It's cheap, and if you stick to your principles and sell only term, it's hard to make a living. At both ITT and Waddell & Reed, we sold the daylights out of low-cost term policies... *and* we sold mutual funds, since those companies were primarily investment companies.

Selling contractual mutual funds helped us make a living. They were commonplace then. In fact, contractual mutual funds really launched the whole mutual fund investment industry. Typically, agents sold 10-year, $100-per-month plans, with half of the sales commission going to the agent in the first 12 months of the sale. With a $1,200-a-year fund, the agent received half the $600 sales charge, or $300. Pretty good money.

Then, in 1972, the Securities Exchange Commission (SEC) dropped a bombshell. It changed the way we did business forever.

The SEC regulation required the company to ask the client if he wanted to renege on his initial investment at the end of the first year. The agent had to show the client his first year's investment value and then give back the client's money, if requested.

For the most part, this put contractual mutual funds out of business. Here's why: If you show a client that an initial $1,200 investment is worth only $600 in the first year because the stock market dips, and he's paid 50 percent of his sales charges the first year, of course he wants his money back.

Most companies dropped contractual mutual funds and went to a "level load" type of fund, where commissions were paid out over the length of the fund as a percentage. This meant the average agent commission plunged to around $50 the first year. For our sales force, going from $300 to $50 resulted in an 80 percent pay cut – drastic – and all because of the SEC's unexpected regulation change. At the end with ITT, we were hurting financially anyway, and this added insult to injury. But what could we do?

After the switch to Waddell & Reed, we began selling their Annual Renewable Term (ART), guaranteed to age 100. Waddell & Reed invented the ART as the first "permanent" form of term insurance. A fantastic product for the consumer and extremely inexpensive, ART worked differently from the 20-year decreasing term product we'd sold at ITT, which had a level premium. A $100,000 decreasing term policy like ITT's product meant the premium remained level at $250 each year of the policy. But the ART featured an increasing premium. If you sold a $100,000 ART policy, the first year premium might be $180, depending on the client's age. The next year's premium would increase to $191, the next year $196, and so on. While a great product for the consumer, ART gave the agent a major commission hit. We fell from making half of $250 to half of $180 – a 30 percent cut.

COMMISSION CRISIS

The commission cutback meant my Southeast team could sell like mad, recruit like crazy, and still barely make a living.

After about five months, I flew to see John Kostmeyer in Kansas City. Waddell & Reed was such a vast improvement over ITT that I hated to complain. Overall, their products and service rated high. But we were working hard and starving to death. From where I stood, I didn't see how Waddell & Reed could keep its doors open. We needed a product that paid more commission. Without a change, and soon, the company faced real trouble. John agreed.

I offered a possible solution. A general agent who worked for Fireman's Fund had told me about a new concept – "deposit term." A small insurance company in Texas developed it to work like this: If the client wanted a 10-year $100,000 policy, he paid a $1,000 deposit ($10 per $1,000 of coverage) as a promise that he would keep the policy the full ten years. In return for the deposit, the agent guaranteed a 7.2 percent tax-free return on his money. At the end of 10 years, the client got back $2,000, guaranteed. It paid great returns for consumers and great commissions for sales agents. I told John I wanted to bring this product to Waddell & Reed, and he gave me the green light.

Insurance products have no copyright protection, so when a company comes up with a new competitive product, other companies duplicate it. That's what we did. I talked to the Texas company, figured out the product structure and gave the information to our actuaries. They made some improvements and created the Waddell & Reed version of a deposit term product. We called it the Guaranteed-10, or G-10 for short. In no time, my Waddell & Reed team was out selling deposit term like crazy.

The G-10 product saved the company. Our commission soared from $90 to $250 – double the ART product.

FAST PAY BONANZA

A huge advantage at Waddell & Reed turned out to be their "fast pay" system. ITT forced agents to wait for the policy to go on the books before issuing a sales commission; it took three months. In contrast, Waddell & Reed paid advance commissions. When you sold an insurance policy, you got nine months (or 75 percent) of your commission paid "in advance." In other words, you got paid *immediately* after the sale.

The advance pay system phenomenally improved the old "slow pay" way, and gave sales agents extra incentive to write more business. Recruiting got easier, too. Handing a new recruit his first paycheck almost instantly motivated him to go out and "do it again." Naturally, sales and recruiting took off.

It reinforced a business truth I learned long ago: The faster you reward good behavior, the faster you grow.

CHARGEBACKS, ROLL-UPS AND THE 5-POINT CHECKLIST

One "catch" plagued the system – getting a "chargeback." If a client dropped the policy before it had been "on the books" 12 months, the company issued the selling agent a chargeback. He then had to pay back his advance commission in full. A "roll-up" charge applied if a downline agent left the company with a sale that didn't stay on the books for one year. In that situation, the chargeback "rolled up" to the Division Manager or Regional Vice President, who then faced paying back the advance commission. Chargebacks wrecked "persistency," a performance indicator closely watched by the company. If lots of policies fell off the books, a red flag went up, and the company investigated sales agents for the quality of business they wrote.

The advance pay system meant managing monthly income flow, and setting aside extra "emergency" funds on a regular basis became extremely important. An unexpected chargeback could wipe out a family budget. Roll-ups could also cause some pretty hard feelings among teammates.

In our office, we set up guidelines. We pinpointed our market and devised a 5-point recruiting checklist. We wanted to sit down with married couples 25 years or older who owned homes, had kids and steady jobs. We look to recruit conscientious men and women who needed our products, wanted to make money and cared about writing good business. People meeting these criteria had more to lose by being reckless or dishonest. Raising a family and paying a mortgage made them more likely to write good business – they had too much on the line to risk losing income through chargebacks. Also, the profile yielded good clients – the kind of folks who needed life insurance anyway. Bottom line, we wanted to hire people who needed life insurance. They spoke effectively to other people who needed life insurance. Just that simple.

Once again, hiring part-time agents worked beautifully. Part-timers had little incentive to abuse the company – they already had full-time jobs and didn't rely on making sales for financial survival.

We also asked the agent – and the spouse – to sign a note committing to pay back the advance commission if the agent received a chargeback. If someone lost a policy, one of two things would happen: The agent would write another policy to replace the lost income. Or, if the agent decided to leave the company, he had to pay back the debt to the company before resigning. That way, the chargeback didn't roll up to the manager, forcing him to pay a debt he didn't cause.

Chargebacks didn't happen often, but when they did, the right people had to be held accountable. A responsible plan eliminated much hurt and anger.

FIELD TRAINING

In my opinion, classroom training is pretty much a waste of time. Trainers typically have little or no "real world" selling experience. They might have fancy degrees and know a bunch of big words, but usually they don't know much about the insurance business. I wanted my team to learn from *our* managers – people who made their living selling our products, who lived by our principles.

When I recruited new people, I always went on appointments and made the first few sales for them. I probably made 40 sales with one of my recruits, Robert Sapp, Berkmar High School's baseball coach at the time. Robert was one of the coaches I recruited with my handwritten letters when I first moved to Atlanta. He had so many contacts it took us months to see them all. I think I recruited another 20 to 30 people just through him. We went together on all those appointments, until he felt comfortable taking out his own recruits. That's the best way to learn.

Field training strengthened the important relationship between the upline manager and the new recruit. I'm a proponent for four reasons.

First, you really get to know a person when you sell and recruit together. Second, everyone ends up with a crystal-clear understanding of chargebacks and the payback system. Third, if an agent leaves the company, the manager still holds a relationship with the client and can comfortably follow up on that person's policy or investment needs. Fourth, the new recruit moves into the field faster.

Our system – using managers to train downlines – built a lot of protection into our organization. It also bonded us. Aside from the troubles we experienced from bad corporate decisions, we rarely knew internal conflicts.

Growth has a way of forcing change, though.

Eventually, I faced a tough decision that triggered our first "in-house" clash.

FIRST PROMOTION

I came into Waddell & Reed as Regional Vice President of the southeast region of the United States. In six months, our region shot from worst to first, becoming the largest, highest-producing office in the company. As RVP, I traveled to the eight Waddell & Reed offices in my region, spread over six states: Alabama, Florida, Georgia, Mississippi, North Carolina and South Carolina. I still ran our Atlanta Division office, too. Soon, it became too much. I was working myself to death trying to do it all.

I made a decision to promote one of my downlines to lead that office. But who?

By this point, I held to a very important leadership tenet: A credible leader in this business had to do two things:

1. Prove an opportunity works by being personally successful at it.

2. Develop at least one successful downline leader, to show others the opportunity is "for real."

Here's where things got tricky. My most experienced manager was Tee Faircloth. Below him, Bobby Buisson, and then five or six other up-and-coming leaders.

On paper, Tee deserved the promotion. A good recruiter and salesman, Tee earned the biggest income in the group. He'd produced several strong leaders who also performed well. But Tee had some troubling personal issues he couldn't seem to overcome – a sticking point for me.

My second candidate was Bobby Buisson, a former teacher and basketball coach. Loyal, coachable, a relentless worker and a great family man, Bobby loved the crusade and threw himself into learning the business. His best attribute? A fantastic attitude. But learning the business came hard for Bobby. He struggled with every aspect of selling and recruiting.

I'll never forget our first Fast Start School at Waddell & Reed. I asked Bobby to be one of my speakers. He spent three weeks meticulously preparing a presentation. When the time came for him to speak, I gave him a long, flattering introduction, my usual style. I loved to spend four or five minutes telling the audience about my guys, what they had accomplished, how loyal, smart and hard working they were. Knowing Bobby's nerves, I really poured it on. When I was done, Bobby walked stiffly to the podium. He read his 15- minute speech – word for word – and as he did, he ran out of air and paused in mid-sentence to suck in his breath. We prayed he would get through it without passing out.

I didn't like anyone to ever read a speech. I wanted speakers to get up and talk, straight from the heart. After that episode, I told Bobby never to write out another speech but instead to be prepared to talk 15 minutes about some aspect of the business that he could talk about for five *hours*. "Bobby," I told him, "just get up, talk fast and be excited! People remember enthusiasm long after they forget the words."

Bobby took the advice to heart. We spent hours together, practicing on stage, going over client presentations, learning the system, working through fears. He simply did not give up. That kind of "bulldog" tenacity went a long way with me.

Bobby struggled financially at first. His first year full-time, he earned $6,000 – less than he brought home as a teacher and coach. He struggled, too, in recruiting downline leaders. A diamond in the rough, for sure.

CHARACTER COUNTS

None of that bothered me. Bobby became my choice to take over my Atlanta office – an office full of future A.L. Williams giants. Bobby – always positive, loyal and dependable, even as he struggled – earned the reward instead of Tee.

It could be viewed that I'd temporarily lost my senses with this decision.

Well, it *was* a tough decision, one of many to follow. But I wanted to send a clear message to our team. I meant to build my business with people like Bobby – people with great attitudes, work ethics, and family values. Our opportunity was so special that a guy like Bobby, who initially faltered in the business, could become a superstar. You can teach a person with character how to be a good producer. You can't teach a producer how to become a person of character. Reputation is everything in business.

Bobby rose to the challenge like a champion. Taking over my base shop, he found himself in charge of a fantastic team, and his income rocketed from $18,000 to $100,000 in one year. He became the second $100,000 earner in our Waddell & Reed organization, after me. Later, he went on to become the top earner in the company and a multi-millionaire. I made the right call.

On the other hand, my choice absolutely devastated Tee. He'd joined the company before Bobby. He'd become the bigger producer. He felt entitled to the promotion. Bitter and defiant after the pass-over, Tee showed no respect for Bobby and made life miserable for him, to the point of disrupting the whole office. He refused to attend any meeting Bobby called, sabotaged his weekly activity reports, called Bobby a brown-noser (and worse) in front of others. I was ready to fire him, but Bobby held me back. His friendship with Tee, dating back to their basketball days at Auburn, meant enough to Bobby to protect his disappointed, gifted associate.

I gave Tee an ultimatum – either leave the company or go work in Tallahassee with Coach Taylor. By this time, Coach Taylor had left coaching, and I convinced him to join our business, putting him in charge of that office. I was confident Coach Taylor could teach Tee a thing or two, maybe help him grow up a bit. To his credit, Tee moved his whole family down there and stayed for a year. He worked hard and did well.

After that, I promoted him to Division Manager and moved him back to Macon, Georgia.

ONE TOUGH DUDE

One issue really made headlines at Waddell & Reed – my decision to promote a lady named Virginia Carter to Division Manager. Ginny had been at Waddell & Reed about a year when I came in 1973. A District Manager then, Ginny knew both sides of the game (she'd briefly sold whole life), and she was a total convert to the "Buy Term and Invest the Difference" philosophy. She was spunky. She was hard working. She was a leader I could count on.

Ginny worked out of a Division office located off of I-85 in Atlanta called Northgate Park, led by a guy named John Pestrocelli. John was a nice guy, but clueless about financial services. He'd moved from New Jersey to Atlanta, leaving an old multilevel marketing company called Bestline. When Waddell & Reed began to hire division managers from outside the company, John got hired, with a salary package and bonus incentive. He convinced several Bestline buddies to come too, including two guys named Art Burgess and Frank Dineen. Ginny knew all of them from her days at Bestline, and she also went after a guy named Bill Orender, who eventually came on board, one of her first recruits.

- - - - - - - - - - - -

"I was 53 years old when Art came, a single mother raising four children, pretty jaded and cynical. The glass ceiling was thick in those days. I'd had several bitter experiences as a woman in the workforce. I watched how Art motivated his team, but I was skeptical at first – I'd heard those words before. I waited to see if he really lived up to his promises."

– VIRGINIA CARTER

- - - - - - - - - - - -

With the exception of Ginny, nobody out of that Northgate office turned in many sales or recruits. They were all starving to death, except for John, of course, on his guaranteed salary. I tried everything to get John motivated, but nothing worked. His heart just wasn't in it. After a year, I knew what had to be done.

Ginny and Frank Dineen became good buddies working out of John's office. Both were fed up with John's lack of leadership. In fact, they asked me to form their own "division," just to get out from under him. I nixed that idea and instead asked Frank to relocate to Tallahassee to work with Coach Taylor and Tee Faircloth. Frank, a young, single guy at the time and a little irresponsible, showed tons of potential. Like Tee, I thought he would benefit from Coach Taylor's "coaching" for a while. So I moved Frank to Tallahassee.

"I remember how that came about," Frank recalls. "Art gave me a choice – either move to Tallahassee or leave. He said I had five minutes to make up my mind. I was all set to say no, but my mouth said yes. I'm not sure why. But once I moved, I jumped from District #111, last in our region, to #4. Huge improvement."

Ginny wanted a move, too. But I presented her with another opportunity. Returning from a field training appointment with Bill Orender one night, Ginny returned my urgent phone message. "Ginny," I shouted into the phone, "if I fire John tomorrow, will you take the Division Manager position?"

On the other end, I heard Ginny suck in her breath. "Well," she said, hesitant at first. Then… "Yes! If you promise you'll help me, I'll do it! But you know the home office will blow up over this."

I grinned. "They will and that's okay. You're the right person for the job. I'll be glad to help you, but I already know you'll do great!"

Next day, I fired John and put Ginny in charge. What a difference! Incredible performers emerged from her office. Just the kind of leader I wanted, Ginny led with a big heart and a positive attitude. She loved the fight, too, boy, and she fought tough. I gave her one of my "I'm a Stud" T-shirts and she loved it. She took it just the right way.

Ginny was right – Waddell & Reed threw an absolute fit over me promoting her, but I had no regrets. So what if Ginny was a woman? Women can believe in this thing just like men. Women can fight just like men.

Ginny became the first of many women to do well in our company. She didn't want to be treated differently. She didn't want to be given something for nothing. She certainly didn't want to be denied something she was tough enough to earn for herself.

It's one of my favorite principles: If you give a frustrated man or woman an opportunity to *be somebody*, then watch out. They find a way to win. You can count on them when the going gets tough.

FLORIDA CONNECTION

Another tough woman also played a huge role in our company's development, but in a different way. Trudy White, a 20-year veteran of Waddell & Reed when we first met, managed our Fort Lauderdale office. Trudy was sharp, and we hit it off instantly. Loaded with company knowledge, Trudy stayed totally on top of things. She knew how to run an office. I relocated her to Tallahassee as Coach Taylor's office manager, and she helped him organize and run things there. She took Tommy's talented but roughneck crew of crusaders – Frank Dineen, Tee Faircloth and Fred Marceaux, an old coaching buddy of mine from Thomasville days – and made them professional. Big job.

About this time, Bobby Buisson mentioned one of his college roommates and basketball buddies, a guy named Bob Miller, in Fort Lauderdale. I wanted to grow our Waddell & Reed office in that city; adding new blood would give the place a boost.

A math teacher and high school basketball coach – always a plus for me – Bob needed extra income. We decided to meet.

"Within 10 minutes, I was ready to join," Bob remembers of that February 1974 meeting. "Art didn't even go through a commission structure. He just talked about it being good part-time income. I started the licensing process that day."

Bobby Buisson smiled when I told him Bob joined. I'm a pretty good judge of character, and Bob seemed like just the kind of person we wanted. Green, but coachable. I had a hunch he might be one of our major players. I jotted him a little note:

How true that turned out to be.

CLOSING A SALE

People don't believe me when I say I hate sales. Let me make the distinction. I loved selling "Buy Term and Invest the Difference," because it sold itself. What I couldn't stand were sales tricks or gimmicks. You know...*Techniques*. I just educated people with facts. No "conventional" sales approaches for me.

A good example. Bob got his Florida license and I flew down personally to field train him. Bob took us to a friend, Dan. When I talked to Dan, I could tell he was a pretty analytical guy. At our second appointment, I quietly laid out the comparisons of Dan's whole life policies and ours.

"What do you think?" I asked. What a closer! Try to find that one in a sales training book! But I knew Dan was a smart guy – he could make a decision on his own. No need for salesmanship on my part.

Dan looked over the numbers. He finally nodded. "Well, it looks pretty good to me," he said. "You're saving me half the monthly cost. You're freeing up $2,000 for savings. I'd be a complete fool not to go with your program!"

Exactly the conclusion I wanted him to draw! I asked Dan if he wanted a term insurance application. Yes, again.

Unconventional? Yes. But that's how I made every sale and it's how I taught my team to make sales. Show the clients the facts. Let them draw their own conclusions. Unless they're "double-dumb," they can't miss that "Buy Term and Invest the Difference" is a family's best way to go.

That night, I sat down with Bob and his wife, Jane, and talked. I asked Bob if he knew how much money he'd just made. Of course, it brought back my own first appointment at ITT, when John Crawford sat there in that Columbus coffee shop and told me I'd made $325.

I could tell Bob had no idea. He was excited about our program, not even thinking about commissions. When I told them it was $600, Bob and Jane's eyes bugged out like mine once had.

At that time, Bob's take-home pay was $1,000 a month. He pulled in an extra $500 coaching basketball. I helped him make $600 in two nights, just by going out and helping his friends. In the months to come, Bob would earn enough part-time to let Jane stay home with their two young children. Truly the greatest part-time opportunity on the market.

STAR PLAYER

Another key player joined our ranks as a walk-on. Bob Turley, in his earlier days, pitched for the New York Yankees. And I mean pitched. He played in seven World Series, earned MVP of the 1958 World Series, won the Cy Young Award and the Hickok Belt (a professional athlete of the year award). I met Turley through a mutual friend in Atlanta, G. Scott Reynolds. Scott had written a book called The Mortality Merchants, a third-party piece totally exposing the frauds of the cash value insurance industry. In the book, he hailed "Buy Term and Invest the Difference" as the right insurance concept for consumers. We had the first third-party piece of literature that openly supported our crusade. Thrilled beyond belief when this book came out, we bought it by the truckload and gave copies to all our clients. Scott and I met, of course – he wanted to know who was buying all his books. And Scott introduced me to Bob Turley.

Bob told me that when his professional baseball career ended it took him a while to find a business he really liked. Athlete and competitor, Turley needed work that offered the same adrenaline. On his own, he found "Buy Term and Invest the Difference" and it hooked him. He had worked actively as a general agent for several insurance companies.

The problem, he explained, came along once a year – the company refused to renew his contract. Why? He sold too much term insurance and not enough cash value! Actually, Bob stubbornly refused to sell any cash value – he didn't believe in it. So he was forced to go from one company to the next, year after year.

Bob signed on with me at Waddell & Reed. I was thrilled; so was he. I brought Bob in at Division Leader and fixed him up in an empty Waddell & Reed office in Sandy Springs, just north of Atlanta. Bobby Buisson and I drove up with a desk... strapped to the top of my little red Audi. We hauled the desk up to Turley's 10th floor office and set it up for him. Turley, in a more conventional way, brought in a secretary and a couple of guys who worked with him before... and they took off.

BALMY FLORIDA

We neared the end of 1974. We were growing, and our Fast Start Schools ran like clockwork every six weeks. Those weekend meetings kept us focused and motivated.

"I remember my first Fast Start School," says Bill Orender, District Leader at the time. "I was brand new in the business. Art had all kinds of banners, streamers and signs hanging down from the ceiling, just like a schoolteacher would do in a classroom. The signs said 'Be Somebody,' and 'Crusaders Die Hard.' All the speakers wore T-shirts. Art talked about how we could change the world. That really impressed me. Nowhere else had I ever heard anyone talk to me about changing the world."

"I brought about eight of my country boys from Albany," echoes Frank Dineen, also a District Leader back then. "They sat there wearing overalls, chewing tobacco and holding spit cups. Bill Orender got up to speak, all prim and proper, looked down at my guys and almost fell of the stage. He said, 'You guys must be with Dineen.' I said, 'Hey, Orender, stick it in your ear. They'll out-perform your guys any day of the week. We shoot guys in three-piece suits in South Georgia.' Very competitive, but all in good fun."

In December, I organized our Southeast Region's very first annual convention. Although one day we would go to the finest resorts in the world, this one was "no frills" – basically a long weekend, expenses paid out of my own pocket. I set us up at a Howard Johnson hotel in Panama City, Florida. Everybody heard we were staying at a beautiful place on the beach with swaying palm trees, balmy temperatures and white sand.

We got off the plane on a Friday night, and it was 32 degrees. So much for "balmy." We waited in the lobby. The Howard Johnson couldn't give us meeting space until the hotel restaurant closed for the evening!

It didn't matter. We spent the weekend talking business together and had a great time. I awarded plaques, trophies and T-shirts, tons of them. Praise and recognition would be especially important at this stage of growth. I wanted to show pride in my team's accomplishments, to pump folks up and motivate them. It had to come from me; I was their leader.

"In professional baseball, we always stayed in the best hotels," remembers Bob Turley. "I'd been to Europe and Hawaii a dozen times. But as far as I was concerned, that Panama City convention was more fun than going to Europe or anywhere else. We didn't have a lot of money – the fun came with the people, the attitude and the energy. It was like being a rookie in baseball all over again. And Art kept the excitement going. He could give that coach's pep talk better than anybody. Instead of touchdowns, we were making sales."

Turley won a six-month sales contest I'd launched back in June. I played it up.

Though a "big name" athlete, Bob started as a bottom-rung Rep in our sales region. Now he was our number one producer. His pacesetting ability to put numbers on the board stretched everyone's thinking.

UNEXPECTED LOSS

The convention left us all on an emotional high. A new year! More growth! I couldn't wait!

Then out of the blue, Waddell & Reed fired John Kostmeyer, my main contact with corporate leadership, the man who had played such a major role in our success. I never got a clear story on why he got fired, except that Waddell & Reed's parent company, Continental Investment Corporation, a real estate company, teetered on bankruptcy in a soft real estate market. Apparently, firing John was part of their cutback solution.

The move set a negative tone for the next two years. I quickly discovered how much John had shielded me from Waddell & Reed politics. I got a good dose of it now. Not a game I played well at all.

THE CORPORATE GAME

In football, I focused completely on doing what it took to win a game. Every Friday night, I put the best 11 players on the field. Whoever earned the position during the week got to play. A good coach never lets politics affect who plays and who doesn't – not even for a son, a friend's son, or whoever. You just don't think that way; *you can't*, if you want to win.

That's how things should work in business, too. You reward the people who work hardest, who earn it. Both ITT Financial Services and Waddell & Reed played office politics instead. Promotions went to the person "in" with the boss. People fought over offices, how many windows, and on and on. It hadn't really affected me directly until now.

I couldn't help but notice the huge disparity in how corporate employees viewed themselves and how they viewed the sales force. Our hard work kept corporate people at all levels in their comfortable, salaried jobs. But their attitude seemed, at best, tolerant. Employees saw themselves as the smart, pretty people with fancy degrees and window offices. Agents ranked a half-step up from used car salesmen. Even top executives thought of us that way. Especially the top executives.

Here we were, working in the field every day and night, weekdays and weekends, making sale after sale, bringing in new people right and left, doing our part to make the company successful. We were growing like wildfire, breaking all the company sales records. To me, our heroes deserved the big rewards – we put it all on the line every day. Our income. Our reputations. Our mortgage payments. Home office people got their salary checks every two weeks while we lived on commissions. Home office hours ended at 5 o'clock; ours went around the clock. To my way of thinking, the corporate leaders showed foolish indifference to our efforts... and needs.

We needed recognition, bonuses and administrative support – anything to make our day-to-day effort a little easier. Instead, we got just the opposite. The big rewards went to executives; we endured cutbacks in commissions, products and support.

It all seemed backwards. As days and weeks went by at Waddell & Reed, I began to yearn for control. I wanted a company that viewed salespeople as "king," where commissions, products and administrators supported the sales force, not corporate bigwigs. I wanted unlimited promotions and sales territories. Instead of commission cutbacks, I wanted my guys to get commission raises.

For a second time, I saw handwriting on the wall. So how would it all change for the better? One way. Create our own company.

PRETTY BOYS

Bob Strader enjoyed a salaried position as "National Sales Director" out of corporate headquarters in Kansas City. Though not part of the sales force himself, Strader watched over us – a fact that irritated me. I think our climbing sales at Waddell & Reed made Bob feel threatened. So instead of working with me, the number one sales guy, he set out to undermine my reputation.

Strader called me a prima donna. He questioned my organization's quality of business, recruiting numbers, sales numbers, the quality of recruits. He made it his business to plant seeds of distrust with Ben Korschot, the president who replaced John Kostmeyer. Bob really seemed to relish his tactics – status quo for a corporate setting. But it got under my skin. It seemed ridiculous, mean and unwarranted. I didn't want the guy's job. I had no interest in a salaried position in Kansas City – with or without a window office. My thoughts headed in another direction – out the door!

I grew more and more certain, based on our numbers. Our region shot from 13th to first in a year, then we beat all the other regions combined – we could stand on our own.

"IMPACT"

A guy named Bob Butterworth worked as Strader's assistant. The two of them loved to deliver corporate messages to me, especially bad news. After all, any changes to field compensation didn't affect *their* wallets.

As months passed, tension escalated with Butterworth and Strader. Any time Korschot changed commissions, promotions or structure, he dispatched Strader or Butterworth to tell me. I disliked Strader, but I *loathed* Butterworth. A former whole life agent and corporate "pretty boy," he would tell you one thing, then turn around and do the opposite.

And where did he get off with that? He'd never built anything, sold anything or recruited anyone... and neither had Strader.

One event really put me on edge with Butterworth.

Rusty Crossland, my Division Manager, operated out of his new office in Marietta. An excellent recruiter, Rusty brought in lots of new people, worked hard, and did a phenomenal job. I felt so proud of him.

About this time, the company launched an "experimental" program called "Impact." Ten Division Managers from all over the company participated, including Rusty. Now, instead of reporting to me, Rusty straight-lined to Butterworth, with paid salary, paid expenses, secretary, office and telephone. His job? Recruit one new full-time person a month, hire and train him, put him on salary, and groom him for Division Manager.

I went ballistic. I lost one of my best recruiters to the company, and to Butterworth, no less! Rusty was so tied to Butterworth, in fact, that he couldn't hire his one recruit a month unless Butterworth flew to Atlanta to review the résumé, sit through the interview, everything.

"Impact" went against all I believed in – salary, paid expenses, full-time. Butterworth knew I didn't like it, and he never missed a chance to rub it in. To his credit, Rusty performed well. In fact, only one Division Manager in the program consistently met quota and budget goals – Rusty. I thought I'd lost him for good.

Meanwhile, our scheduled Fast Start Schools pressed on. Frank Dineen would charge in with 20 people and Rusty, two… and Rusty could hire only one!

LAST STRAW

Changes came down from the top more and more often. Like ITT Financial Services, Waddell & Reed began a meltdown. Parent company Continental Investment Corporation (CIC) finally went bankrupt, and to cover losses, corporate cut our commissions and bonuses. The effect? Devastating. Agents had to write twice as much business… to make *half* as much money. Again, a parent company sacrificed the hard-working sales force for its mistakes.

I didn't like it. At all. Nor did I like how I learned about changes. Imagine news of a 10 percent commissions cut or a promotions freeze for the next quarter coming in by interoffice memo or a phone call from Strader or Butterworth.

How could I be expected to explain another cut in pay when I didn't understand it myself? How could I possibly keep my sales team motivated?

I went to see Korschot. He at least owed us the courtesy to fully explain the changes and clarify why we had to make them. I was one of 13 Regional Vice Presidents – we all needed to understand the latest change so we could explain it. In my opinion, the least Korschot could do was take the time to talk with us himself instead of sending news by an assistant's assistant.

Korschot agreed. He confirmed he would not announce any more changes without notifying leaders first. I thought we were straight on it.

We weren't.

It was fall 1976, our annual Southeast Region convention in St. Petersburg, Florida. Everybody was pumped. In spite of all the corporate troubles, our growing sales team showed profits. I lavished them with praise and awards.

And I had a big surprise, Venita Van Caspel, as our keynote speaker. A nationally known financial advisor who publicly touted term life insurance over cash value, Venita promised to be a potent speaker. Here, thrillingly, stood a living, breathing, third-party endorsement for our "Buy Term and Invest the Difference" crusade. I couldn't wait for the meeting to start.

Then the phone rang. Butterworth. My face froze. His news? Execs had decided to cap monthly advances at $1,000. What? Some of my guys made $4,000 and $5,000 in advances every month. Finally, they could make a decent living. A monthly earning cap of $1,000? Beyond insulting.

He had more. Waddell & Reed planned to eliminate all new offices for 1977. That meant *no promotions*. At least 30 of my agents qualified for promotion!

Butterworth saved the worst for last – bonus cutbacks for the next year. Bonuses made up one-third of our incomes. Suddenly, we faced losing one-third of our income for doing the same amount of business.

"So that's your news for the day, Williams," Butterworth practically sang.

I stood there, fuming. In the midst of our great meeting, I had to deliver this horrible news. But something irked me even more. Once again, devastating company news had sailed in on a casual phone call. Korschot had given me his word. But here it was, the same old crap.

I got mad... and ugly. I told Butterworth to deliver a message to Korschot. I said, "You tell Korschot that I said he can go stick it where the sun don't shine."

I didn't quite use those words.

Butterworth sputtered a bit. I wasn't known for vulgar language. "Are you serious?" he asked, half laughing.

Boy, was I. Through gritted teeth, I said, "You go tell him those... exact... words."

And he did.

Strader, in a meeting with Korschot, heard Butterworth deliver my tender little message. Sure I'd had a mental breakdown, Strader got on a plane and flew directly to St. Petersburg. When I saw him walk into our meeting, I unloaded on him. Big time.

The scene caused an unbelievable uproar. But, honestly, I wasn't worried. In such a huge mess, it didn't make sense for Waddell & Reed to run off their number one guy. Still, for me, this fiasco was the last straw. It was déjà vu all over again – just like at ITT Financial Services. The exact same situation. *Unbelievable.* Continental Investment Corporation (CIC) took the profits from a sales force going great guns, breaking all the records, to pay off their problems. Just like at ITT, corporate problems held back our growth as a sales force.

Lower commissions. Cut bonuses. Limited promotions. Limited sales territories. Shrinking home office support. Opportunity in one of the only growing areas of the whole corporation – *reduced* instead of expanded? It didn't make sense.

The time had come to leave and do better for people. It wouldn't take much.

As I suspected, CIC had no intention of running me off. Just the opposite. Terrified I might leave, anxious to do anything to keep me, they flew me up to their huge luxury office tower in downtown Boston and lavished me with food and attention for an entire day after the bombshell meeting.

We talked. CIC threw out all kinds of bait. Would I be interested in the President's position (Korschot's job)? Would I like a $100,000-plus per year salary with lots of perks? What would I think about the Vice President position? They even offered me the National Sales Director's job – Strader's job. Ha! His worst nightmare confirmed!

Outside, I remained polite, thoughtful and complimentary. I listened. I played like part of the team. Inside, though, I boiled. Look how the company operated – limo service, huge office suites, food service carts loaded with hot tea and clam chowder, on and on – every luxury perk imaginable. These people lived like kings, while we got scraps in the field. Somehow, they could heartlessly cut our profits but not their own overblown budget.

This day would prove to be a waste of their time. I had no intention of taking a corporate position. I was leaving. Nothing they could say or do that day would change my mind now. I wanted something better than a job. I wanted to build my own company. I wanted a business that let salespeople be "king."

I would've thoroughly enjoyed telling them so. But timing, after all, is everything. October 1976, I had already started making plans. But I needed to find a company to take our business. Also, year-end bonuses mailed at the end of January. I wasn't about to leave until we all received that hard-earned reward.

So, I had four months to get organized. As I sat there quietly listening to the suits talk, my mind raced.

I *knew* what I wanted. I *knew* it would work.

In Boston that day, I left them convinced I'd calmed down. Hostile words? Forgiven. My reaction? Understandable. It had been a tough year at Waddell & Reed, and sometimes folks let off a little steam. Now everything would be just fine.

That's what they thought.

Six weeks later, I had an underwriter. Very soon, the door would be swinging shut behind me, no looking back.

11 Financial Assurance

The next four months turned out to be some of the happiest – and most frustrating – of my life.

Ten years of hard work had proven what I believed to be true. "Buy Term and Invest the Difference" benefited families. Recruiting part-timers benefited a sales force. Individual responsibility benefited individual achievement.

We broke sales records at both ITT Financial Services and Waddell & Reed, in spite of all the corporate setbacks. We were onto something colossal. We'd found a better mousetrap, a better way to build a company.

I began to harbor a dream. I'd really never seen a way to challenge the big guys, like Prudential or New York Life. Now, it hit me like a big middle linebacker – we could become a national sales force, not just regional. We could beat Prudential! We could dominate this whole industry.

We lacked only one thing – a company willing to give us a chance.

Fast and thoroughly, I put together a detailed game plan of our concepts and accomplishments and started making phone calls. I could barely breathe! This was it – the big time. I thought I'd talk to two or three companies at most, then we'd have a deal.

Boy, was I wrong.

SHOPPING AROUND

I went to several key life insurance companies that sold term insurance – Kemper, Keystone, Fireman's Fund, Hartford, Travelers, IDS, Robinson-Humphrey, Fidelity, Templeton. These companies, for the most part, wanted to expand their sales base. Most did not have a sales force. Initially, they met my meeting request with open arms. I carefully explained our system, our track record, our approach. I made it crystal clear we would strictly be a "Buy Term and Invest the Difference" company. We would replace whole life policies with term.

"We'll go out there and go to war," I told a room of executives. "Our crusade means to right a wrong in the industry. Best of all, our 10-year track record proves we are onto something big!"

Practically jumping up and down by the end of my presentation, I fully expected the same reaction from executives. It didn't happen. After four or five such meetings, I spotted the pattern. About the time I mentioned certain words – term, comparison, crusade – arms folded and smiles faded. Companies might be interested in our sales force… but not in our cause. Hearing the words "cash value life insurance is a rip-off" made them break out in a cold sweat. The very thought of preparing written price comparisons between cash value policies and term made them shake. Comparisons just weren't done. They smacked of competition. And competing with a fellow whole life agent? Unthinkable.

One experience stood out. The chairman of Keystone Life, a very reputable Boston company, wined and dined me, and I showed him the whole game plan – sales records, business plan, market statistics, goals. Keystone had a great name and great products, especially in mutual funds. One thing they didn't have was a sales force.

When I left the chairman that day, he was excited and I was excited. Everything looked great – I really thought we had a deal. A few days later, he flew to Atlanta. We met for a fancy dinner downtown. I just knew he was going to say yes. Instead, he looked me straight in the eye.

"Art," he said, "I have no doubt you are going to fail."

I was stunned.

His words stung as hard as a slap across the face. It would've been one thing to politely decline my offer. But his cold statement cut to the core. He even went on to lecture me. "Regulators will *never* allow you do what you want to do," he insisted. I really could've punched him.

Keystone wasn't the exception. Every single company I met with turned me down. All claimed to be desperate for more business, but nobody wanted to try this. It was all about the regulators.

All big companies sold whole life. Most insurance regulators and commissioners were beholden to big insurance companies. Most got help for their elections campaigns from big insurance. They certainly wouldn't risk taking a stand against whole life.

I picked up their second fear. Despite our shining track record, companies considered part-time sales agents to be a radical – and ridiculous – notion. Insurance agents should all be full-time professionals. No exceptions.

Thirdly, companies didn't seem to believe a sales force could survive financially selling only term insurance. They firmly doubted that my new concept of a "term only" company would work.

Advance commissions? A fourth issue. It takes huge amounts of up-front cash to pay out advance commissions so it was not a common practice. Waddell & Reed, among only a few, paid advances. Once again, the new concept made mainstream companies uncomfortable.

One final issue. I made it very clear I wanted to build a company with salespeople, not the home office executives, in charge. I wanted unlimited recruiting, unlimited RVP promotions and unlimited new offices. We'd have no protected territories, no limits on growth. In my proposal, the company would provide products, process business and pay our sales force.

Well. Such a concept flip-flopped the power structure of every company out there! No life insurance company in existence put the sales force in charge, then used the home office people strictly as support. Put all the control in the hands of the sales force? Executives' comments went pretty much like this: "You want to use our products, all our money, and all our people to process the business… and we don't get any input? You get total control of the company? NO WAY!"

For two months doors slammed in my face. Frustrated, I was almost ready to go back to coaching football. Rather than take a shot at dominating an industry, companies focused on risks and controversy. Where in the world could I find a company to take our business?

STRIKING GOLD

Then one day a name popped into my head: Bill Adkins. Back when I joined Waddell

& Reed, Bill was the president of United Investors Life Insurance Company – Waddell & Reed's life insurance underwriter. Bill created the first permanent form of term insurance, Annual Renewable Term to age 100 (ART). That excellent product lured me to Waddell & Reed. I got to know Bill Adkins, and we became great friends. He was a terrific salesman, a good man and a firm "Buy Term and Invest the Difference" believer. But for some reason, Waddell & Reed fired Bill about the same time they fired John Kostmeyer.

The thought of Bill gave me fresh hope. I tracked down his telephone number and wondered why I hadn't thought of him earlier. With his career in the industry, he probably had a good long list of contacts. My "Friday night feeling" started to creep back, just a little.

That phone call turned out to be a "moment of destiny." I had been about to give up, about to forget it all, but decided to give it one more shot and make one more phone call. It turned out to be "the gold mine."

Pleased to hear from me, Bill explained he'd become the president of Financial Assurance Inc., a small life insurance company based in Kansas City. He didn't give me any contacts; he *was* the contact.

In days, I sat in Kansas City, talking to Bill and Joe Jack Merriman, owner of Financial Assurance. As at other companies, I laid out everything I wanted – every radical, controversial, experimental idea.

I asked Financial Assurance for their products, their financial resources and their business processing support. In return, I would build them a national sales force. They nodded. They listened. They asked questions. Then, we talked some more.

This time the conversation felt different. Their questions asked, "How can we make this work?" instead of "Are you out of your mind?" They weren't scared by anything I said. Instead, they were totally turned on, especially about the national sales force. *They saw the vision of what we could do*.

I had my company.

NEW IDEAS THAT LAUNCHED A COMPANY…

- 100% term products
- Part-time sales force
- Unlimited recruiting
- Unlimited RVP promotions
- No protected territories
- 100% free enterprise
- 100% licensing fees
- Sales force in charge of company

…*And Changed an Industry*

HAPPIEST DAYS

Starting mid-November 1976, I began to meet with Bill Adkins almost every weekend in Kansas City, and we started designing a new kind of company from the ground up. Once again, just like Baxley and Kendrick, we'd take an organization doing next to nothing and build a team. It energized all of us. We met at a hotel two or three days at a stretch and worked non-stop. Financial Assurance had sharp business leaders who believed in the same things I did. Connecting with Financial Assurance turned out to be a huge part of our "destiny" – a perfect fit in ways none of us could've imagined.

Joe Jack Merriman, a former president of Waddell & Reed, had little to say for that company. Bill harbored a deep grudge – Waddell & Reed fired him over their financial problems with Continental Investment Corporation. That I would leave Waddell & Reed's biggest sales region and likely bring a sizable number of agents sweetened the pot for Bill. No one ever said it, but I felt that Bill and Joe Jack both had a "mad on" when it came to Waddell & Reed. They relished an opportunity to "stick it to" their old company.

Another interesting "coincidence:" Financial Assurance operated in only 13 states – but those 13 states just happened to be in the Southeast region, where all my agents worked. Financial Assurance didn't have a sales force, just a few independent agents. A disadvantage? Hardly. Taking on our sales force posed almost no risk for them in losing other business.

What providence to find a company that wanted our business. Bill and Joe Jack were great people, fierce proponents of "Buy Term and Invest the Difference," firm believers in our track record, unflinchingly willing to try my radical concepts. They wanted business badly enough to shoulder our risks.

On a handshake, Joe Jack Merriman agreed to put out $1 million in up-front funds. This would easily cover advance commissions for 1977, our first year of business. Smiling, we agreed we'd never spend that much money in a year.

- - - - - - - - - - - -

"Best decision I ever made – build our company 100 percent free enterprise. It became the foundation for running the entire business."

– ART WILLIAMS

- - - - - - - - - - - -

THE MAGIC FORMULA

Two burning issues needed resolution. First, what kind of package could I offer career salespeople to entice them to leave an established company and risk starting over with mine? Second, we needed a company infrastructure to support a sales force with unrestricted territory, unlimited recruiting, unlimited promotions, and a way to build their own businesses over time. I wanted as many people as possible in the Waddell & Reed Southeast Region to join me. With a major career move, what could we offer to offset the overwhelming risk?

Here's what I knew, after working with hundreds of people in the last few years: Most

people wanted to be their own boss. And they wanted control over their income.

So, we broke it down like this…

WADDELL & REED PROBLEM: PAID EXPENSES, LIMITED COMMISSIONS

NEW COMPANY SOLUTION: 100% FREE ENTERPRISE/PERSONAL RESPONSIBILITY

Waddell & Reed offered its salespeople a J-O-B – a job that absorbed the high costs of training, licensing and office expenses. To cover killer expenses – office rent, phones, secretary, and training – Waddell & Reed pulled the money out of the commission pool, cutting cash flow to the field. I did not want that. I wanted a company structure that spurred unlimited growth.

Instead, our sales force would take responsibility for office expenses, licensing, training, rent – everything. Nothing would bill back to Financial Assurance.

In return, two phenomenal things would happen. One, personal responsibility would take over. When it's your money, you tend to spend it a little more wisely. You rent a smaller office space or use a spare room in your home.

Two, commissions would automatically rise. Money would not be stretched between expenses and commissions, so more money could pay out to the field. Sales force agents would get straight commission. The more they produced, the more money they would earn. Bill and I figured agents would earn *three to four times more* in commission with our company, even after expenses. Income would be more secure too, with no need to cut commissions.

SCOREBOARD

Wadell & Reed opened 2-3 new offices a month.

A.L.Williams opened 2-3 new offices a day.

WADDELL & REED PROBLEM: PAID ALL START-UP FEES FOR NEW RECRUITS

NEW COMPANY SOLUTION: NEW RECRUITS PAY OWN START-UP FEES

Like most insurance companies, Waddell & Reed covered all the costs of licensing and training for new recruits. About 99 percent of new recruits came in full-time and took a monthly salary. This huge upfront financial investment made companies highly selective. They administered personality and achievement tests to potential recruits. Northwestern Mutual claimed in one of their ads to spend $200,000 to license and train new recruits.

At A.L. Williams? We would pay zero – no licensing, no training, no salary. New recruits would start part-time, with no risk to themselves or to A.L. Williams. It opened the door to recruiting unlimited numbers of people – a sales force as large as we could grow it.

SCOREBOARD

Wadell & Reed recruited 15-20 new people/month.

A.L.Williams eventually recruited 15,000-20,000 new people/month.

WADDELL & REED PROBLEM: PROMOTION LIMITS AT ALL LEVELS

NEW COMPANY SOLUTION: UNLIMITED RVP PROMOTIONS

Waddell & Reed's infrastructure simply couldn't afford to pay all the expenses to open more full-time offices. Because of this, they limited Division Manager promotions to just two or three a year in our six-state region. (I usually had 30 or 40 people waiting on a promotion to those positions!)

Our 100-percent free enterprise solution completely eliminated promotion limits. Bill and I built an organizational model with four levels, just like Waddell & Reed – Representative, District, Division, Regional Vice President. Set guidelines freed us to talk to new recruits about a move up to RVP. The new Rep could start out part-time, then work into a full-time RVP position – when he was ready! No more waiting on management.

SCOREBOARD

Waddell & Reed had 13 RVPs – total.

A.L.Williams eventually had 8,000 RVPs.

WADDELL & REED PROBLEM: NO REWARD FOR BUILDING NEW LEADERS

NEW COMPANY SOLUTION: OVERRIDE COMMISSION SYSTEM

Waddell & Reed's Division Managers didn't want to promote their downlines – it lost them money. For example, if Virginia promoted Bill Orender, he would've left her office, started his own… and taken his income with him. She would no longer receive any income from his production. Virginia would've worked hard, produced a good guy for the company, and then lost money by promoting him! The system held people back.

I wanted to reward leaders for promoting their top producers. Also, I wanted to give the sales force a way to build secure incomes based not just on their solo production, but on the production of all their downlines.

My solution: a generational override system that gave an RVP an extra 15 percent override commission on income from any downline he promoted to RVP. Revolutionary!

Now agents had a pure incentive to promote downline people: additional income. No more holding back. This wasn't a dead-end sales job, but a chance to make any kind of income you desired.

SCOREBOARD

Waddell & Reed had 3 levels of overrides.

A.L. Williams eventually built 16 levels of overrides.

WADDELL & REED PROBLEM: PROTECTED SALES TERRITORIES

NEW COMPANY SOLUTION: FREEDOM TO BUILD WHEREVER

Protected sales territories were a trademark of the traditional insurance industry. In our new company, protected sales territories would not exist. We wanted a national sales force where a properly licensed sales leader could live or do business wherever he wished. The market was so huge; I saw no way to saturate it.

SCOREBOARD

1977: A.L.Williams ranked last of 2,000 life insurance companies.

1984: A.L.Williams ranked first of 2,000 life insurance companies.

WADDELL & REED PROBLEM: LIMITED GROWTH AND INCOME

NEW COMPANY SOLUTION: THE MULTIPLICATION GAME PLAN

I wanted to launch our company with seven RVPs – eight, counting me. Our brand new organization would hang out a shingle with just five fewer than the 13 RVPs Waddell & Reed had in their entire company!

Even bigger and better, we had a plan that would soon lead to hundreds, even thousands of RVPs. How? Multiplication.

Here's the math:

- 7 RVPs each build 7 RVPs, equals 49 RVPs.

- Those 49 RVPs develop 7 RVPs each, equals 343 RVPs.

- If each of the 343 RVPs recruited and developed 7 RVPs, their organization would multiply to 2,401.

- Take that number by 7 and it grows to 16,807.

- Again, multiply by 7. The organization swells to 117,649.

SCOREBOARD

In 12 years, we had 225,000 licensed people.

The other 2,000 insurance companies had that same number of licensed people – combined.

WADDELL & REED PROBLEM: SLOW PAY / TWICE-A-MONTH PAYCHECKS

NEW COMPANY SOLUTION: FAST PAY / TWICE-A-WEEK PAYCHECKS

We had to improve the pay system. I knew from personal experience that the faster a new salesperson got paid for a sale, the more on fire he would be for the next one. I knew of no insurance company that paid more than once a month. Our revolutionary system paid agents twice a week for insurance sales and once a week for mutual fund sales – a first in the industry.

SCOREBOARD

Waddell & Reed paid 2 paychecks a month.

A.L. Williams eventually paid 16 paychecks a month – different paychecks for each new product sold.

WADDELL & REED PROBLEM: OUT-OF-DATE PRODUCTS

NEW COMPANY SOLUTION: NEW, MORE COMPETITIVE PRODUCTS

Bill and I created more competitive ART and deposit term products than Waddell & Reed. Our new products proved better for families and more lucrative for the sales force. For example, our deposit term product would pay a $500 commission, compared to Waddell & Reed's $300.

SCOREBOARD

A.L. Williams cut the cost of its life insurance products 10 times in 12 years.

WADDELL & REED PROBLEM: CONSTANT CUTBACKS ON COMMISSIONS

NEW COMPANY SOLUTION: BIGGER COMMISSIONS, NO CUTBACKS

My experiences with ITT and Waddell & Reed taught me one thing for sure. It was wrong to make the sales force automatically pay for any financial setbacks experienced by the company or the parent company. I made up my mind it would never happen here. Every nickel of commission money went to pay the sales force. The result? Higher commissions, no cutbacks.

SCOREBOARD

It took Waddell & Reed 20 years to become a $1 billion life insurance company.

It took A.L. Williams 10 years to become a $300 billion life insurance company.

WADDELL & REED PROBLEM: NO LIFE PRIORITIES

NEW COMPANY SOLUTION: CORRECT LIFE PRIORITIES

In my part-time days with ITT, I put a few vice presidents on a pedestal for a while.

Surely those well-spoken businessmen had it all together.

I found out differently when I went full time. Many executives battled the bottle. Many divorced, some two or three times, leaving messed-up kids. They looked on top of it at the office, but their personal lives made them seem hypocritical to me.

In our company, we set priorities: God first, family second, business third. I wanted it clear from the beginning that sacrificing a happy home to succeed in business was not "winning" in my book.

SCOREBOARD

A.L. Williams established the Partners Organization early on as a support program for spouses of our agents.

Husbands and wives attended meetings and trips and took part in company events.

WADDELL & REED PROBLEM: NO COMPANY STANDARDS

NEW COMPANY SOLUTION: HIGH COMPANY STANDARDS

ITT and Waddell & Reed served alcohol at meetings and it sometimes caused problems. We established a no-alcohol policy for our company, just to eliminate the issue. I didn't mind if people drank on their own time; I just didn't want to deal with it during meetings.

- - - - - - - - - - - - - - - -

What potential! I didn't know of another company with unlimited territory, unlimited promotions, unlimited income, unlimited growth, big commissions, good products, fast pay. We focused everything on improving the salesperson's life. Everything. Our motto said it all: "A Company Where Salespeople Are King."

For the first time in insurance history, salespeople would run a company.

I couldn't wait to get started.

LAYING PLANS

For many reasons, I didn't tell my Atlanta sales team about Financial Assurance. First and foremost, I wanted to take as many people with me as I could. To do that, I needed a detailed game plan in place for leaving. I spent many days agonizing over what we would offer people and how I could entice them to come along. I also didn't want to risk someone "spilling the beans" and ruining the exit plan.

Meanwhile, I began quietly meeting with Bobby Buisson, Bob Turley and Virginia Carter to discuss "start-up ideas." Bobby and I would swing around and pick up Ginny at her office, then drive to Bob's Sandy Springs office, meeting in guaranteed privacy. I didn't tell them about Financial Assurance and all our planning, but they felt something happening behind the scenes. They were only too glad.

One day, Bob Turley told me that one of his best guys, Larry Weidel, was ready to bolt. "He's fed up, Art," Bob said. "He wants to go to Fireman's Fund. Says they offer double the commission on deposit term contracts. Can't say I blame him."

"Don't let him go, Bob," I urged. "Big changes are coming. Just tell Larry to hang on a little longer."

I could tell Bob was restless, too. I kept them engaged in our clandestine meetings, talking about *everything* – commissions, products, promotion structures, application processing, recruiting, licensing issues, offices, expenses, etc. I knew those loyal lieutenants would keep our discussions private. Good thing, too. If Strader or Butterworth got wind of this plan, I would certainly be fired… and the whole thing would likely go up in smoke and ruin our chance to make a clean break.

Nearer year's end, Waddell & Reed announced more sweeping changes. They totally revamped bonus structure, drastically affecting our income. They cut the annual number of Division Manager promotions from three to two. To top it all off, they cut our office expenses even more.

To see Korschot and Strader cut those expenses again seemed almost cruel. The system worked on production. A Division Leader's office ranked A, B or C, based on monthly production. Ranking determined the amount of money the office received each month to offset office expenses.

Naturally, Ginny, Bob and Bobby all ranked "A," the top division. Initially, their offices received $1,000 a month to cover a full-time secretary, telephone, postage, letterhead and so on. In reality, of course, this amount didn't even come close to covering the cost of one secretary.

A few weeks later, the company reduced the sum again – to just $600 a month. It seems the "brains" decided that $1,000 was too much to pay the big producers, since they were already "doing well." The other $400 then went to offices not doing well! Management punished the producers… and rewarded the non-producers!

But the bloodletting wasn't over yet. Another announcement: office expenses cut to $400.

A few weeks later, they slashed it to $300. *Outrageous.*

Bob Turley heard the news… and went straight out and got a general agent's contract with Kemper. He couldn't stand it another day.

I couldn't either. I gathered Ginny, Bob and Bobby and told them about Financial Assurance. I told them we'd leave when we had our bonus checks. I painted a picture of our new company – a 215 percent RVP contract, commission checks twice a week, unlimited freedom to promote new RVPs, overrides.

I saw total relief and excitement. For the first time in many weeks, that "Friday night" spark came back in their eyes.

Our moment had arrived.

On February 1, 1977, Bob Turley flew to the home office in Kansas City and picked up all the bonus checks for the Southeast Region.

When the plane landed, Bob made a phone call to Strader and resigned. He packed up his office and moved to a new one just down the road in Smyrna. He was in business the very next day. His two Division Managers, Larry Weidel and Walt Ilginfritz, left with him.

Time for the rest of us to make the jump.

That's when things really got interesting.

RESIGNATION

On Thursday morning, February 10, 1977, I placed a 30-second phone call to Bob Strader. I was leaving. I'd been waiting to make that call for months.

At first, Strader seemed elated to hear my news and made no effort to hide it. Fine. I was happy, too. Happier than I'd been in months.

Then a slow dawning came over Strader. He realized I probably wouldn't go alone. That afternoon, he and Butterworth landed in Atlanta on a private plane. From a temporary office in a hotel, Strader started calling in sales leaders in a desperate attempt to salvage what they could of the Southeast Region. Soon Ben Korschot, Charlie Atwell (a longstanding and beloved home office executive), the president of the mutual fund company, the president of the life insurance company, several RVPs from other sales regions, even CIC's chairman of the board flew in to join them.

It was sad in a way. It took the threat of total disaster to prompt the executives to take care of their people. In they flew, with big promises and a bottomless checkbook. Suddenly, they wanted to promote Districts and Divisions. Now they even wanted to promote multiple RVPs. What irony. They had just stripped us of commissions, benefits and expenses, yet here they came, desperately spending thousands to save us, promising the kind of support we needed.

For most of us it was too late.

My resignation lay behind me. Time to execute the rest of the exit plan.

With Bob Turley already off the scene, Bobby Buisson was the next to leave. Ginny agreed to be my "eye" on the inside for about a week, then she too would officially resign. I quickly began contacting all the Division Managers, District Leaders and Reps in the Southeast Region with our new opportunity. Strader had every right to panic over a possible mass exodus. The company's most dynamic talent just happened to reside in my region.

Waddell & Reed executives swarmed over every sales agent in Atlanta. I knew I had just a small window of time. I wanted as many of my sales team to come with me as possible, yet I also knew the risk it posed. I made it very clear to everyone I talked to that the opportunity with Financial Assurance could lead to something big, something really special. But… there was also a *big chance* it might not work. I wanted everyone to understand this going in – the odds of us making it were *small*.

But, boy, if we did make it, success would be unbelievable.

QUICK TRIP

I asked Bobby to call Randall Walker in Carrollton, a good hour and a half away from Atlanta. Bobby was Randall's upline, and I knew Bobby could explain the situation just fine. I wanted our "group" to meet as soon as possible. As I heard later, it took Randall all of about five seconds to decide to come with us.

A second order of business was a trip to Macon. I called Frank Dineen, a District Manager in Albany, asked him to drive to Macon and pick up Tee Faircloth, the Division

Manager, and meet me.

Frank Dineen tells about our get-together this way:

"The place Art told us to meet him was on the Bibb County line, next to this Dempsey Dumpster, the only thing around for miles. Tee and I sat there and got good and hot. Finally, Art roared up in his little red Audi.

"He jumped in the back seat and said, 'You can't believe what's happened! We resigned from Waddell & Reed! Things are really hitting the fan. Bob Strader and Bob Butterworth flew in from Kansas City. They'll try to convince you to stay. But we're going to leave and do something really special with our lives. Most of the people in Atlanta are coming with us. So are you in or you out?'

"Both of us said, 'I'm in,' quick as that.

"Art said, 'Great, here's your resignation papers. Just sign them and I'll mail them when I get back to Atlanta.'

"Art slapped the papers over the back of the seat, and we signed them. Then he said, 'By the way, you're both RVPs!' Then he jumped back into his little red car and zoom, he was gone.

"We looked at each other. 'What's an RVP?' I asked Tee. He shrugged. We didn't know, but we were in!"

Both men were soon to discover – their new promotion to Regional Vice President represented a major step-up. An open door to big opportunity, even financial independence.

MAJOR SURPRISE

Next, I drove to Rusty Crossland's new home in Marietta. Rusty's salary position made his situation different from that of other agents in my region. Before he went corporate, he'd been one of my top recruiters. Losing him to Butterworth had been a real blow. I went from working side by side with Rusty every day to seeing him briefly once every six weeks at Fast Start Schools.

Rusty performed extremely well, and Butterworth seemed happy with him. As far as I knew Rusty was happy, too. I really wanted Rusty, but I had my doubts he would come. I knew the kind of pressure he would get from Butterworth. But I still wanted him to know what was going on.

I sat down with Rusty and his wife, Teresa, at the kitchen table.

"Art laid out a plastic covered folder," Rusty recalls. "On the front page was typed 'The Magic Formula for Success.' He opened the folder and explained what we could do as independent contractors with Financial Assurance. There was never even one second's thought on my part. When he was done talking, I said, 'Okay, I'm in. Where do I sign?'

"I think Art was surprised. After all, I'd been the poster boy for Waddell & Reed."

Rusty was right – he shocked me! I fully expected him to ask for a week or two to think about it. Without even blinking, he said yes. I was so stunned I almost fell off my chair! I will never forget that moment. Rusty and I had always been close, but we bonded in a special way right then.

While Rusty surprised me, Butterworth didn't. He called Rusty right away, offered to double his salary, pay more office expenses, give him an 800 number, a bigger office, unlimited recruiting, whatever he wanted – literally, an open checkbook.

Rusty firmly turned it all down. What a champion.

TURNAROUND

When I got home that evening, Angela handed me a fistful of messages – all from agents who'd decided to come with us. Tired as I was, I flipped through them. One name grabbed me: Bill Orender. For Bill, one of my personal favorites and a giant in our organization, the decision had proven harder. Bill first accepted the company's offer of RVP. As he explains:

"I was going to leave, then all the Waddell & Reed people rushed in and offered me Art's job, plus a guaranteed salary, paid expenses, a company car. I had a wife and two little kids – it was a very attractive offer. So I decided to stay.

"I told Art, and he seemed really nice about it. I told Virginia Carter, and she was brokenhearted. That night I got up at 3 a.m., totally bothered by this thing. I took a Ben Franklin approach and wrote out reasons why I should stay and why I should leave.

"Finally, the last thing I wrote got me: 'If you take a paycheck, they own you.' I didn't want any part of that. So I went with Art."

Bill's change of heart humbled me to the core. He could've taken the easy road and the big paycheck. But he saw the vision of what we could do, not short-term but long-term, and chose to take the harder road with all of us.

When people ask me why A.L.Williams became so special, I tell stories about people like Rusty and Bill.

From the beginning, our people bonded in tough situations and built relationships that have lasted a lifetime.

COACH TAYLOR

Something terribly painful happened in this time, too. When Coach Taylor came to work for me at Waddell & Reed, it worked great for both of us. The Tallahassee office grew under his leadership, and he'd done a fine job of "raising" Tee Faircloth and Frank Dineen.

But Coach Taylor was getting older. Recent heart bypass surgery had slowed him down, and he was edging toward retirement.

My goal was to work it out so Coach Taylor got my old job as RVP of the Southeast Region. He'd have a great income, good benefits, a secure retirement. At his age and health, it would be a perfect fit for him. I knew, too, that Waddell & Reed would be looking to promote someone to RVP who could hold the Southeast Region together and Tommy could, if anyone could.

That was my plan, but plans don't always work out like you want them to.

Early Friday morning, the day after my resignation, I flew to Tallahassee to meet Coach Taylor. At his office, I told him the whole story – that I had resigned from Waddell & Reed, and was starting a new sales company with Financial Assurance. I would take many of our teammates with me, but only with their full understanding of the extremely high risk involved in this venture. I would promote seven District Managers to RVPs – my core group for the new company.

Then came the part I dreaded. I told Coach Taylor he wasn't getting the same offer. I explained why, that I wanted him to stay at Waddell & Reed and take my old RVP position, if it worked out. I made it clear that I didn't want him to come with me because I just couldn't bear the thought of being responsible for his personal financial failure in the highly likely event that everything fell through. I explained two reasons why staying at Waddell & Reed would be best for him – a $100,000 salary and super health benefits. He needed both. He could finish out his working years in a secure position.

Coach Taylor listened. When I was done, he excused himself to go to the bathroom. A moment later, I heard him sobbing. I sat there and fought back my own tears.

What an awful moment. Yet I felt I made the right decision. I wanted what was best for Coach Taylor. I couldn't offer the security he needed. Still, I knew how very hard it was for him to hear that I preferred he stay with Waddell & Reed right now, rather than follow me to the new company.

I knew because it was every bit as hard for me.

WEEKEND VISIT

I got home late Friday afternoon and Angela again handed me a dozen messages from people who had resigned from Waddell & Reed and were coming with us.

The news overwhelmed me. *Everybody* was coming – immediately. I hadn't planned on this at all. Even then, the surprises weren't over.

The next morning, Fred Marceaux and Trudy White pulled up in my driveway. They had driven all the way from Tallahassee to talk to me about the new company.

"We thought we'd never get here!" yelled Fred, as I walked out to meet him. "Who ever heard of Snellville anyway? I thought we were going to run out of gas on that little two-lane road!"

I laughed. Fred… What a gem. One of my handpicked RVPs, he would get us going in Florida. A "bulldog" competitor, relentless worker, and totally passionate for "Buy Term and Invest the Difference," Fred couldn't wait to "get after it."

But Trudy's appearance was a bit of a mystery. She had been Coach Taylor's assistant for years. I'd already talked to her about staying on with Coach Taylor at Waddell & Reed. I told her throwing away all that hard-earned security would be foolish. But Trudy had other ideas.

"So why are you here?" I asked her.

"Frank Dineen called me and told me you'd resigned," she said, chin high, apparently miffed I hadn't called her myself. "At first I thought, oh no, what happens now? But then I decided. I'm coming with you. Period."

I begged her to change her mind. We talked for hours. But in the end Trudy won. She fixed a steely gaze on me and said, "Art, I don't care what you say. This new company is going to work, and I want to be part of it."

So, that morning, standing in my driveway, I hired Trudy White as our first employee. It was the only way I could make her go home.

Not long after, Coach Taylor decided I was right about staying put. On my recommendation,

Waddell & Reed hired him as the Southeast Region's RVP. They gave him a great incentive package. He stayed at Waddell & Reed three more years before joining me again.

Yessiree, we were off and running. But none of us, not in our wildest dreams, could have predicted all that happened next.

We really were about to change the world.

Part IV - Launching the Dream

"The truth is incontrovertible.

Malice may attack it…

Ignorance may deride it…

But in the end, there it is."

– WINSTON CHURCHILL

12 No Name, Just Cause

In 1970, just starting full-time with ITT in Atlanta, I attended a sales meeting where the speakers recommended a book, *Think and Grow Rich*, by Napoleon Hill. Hill was an interesting guy – he spent almost his entire adult life studying the common characteristics of highly successful people. In his book, he proposed that all his research subjects used basically one formula to become wealthy. If you read this book (and I recommend you do), you will discover what I did: this "formula" is not easy to find. You have to read the entire book and figure it out. The whole thing gets very intriguing.

When I did decipher Hill's "mysterious" concepts, something clicked. I began to apply them to my own life. They resembled how I'd trained my football teams. They made perfect sense for growing a sales force. I asked everyone in my organization to read that book and bought copies to pass around. When we recruited new people, they read it, too.

Unlike Hill, I didn't make my team struggle to figure out the formula. My original business goal centered on achieving financial independence. It's why I saved $42,000 working part-time. Hill's philosophy inspired my own personal financial planning. Then I began to teach that same plan to every person on our sales force.

Success extends beyond financial principles to mental principles – perseverance, hard work and good choices. You decide what you want out of life, then name the price you're willing to pay to get it. In a word, it's about attitude.

You can help anybody grow and get better… except the person with a bad attitude.

As we launched the new company, Hill's philosophy influenced our everyday thinking. Here we stood, a tiny little David shaking our "Buy Term and Invest the Difference" slingshot in the face of Goliath, the monstrously large whole life insurance industry. As a company, we might not make it. But if we did, it would happen because we truly thought of ourselves as a different kind of company. From my point of view, attitude would determine if we stayed in business for good… or bite the dust after a month or two.

It was that important.

CHOOSING THE SEVEN

Attitude determined my choice of seven "founding" RVPs.

I made it clear from the beginning that big rewards depended on more than hard work at the office. High standards in every area of life mattered, too. I wanted a business with people who really valued their families, who lived strong personal beliefs and earned good reputations in their communities. Everyone would see rewards for business production… but the big money would go to people who achieved all of that plus a little bit more – champions in business and champions in life.

Bob Turley, Rusty Crossland, Ginny Carter and Tee Faircloth stood out as outstanding recruiters and producers. Bobby Buisson, Fred Marceaux and Frank Dineen got high marks as super hard workers, loyal and committed. All seven were strategically located for mass expansion – Tee in Macon; Frank in Albany; Rusty in Marietta; Bob, Virginia and Bobby in different areas of Atlanta; Fred in Tallahassee. With no protected territories, opportunity stretched from here to the horizon. They could each recruit and build as fast as they wanted, wherever they wanted.

THE "SECRET FORMULA" FOR FINANCIAL INDEPENDENCE

Step 1: Have a specific goal. I earned $10,700 a year as head football coach and athletic director in Columbus, Georgia. After lengthy consideration, I determined my specific goal. I wanted an income of $30,000 a year, guaranteed for life.

Step 2: Set a specific time to achieve goal. At age 28, I decided to work and sacrifice for 10 years to achieve my goal. I would be financially independent by age 38.

Step 3: Write down your goal. Make it specific. Write it down on paper as a commitment. (I wrote out my goals on a piece of cardboard and kept it in my daily calendar. I carried it around for years.)

Step 4: Develop a plan to achieve your goal. Working part-time for 2 1/2 years, I saved $40,000. If I saved that $40,000 for 10 years at 10% interest, I would have $100,000. **$40,000 x 10% x 10 years = $100,000**

If I accumulated $300,000 in cash savings, and received 10% interest, I could withdraw $30,000 a year and never touch my principal. This $30,000 could go on forever. But I needed $300,000. I had only figured out how to get $100,000 by investing the $40,000.

I was still $200,000 short. At 10% interest, I would have to save $1,000 a month for 10 years to get the additional $200,000.

$1,000/mo at 10% interest x 10 years = $200,000

Now I had my final plan. Invest my $40,000 for 10 years and invest $1,000 per month for 10 years. $300,000 would equal $30,000 a year for life.

Step 5: Decide the price you are willing to pay to achieve your goal. Saving $1,000 a month was tough, but I knew that's what it would take to achieve the goal.

My price: Give up coaching to work full-time helping people build financial security. It worked for me and my family.

Step 6: Focus on reaching your goal. Every day I worked toward achieving a financially independent lifestyle. My dreams made me keep trying when I could have quit.

STARTING WITH NOTHING

On the first morning of our new company, I gathered everyone at Bob Turley's office. (Didn't even have my office set up yet!) We had no name. No money. No offices. No corporate structure. No business cards. No stationery. All the stuff it takes to set up a business – we didn't have most of it.

Here's what we did have: Angela and I had set aside $200,000 of our own money to cover any financial crises that might come up. We had Financial Assurance's promise to underwrite our business. We had one employee, Trudy White, two telephone lines and a small pile of rate cards and insurance applications from Financial Assurance.

Even the first batch of apps was goofed up. They didn't say "Financial Assurance" at the top. We crossed out the name of some other FAI-owned company and hand-wrote "Financial Assurance" ourselves!

And attitude? I mean to tell you, the air in that little meeting room buzzed. Excited to be there, free of Waddell & Reed, and talking about our own company felt amazing! We were on fire. I think I knew from that first meeting it would all work. We could change forever the financial devastation death left at the doors of families. We could take on the life insurance industry and win. We could build a national, maybe even international, sales force. *We could beat Prudential!*

I looked at Rusty Crossland, sitting in the front row – I knew the secure job he'd left behind. I looked at Randall Walker – he didn't even ask his wife, Mary, before he said yes. There sat Virginia, in her mid-50s, starting over with me. Bob Turley, the former professional baseball player, now played for our team. Trudy White, so fiercely determined to be part of our dream that she left behind a safe retirement. And Bill Orender, leaving a $100,000 job offer to start over as a lowly Division Manager.

THE ORIGINAL SEVEN RVPS

Bobby Buisson

Virginia Carter

Rusty Crossland

Frank Dineen

Tee Faircloth

Fred Marceaux

Bob Turley

I still get emotional when I think about that special group. They came in and went straight to work. They didn't look back. Waddell & Reed dangled six-figure incomes, cars and fancy titles under their noses. I offered… what? Total intangibles – hope, opportunity, a chance to be your own boss, a long shot at financial independence.

I held my thumb and forefinger about a quarter of an inch apart. I said, "Look, the odds of us making it are about this big. The risks? Off the charts! But if we make it, it's going to be gigantic." That's all they needed to hear. They knew they stood on the ground floor of an unlimited opportunity.

Man, I loved those original people. They represent for me the perfect examples of people who win with their hearts, not with their heads.

- - - - - - - - - - - -

"Art said it over and over…

'Be somebody. Do something special. Make a difference with your life.' Where else do you go to hear those things? No other company I knew ever talked like that."

– BILL ORENDER

- - - - - - - - - - - -

At the end of that first meeting, I announced a surprise – our first company incentive trip. Financial Assurance offered to take our top 20 couples to Hawaii, a trip already planned for some of Joe Jack Merriman's top producers. Adding us probably cost FAI an additional $200,000, a gigantic "people investment." But they were serious about treating us right. A first-class trip, our first venture outside the continental United States – well, let's just call it a fabulous way to kick off our new company!

THE WORK

We left that meeting on a dead run. Those first few weeks? *A blur.* The team had always been hard workers, but until we launched A.L. Williams, none of us knew we could work *that* hard.

I had total responsibility now, not just for my family, but for all the people who made huge sacrifices to come to work for us. Up at 5 a.m., I'd hit the road, return home at eight or nine o'clock that night with no dinner (and I love to eat), with a dozen "emergency" messages from people demanding I call back, even at 1 o'clock in the morning. I'd drop into bed for four or five hours, get up, then be gone again for another 20-hour day.

Terrifying? Yes… if I'd had time to think about it. But I was in a "zone." Twenty hours a day, seven days a week, I talked on the phone, met people for meals, visited prospects, recruits, my team.

I called Waddell & Reed people, ITT people, associates in other businesses, coaches, old school buddies, friends, family. I spent about 30 minutes on average with interested people, and by the time I got through, they must have felt hit by a tornado. I'd leave, then they'd start thinking it over and come up with a million questions.

In that "zone," I didn't know what day or time it was. Crazy! But I couldn't operate any other way. The people I met were dying in their dead-end jobs; they wanted a better way. So I just kept going. Exhausting, yes, but totally thrilling. It boggled the mind – a "high" like you can't believe. As good as beating Waycross!

The good news? Everybody jumped in immediately. The bad news? Everybody jumped in immediately.

Originally, we expected people to join in waves over a three-month period. We'd train the first group, bring in the next group. The first group would help train the second group, and so on. This incredibly well thought out plan would let us build the new sales force logically and methodically… and that plan flew out the window on Day One.

THE APPS

Our traditional company story holds that on February 10, 1977, we started with "85 original people." When I left, Waddell & Reed employed some 800 people in our Southeast Region. Of that group, 85 people left to join us. It may have been a few more or a few less – we were way too busy to stop and count.

By the end of the first week, we had at least 100 people selling and recruiting. Friday, we ran out of apps and rate cards. I called Bill Adkins in Kansas City to ask for more – he thought I was making up numbers.

Our original business plan called for 20 licensed people and 25 apps the first month. We had 100 licensed people and 100 apps by the end of the first week. I never dreamed so many people would join so soon.

I begged Bill Adkins to send us more apps (preferably with the name "Financial Assurance" at the top) but somehow he didn't share my sense of urgency. I decided to make a personal visit to the home office. We'd troubleshoot our new twice-a-week-paycheck system… and bring home our first paychecks.

I grabbed that fat stack of apps and flew to Minneapolis.

THE HOME OFFICE

Joe Jack Merriman was a tall, dark-haired handsome guy. Everything about him said first-class, including his lovely wife, Elaine. His elegant office, located in a downtown tower, offered a terrific view of Kansas City. Joe Jack invited me to his home several times and treated me to dinner occasionally at the exclusive Cattleman's Club.

Many times, we discussed Financial Assurance's Minneapolis office. Joe Jack always described it as the "real" home office. I pictured it in a fancy office tower in Minneapolis, probably similar to Waddell & Reed's home office, which took up four floors in Kansas City's glitzy Crown Center. This trip, Bill Adkins and I met in Minneapolis.

To my surprise, we pulled up in front of a little bitty old brick building. The sign in front puzzled me. Apparently, only half the building housed Financial Assurance. I walked in and just about died. Fanatical, one-track minded about getting this thing started, all go-go-go with no time for details – I'd simply taken it for granted that Financial Assurance boasted a large, impressive, big-league home office.

I stood with my mouth open. Four tiny offices occupied a space barely bigger than my old *office* at Waddell & Reed. I counted just five employees – an accountant, a person in charge of licensing, two administrative people, and one part-time underwriter. I looked at Bill and wanted to scream,"*You've got to be kidding!!*"

Miraculously, I'd found a company willing to take us on and do every controversial, revolutionary thing I'd dreamed up. I'd spent hundreds of hours with Bill Adkins, the genius inventor of ART, and Joe Jack Merriman, a phenomenal businessman, designing the perfect company – every aspect to a "T." All these people in Atlanta now worked for this "perfect" company, with more coming on board all the time.

Then… I saw Minneapolis. What a shock! Financial Assurance barely existed. I expected a Prudential-like tower. Instead, their home office looked like a mom-and-pop store. I had to look hard to find a copier!

I made two decisions instantly. One, we would build our own home office as soon as possible. Two, nobody from my sales force would ever come to Minneapolis.

Not even Art Williams could sell the looks of this place.

The Minneapolis staff processed an average of 25 apps a month – about one a day. What would they think when I dumped my stack of 100 apps in their laps – business from just one week?

Thank goodness, I found the right attitudes here, too. They couldn't wait to get started. I handed my apps to the underwriter, a nice guy named Bob Leseman with Coke-bottle glasses, and he went to work. Bill and I sat down with the rest of the staff.

Computers didn't exist here. To submit commission statements, Angela had typed up a commission slip that listed the four levels – RVP, Division Manager, District Manager and Rep – with commission percentages listed by each. We made copies and handed them out, along with apps and rate cards. For sales, the RVP filled out the slip, wrote in the correct commission amount, and then stapled it to the app. Total honor system.

Financial Assurance checked slips and hand-wrote paychecks, one by one. They never balked at one check. This manual process went on for months, until eventually the office computerized. With one computer.

Before I left Minneapolis, I rounded up every app and rate card I could find – about enough to pass out one or two apps per salesperson. They didn't last long. Back in Atlanta some of our guys now wrote 10 apps a day. We found a local printing company to run more, but it took forever. They politely promised turnaround in days – I needed apps in hours. I'd get one batch back from the printer, thinking I had a real stockpile, only to return in two days needing more.

I made weekly trips to Minneapolis for months, building relationships with the staff there. Plus, I had promised twice-a-week paychecks, and I wanted to make sure we delivered. Financial Assurance kept its word – they never missed a beat cutting our paychecks, even after we switched to overnight mail.

Welcome to just the most exciting, thrilling, confusing, chaotic situation in the history of insurance. It felt almost impossible to believe… But we were in business – writing apps, putting business on the books, and getting commission checks faster than any company ever had before.

THE SALES FORCE

We worked from Bob Turley's office. We also worked from Ginny Carter's home, centrally located, with lots of space and privacy. I wish I had a nickel for every phone call I made. I talked a blue streak from dawn 'til dusk.

I'd call up people and just sell the dickens out of everything. I'd tell them what we were doing, how great it was, what a great opportunity we had, how we had everything going our way. I'd hang up, then get on the phone with Financial Assurance and scream like a maniac for more apps. I'd hang up from that call and dial more people, confident and happy, wooing them to come join us. Next, I'd be back on the phone with Financial Assurance, blistering them again, pleading for more paperwork. I was too busy to think how I might look to others.

One sales guy, Ken Durham, took it all in. Ken had a flair for comedy and he could imitate anybody – how they talked, walked, everything. To the amusement of many, including me, he developed a "historical reenactment" of the birth of A.L. Williams, imitating me talking and laughing one minute, then screaming and pounding the table the next. He did it well. He did it for years. Ken had me down cold. In fact, sometimes he fooled people on the phone, imitating my voice so well they thought it was me.

We lived on the edge in those early days. We worked hard, but we had a lot of fun, too. There's nothing quite so refreshing as a good laugh at your own expense.

FIRST OFFICE

Joe Jack Merriman had promised $5,000 for office expenses, which seemed like a fortune, but I wanted to cut corners any way I could. No Crown Center for us. We finally found an office building in Tucker with some space. People accuse me of being cheap. Darn right, when so many folks depended on me.

The whole office wasn't much bigger than the average family living room. Our space was small. And cold. And noisy – the building was under renovation. The front door didn't latch, and the wind would blow it open. We propped it shut with a Coca-Cola crate, but with people constantly coming in and out, we all just learned to dress warmer.

Angela and I shared a tiny corner office with a glass door. The rest of the salespeople and Trudy spread out next to a row of windows. We had a few desks and two phones, and one little "room" with no windows and dim lighting, a "dungeon" for the copier and office supplies.

Well, we may not have had comfort, but we had business. Buddy, it was insane. We had four promotion levels, but no standardized system yet for promoting people. I told folks to use their own good judgment when it came to promoting people in their organization.

"Look," I said, "this is your business. Promote people when you want to."

They did. In fact, the promotions just didn't seem to stop.

What a time. Here we were, shot like a rocket off a launching pad… but we didn't even have a name.

We discussed it every day. I made a few stipulations. I didn't want the words "insurance" or "financial services" in our name. We were non-traditionalists – we didn't want that negative "insurance agent" label. We all liked non-descript company names like E.F. Hutton and Waddell & Reed. They sounded more credible, like law firms. Still, nothing sounded just right. So we kept thinking.

A few days after start-up, we gathered at Bill Orender's home for a party, the wedding engagement of Virginia's daughter, Rickie. The subject of our company name came up and, out of the blue Art Burgess, one of Ginny's guys from way back, came up with something.

"Art, what's your middle name?" he asked.

"Lynch," I said, puzzled.

His face lit up. "That's it! How about we name it A.L. Williams? After you? You founded the company, right?"

At first, Angela and I protested. Everyone in that room had a hand in founding the company. But the more we talked about it, the more we liked it. It solved our dilemma, too – people wouldn't look at the name "A.L. Williams" and think insurance.

A little later, Kevin King, our part-time chief legal counsel, finalized it legally. We became "A.L. Williams & Associates Incorporated."

THE PROBLEMS

As the first few weeks tore by, apps began to multiply. In the first month, we wrote 300 sales… and the pace accelerated. The sales force had expanded to more than 200 people; that number climbed every week, too.

What a sight! We ran to the printer for apps, rate cards, bank drafts, commission statements, recruiting papers, promotion papers and now business cards and signs. A million little details that we didn't anticipate popped up. We solved problems on the fly, and stayed focused on the big stuff – surviving day to day.

Great for us… but bad for poor old Bob Leseman up in Minneapolis, completely snowed under with underwriting in that snowy city.

I will never forget pulling into the parking lot one cold morning to see Bob stagger out of his car with a three-foot high pile of apps. He'd taken them home the night before. I saw blind panic behind his thick glasses. Bob began to hire additional underwriters, which posed another problem. It's difficult to find good underwriters in the first place. Then it takes time to train them.

The last thing we needed – one big slowdown – hit us hard.

POLICY COST ANALYSIS

It didn't take two months for the war between the life insurance industry and A.L. Williams to begin in earnest.

The industry initiated a quiet little law that required insurance agents to provide a prospective client with a written comparison of his current policy and the new policy that would replace it.

For example, if a family had a $25,000 whole life policy and Virginia Carter tried to replace it with a $100,000 term life policy, Virginia had to show the family a written comparison of the two policies before she could close the sale. Then the client had to sign a consent form, agreeing to the replacement!

No other industry required a competing seller to notify the competition when it replaced their product – much less sign a consent form. Can you imagine going to a car dealer to trade in your Ford for a Toyota… and the salesman saying, "Wait a minute! Before I do that, I'm required by law to call Ford and get their permission for you to sell their car and buy this other one. Then, if you still want to buy the Toyota, sign this form."

Ridiculous! Totally anti-free enterprise. Before a client could replace his own policy with a better one, his agent had to step through the dreaded process of policy cost analysis. Nothing more than a political pay-off to the insurance industry… and a veiled means of trying to slow our sales.

A tricky thing for agents, too. The agent had to mail in the client's actual whole life policy. No sale could happen quickly if this part of administration didn't move quickly.

Joe Jack felt uncomfortable with agents filling out the comparison forms, worrying that mistakes could cause the insurance department to fine Financial Assurance, or even kick the company out of the state. So he hired a small organization in Kansas City to handle policy analysis, and he required the sales force to send the forms there.

Small was the word. Run by one guy, Paul Andrews analyzed each old cash value policy, compared it with the replacement term policy, wrote up a report, then sent it back. Like Bob Leseman, Paul Andrews became instantly overwhelmed. Suddenly, it took weeks to get back policy comparisons – if they came back at all.

Here's what happened in some cases. An A.L.Williams agent would go into a home, show a family how they'd been ripped off with a "trash value" policy, explain how they could have lots more coverage (for the same price) with a term policy. He'd then pick up their policy, send it off to Kansas City for a written comparison, and… never see it again! The agent then found himself in the awkward position of having to return to the prospective client and tell him he'd lost their policy. Embarrassing! Many clients went ballistic over losing what they considered a valuable document.

Now this scenario didn't happen much… but it did happen too much. It really put our agents in a spot.

Eventually, Paul Andrews hired a whole room full of people to analyze policies. On one of my visits to Kansas City, I took them a cake to thank them for their hard work. About 30 people packed that room, jammed in with tables, boxes and more boxes, analyzing policies.

Still, it took them three months to catch up.

THE LICENSING

In Georgia at that time, a person could get a six-month temporary license to sell insurance. He first turned in a "hiring pack," as we called it. The new package of paperwork requested a temporary insurance license. The paperwork went to Financial Assurance's internal licensing department (another one-person department!) for processing. If FAI approved the license application (it required a credit and background check), the company issued an "appointment" and sent the paperwork on to the Georgia Insurance Department, which issued a temporary license to the new agent.

Normally, this process took a couple of weeks, max. And if the potential agent didn't get a "rejection" phone call or card in the mail in 12 days, it was assumed the temporary license was granted. A person got a card or a phone call only for failing to qualify. Even without the paperwork, the agent could start selling life insurance.

Along about April, we realized some – well, maybe a bunch – of our new people hadn't received licenses. Because we recruited so many people so quickly, paperwork bottlenecked, first at Financial Assurance's licensing department, then at the Georgia State Insurance Department. Licenses just weren't getting issued in the usual time frame – both departments normally issued only about a few licenses a month! We swamped them with dozens, then hundreds. So, some of our new recruits, or "greenies," assumed they were licensed when their 12-day "waiting period" passed.

Some of them jumped the gun, selling before their documentation cleared.

We also got another surprise – Financial Assurance's deposit term product wasn't officially registered in the state of Georgia! It was the same story – paperwork submitted to the state, but no official product approval.

What a deal – a portion of our sales force wasn't even licensed. And all of us sold an unregistered product, by the truckload.

THE MEETING

These problems, along with the slow turnaround on policy comparisons, slow policy issues, and inconsistent monthly bank drafts drew some volatile reactions. Tempers flared. Some folks accused me of a raw deal.

Can't say I blame them. We were all stretched, trying to keep up. But I couldn't stand people thinking I'd lied to them or been unfair. I was killing myself trying to make sure Financial Assurance met its obligations to our people.

At the same time, I understood these problems came with start-up. In time, we'd resolve them.

One thing we could *not* do was get down. Bad attitudes would kill us faster than any lesser problem we faced.

I called a manager's meeting. I crammed as many people as I could into that drafty little office. People stomped in mad, upset, ready to jump down my throat.

Well, I never gave them a chance. I stormed to the front of the room, slammed down a stack of papers, and glared at the group. "We're not here today to talk about problems!" I yelled. "We're here to talk about doing it *big*!"

I focused the next two hours on what we really needed to do – get to work. "Yes, we've got problems," I said bluntly. "Who doesn't? But, remember this, folks. So many people out there need our products and opportunity. We have to think and act like winners. It's my job to solve problems; your job to make sales and recruit."

I reminded them how far we'd come. "We are *free*! We work for A.L. Williams now, 'where salespeople are king.' We just came out of prison in corporate America! We used to sit in sales meetings at Waddell & Reed, listening to corporate people talk about product profits and a bunch of meaningless crap like that. We used to sit around with people who didn't understand us, didn't even *like* us!

"Now we're at A.L. Williams. Now we talk about what really matters! What do you need? What can we do better? How can we recruit more people? How can we get you more income? Do we need better products?

"Now we have total control. Remember? We are making history. We are going to beat Prudential. Nobody else in the entire world had ever tried this. How can any of that be a problem? All we have to do is go for it!"

The meeting ended. People quietly picked up their stuff. They left... and I could see a new look in their eyes.

Now they "got" it. A.L. Williams was special. We had a shot at living a dream... even if parts of it seemed a bit nightmarish at the moment.

"Art in that meeting gave the most unbelievable example of taking charge I've ever seen. Spectacular. Nobody gave Art one word of crap. To me, at that point, the company began. For the first time, we really united. If Art had been weak at that moment, the company might never have happened."

– LARRY WEIDEL

INVESTMENTS

Later that month, we held a three-day meeting in Atlanta to introduce West America Financial Services, a local investment company we'd picked to provide mutual fund and investment products. Because I preached that our sales force should own the products we sell, I asked Claude Peay, head of West America, to let people attending the meeting buy his company's front-end load monthly mutual fund, Fidelity Destiny, at cost.

He agreed, and many of our agents bought Fidelity Destiny. It got us going on the investment side of business.

Ironically, this company also sold cash value life insurance.

A couple of months later, West America held a convention in Acapulco and invited Angela and me to attend. At their big banquet, they actually gave out awards to agents who had converted the most term insurance to whole life!

I sat there, amazed, but somehow kept my mouth shut. Welcome to traditional life insurance. Whole life was "permanent," and term was "temporary." The big companies clearly meant to replace temporary with permanent. So what if it left families ruined when breadwinners died?

Well, A.L. Williams was about to change all that.

THE PILOT

Bob Miller heard about the West America meeting and flew up from Fort Lauderdale. I was delighted; I had an idea about him. Fred Marceaux's Tallahassee office was our only full-time presence in Florida. Adding one in Fort Lauderdale could help us expand.

Bob spent the weekend at our house. I explained that I wanted him to build a "scratch" RVP office in Fort Lauderdale, a pilot that would give us a blueprint for opening new RVP offices all over the United States. I told Bob the honest truth – we had no budget. He'd have to tackle this task with absolutely no financing. In return, I offered Bob a full RVP contract, which would at least let him earn a higher income as he transitioned full-time into A.L. Williams.

My strategy went broader than one office. I really wanted Bob as a recruiter, not a salesman. I wanted him to start out with a small office in his home and recruit as many new people into his organization as possible.

While justifiable and reasonable to me, I knew that promoting a part-timer straight from District Manager to full-time RVP would raise eyebrows. But I was asking Bob to carry out a very hard task – start a pilot office for "free." I decided to call Bob's office the "Florida Division." On paper he would be a Division Manager, even though he had an RVP contract. I would let Bob see what he could do with this challenge before we officially promoted him to RVP.

THE COMPETITIVE SPIRIT

Even in constant change and upheaval, two things kept me in touch with our exploding sales force. We stuck to our regular schedule of Fast Start Schools. And I introduced "Leaders Sheets," a twice a month front-and-back "newsletter" from our home office.

Fast Start Schools, always held at the Presidential Hotel off I-85 in Atlanta, took off with the birth of A.L. Williams. Every six weeks RVPs, Division Managers and District Leaders streamed in with carloads of people. All new recruits attended. As people flooded into the meeting room, I asked various leaders how many people they'd brought, especially interested in numbers of new recruits.

I announced the numbers from our stage: "Crossland brought 15 new recruits. Now that's pretty good. But Dineen brought 18, and Carter brought 20. Well, that's almost number one. Turley brought 25!"

That kind of stuff stirred competition among the ranks, as I'd hoped. I could always tell whose numbers were high and low. If Marceaux shipped in three carloads of people, he'd look me in the eye, grin from ear to ear and shout, "15!" In an off month, I'd get a downward glance and barely a mumble. Leaders either loved to see me coming or hated it.

It all had a point. "Greenies" held the key to our success. Those new people sat there, listened to me go through numbers on stage, and grew convinced this was something big. Those new people left a Fast Start weekend with their heads spinning.

"Fast Start Schools gave our new people a bigger picture," says Frank Dineen. "They'd realize they weren't the lone ranger out there in the boondocks, talking in the wind. They were part of something growing, something exciting."

The weekends united the rest of us, too. Our time to get together, get a "mad on," tell our war stories, catch up with each other. We all looked forward to Fast Start Schools. They gave us the regular competitive surge we needed to keep going.

THE BULLETINS

Leaders Bulletins served a similar purpose. Angela and Trudy got on the phone every other week, calling the RVPs to get sales, recruiting and premium numbers on every sales guy in their offices. We'd list the top 20 in every category. Trudy would type it all up, make copies and mail them. To drive competition, I always wrote comments on the original, circling the #1 producer, pointing out who moved up or who dropped in their numbers. If someone really tumbled, that person became "Turkey of the Month." All in good fun, of course, but the teasing nevertheless spurred all the RVPs to do better and better.

By now, we'd been up and running almost three months. I felt we'd hit a reasonably steady stride.

Then lightning struck on a clear day.

The phone rang. Johnnie Caldwell, Georgia's state insurance commissioner was on the line. "Art Williams?" he said. "I'm about to put your company out of business."

GREAT BEGINNINGS
1st Leader's Bulletin
MARCH 1977

107

13 The War Begins

Johnnie Caldwell demanded my immediate presence in his office at the State Capitol.

When I got there, he pulled me into a roomful of lawyers, sat me down and said, "Art, you're a crook, and I'm going to put you out of business. You're out there twisting insurance."

This unexpected confrontation threw me a bit, I'll admit, and Caldwell looked intimidating. But twisting was a worn-out subject with me, and I'd been through too many kitchen table confrontations to be scared for long. Especially when I knew I was right.

"Well, Mr. Caldwell, if you can do that, I'll go back to coaching football," I said flatly, "but I don't think you can. You can't call it twisting if you give clients a better insurance deal, can you? Every time we replace a whole life policy with a term policy, we give some family out there more coverage. For some reason, we've never received one consumer complaint over clients getting a better deal with us. So if you still think I'm a crook, I've got $200,000 in cash and, if I have to, I'll spend every nickel of it exposing you for the phony you are." I stood up and left.

Caldwell immediately issued subpoenas to 85 members of our sales force. Within days, they appeared in his office, swore on a Bible, and submitted to hours of grilling on their selling practices. In his opening statement for the hearings, Caldwell accused us of selling "an illegal flimflam product" – deposit term.

Kevin King explains the hostility. "Deposit term was a straight life insurance product. You paid for it and if you died, the company paid the death benefit. It was a big seller. Deposit term sales caused the replacement of many cash value policies. The problem? Cash value policies paid a renewal commission for life, so naturally all those replacements made whole life agents mighty unhappy. The utter audacity that somebody else would sell a good policy to replace their bad policy was incongruous with their worldview."

Even though A.L. Williams had only been in business a short time, members of the Georgia Association of Life Underwriters (GALU) knew us well. Mostly traditional life insurance agents, the GALU had followed my progress through 10 years and three companies. They saw how much business we replaced and they couldn't stand it. To them, replacement broke a code of honor. You just didn't do it.

"It was an industry mentality," adds Kevin. "No decent, self-respecting whole life insurance agent would ever sell a policy that would replace the original policy. It was unheard of. You never replaced, you just sold the client another policy. The fact that the client might end up with ten $10,000 cash value policies? No problem. Each agent back down the chain expected that his policy would stay in force forever, because that gave him his income."

"A.L. Williams really broke the mold in the industry with replacement," Kevin concludes. "The fact that we did it over and over was offensive to whole life agents and the word 'replacement' became a pejorative – not a nice thing. In fact, it was a perfectly wonderful thing. It forced competition, badly needed and long overdue."

One Sunday. I woke up to see my picture plastered on the front page of the *Atlanta Journal-Constitution* with a headline that blared: *A.L. Williams Under Investigation*. Interestingly, the controversy put a guy named Harold Skipper in the local spotlight. Skipper taught insurance and risk management at Georgia State University. Since the Life of Georgia Insurance Company had set up an endowment fund that paid his salary, he basically served as a paid spokesman for the whole life industry.

Skipper, in my view, took advantage of his position. He spoke out regularly in opposition to our cause, products and concepts. In one Atlanta Journal-Constitution article, Skipper wrote deposit term reminded him of "an insurance pitch in the 1950s and 1960s that urged consumers to 'buy term and invest the rest in mutual funds.'" He claimed the "deposit" in "deposit term" was not a deposit at all. "You can take a whole life policy, require a $500 deposit – actually a higher-than-average first-year premium – and promise $5,000 back. It's actuarial hanky-panky, and you can do that with any insurance policy in the world," he wrote.

How typical. Why would someone fed by the traditional industry see anything positive about a product that was good for the consumer?

The war would rage for years to come.

THE HEARINGS

The hearings went on, grueling and stressful for us all, though oddly they never called me to the stand. Each subpoenaed agent endured hours of questioning by Caldwell and his insurance deputies and lawyers. Kevin King and a lawyer from Financial Assurance sat through every hearing with every agent. Most questions concerned selling deposit term, but other issues, like agent licensing and product licensing surfaced, too.

After many weeks, Caldwell threw up his hands. He found no "smoking gun."

Caldwell was smart enough to see we were really okay people, out to do something good for the American family. He did his homework, too. He found out how many of the whole life policies we replaced fell short – some of them only really worth *$500 or less*. Families benefited when we replaced those sorry policies – and that fact was hard to ignore.

Caldwell's investigation did reveal that some new recruits sold policies before getting confirmation of their temporary licenses. Those typical start-up problems had to be addressed.

But what we didn't have proved significant – consumer complaints. Nobody had called up the Georgia Insurance Department and accused us of fraud. No client had been cheated out of money at the hands of our agents. Under a magnifying glass, we turned out to be a legitimate company with legitimate agents selling legitimate products.

Matter of fact, our clients *loved* us.

Kevin's assessment: "Johnnie Caldwell was a smart and skillful politician. He understood right away that this was a matter of competition. He knew in his heart of hearts that if you want an opportunity to compete, you ought to have it."

The investigation concluded. A couple of our agents paid a few hundred dollars in fines. No one lost a license. It turned out to be "nothin' about nothin'"... and yet a big deal, just the same.

We proved ourselves by every legal standard to be a legitimate, fundamentally sound business.

THE GEORGIA ASSOCIATION OF LIFE UNDERWRITERS

Since 1967, I'd built three sales teams on the replacement concept, A.L. Williams being the third. We all had a few confrontation stories to tell.

Frank Dineen walked out of his Albany office more than once to find his tires slashed. He found his mailbox full of horse manure and cut-up Financial Assurance policies. Other agents received anonymous phone calls or found threatening notes. We turned juvenile intimidation tactics into positives for our sales force.

That happened at one Georgia Association of Life Underwriters meeting. Ginny Carter's brother, a licensed whole life agent and GALU member, tipped us off that the next GALU meeting featured a seminar on replacement. He purchased tickets for me, Ginny, Bobby Buisson and Frank McIntosh. One of the few outspoken consumer advocates for "Buy Term and Invest the Difference" at that time, Frank first endorsed A.L. Williams. He made his living as a consultant and expert witness for lawsuits and hearings involving life insurance issues. As founder and president of Insurance Research Service (IRS), he sold his own pro-term books and brochures.

Frank was a true crusader and sort of our antidote to Harold Skipper. We didn't pay for his endorsement, but we did buy lots of his books. Frank also founded the National Association of Term Life Underwriters, a term-only alternative to the large and powerful National Association of Life Underwriters. When we found ourselves in a confrontation with a whole life agent who whipped out his NALU membership card to impress the client, we took great delight in pulling out our NATLU *charter member* cards.

The breakfast meeting took place in a downtown Atlanta hotel, and it didn't bother us at all to walk in with big, muscular Frank, an ex-boxer from Brevard, North Carolina. We strode to the front of the room with a large tape recorder. We sat down. We turned it on.

Probably a couple of hundred people there knew us. The deputy insurance commissioner ran the meeting, and when he called for questions, the same one kept coming up: "What are you going to do to stop these A.L. Williams people from replacing our policies?" We made sure we got his answer on tape.

The deputy dutifully (and correctly) explained the odd regulatory procedure that required all licensed agents to pick up a client's whole life policy, prepare a written comparison, return the original policy with the comparison to the client, then notify the competing agent that his policy was being replaced, and ask the client to sign a replacement consent form.

Nobody complained about us following the regulation – because we did, to the letter. Actually, as time-consuming and annoying as they were, policy comparisons *helped* us. A negative that became a positive, policy comparisons proved to be the perfect educational tool, since term always came out better than whole life.

Whole life agents couldn't beat us on paper. They couldn't beat us at the kitchen table. So, at the GALU meeting, they huffed and puffed and asked the deputy again: "We know the regulations. But what are you going to do to stop them from replacing our policies?"

The answer? Nothing.

THE PHONE CALL

On the first Friday in June 1977, I sat in my hotel room at the Presidential Hotel preparing for a Fast Start School. The phone rang. Joe Jack Merriman.

Immediately, I sensed the tension. "Art, we can't take any more business," he stated. "I budgeted $1 million for the entire year. It's been four months... and we've spent $3 million. This thing is getting too big."

He paused. "It's over."

I slumped in a chair, devastated. It was true – we'd spent three times the annual budget in four short months. Unbelievable.

Joe Jack's valid concern forced me to remember his position. At Financial Assurance, Bill Adkins was the upfront guy, a real crusader who passionately hated the whole life industry.

He loved A.L. Williams.

But Joe Jack was the owner. Behind the scenes, he carefully analyzed how much we brought in every month and how much he paid out. When Bill begged him to approve hiring more underwriters and policy analysts, Joe Jack drug his feet. Weeks slipped by before he finally signed off. He held the purse strings; the rest of us played catch-up. But that was his job. As a businessman, he had to make money.

Here's the problem. Life insurance accounting takes huge amounts of upfront money to underwrite new business. A new policy costs at least $3 (in commissions and administrative costs) for every dollar of premium. It takes five to seven years before a policy begins to make money... and then only if it stays on the books. Joe Jack would make plenty of money eventually. But the initial payout in commissions and administrative costs at our unbelievable rate of growth was killing him.

I looked around the room, strewn with notes and numbers prepared for two and a half days' worth of "blowin' and goin'" for 500 fired-up A.L. Williams people. Five hundred people! What was I supposed to say to them?

"Look, Joe Jack," I said, thinking fast. "This thing is just too good. Let's take the weekend and think about it. Let's talk on Monday."

Reluctantly, he agreed.

The phone call shook me to the core, but I kept the news to myself. We blasted through that meeting, positive as ever.

Monday morning, I flew to Kansas City. Joe Jack reminded me again of the $3 million he'd spent in just four months.

"You're doing 500 apps a month," he said reproachfully. "I didn't want that. We're a small company, 25 apps a month. The most we want is 100 to 200. You agreed to that in our business plan. It's too big, and we can't go on."

Somehow, I convinced Joe Jack to hang on a little longer. Our meteoric growth shocked me, too. But did we really want success to kill a company? Finally, Joe Jack agreed to keep financing us. But I could tell he'd had enough. It was never his goal to get big. Financial Assurance, a $9 million in assets company, would be content to stay there. In my bones, I knew our "marriage" had ended.

I didn't tell the sales force. Why mention our fragile state? At meetings, I continued to sell the dream of building it big and beating Prudential. Joe Jack had heard those same words many times, but now I realized he didn't believe in those dreams. Not the way we did.

I lived in dread. At any minute the phone could ring and we'd be out of business. And what options did we have beyond Financial Assurance? Not one. It had taken a miracle to even get this far.

But I didn't lose hope. Something deep inside me kept saying, *Art, it's going to work out*.

And in walked Boe.

THE BIG GUY

A man named Charles "Boe" Adams kept noticing the name "A.L. Williams" on the marquee of the Presidential Hotel. It intrigued him.

A towering man with a booming voice, Boe worked as the southeastern regional vice president for National Home Life, based in Malvern, Pennsylvania. He managed general agents in 13 southeastern states, including Georgia. One day on his way home from his nearby office, he decided to stick his head into one of our Fast Start School meetings.

He liked what he heard… for a good reason.

National Home Life was part of a larger company, National Liberty Corporation, owned by Art DeMoss, a Christian entrepreneur. Licensed in all 50 states and renowned as the world's largest mail order life insurance company, National Home Life wanted to add a sales force. Boe had his eye peeled for some good general agents.

Or maybe even an entire sales force.

Through a friend, Boe contacted Bob Turley and made a trip to his office. A couple of general agents, Ed Randle and Tom Powers, came along. Boe had two purposes, one was to throw a little hook out to Bob, enticing him with higher contracts. Bob didn't bite. The other? Find a way to meet Art Williams.

Something else interesting happened at that meeting. Boe understood advance commissions.

He surmised that Financial Assurance was very likely running low on money. Government regulations require life insurance companies to keep enough cash in reserve to cover all the business on the books in the event of a catastrophe. Advance commissions, as noted, eat up huge amounts of that cash. At the rate A.L. Williams wrote business, Boe figured (correctly) that without additional financing, rocky days might lie ahead.

True to his word, Bob Turley arranged a time to meet Boe. Boe and his wife, Myrna, had just moved to Atlanta and Angela and I joined them for pizza at their new house in Tucker. Art DeMoss showed up, too. Instead of talking business, Art DeMoss and Boe shared their Christian testimonies. Their professions came as a surprise. I didn't disapprove or disagree; I'm a Christian myself. Angela and I just didn't expect that at our first get-together.

The evening proved to be a moment of destiny. (I'll explain why in the next chapter.) Boe and I knew our paths would cross again.

In fact, they crossed very soon.

THE BLOW-UP

In his latest article in the Atlanta paper, Harold Skipper tried hard to make hay out of the fact that Financial Assurance didn't have an A.M. Best rating.

The A.M. Best Company, an independent ratings service, analyzes the financial strength of insurance companies in the marketplace. Companies with a high Best rating use it as a selling point. In the field, A.L. Williams' agents took a beating. Competing agents told clients that their company had an "A+" rating… but the A.L. Williams underwriter didn't have a Best rating at all.

It was true, we didn't. Small as it was, Financial Assurance fell below A.M. Best's standard for evaluation.

This did not sit well with Joe Jack. He contacted Moody's, another independent risk analysis company. For a small fee, Moody's reviewed Financial Assurance and gave us an "A+" rating. Even when it seemed silly, we countered the competition.

My next visit to Kansas City, Joe Jack treated me to lunch at the Cattleman's Club, and I thanked him. The Moody's rating would certainly give our guys a boost, and it was a nice gesture on his part, considering the shaky state of our agreement.

Usually, Joe Jack never mentioned the sales force. That was Bill's job. Our conversations concentrated 100 percent on home office issues – financing, hiring new employees and underwriting. Sales never came up.

Until today.

Out of the blue, Joe Jack said, "Art, I think it's time to slow down your recruiting. You really need to be more selective in who you bring in."

He pulled a card from his suit jacket – some sort of personality test he wanted everyone to use, designed to help "improve the quality" of our people.

He never even finished. "Joe Jack," I blew up, "you have never recruited one person in your life! How dare you tell me how to recruit!" We stood up and screamed our lungs out right there in the club before I finally remembered it might not be the best time to tick off Joe Jack. I mumbled some sort of half-hearted apology and sat my butt down.

I just didn't see how much longer we could go on.

THE BILL

Ironically, yet another crisis with the Georgia State Insurance Department broke the strain.

In September 1977, the Georgia Association of Life Underwriters pulled all their "insider" strings and managed to pressure Caldwell and the state legislature into drafting a bill to permanently outlaw the deposit term product in the state of Georgia.

Wow. The news stunned us. This fight had just jumped to a whole new level. The proposed bill didn't just affect A.L. Williams, but every insurance company in the country licensed to sell deposit term in Georgia – Fireman's Fund, Kemper, Waddell & Reed, National Home Life, and many others. They all jetted representatives to Atlanta, and we quickly organized meetings to fight this thinly veiled attack.

I told the Financial Assurance guys. Bill looked shocked, even a little scared. But Joe Jack got flat out mad.

Sitting in my office, Joe Jack pointed a finger at me and said, "They can't outlaw deposit term. This is a good product, a better deal for families, and we can prove it." He gave me the green light to fight the bill. I'd never seen him so determined. I'm sure it's what kept us on his payroll a few more precious months.

I called an RVP meeting, plus Bill and Joe Jack. Bill explained the situation. Naturally, it upset everybody. They looked at him. "What can we do?"

Knowing Bill, I fully expected him to roll out a plan... or at least say something positive.

Instead, he threw up his hands. "I don't know."

I shook my head in disgust. Joe Jack, on the other hand, seemed firm. "Outlawing deposit term is impossible," he told us. "I'm willing to fight this all the way to the Supreme Court if necessary." My ears welcomed those words, because I certainly had no intention of giving up. We were "in trouble" for doing something right! We just had to figure out the best way to fight it.

Pressure ran high. The legislation to kill deposit term was already in a Senate committee. Insurance industry lobbyists and some of the state legislators pushed their agenda hard in every room they could fill with smoke. They wanted a vote as soon as possible.

I had an idea. I remembered that a friend of mine from Cairo now worked in the office of Governor Busbee. I called him, and asked for a big favor: Could I get a private meeting with the Governor?

To my relief, my friend said he'd see what he could do.

I also turned to Bob Turley. As a former professional baseball player, Bob had many acquaintances in prominent positions. He knew a state legislator, Jimmy Neismith, a senator from south Georgia. Jimmy arranged a meeting for us with a couple of state representatives at a hotel in downtown Atlanta. I planned a short presentation on our company and concepts, focusing on the good we did for families and showing how the issue was really about competition. I thought maybe we could sway them to vote against the bill.

INDECENT PROPOSAL

Boe Adams, representing National Home Life, attended every group meeting we held about the proposed legislation. He agreed to meet with the legislators and he also invited a state senator from Columbus he knew. So our meeting consisted of Bob Turley, Boe, Jimmy Neismith, three other state legislators, and me.

We went to the hotel. I gave my presentation. They listened. Afterward, one of the senators calmly said, "Art, it's no problem to stop this legislation. For $15,000, I can get this bill thrown out."

The air seemed to suck out of the room.

In a controlled voice, I said, "Gentlemen, thank you for allowing us to come down here and tell our story. But let me tell you something. Fifteen thousand dollars is not that much money in terms of company funds. But accepting your offer is wrong.

"The only thing we've got going for us is the fact that what we're doing is right for consumers. Big insurance companies have ripped off the American people like you can't believe. Our only hope is that enough good politicians and regulators out there will see the truth and refuse to give in to a corrupt industry. The day I have to pay off somebody to stop something that's wrong is the day I get out of business."

We walked out then and there.

My first exposure to political bribes made my stomach turn. I disliked politicians. That meeting did nothing to change my view. But too many families and good people were at stake to give up.

In the next few weeks, I gave my presentation to as many state legislators as possible. I told them one by one the truth about deposit term. I asked them to vote against the bill. The slow sticky process, trying to see them all, dragged on. When I did get an appointment, most lawmakers nodded and appeared to be receptive, but how could you tell? Money was their motivation. If you helped them financially to get elected or re-elected, they got deeply concerned about your problems. Just "doing right" for families didn't win their support.

The whole experience soured my feelings about politics even more. It opened my eyes to yet another "evil industry."

THE CONVENTION

Back at the office, Angela and I busily planned the first A.L. Williams convention, to be held in Point Clear, Alabama, in mid-December. For the first time ever, we'd treat our team to a meeting at a truly first-class location. A leading resort destination, Point Clear ranked with Sea Island or Charleston, and the Grand Hotel offered total luxury. We'd spent conventions before at rinky-dink beach hotels in mid-winter, to get the lowest rates. We'd still go off-season, but that was the only concession.

By this time, our sales force numbered around 700. We invited 78 top-producing couples to attend (about 80 percent of the fulltimers). I paid the $30,000 meeting cost from my own pocket.

Past conventions with ITT and Waddell & Reed truly frustrated me. The corporate people spent hours and hours talking about company goals, company profits, cutting expenses. Absolutely meaningless to salespeople working their tails off to get that one open Division Manager position. Never once did a home office executive stand up and say, "Here's what you can do to insure more American households, recruit more people, make more sales, get more promotions and build financial independence for your family."

They would certainly hear it at ours.

Recognition would be huge. We were writing 10 times more business, recruiting 10 times more people than we ever dreamed.

People who made $10,000 or $20,000 at Waddell and Reed now earned $40,000, $50,000, $75,000, even more. Tee, Bobby, Rusty, Bob, Ginny and I earned well over $100,000. I gave out all kinds of awards for these achievements.

That meeting marked three historic events. First, I introduced Randall Walker as our 8th Regional Vice President, the first RVP promotion since launching A.L. Williams a year ago. Second, I announced a new 15 percent RVP override. I'd built the RVP override into our compensation system from the beginning but I'd never told the sales force about it. I wanted maximum impact! When I shared the news that night in Point Clear, the entire room erupted. The dramatic moment made me glad I'd waited.

Third, I introduced the "replacement leg." My original plan called for everyone to build 7 to 10 RVPs. Requiring the new RVP to leave behind a replacement, we created a system of unlimited opportunity. Each agent could build unlimited income by promoting leaders in his organization, then generating more income through overrides. This system turned us into a sales management company. Salespeople are out of work every day. But a sales manager in A.L. Williams could create real financial security by building leaders under him who in turn produced more leaders and so on. The sales manager earned an override on every sale in his organization. Eventually, A.L. Williams created 16 levels of overrides. It was our way of building a company, rewarding good work by "pushing up people."

The announcements still stand as a milestone in our company. We all grasped the priceless independence and opportunity we'd gained through A.L. Williams. We represented free enterprise at its finest.

REPLACEMENTS & OVERRIDES

When a Division Manager moved up to Regional Vice President in A.L. Williams, he left behind a successor to replace him as he left to start his own organization. This encouraged RVP promotions for two reasons.

1. The upline RVP benefited financially, receiving a 15% override on all business produced by the new RVP.

2. The RVP didn't lose the DM's entire organization through the promotion. Typically a top producer was tapped as the "replacement."

THE TALKS

As 1977 passed into 1978, state legislators still hawked the bill to outlaw deposit term. The ordeal had already dragged on longer than the hearings. But the cloud had a silver lining – Boe Adams.

Boe and I often met to discuss the bill… and we privately talked about a possible carrier change to National Home Life. Art DeMoss was open to the idea. It thrilled me to consider all National Home Life offered us: 50 states, a vast mail order infrastructure, national name recognition (Art Linkletter was their television spokesman), a huge home office, great products and a great name.

Art DeMoss seemed like a sure bet. He had already built the largest mail order insurance company in the world. His national advertising had made National Home Life a household name. In addition to television ads, NHL inundated every city with a population of 30,000 or more with weekly newspaper circulars and supplements. Now, according to Boe, Art DeMoss' dream had grown. He wanted to build the largest insurance company in the world. He stood ready to commit his company's resources to us. On paper, it looked like a match made in heaven.

The discussions grew more serious. I told Joe Jack about National Home Life and the likelihood of them taking some of our new business. I explained we wanted a gradual transition from Financial Assurance to National Home Life. Joe Jack amazed me. He felt completely comfortable with us selling for both companies. In fact, he was relieved.

So was I. Unbelievably, Joe Jack had continued to pay our advance commissions long after wanting to call it quits. Now, a new insurance carrier could take our business to the next level. The pieces had fallen into place. Just when it all should've been over for good, A.L. Williams fought through to a bigger, even better opportunity.

THE RESOLVE

In February, I received a phone call from the Governor's office: I had 30 minutes with Governor Busbee. I knew this could make the difference in our survival. The deposit term crisis had hung over us for months. Could this meeting possibly swing things our way?

Governor Busbee greeted me warmly. He asked about my family in Cairo. Apparently my friend had briefed him on my background. We chatted pleasantly a minute, then I went through my presentation. (I had that thing down pat by now!)

"The deposit term product has proved itself a blessing and a benefit to the citizens of Georgia," I told him. "It offers them significantly higher insurance coverage at far lower cost, and a tax-free payback, if they keep the policy for the length of term. Outlawing deposit term would not only harm the families who have purchased it, it would also cripple competition in the marketplace.

"And not just in Georgia," I added. "At least 15 other states are following Georgia's lead, trying to outlaw deposit term."

Governor Busbee's response felt different from that of other politicians. He listened intently, expressed genuine interest in my story. At the end of our meeting, he shook my hand. He said he'd look into the matter and get back to me.

He kept his word. In a week, we received a call from the Georgia Insurance Department: The bill to outlaw deposit term had been dropped. As suddenly and mysteriously as it started, the deposit term crisis in Georgia ended. The decision caused a chain reaction, and other states dropped their bills as well. Whatever Governor Busbee did worked. The issue never came up in Georgia again.

What a relief! For the first time in many months I could focus entirely on the sales force. By the time summer rolled around, National Home Life had become an everyday part of our lives. The sales force sold more and more NHL products and fewer of FAI's. By August, the transition was complete. I asked Boe to join me full-time at A.L. Williams and he did.

Joe Jack felt satisfied with the decision, no hard feelings. Financial Assurance continued to process our business on their books. Joe Jack was completely ready to slow down. He kept a few general agents, but cut the business back again to a small operation.

We were set! A.L. Williams geared up for unlimited growth with a new company. National Home Life promised a reserve full of money, a national reputation and the support of 1,800 employees. We're ready and able, they said, to handle this thriving, growing agency.

Fantastic!

But that's not what happened.

14 Boe

The providential meeting with Boe Adams dramatically and unexpectedly changed the course of our company's history: Boe was the perfect guy at the perfect time to fulfill a unique leadership role inside the company. In time, Boe would become the all-time "MVP" of A.L. Williams.

It may sound strange, but finding Boe felt kind of like finding Angela. When I met Angela, I never wanted to marry anybody else. I just knew she was the girl. We shared a depth of understanding that didn't exist with anyone else. We clicked.

It clicked with Boe, too. I could point to lots of super leaders in A.L. Williams; I'd worked with some of them for years. But Boe and I had something different, a connection that went far beyond the field side of the business.

For starters, his background was so much like mine it seemed almost eerie.

Back home in Arkansas, Boe started out as a high school coach after a stellar college basketball career. He supplemented his income selling life insurance part-time. Somewhere along the way, he ran across "Buy Term and Invest the Difference" and sold term with a small life insurance company in Texas.

Going full-time, Boe quickly moved up the ranks and became CEO at the age of 27. Based on his own success as a part-time salesman, he believed he could build an agency with part-timers. And, just as I'd experienced, it worked. By age 30, Boe ran his own company, led a small "Buy Term and Invest the Difference" sales force, and earned a million bucks. The day we met, he automatically understood the A.L. Williams crusade and what it hoped to accomplish. He'd basically hoped the same things at his own company. Unreal.

Something else about Boe set him apart… the tested heart of a warrior. While CEO of his company in Texas, a business reversal cost him his business, his fortune and his reputation. Before he met Art DeMoss in the mid-'70s, he'd hit rock bottom. Art recognized Boe's enormous talent and gave him a place to start over, building the agency side of his insurance business. He also led him to the Lord.

I guess a lot of people in the business world would look at Boe and think, "Well, he blew it. He's a loser. Don't waste your time on him."

Not me. I looked at Boe and thought, "That guy's a winner." To make it big is incredible all by itself, because it's so hard. Then to lose it all…

Not everybody can walk through fire.

After a devastating crisis, most people never find the courage to get back up and start over. If you find a person who can, then you've found the strongest, toughest, most unbelievable leader in the world.

Boe was that kind of guy. And I've often thought that if Boe hadn't suffered that setback, he would've continued on another course, building his own company in Texas. Our paths would never have crossed. Without Boe, A.L. Williams may well have died before it ever really lived.

MR. INSIDE & MR. OUTSIDE

Back in 1940, legendary head football coach Earl "Red" Blaik took over Army's failing football program and turned it into a national powerhouse, winning three national titles from 1944 to 1946 with an amazing 27-0-1 record. A large part of his success lay in the superstar ability of two athletes, Doc Blanchard and Glenn Davis. Known as "Mr. Inside" and "Mr. Outside," Blanchard, a fullback, and Davis, a halfback, combined for 97 touchdowns and 585 points in their three years together at Army... statistically the best rushing duo in NCAA history. Separately they were stars; together no one could stop them.

Boe and I became Blanchard and Davis, the perfect team to run A.L. Williams.

Boe's real gift lay in building back-office support. A genius with numbers, he understood the money side of the business better than I did. We needed tons and tons of money to keep A.L. Williams growing, and Boe – Mr. Inside – knew how to get it.

I now felt free to play my best role – Mr. Outside: building, promoting and motivating the sales force.

For 12 years, Boe and I would function like two pistons in an engine. We knew our roles, and we stuck to them. It's part of what made A.L. Williams work so well.

Boe didn't just endure our freakish growth, he *embraced* it. He loved it, thrived on it, pushed for even more.

Early on, I told Boe, "Look, we're going to revolutionize the industry! We're going to beat Prudential! We're going to write a billion dollars of business in a year!"

That seemed like crazy talk in just our second year of business. But Boe believed. He didn't even bat an eye.

Eventually we wrote a billion dollars of business a day.

MOVING THE ARMY

I like to think of it this way. Before Boe joined the company, we resembled a Boy Scout troop. You woke up in the morning, folded up your tent, and went on your way in a matter of minutes. Things stayed small and simple.

But as Boe came on board, our numbers began to rocket. I became the "recruiting" general and Boe the "administrative" general. I brought in the troops and motivated them; Boe kept that growing army moving forward with the right supplies. Boe devised the back office systems to process millions of apps, license thousands of agents, handle thousands of death claims, and pay millions of dollars in commissions to thousands of families. Such a complex operation took massive amounts of manpower to run.

Beyond that, Boe made sure we never ran out of money. No matter what whopping amount went out in commissions to the sales force, we never missed a paycheck. And we never asked the sales force to slow down.

Never.

THE "BOE" OF NEGOTIATION

Something else set Boe apart – his extraordinary ability to cut a deal. I could hold my own, but Boe? A *master*. His negotiation powers absolutely kept the company running and the commission checks flowing during two ultra-crucial transition periods when technically we should've been out of business. (Those stories come later.) Bob Miller tells a story that captures Boe's amazing capacity to play one group off another to get what we needed.

"Not long after I moved to Atlanta and started working as an in-house National Sales Director," Bob says, "Boe invited me to go with him on a three-day negotiating trip to the Breakers Hotel in Palm Beach, Florida. He had arranged a meeting with the chief actuary and legal counsel and a couple of their assistants of PennCorp, our product company at that time. The purpose of the meeting was to negotiate for about five things – we needed to hire more employees to process business, we needed a product upgrade, more commissions, and a couple other administrative things, like two more staff lawyers, things like that.

"He told me to not say anything but to just watch. I felt like I was a fairly intelligent guy, but not far into the meeting I was lost. I knew if I was lost, the PennCorp guys were lost, because I knew what Boe was trying to do. Boe went in there asking for a laundry list of 50 things, yet he really only wanted five. None of it was written down. Every time he would bring up a point and they would counter his point, Boe would change the subject and move to the next thing. When they tried to counter that one, he'd move on again. He never let them finish. He rattled off all kinds of statistics, just pulling them out of his head. I don't know where he came up with all that stuff. Some of it was true, some of it was B.S., but they didn't know which was which. He had them so confused. Total control.

"After two and a half days of this, we sat down and they conceded in a big heap of exhaustion to 12 of Boe's requests. And then he told them how stupid they were. He said, 'You idiots, you shouldn't give us these 12 things. Take this one back or it will cost you millions. And take this one back or you'll get fired.' And he went on like that, until he gave them back four items.

"We walked away with three more items than we came for. The PennCorp guys went home, completely worn out and relieved, totally convinced Boe had just saved their necks."

"YES, WE CAN"

One final quality made Boe special – the thing that helped me the most through the years. His "can-do" attitude.

The top guy in charge is always in a tough place. To the troops, you must always be positive, always be tough, always be selling the dream.

Behind the scenes, it's different. You're scanning the horizon, looking for what might go wrong, thinking through every worst-case scenario. I carried some pretty heavy weight on my shoulders and sometimes the worries got to me. When Boe and I talked, his answer always came out the same: "Art, this can be done." However big or complicated the issue, Boe stayed out in front of it.

In a money crisis, Boe would say, "Art, our company's going to be even bigger than you think." We'd have a field disaster and Boe would say, "Art, we can beat Prudential even sooner than we planned." His attitude always freed me.

What's the mark of a big-time leader? You deliver. No matter what. You deliver the goods. Every time Boe said yes to me, it added to his workload. In the middle of 25 projects, we'd hit a new crisis. Boe just took it on. He loved being in a position to handle challenges. He paved the road, because he had the big dream, too.

Here's the best way I can describe it: Without Boe's leadership, A.L. Williams would not have become what it did.

Boe Adams was and is A.L. Williams' Most Valuable Person.

15 National Home Life

National Home Life opened up a whole new world. We went from a regional company to a national one, at a critical time. With 95 percent of all A.L. Williams' business still in Georgia, a simple legislative or public relations issue could conceivably put us out of business. The close call with the insurance department over deposit term had proven that. We needed to outgrow the risk, so I temporarily put a freeze on all Regional Vice President promotions in Georgia. The next RVP promotion would come with a catch – a move out of state.

Bill Orender stood next in line for RVP. In June 1978, I called him to my office. "Bill, congratulations! You are going to be our first expansion RVP," I announced happily. "I'm promoting you to RVP and I want you to open up a whole new part of the country for A.L. Williams – go anywhere you want, as long as it's out of Georgia."

I sat back and waited for his reaction, a little nervously.

I needn't have worried. Bill took the challenge like a champion. He immediately researched demographics in other parts of the country and decided on Dallas. In July 1978, he packed up his wife, Carol, their five-year old, two-year old and six-week old baby and drove two days to Texas. By Monday, Bill was on the phone setting up appointments.

"We didn't know anybody in Dallas, not a soul," Bill recalls. "Didn't matter. I had missionary zeal and evangelical fervor. I got there and went to work."

By the end of Bill's first month, he had 10 recruits. He earned $5,000 his second month and never looked back.

Bill set the pace. In a few months, Jack Schulman, a Division Manager under Tee Faircloth, set up shop in Houston. Ron Wright in Bobby Buisson's organization did the same in New Orleans. Jim Martin, another Buisson downline, moved to Plano, Texas.

Our people suddenly became pioneers… it was "Westward Ho" for A.L. Williams.

THE ADMINISTRATION

Art DeMoss was recognized in the industry as the "founding father" of direct mail insurance sales. Far ahead of rival Colonial Penn Life, National Home Life put itself on the map becoming the first company to successfully sell life insurance products without agents. Though the traditional industry snubbed direct mail selling, it held National Home Life in high regard for its business practices.

Art DeMoss surrounded himself with good people. A hand-picked board of directors handled day-to-day decisions on the direct mail side of the company. Bob Safford, an insurance executive from Michigan, built the upstart agency, and Stafford added Dick Morgan, an experienced insurance executive from Mississippi, to run agency operations. Art DeMoss had managed to sign Art Linkletter as national spokesman for National Home Life. Linkletter enjoyed a broad following as one of the country's most popular and well-known entertainers. His frequent radio and TV endorsements transformed National Home Life into a trusted, household name.

So, Art DeMoss knew how to run a good business… and also knew how to step away. An accomplished, self-made multi-millionaire, Art DeMoss in recent years spent most of his time developing Executive Ministries, a Christian outreach program aimed specifically at top-level executives. He kept a heavy speaking schedule, supporting religious groups like Campus Crusade for Christ, The 700 Club, Jerry Falwell and Liberty University, teaching them how to grow their organizations.

Now, as National Home's phenomenal growth numbers started to level off, Art DeMoss turned his energies back to the company again. He realized that National Home Life eventually would saturate the market. Since mail order policies stay on the books an average of four years – a much shorter time than traditional policies – Art DeMoss wisely looked ahead to the long-term potential of A.L. Williams. He had a big vision… and money to spend on it.

But we also had an internal problem. Direct mail processed tens of thousands of apps per month and made money like gangbusters, with an instant 15-20 percent profit margin. In comparison, our start-up sales agency looked small and, out of necessity, it cost money up front to put business on the books. The direct mail people resented every dollar that went to us. They had no understanding of the differences between their business and our sales force. Worse, they didn't care to learn. We were annoying, unwanted stepchildren.

This problem grew more and more apparent as the months went by. Bob Safford and Dick Morgan were excellent guys to be in charge of the agency, but NHL's top brass kept them on a leash. With mail order booming, why invest money to put agency business on the books?

Their narrow vision affected A.L. Williams. While 1,800 employees worked at the NHL home office in Malvern, only about 20 worked our business. So, commissions paid slow. Licensing drug its feet. Bank drafts were inconsistent. Apps got lost.

We had a mess. Clients called, hopping mad… and our sales agents felt the same way.

Here's a situation Bob Miller put up with. "We set up clients on 'automatic payment' where we drafted the monthly premium payment directly out of their bank account, so they wouldn't have to write a check every month." Bob explains. "A lot of people were unfamiliar with bank drafts, so we had to talk them into it. Then the computer would mess up. Instead of taking out $50, it would draft the whole year, or $600. The client wouldn't realize it until the next month. He'd be overdrawn and screaming mad. We'd get it straightened out. Then, the next month, it would happen again. Usually these people were friends of friends, because that's how we recruited, so it was even more embarrassing. I paid all the overdrafts for one client, just to make him feel better."

Enough! I finally told everyone just to count on losing 10 percent of the business they wrote. "It's all part of start-up," I said. "We're growing so fast we have to expect some problems." And it was true. We didn't measure our growth annually because we were compounding *monthly*.

Frustrating? You bet. National Home Life told us from the get-go they wanted as much business as we could give them. We can handle it, they said. But they couldn't. Or wouldn't. We'd stepped in the same old administrative mess.

What made it more baffling was that everything else really was better at National Home Life. Where Financial Assurance had one little computer to run operations, NHL had a giant room full of state-of-the-art computer systems. FAI had one underwriter; NHL had dozens. FAI, regional and unknown, worried about running out of money; NHL – loaded and nationally recognized. Where FAI had no A.M. Best rating, NHL had an A+ rating. They offered us lots of great stuff.

Still, despite all of these benefits, the negatives outweighed the positives. They couldn't support us. Worse, they didn't understand our business.

THE AGENCY

We ran into agency problems, too. Bob Safford's agency within National Home Life operated separately from A.L. Williams. He had several hundred general agents in various parts of the country selling NHL products. Interestingly Safford's team sold both term and whole life.

Bob's agency was a different animal altogether. In October 1978, Bob invited me to Fayetteville, North Carolina, to see his best sales organization in action, selling and prospecting.

"Art, I'm going to show you the office of the future," he told me with great pride. I was excited... until I got there.

I stepped into a boiler room operation. Twenty agents sat around telephones, calling from lists and reading scripts, trying to set up appointments. I wanted to throw up. Here sat the tired "old school" way of building a sales force – the complete opposite of A.L. Williams. For years, I'd pounded the podium on warm market referrals – *no* cold calls, *no* solicitation, *no* talking to strangers. The road to sales went through friends, and friends of friends.

Watching Safford, it hit me: *These people don't understand us. What if they never understand us?* I felt very uncomfortable.

Oh, Safford was a good guy; he just didn't know the way A.L. Williams did business. But, if this thing was ever going to work with National Home, Safford and everybody else would have to learn our system, because we had truly come up with a better way to sell life insurance.

Boldly, I took the opportunity on that trip to explain the philosophy to Bob Safford. I'll give him credit. He understood the differences. He bought into it, too, and began teaching his agency guys to sell and recruit "the A.L. Williams way."

In Atlanta, I sat down with Boe.

"Look," I said, "we have to get our own home office – one that is totally dedicated to handling A.L. Williams business and nothing else. We are a unique company, with unique problems. Trying to fit what we do into another organization just doesn't work. We're like mixing oil and water."

Boe looked at me, challenged, and nodded.

"You're right, Art," he said. "To support our growth, we have to become totally independent under the National Home Life umbrella. Either that... or we find another company."

We both knew what that would mean. We had dwindling options. We couldn't continue to fix back shop problems by changing companies. It cost money, and starting over totally broke the momentum of our sales force. So either we found a way to keep growing... or we died.

Boe immediately called Art DeMoss about the possibility of building us our own home office.

ATLANTA DATA SYSTEMS

Since our Financial Assurance days, with Boe's help, policy analysis had greatly improved. Paul Andrews and his stacks of hand-written extractions lay behind us. Agents who once sent in actual policies (always a problem with clients) now filled out a form with the necessary comparison data, mailed it to the company, then quickly received a computer-printed replacement form with side-by-side policy comparisons, extrapolated cash values and policy futures. Much better. Much faster. Just one problem: in less than a year, we'd overwhelmed two big companies with our volume.

"Why pay someone else to do this?" I asked Boe, after the second company fell apart. "How about we set up our own policy analysis company?"

"That's right," he said. "Let's do it." He drew up plans to create a separate corporation to process policy analyses for A.L. Williams. To fund the start-up, I went to the top nine producers in the company and asked for $5,000 each, promoting it as a financial stake in a new corporation with shares that paid dividends – a good return on their investment. Boe and I also contributed. We spread out the risk and created ownership.

Money in hand, Boe eventually hired his nephew, Mike Adams, and moved him to Atlanta from Arkansas. Fresh out of college with a liberal arts degree, Mike didn't know anything about computers. He learned. Fast. He rolled up his sleeves and designed a customized computer system. By January 1979, Atlanta Data Systems, or ADS, opened for business with two employees in one 500-square-foot room. In a few weeks, it electronically churned out thousands of policy comparisons for our sales force.

Computerizing policy data created a new challenge – project dividends. In the old days, agents had to match a client's whole life policy with a similar policy listed on Diamond Life Bulletins from Flitcraft (an analytical insurance periodical) and try to determine the dividend per thousand. Talk about a nuisance. We ran into hundreds of policy variations from dozens of companies. If an estimate got even a little off, the competing whole life company raised a fuss with our guys at the kitchen table.

Boe appealed to NHL's senior actuary, Bob Whitney. Whitney, Mike Adams and Dick Kinnard, Boe's assistant, came up with a way to automate policy data from the 50 or 60 "top par" insurance companies. They also devised a formula that simultaneously compared the dividends of five companies with similar policies – a huge boon for our agents.

What a breakthrough! We cut our turnaround time on policy analysis from days and weeks to less than 72 hours. Complete internal control made the difference.

CONTROVERSY

While Boe worked side by side with me in Atlanta, he still held his regional vice president position with National Home Life. He led a talented group of agents – Ed Randle, Birmingham; Dick Walker, Tampa; Bill Olive, Palm Harbor; Ara Kalpak and Tom Powers, Atlanta; Dennis Richardson, Houston; Mike Tuttle, Bob Culp and Bob Toney, Dallas; Tom Halpin, Philadelphia; and Ken Asay, Orem, Utah. Smart and capable, they grew extremely interested in joining our "Buy Term and Invest the Difference" crusade.

Ed Randle remembers our first meeting. "Boe told me about Art Williams," Ed says. "I thought Art would be 10 feet tall and look like a superstar. The first time we met, he came out of this little office, no bigger than 12 by 12. He was short, balding even then. But he greeted me like a long lost friend. He said, 'Ed, we can go out of here and maybe change something that's wrong and help a lot of people that nobody is paying any attention to today!' That touched me. Then he looked right at me and said, 'And in the process, I believe we can get stone wealthy.'"

So… to bring in Boe's agents or not to bring them? Boe's sales team as part of A.L. Williams would boost expansion plans, but create company controversy. A tough call. I'd staunchly held from the beginning that all new recruits start part-time on the ground floor, then work (and work and work) their way up to the prestigious Regional Vice President position. No matter what else they had done before in their lives, they started on the bottom rung at A.L. Williams. Everybody took the same shot at making it big. Staunchly, I had opposed recruiting life insurance agents, too – we always had to "untrain" them to do business our way.

Still, Boe's team had some of Boe's steam. I made the call – all of Boe's guys would merge into A.L. Williams… and all would join as RVPs.

I heard the howls from every part of the company, in every territory.

Bringing Boe's guys in as RVPs gave the sales force an impression I had changed my mind on both ground-floor entry and hiring "old-line" agents. I hadn't at all. I just recognized the situation with Boe's general agents for what is was – a unique circumstance. One we needed to take advantage of.

"Bringing in Boe's guys is a one-of-a-kind opportunity," I explained at a special sales force meeting. "Yes, these guys are life insurance agents – traditional agents. But they are Boe's agents. They already understand the crusade. They get A.L. Williams. This is a great thing for the company… and it doesn't hurt you a bit. We can't possibly saturate the market, and this allows us to diversify into new territories immediately. We can double our expansion effort."

I heard a good bit of grumbling. But, true to my word, I still brought new recruits in as "ground floor" Representatives. I still discouraged the recruiting of life insurance agents.

The tough decision proved to be one of the most important of our early years. The National Home guys came in and worked hard, producing 50-60 percent of the sales, in some cases. This time, fourth and one, I made the right call.

FUTURE GROWTH

Boe stood apart a little at National Home Life. He'd brought A.L. Williams on board. He enjoyed a close relationship with Art DeMoss. The executives at the home office in Malvern respected him. But not all of them really understood Boe's vision.

At our initial presentation to National Home Life, I explained that by the end of 1977, our first year of business, A.L. Williams had put $350 million of business on the books.

"We'll probably double that by year-end 1978," I predicted.

Boe stepped to the lectern for his turn. He too projected huge growth potential for A.L. Williams. As he finished, I sensed a very polite skepticism.

Dick Morgan, NHL Agency Operations, heard that first presentation. "Having been in the insurance business for a while on the operations side," Dick remembers, "I'd listened to a hundred agencies, and they always came and blew a lot of smoke about what they were going to do. Art came and did the same thing. I listened and divided his numbers by four. That's what my experience told me to do. But in a very short time, I realized

I should've multiplied his numbers by four. A.L. Williams wasn't blowing smoke at all."

The A.L. Williams home office discussions between Boe and Art DeMoss continued behind the scenes. Over and over, Boe told Art that if he were really serious about building a huge agency system, he had a gold mine.

"These A.L. Williams people are the best in the country," he told Art. "They're going to do it for you… but you're going to have to build them a home office, and you're going to have to sign an exclusive contract."

Boe was right about the exclusive contract. Still, I chafed at the idea of signing such a thing. From the beginning, we'd been determined to keep A.L. Williams an independent sales force. We wanted control, to give a company our business as long as they could take it, then move on to a different company if they couldn't.

Our non-stop growth had revealed my naiveté. A.L. Williams grew so big, so fast that we could break a company. Who was going to give us a home office and all the support and money we needed without some kind of assurance of our loyalty and all our business?

Boe made sense. I realized probably it was time to make a deal with the right company and become a captive sales force. We would exchange independence for support, stability and financial backing. I really saw no other way to sustain our sales force.

National Home Life was the logical partner of choice. And Boe told me DeMoss was very interested, although I didn't hear it from him personally.

POINT CLEAR II

By December 1978, we made 1,000 sales a month. We had 2,800 licensed Reps selling in 21 states. At our second convention in Point Clear, Angela and I treated 125 top couples to the year-end celebration at the Grand Hotel. Again, I gave out lots of awards, including four RVP promotions: Ron Wright, Art Burgess, Ward Peters and Bob Miller.

What a fun night for Bob. I completely surprised him with an "official" RVP promotion. He deserved it. He'd done a great job with his pilot office. His two top recruits, Greg Fitzpatrick and John Roig, had already jumped full-time.

Clearly, even with some frustration at National Home Life, the sales force was thriving. In March 1979, we received production numbers for year-end 1978: A.L. Williams put $630 million dollars of new business on the books, measured as "face amount of policies submitted."

Just as Boe and I predicted, we'd nearly doubled our production from one year ago. If we stayed on pace, we'd break the $1 billion mark in 1979 – just two years into our business.

MORE OPPOSITION

The rest of the life insurance industry numbered around 300,000 licensed agents in 1979; A.L. Williams a "peanut" by comparison. In a powerful, multi-billion-dollar industry with a 100-year track record, our two years of business looked pretty trivial.

With Financial Assurance, we held licenses in 13 states, did business in just three, and 95 percent of our business came from only one, Georgia. Elsewhere, the name A.L. Williams brought shrugs.

All that changed when we moved to National Home Life. We stepped onto the national playing field of all 50 states. Suddenly we ran into more opposition. Our "plague" was beginning to spread, and the competition didn't like it one bit.

The regulatory crisis that started with Commissioner Caldwell in Georgia suddenly grew fifty-fold. In the 1970s and 80s, life insurance was the only industry in the marketplace that sold products nationally but that each state controlled. Each state, Alabama to Wyoming, had its own insurance commissioner and department.

Insurance commissioners, also known as regulators, typically came out of the traditional life insurance industry as former agents or company executives. Most took office as governor appointees, with strong behind-the-scenes connections to powerful insurance companies. Naturally, many insurance commissioners blatantly acted on behalf of the industry that put them in office (their past employers) and worked hard to make sure insurance interests – not consumers – got the big pieces of pie.

Legislators should write and enact insurance laws, of course, but a dirty little secret of some state lawmaking bodies is this: insurance executives or lobbyists are often the real authors of insurance legislative bills. Many times, such bills pass through the legislative process and became law without public knowledge. Committee chairmen and other members of the state legislature often win election on generous campaign contributions from insurance companies. They rubber stamp a law favorable to the industry without question. Money talks.

As A.L. Williams expanded into new states, we quickly found ourselves clashing with state insurance departments. One amazing example: In Delaware, legislation appeared on the house floor to outlaw part-time insurance agents.

Talk about slanted. A.L. Williams didn't even do business in Delaware at the time! Who else but A.L. Williams used part-time agents to sell life insurance? We dispatched National Home lawyers to Dover and they successfully removed the bill.

In Alabama, bowing to pressure from state and local underwriter associations, state insurance regulators proposed a bill outlawing deposit term as an "illegal product," similar to our Georgia crisis. Our lawyer, Kevin King, asked a judge in Montgomery for an injunction against the bill. The judge said yes; the bill went away.

In Florida, the state legislature tried to outlaw deposit term by tacking the proposal onto an unrelated bill. Dick Walker and his ALW team drove to Tallahassee and presented testimony before a subcommittee. The bill dropped.

Between 1977 and 1981, at least 15 state insurance departments attempted to outlaw the deposit term product. None succeeded.

Even so, these distractions sometimes cost us energy and resources we could have used protecting more families and building more business for our enterprise.

SENATE SUB-COMMITTEE

HEARING ON LIFE INSURANCE

Washington, D.C.,

February 20, 1973

"For almost 70 years, the life insurance industry has been a smug sacred cow feeding the public a steady line of sacred bull. Through deceptions and inadequate information, the life insurance industry dupes husbands into shortchanging their wives and children by buying too much of the wrong kind of insurance (or too little of the right kind) at excessive prices."

– RALPH NADER,

CONSUMER ADVOCATE

"To say that the life insurance industry represents a sacred cow that is spreading sacred bull over the American economy is to pay it an undue compliment. Although I can endorse most of what Ralph Nader said before this subcommittee on Tuesday, I think his figure of speech is overly generous to the life insurance industry. Both the cow and the byproduct of the bull are valuable and useful farm commodities. The impact of the life insurance industry should be measured by more critical prose."

– HERB DENENBERG, PENNSYLVANIA

INSURANCE COMMISSIONER

NEW NEGOTIATIONS

Lots of general agents around the country sold National Home Life products but weren't particularly loyal. This freedom comes with being a general agent – you can sell products from many companies.

Joel Cristy in Miami, a friend of Boe's, sold a little life insurance for NHL, but he preferred accident and health (A&H). He'd signed a general agent contract to sell A&H insurance for PennLife, a product company owned by PennCorp. He did well with it.

One day, talking to Boe, Joel happened to mention his new affiliation.

"You know, Boe, you really ought to meet the president of PennCorp, Stanley Beyer," Joel said. "PennCorp works a lot of part-time agents. You two might have something in common."

Joel arranged a meeting, and within days, Boe sat down in Santa Monica, California, at an exploratory meeting with the president and chairman of PennCorp Financial Services.

It went well. Very well. Boe's reaction says it all: "Art, I've seen something incredible. You've got to meet Stanley Beyer."

PennCorp, around since 1939, featured $2 billion in assets, 2.5 million policyholders and thousands of employees and sales representatives in the United States and Canada. It owned several insurance companies, including Massachusetts Indemnity and Life Insurance Company (MILICO). PennCorp offered accident and health, credit, property and casualty, but it's bread and butter – high-indemnity, high-premium disability policies – sold to doctors, lawyers and professional athletes. This so-called "occupational disability," underwritten by MILICO, boomed in the mid-70s, but had steadily tapered off since. Although licensed in 49 states, MILICO did very little business these days. Looking at A.L. Williams on paper, Stanley Beyer had an idea.

Boe and I flew to Santa Monica. At first sight, I knew instantly: Stanley Beyer was different. The executives at ITT and Waddell & Reed? Corporate guys. Joe Jack Merriman? A financial guy. Art DeMoss? A direct mail guy.

But Stanley? A *sales guy*. He had come up through the ranks as a door-to-door salesman, the toughest kind, and used his sales experience to build a huge, successful company. Meeting him felt like meeting Boe – we clicked. He understood salespeople; he knew what motivated them.

When we walked into his office, I looked up. A banner over his desk read "Penn-Corp, Where the Salesman is King." My heart skipped a beat.

We began with a discussion of our core concepts. That took about three minutes. Even though PennCorp sold no life insurance, Stanley intuitively grasped our crusade. Years before, it turned out, he started using a split-funding concept with his sales force similar to "Buy Term and Invest the Difference." He had part-time contracts with lots of general agents, but he'd never considered building a sales force with part-timers.

He liked the idea. We explained advanced commissions; he liked that concept, too. Stanley saw our sales figures, a company on fire with growth, while his sat sort of stuck in the mud. Selling disability, he appealed to a tiny niche market. Now, the life insurance market, with appeal to a limitless middle-income market, might be a perfect vehicle to take him to the top.

To close our visit, Stanley toured us around the home office, a professionally decorated, antique-filled six-story office tower in downtown Santa Monica. His nearby home proved equally stunning. Stanley's next-door neighbor was Henry Mancini, and Stanley and his wife often socialized with the famous composer and other Hollywood notables. Stanley was "big time." He operated on a different level. He impressed and excited us.

In the next six months, negotiations with Stanley about a possible carrier switch to PennCorp picked up speed. The pivotal piece: Stanley would spend the millions necessary to build us a home office… *if* A.L. Williams would sign an exclusive contract with PennCorp.

Boe, meantime, carried on the same negotiations with Art DeMoss. According to Boe, Art DeMoss too would do whatever it took to keep A.L. Williams… including building an A.L. Williams home office in exchange for an exclusive contract. Although Boe liked PennCorp, he felt strongly we had a better deal with DeMoss, since our relationship was established. Our products were already licensed with National Home. We'd avoid the headache of "switching over" – no slowdown, no re-licensing, just continued association with the addition of our own home office to process the business being written. Even so, Boe masterfully kept up negotiations with Stanley. Boe and I made more trips to Santa Monica, meeting with Stanley and his key executives, Burt Borman, Lee Myers and Treacy Beyer. We talked often on the phone, too. By this time, we were making 1,800 sales a month. Very soon, I predicted, we'd see 4,000 sales a month.

I waited and watched and absolutely marveled. Little 'ol A.L. Williams, a "nuthin'" company started by 85 "nobodies" just two years before, now attracted two huge, national financial services companies willing to bet their futures and millions of dollars on us.

We waited, ready to make the next move toward our destiny.

BOMBSHELL

In July 1979, Boe and I hosted a mid-week RVP meeting in Dallas. By now, some tremendous field leaders had separated themselves from the pack and moved up in the company. I wanted to make a big deal out of them during our sessions.

A few examples of the "walk-on" potential at A.L. Williams.

• Hubert Humphrey, a conductor from Macon, started part-time. He earned $20,000, surpassing his annual railroad salary of $18,000, in less than four months. Going fulltime, his A.L. Williams income passed the $200,000 mark by mid-1979.

• Dennis Richardson, a NHL convert from Dallas, created a one-night version of the Fast Start School, called an "Opportunity Meeting." He brought in hundreds of new prospects every week.

• Ronnie Barnes, from Chattanooga, Tennessee, saw his 1978 A.L. Williams income hit $100,000, well past the $12,500 he'd earned teaching school.

• Doug Hartman, a former business owner in California, earned $60,000 his first year in A.L. Williams.

So, across the country our sales force just exploded in growth, and it charged the atmosphere.

That day in Dallas, though, something happened that sparked a full-scale electrical storm.

A news story broke – a "bombshell" that devastated the traditional life insurance industry and gave our cause a powerful vindication.

On July 10, 1979, the Federal Trade Commission in Washington, D.C., released a 455- page Staff Report on Life Insurance Cost Disclosure. The report culminated a two-and-ahalf year investigation to determine if consumers got enough cost information about whole life insurance from companies selling it. Two findings revealed that, without question, insurance companies kept families totally in the dark.

Highlights[1]:

• American consumers are **losing billions** of dollars yearly as a result of ill informed and inappropriate life insurance purchase decisions.

• The average rate of return paid to whole-life policyholders in 1977 was estimated to be **1.3 percent.** The rate of return is extraordinarily low, considering it's essentially tax-free.

• People who buy policies and then let them lapse within the first 10 years face **severe economic consequences** in lost interest and, in some cases, loss of principal. Losses due to first-year lapses alone exceeded $200 million in 1977.

• Consumers do not know the rate of return they will earn on the savings element of their whole life policies and the situation **prevents comparison shopping** with other types of savings or investments.

• The rate of return on new policies is in many instances **substantially below alternatives** readily available in the marketplace. The rates of return on older policies, especially non-dividend paying policies, are far worse.

• The consumer is given virtually **no meaningful information to compare** the true costs of similar policies or compare the benefits of the cash-value purchase with alternate forms of savings or investments.

• **Effective price competition does not exist in the life insurance industry.**

THE FTC HEADLINES HIT EVERY MAJOR NEWSPAPER!

'Whole Life Insurance a Bad Investment,' Yields Only 1.3% Return, FTC Reports

– *Los Angeles Times*, July 11, 1979

FTC Staff Says Consumer Losing Money by Keeping Savings in Insurance Policies

– *Wall Street Journal*, July 11, 1979

Americans Lose Billions on Insurance, FTC Says

– *Houston Post*, July 11, 1979

FTC Finds 'Whole Life' Insurance a Bad Investment

– *Dallas Morning News*, July 11, 1979

FTC Study Assails Whole Life Policies

– *Palm Beach Post*, July 11, 1979

Presenting his staff report to the Senate Commerce Committee, FTC chairman Michael Pertschuk stated, "I think it is fair to say that no other product in our economy that is purchased by so many people for so much money is bought with so little understanding of its actual or comparative value."

Whoa! The sleeping giant of truth just woke up and roared.

All these years the traditional life insurance industry had been using all its muscle to ruin the A.L. Williams name and reputation. Now the FTC held up tangible, third-party proof that legitimized our "Buy Term and Invest the Difference" concepts.

Confirmed: Cash value was a rip-off! What a breakthrough!

We put the FTC report on top of every client's kitchen table. We passed out flyers by the thousands. The report supported everything we claimed. Its credibility just couldn't be denied. Every man and woman in A.L. Williams felt a new conviction that our crusade was 100 percent right for consumers.

The traditional industry, on the other hand, blasted the FTC on every front.

The report blindsided the National Association of Life Underwriters (NALU). The NALU had not expected the report to highlight industry rates of return; it immediately went on the attack. Jack Bobo, NALU's executive vice president said, "Without question, the most disturbing event occurring in 1979 was the release, on July 10, of the long expected report by the FTC staff regarding their study of life insurance." Naturally, the NALU claimed the report was "based on totally misleading figures," and "put the industry in a very bad light with an apparent bias favoring term life insurance."[2] Within three hours of the report's release, NALU released thousands of counter brochures called "A Response to the FTC" – its "Hail Mary" effort to debunk the report.

The NALU filed a statement with the Senate Committee, challenging the integrity of the FTC report. The action generated hundreds of counter articles by the press, and Bobo instigated a highly prolific letters-to-the-editor campaign with NALU members all over the country.

In August, Phil Donahue hosted Norman Dacey, author of *What's Wrong With Your Life Insurance* and well-known term advocate, on his popular afternoon TV talk show. Dacey skillfully highlighted the findings of the FTC report and the advantages of "Buy Term and Invest the Difference." VCRs had just come on the market, and A.L. Williams agents everywhere taped the show and played it over and over again. Another perfect third-party endorsement.

NALU, not to be outdone, managed to get its newly elected president, Thomas Wolff, and Prudential CEO Robert Beck, on "The Phil Donahue Show" to present the traditional industry's viewpoint. After the TV appearance, NALU claimed its two guys succeeded "in discrediting both Dacey's views and the FTC's misleading statements." NALU also claimed its henchmen "ably presented the life insurance business as one conducted by people who are responsible, concerned and keenly sensitive to people's needs for financial security."[3]

Did they? Why did our subsequent sales start to rocket off the charts? Consumers now *knew* the real story behind "trash value" life insurance. With a choice, they came to A.L. Williams every time.

The NALU didn't stop using all its power and influence to control the damage. In October, Wolff and four insurance company presidents representing the American Council of Life Insurance, along with Federal Law and Legislation Committee Chairman Rice Brown, appeared before the Senate Commerce Committee to refute the FTC report. They made a big point of challenging the actuarial assumptions that led the staff to claim a 1.3 percent return on investment.[4] And guess what? Money in politics still talked. NALU's lobbying efforts moved the Senate committee to ban the FTC's ability to conduct any independent study of the insurance industry in the future. Amazing! This landmark decision applied to no other industries, but gave insurance companies total protection from further investigation.

Still, when the dust settled, the traditional industry could not undo the damage done by the FTC report. Their credibility suffered a mortal wound: Cash value insurance lay publicly exposed as a rip-off.

Traditional whole-life insurance would never really recover.

SHOCK

In this incredible swirl, negotiations with National Home Life and PennCorp came to a head. In California, Stanley Beyer waited patiently, checkbook in hand. He would even build our home office in *Atlanta*. It would be more efficient and affordable to build a new one in our part of the country, he told us.

In Pennsylvania, Art DeMoss sat ready, too. He'd spend whatever it took to develop the sales force into a large business division, separate from the mail order business. He told Boe he'd throw in a home office, as well. He scheduled a meeting with us for the following week.

What a position! I couldn't help but think back to 1976, when I spent four long months going from company to company, begging them to take our business. Now, not three years later, two huge companies stood ready to tie their futures to ours.

All of it changed one afternoon, in the blink of an eye.

On Saturday, August 18, 1979, Art DeMoss died suddenly of a heart attack while playing tennis at his home. He was 54 years old.

Boe called me with the news. I drove over to Boe's house, and we just sat and looked at each other. It's hard to describe that feeling. Total shock. Art DeMoss was a fine man, a great leader and businessman, a fantastic husband, father and Christian. His death hit Boe especially hard.

It hit me hard, too, in another way. Suddenly, I faced a very real – very frightening – possibility: A.L. Williams was history.

With Art DeMoss' death, it was very likely that National Liberty and National Home Life would be put up for sale immediately. The company, of course, would stop accepting new business. Our contract required NHL to give us a six-month notice before it stopped advance commissions to the sales force. But Boe and I had no clue if the contract still applied in this situation.

----

1 www.advisortoday.com, "Voices From the Field," Chapter 8: "FTC Releases a Study Critical of the Insurance Industry."

2 Ibid

3 Ibid

4 Ibid

PennCorp's offer still sat on the table. A snag in our discussions, however, now loomed very large – it would take Penn Corp 18 *months* to build a home office.

We didn't have 18 months. Look at us! We didn't have any sizable office space rented in Atlanta. We didn't have a computer. We didn't have staff. We didn't have "nuthin." We couldn't sustain a sales force for 30 days without advances, much less 18 months.

Boe and I sat there and grieved.

A cold hard fact made those hours even worse: A.L. Williams, in all its brief glory, could be out of business.

This time for good.

16 Penncorp

One day, you can hold the world in the palm of your hand. Next day, your hand can be empty.

Sure enough, on Monday morning, National Home Life and National Liberty Corporation went up for sale. A.L. Williams was out of business.

Everything depended now on Stanley Beyer.

First, though, we had to keep our doors open until we struck a PennCorp deal… if we struck a deal. On Tuesday, Boe flew to Malvern and met with the NHL executive officers. He would give them one of his greatest negotiating performances.

Boe's goal was to convince National Home Life to keep taking new business – and paying advance commissions – for six more months. It was mad, a crazy thing to ask. Anyone in insurance knows that once you put a company up for sale, you don't want new business. The cash drain only hurts the sale value of the company. But Boe pointed to the six-month clause in our contract and made his case.

First, he explained that PennCorp's insurer, MILICO, would soon be processing our A.L. Williams business. That statement relieved enormous pressure. Steady business for MILICO undergirded any potential sale for NHL.

Next, Boe promised that A.L. Williams would not replace any National Home policies already on our books.

Now, it was time for a bit of Boe magic.

"Look," he told the grieving execs, "if you're smart, you'll let us continue to give you our best business – the business from our full-time agents – for six more months. We're recruiting lots of new people every month, and we'll get those greenies licensed. But we'll assign all their business to PennCorp, not you. Rather than cut you off totally, we'll keep business coming in during this transition. We'll work it out so you get only the best business we write."

The NHL executives agreed to it.

Those guys still must have been in deep shock. If they'd thought about it, they would've seen right through Boe's "logic." Right then, it proved a great gift that the National Home executives never really took the time to understand our business. Boe walked out of the meeting that day with the heart of A.L. Williams beating in his hand.

We had six more months. And this should be said – Boe did lots of important things for our company over the years, but this stands as one of his finest hours.

- - - - - - - - - - - -

SHARED PHILOSOPHY

"In 1979, I met Art Williams. For the first time, I found an individual whose enthusiasm, intensity and devotion to the men in the field was a carbon copy of what we stood for."

– STANLEY BEYER

OPPORTUNITY MAGAZINE,

SEPTEMBER 1980

- - - - - - - - - - -

$100 MILLION CONTRACT

Our luck held on the phone with PennCorp, too. Stanley listened, thought briefly, then committed to build our home office.

In six months.

He confessed, even as he said yes, he didn't think it was possible. We weren't sure ourselves – to our knowledge such a thing had never been done before.

Ah, details. When did they ever slow down A.L. Williams?

On Saturday, September 8, 1979, Boe and I flew to Santa Monica. I signed a $100-million general agency agreement with PennCorp Financial Services, making MILICO our new product company. We drew up the contract so fast that the draft we signed had handwritten notes in the margins. A final draft was never typed. We didn't have time.

Never truer. We now had until March 1, 1980 – a little less than six months – to simultaneously stay in business with National Home and complete the home office with MILICO. Without a blowing and going new office on that date, we would be out of business. Again.

What a roller coaster. First… We were on top of the world. Then… We were flat out of business. Then… We were back in business with a new company. All in three weeks. We all felt a little dizzy.

The PennCorp deal called for a special meeting with the sales force. I put a lot of thought into what to say.

I wanted to shout it from the rooftops: "Look, we're going with PennCorp! Everything we dreamed about is fixing to become a reality!"

But I couldn't. Still writing with National Home Life, I didn't want to do anything to risk National Home cutting us off. We walked a tightrope with them for the next six months. I lived in utter dread of getting that "it's over" phone call from their execs.

Instead, I simply explained that in the next six months we would transition from selling life products for National Home Life to PennCorp. "This will give you an opportunity to sell for two *great companies* – the best of both worlds," I explained.

The sales force took it all in stride. We continued to sell and recruit with no let-up. Some organizations switched over to PennCorp products immediately; others sold both for a while. It all happened with relative ease for the guys in the field. They knew what they needed to know. It was up to Boe and me to worry about the rest of it.

Behind the scenes, we went to work in Atlanta hiring everybody we could hire. We needed people in every position – licensing, underwriting, new business, policy issue, field compensation, policy owner services, premium billing and collection, communications, compliance and on and on. Impressed with their work at National Home, I convinced Dick Morgan, Bill Keane and Bob Whitney to join us in similar roles at A.L. Williams. Oliver Horsman, a public relations and consumer expert from NHL, joined us in the compliance area. We hired Dick Kinnard, Boe's long-time assistant, and put him to work buying desks and office equipment.

Boe called his extended family in Arkansas and hired nearly every relative he could find. Angela and I persuaded Sydney Ogletree, Angela's sister, to move up from south Georgia, as well as my brother Don Williams and his family, now living in Blakely, Georgia. Other relatives pitched in, too.

Later on, people criticized us for nepotism. Truth is, if we hadn't hired our family members to come in and work, the home office never would have gotten off the ground. They came in and worked around the clock – endless hours – and for very little pay in the beginning. Quite a sacrifice. Many family members performed exceptionally well, too. By the time Sydney finished her tenure with A.L. Williams, she'd run every major department in the home office, including Human Resources.

We hired 40 people – still not enough. Arguments flared. Did we really need to hire 20 more people? Stanley said no. He sent Treacy Beyer in from Santa Monica to help solve the problem. It turned out we did… and even 60 people couldn't keep up! People worked 18- hour days, seven days a week, doing everything possible to meet the March 1 deadline.

The next big issue? Where to find 10,000 square feet of office space. Boe put his wife, Myrna, on that one. She worked with Richard Bowers, a young real estate agent just starting out in the commercial business. Richard wasted no time, finding a very suitable property on Northlake Parkway, a thriving area located just off Atlanta's I-285 "perimeter" interstate. Richard leased us 7,000 square feet of office space. (It would soon grow to 40,000.) Bowers, incidentally, went on to build one of Atlanta's top commercial real estate firms.

Talk about a long, stomach-churning six months. At the same time, the work felt exhilarating beyond belief. Every person we hired to run our home office was another huge step toward independence.

No doubt about it, we stood on the threshold of history!

If we could just survive a few more weeks.

- - - - - - - - - - -

A CAPITAL INTENSIVE BUSINESS

"The kind of business Art Williams wrote required an enormous amount of capital. The first year a policy stayed on the books, we spent $300 for every $100 of premium on commissions, expenses and setting up the reserve fund, required by law. "A company needed lots of money to play in Art's league. If he continued to grow meteorically, then the company would begin to earn back the capital fairly quickly as the policies stayed on the books over the years. But every year we needed more money than the year before due to constant growth. We had to keep pushing into the future years to figure out the earnings. "This is not to say it wasn't profitable. Insurance companies account for all of this so they can show earnings even early on. But it takes a lot of capital to make it go. Even more with A.L. Williams."

– TREACY BEYER, PENNCORP EXECUTIVE

MISSISSIPPI

Smack in the middle of all this, big trouble brewed up in Mississippi. RVP Bill Anderton, an old college buddy of mine from Mississippi State, worked out of Jackson. Going great guns for A.L. Williams, he rose to be the number three producer in the company, replacing about 100 whole life policies every month and adding new recruits by the week. The flood of policy replacements drew the ire of local life underwriters associations, and they wasted no time in complaining to George Dale, the state insurance commissioner.

Mr. Dale, a decent guy, was new to the job. Like so many elected insurance commissioners, he knew very little about the insurance industry. In fact, he left work as a high school teacher and coach to run for office. Naturally, big insurance companies in Mississippi pretty much paid for his campaign. So, when their agents starting pressuring him to "do something about A.L. Williams," he listened.

In August, one of Bill's downline managers, an up-and-coming producer by the name of Joyce Banks, submitted a required policy comparison to ADS. It replaced a Connecticut Mutual whole life policy with a National Home Life deposit term policy. Following procedure, she gave the comparison paperwork to the client after she got it back from ADS and let them look it over. The competing Connecticut Mutual agent, trying desperately to stop the replacement, grabbed the ADS printout and spotted something. What dividend tables had been used to calculate this comparison?

It was nothing more than a computer error. There were literally hundreds of dividend tables to choose from in comparing policies. Insurance companies constantly introduced new policy names and configurations. Sometimes an exact policy match proved hard to compute.

Looking carefully, it became clear to us that the wrong set of tables had been used. Equally clear to any fair-minded observer was the total lack of malicious intent on anyone's part to mislead the client. It was just an honest, if unfortunate, mistake.

The competing agent seized his opportunity. ADS printout in hand, he filed a formal complaint with Commissioner Dale, accusing A.L. Williams and National Home Life of giving the client false and misleading information. Dale promptly ordered a hearing and suddenly, it was all over the front page of Jackson's *Clarion-Ledger*: A.L. Williams charged with "deceptive marketing practices" in trying to sell deposit term"– an "unconventional form of life insurance."

War broke out in Mississippi. And it got ugly fast.

Commissioner Dale summoned Bill Anderton and Joyce Banks to his office for a long grilling on their business practices. Dale announced the possibility of ordering a "cease and desist" on all deposit term sales in connection with A.L. Williams and National Home.

That, he said, would depend on the outcome of an August 30 hearing he'd scheduled.

The *Clarion-Ledger* covered the story every day. Competing agents gleefully carried headlines in their briefcases: "A.L. Williams and National Home Life Under Investigation." "Deposit Term Sales Sparks Insurance Controversy."

On August 30, Dale launched an all-out investigation into our selling practices. The spin in the public square got even nastier, circulated by hundreds of life underwriter association members representing at least 50 traditional insurance companies. Their message: "A.L. Williams, along with National Home Life, is a crooked company that lies to people, issues bogus information to make them lapse their whole life policies and then steals their cash values."

Clients panicked and began to drop their newly purchased policies left and right.

The fall-out proved catastrophic for Bill. In addition to cancelled policies, he began to lose his sales force. Agents in financial straits with all the unexpected lapses had to quit… and all their chargebacks and debit charges rolled up to Bill. He stood an inch away from financial ruin.

It got even worse. On September 20, Commissioner Dale made good on his threat to order a "cease and desist" on the sale of all deposit term policies from National Home Life. The *Clarion-Ledger* blared its front-page story: "State Bans Firm's Unconventional Insurance Sales."

An A.L. Williams death blow, or so it seemed, to the smug local president of the Jackson Association of Life Underwriters: "I think the commissioner has spoken in a way that protects the consuming public," the paper quoted him.

Bill Anderton knew he had my total support, and the company's. We showed it, too. We sent Kevin King to Jackson to meet with the Commissioner and defend our interests. Dick Morgan, a personal friend of George Dale, went with Kevin and so did several National Home representatives. Two or three times a day, I called Bill to see how he was holding up. At one point in the ordeal, he looked a little wild-eyed as a TV reporter questioned him about A.L. Williams and "any prior convictions on his record."

He had none, of course, but the slimy insinuation was there.

The cease-and-desist lasted two weeks. Then, just as suddenly as it erupted, the storm passed.

The Commissioner released an official statement. After hearings and a long look at evidence, Dale cleared A.L. Williams and National Home Life of any and all wrongdoing, including fraud, false or misleading information, or malicious intent. The problem? A simple numbers error, the Commissioner stated. A.L. Williams was free to conduct business as usual.

The *Clarion-Ledger* buried that tiny, eight-line article in its back pages.

Pure politics. The industry, as usual, refused to compete with us at the kitchen table. It trumped up charges instead, to cast suspicion on our selling practices and turn confused families against us. A small computer error had mushroomed into a two-week ban on our business in the entire state of Mississippi!

The day after the announcement clearing us, we flew a bunch of A.L. Williams people into Jackson. We threw a huge rally for Bill, Joyce and all the Mississippi teams. What fun. I used the episode to motivate the socks off everybody.

"These people were trying to put us out of business," I yelled into the huge crowd. "Well, guess what? It didn't work. What happened here just makes us tougher. We can't run from problems. This is a war and the other side is not going to quit fighting. Neither are we. But what we do is right for those families you see every day out there… and no insurance company or regulator is ever going to take that right away from us."

It must have worked. The next month, our A.L. Williams business in Mississippi doubled. Bill went on to completely rebuild his organization and pay back every bit of debt he owed the company. He even earned a trip to Rome. Joyce Banks relocated to Ohio and became an RVP there. In all, what a credit to our team in the Magnolia State.

The Mississippi cease and desist was over for good.

But the competition would find amazing ways to bring it back up for many years.

NEW LEVELS

In October, I surprised the sales force by announcing a new position level – Senior Vice President. One step above Regional Vice President, it carried more prestige and higher override commissions. I made the guidelines pretty tough and named Bobby Buisson, head of the company's fastest growing hierarchy, as the company's first SVP. With many leaders at the edge of an RVP promotion, it was a perfect time to hang out a bigger carrot.

We changed the venue for our third annual company convention from Point Clear to The Cloister on Sea Island, off the coast of Georgia. Spectacular, The Cloister for 50-plus years enjoyed its status as one of the world's top luxury resorts, hosting world dignitaries, business leaders and celebrities from all over the world. In December 1979, it hosted the top producers of A.L. Williams.

Sea Island became one of our greatest conventions – truly life changing for the 175 couples that attended. First, I announced four RVP promotions: Hubert Humphrey, Ronnie Barnes, Dick Walker and Bill Anderton. Our company RVP total stood at 32 – four times our starting number.

Another milestone: Year-end numbers showed $1.8 billion in new business for 1979 – more than double our 1978 production. Nearly two billion in business!

Our sales force, now at 4,000 licensed reps, nearly doubled during the year, too.

Sea Island made history for another reason. It marked the launch of our Partners initiative, one of the most significant programs A.L. Williams ever started.

For a couple of years, I'd gotten mild complaints from some of the sales guys – their wives found it hard to be supportive. From the wife's perspective, she was stuck at home to do all the work while her husband went out night after night on appointments. The grass didn't get cut. The kids missed their dads. Every conversation centered on A.L. Williams. And where were those big paychecks they kept hearing about?

It had been the same way for Angela and me. Before Angela really understood "Buy Term and Invest the Difference," she questioned the long hours, weekend appointments, the lack of money coming in. I told her – all the time – how "big" this would be… and she gave me her share of arms-folded glares. It took some time and convincing.

Once Angela did fully understand the crusade and the opportunity, she rolled up her sleeves to help. We worked as a team, and it made the late nights and weekend hours easier to bear for both of us.

After I went full-time, Angela not only managed our home and children, but also ran the office. There's no telling how many policy extractions she typed, flyers she copied, or phone calls she made. She worked as hard as I did. Building A.L. Williams wouldn't have been possible without Angela. Absolutely 100 percent together in this thing, we were partners – in business, in marriage, in everything.

The more I listened to the frustrations of couples in the field, the more I realized Angela needed to tell her story. She was the perfect person to help spouses understand A.L. Williams.

Angela never wanted the spotlight. She felt reluctant in other years to step forward. Listening to me stumble through a couple of weak attempts at spouse meetings finally convinced her. "I'll never forget Renee Weidel at Point Clear one year," Angela remembers. "Art called for questions. Renee stood up, a baby in her arms, and said 'Art, you tell us we have to pay the price to win. Well, I want Larry to win. We want to succeed. Tell me, what do *I* do to win? What is my price?' Her tone was kind of desperate. Art stammered around, trying to answer her. He wasn't used to getting that kind of question, especially from a wife. I thought, Art doesn't even realize what price Renee has to pay. For the first time, it hit me – maybe there is a way I can help."

This year, for our third convention, Angela agreed – time for her to lead a spouses-only meeting.

Neither of us had any idea what a difference that get-together would make.

At Sea Island, when the spouses heard about Angela's meeting they couldn't find a seat fast enough. I was running an agent session at the same time so I didn't sit in, but the packed meeting hit a nerve with all 50 spouses who attended. And that's putting it mildly.

"My heart was in my throat, but I took a deep breath and talked for an hour," Angela says. "I told my story and how I came to understand Art and what he was trying to do with the business. I explained the principles that A.L. Williams was built on, how they came to be and what they meant to us as a family and what they could mean to each of their families. I talked about my parents and the sacrifices my mother had made. Then I shared some personal stories about A.L. Williams people and the hardships and rewards of a sales business. I wanted them to understand this business is tough and requires a great deal of commitment from both the husband and the wife. I guess you could say I 'preached pretty good!'"

Some women cried. Some left the room a little angry, a little ashamed, even a little hurt. Later that day, several Division Managers approached Angela. "I don't know what happened in there," one said, "but you really inspired my wife. We want you to talk at the Fast Start Schools. Would you?" Angela nodded.

The Partners Organization, there and then, officially launched.

Angela began speaking on a regular basis. Conventions. Fast Start Schools. Partner committees. Discussion panels. Overnight events.

She organized Partner meetings for business; some for plain fun. She employed the leadership skills of spouses like Jane Miller, Red Buisson, Norma Humphrey, Renee Weidel and others. More and more Partners stepped up to share their personal stories, and the whole thing just took off. Angela quickly learned to set aside time at every meeting just to answer questions about the business. Partners begged to learn practical things like how to run an A.L. Williams office, live on a commission income, recruit new people, train and license them, keep teams growing. Others wanted a better understanding of term insurance and mutual funds. Some just needed a good dose of encouragement.

Buddy, those Partners became true believers. What they learned on the national level they took home to their downline Partners, organizing Partner meetings in their local offices. The 180° change in attitude astonished everyone. Partners helped their husbands run better offices, manage their time, improve their incomes. We'd flipped a powerful switch, just by tapping the energy and commitment of our spouses in a whole new way.

As much as any other business decision Boe and I made, the Partners Organization contributed to the overall growth – and mental health – of our sales force.

FIRST PARTNERS MEETING

"Jill and I grew up in Laurel, Mississippi. We got married in college. In fall 1979, I started my senior year at the University of Southern Mississippi, managing a health club full-time. Jill worked at a bank. A buddy of mine was part-time with A.L. Williams and he invited me to a Fast Start School in Jackson. I sat there, watching Art Williams on stage wearing a 'Do It' T-shirt. I kept waiting for the president of the company to come.

"When I realized who he was, I started listening. It blew me away. Everything Art said about freedom and owning your own business made sense. I'd always wanted my own business. Jill wasn't thrilled but I signed up and started selling part-time. I made $3,500 my fourth month and was ready to go full-time, but Jill wanted me to finish school and get a good job.

"I won the trip to Sea Island, but Jill remained very negative and refused to get off work. I had to call the bank president to get her a day off. I almost had to put her in the car.

"We drove 12 hours all night to get there. She'd sat through lots of Fast Start Schools and meetings by then. Nothing had turned her around. Until Angela's Partner meeting. I practically dragged her to it, like you could see the heel marks all the way to her chair. But when she came out of that meeting she was very emotional. She threw her arms around me and apologized then and all the way home.

"To this day I don't know what was said in that meeting, except that Jill saw this opportunity as something we could do together. Right then we decided to go full-time. She quit the bank. I quit the health club and school. I had one semester left. We opened our first office. That was the impact that Sea Island and the Partners meeting had on us."

– DAVID LANDRUM, RVP

THE SWITCH

We did discover one advantage in building a home office from scratch in six months.

You buy everything new – especially the computers.

As a huge mail order company, National Home Life ran huge computer systems. To prepare for a massive upgrade, they had just finished a two-year comparison study on the latest and greatest IT systems. Two former NHL execs, Dick Morgan and Bill Keane, crossed over to A.L. Williams with the study in hand. So when the time came to pick a computer system for A.L. Williams, we had the answer: Life System 70.

IBM's largest mainframe was the most state-of-the-art computer system money could buy.

Boe's connections let us sidestep a two-year waiting list to get one from TCC, a general life insurance software and processing company in Austin, Texas.

The Life 70 System put us light years ahead of the competition in processing business. It was incredible – so incredible nobody really knew how to run the thing. By January 1980, seven people worked at the new regional MILICO office at Northlake, most focused entirely on learning how to install and operate the new computer.

On March 1, Boe made an announcement – we had the system up and running! It even processed its very first life app under the MILICO name – one from Bob Miller's organization. I gave Bob a plaque to honor the occasion… and, just like that, our new home office opened for business!

We made it – right on deadline. But the job wasn't over quite yet. Boe drew me aside a couple of days later. "Art," he drawled, "when you and Stanley said get it done, we got it done. Now is it perfect? No! Technically, we're in business. But it's going to be weeks until the entire operation runs at 100 percent capacity."

Beyond exhaustion, Boe and his people continued to work around the clock.

Was the new home office going to work? Well, you tell me.

By the end of March, our staff and system had processed a record-breaking 2,500 apps. These numbers shocked even Stanley.

"How many apps a month do you think you'll be doing by year-end?" he asked Boe and me.

"I'd say 4,000," Boe predicted.

Boe was right a lot of times. But this time he was wrong.

Way wrong.

ROME

In April, Angela and I and Boe and Myrna hosted A.L. Williams contest winners on an incentive trip to Italy, sponsored by National Home Life. The trip had been planned long before Art DeMoss' unexpected death. Because the trip rewarded productive ALW sales agents under the National Home banner, we went ahead with it.

Right before the trip, I told the sales force all about Stanley Beyer. I came clean on the $100-million-dollar contract, the carrier switch with PennCorp. I broke the news about the brand new home office already processing our new business.

Then I announced that by May 1, 1980, all sales with National Home Life would stop. We would sell PennCorp products exclusively.

Here we were, with a company we were leaving, trotting around together in Rome and Florence, supposedly having a great time. Most people did, actually. But not me.

I could only think about getting back to Atlanta and finishing that home office and getting up to speed with PennCorp. The banquets, the sightseeing – I put up a good front, but my stomach stayed in knots for 10 days. After the plane finally landed in Atlanta, I just about wrecked the car zooming over to that office building on 2260 Northlake Parkway.

PERMANENCE

A week later, Boe stuck his head in. The home office was done. One hundred percent operational.

"Come over tomorrow and move into your new office," he grinned. Relieved beyond belief, I nodded.

Springtime in Atlanta is always beautiful, and the next morning seemed exceptional – warm, blue skies, blooming pear trees, azaleas bursting with color. My heart jumped when I pulled into the parking lot and saw that big 'ol beautiful office building sitting there. I walked in with several A.L. Williams employees. I watched as they opened their offices, turned on new computers and copiers, flipped open file folders, got busy with the day's work. I shook hands with Kevin King in his new permanent law office on the first floor. Bob Whitney waved from his one-man (soon to expand) actuarial department. Bill Keane and Dick Morgan showed off the Life System 70. It took up its own whole room. Lights blinked, the vital signs of a brain processing 2,500 life apps a month. Boe, beaming, introduced me to a full staff of underwriters, already hard at work. I had a flashback of poor beleaguered Bob Leseman from Financial Assurance, buried under a pile of apps in Minneapolis.

We'd come a long way, baby!

My office? The nicest I'd ever had, with decent furniture and framed pictures on the wall, roomy enough for a conference table and chairs. The emotion I'd fought back all morning suddenly spilled out, and I blinked back tears of joy.

We made it, I thought. *A.L. Williams has arrived*!

Twelve years of trial and error. Starting at nothing. Breaking every sales record. Dominating every company. Surviving crisis after crisis. Doing the impossible day after day. Growing bigger every month. Now… we were here to stay.

I thought back to Joe Jack Merriman's phone call: "*Art, we can't take any more business.*"

I remembered the meeting with Johnnie Caldwell at the state capitol: "*Art, you're a crook and I'm going to put you out of business.*"

I remembered meetings where I stood in front of the sales force, held up my thumb and forefinger, saying, "*We are THIS CLOSE to being out of business. We better get it while the gettin's good.*"

I thought about sitting with Boe the day Art DeMoss died.

In my mind I saw it all. The controversies, the administrative nightmares, the lack of money. How many times had I put my head on a pillow, wondering if tomorrow we'd be out of business?

All that changed today. We had the $100 million contract. We had our own home office. We had the backing of a big, powerful company totally invested in our well-being, a company willing and able to stand up for the principles we believed in. This structure now in place would let us dominate the industry. PennCorp had put its future on the line for us. Together, we would do right for families. Together we would fight the enemies of our cause.

From here on out things would be different.

I'd sensed it this morning. Saw it as I walked through the hallways, offices and work areas. *Confidence.* Everywhere. Filling the air.

Our people knew it. We were getting off a prop plane and climbing into a jetliner. Yesterday, we hoped to survive. Now we had a place in history. I could die a happy man.

"*Am I good enough to keep this thing going?*" That haunting question… answered.

The era of crisis management was over. On to building an industry giant.

Part V The Glory Years

"If you're afraid of the future, then get out of the way, stand aside. The people of this country are ready to move again."

– RONALD REAGAN

17 Greatest Growth Year

William James once said, "If you want to make a big change in your life then you have to make immediate and exaggerated changes in your activity."

In 1979, Larry Weidel (still at the Division Manager level after years as a personal producer) moved his wife, Renee, and their two young sons to Greensboro, North Carolina. Larry realized that to really succeed in this business, he had to start building an organization. So in Greensboro, he began to recruit like never before.

By the end of the year, he'd recruited 56 people. By July 1980, his organization had 147 new recruits. His income that month topped $22,000.

A month later, recruits jumped to 235. Larry was on a roll. I awarded him a much-deserved Regional Vice President promotion.

At the end of 1980, his organization boasted nearly 1,800 recruits. One year later, his team recruited more than 7,000 people. Larry soared to SVP. He earned more than $300,000 in 1981, securing his place as one of the top leaders in A.L. Williams. His decision to recruit big changed his life. Larry took a huge risk, put his family and career on the line, and earned back something amazing. Larry's growth surge stirred hundreds of RVP wannabes to "build it big" by recruiting.

It also caused a commotion of quite another kind.

Within weeks of Larry's jumpstart in activity, hundreds of complaints about replacement poured into the North Carolina Insurance Department. Insurance Commissioner John Ingram's quick look into the matter showed the protests coming not from consumers, but from whole life agents. Why? Ingram called on Special Assistant Barry Clause, who formed an informal task force to investigate the replacements. The task force consisted of two representatives each from the North Carolina Insurance Department and the Attorney General's office. In June 1980, under Barry's direction, the group began a major investigation into both A.L. Williams and MILICO.

Barry knew life insurance solicitation and replacement. He'd spent three years working with the National Association of Insurance Commissioners, serving on two task forces that reviewed cost disclosure regulations and sex discrimination in insurance. A real student of the business, Barry understood life insurance – structure, marketing and sales. When A.L. Williams and replacement came to his attention, he jumped. In his mind, our agents were doing something against regulations. He set out to prove it.

Over the next few months, Barry and his crew interviewed about 350 consumers, dozens of agents both in A.L. Williams and other organizations, and insurance regulators in other states. He attended Fast Start School meetings and local RVP meetings, interviewing the agents afterward. He spent many days at our home office, talking to staff members from both Atlanta and Santa Monica, reviewing our entire operation. I didn't worry about it too much; we'd won previous battles over replacement. Still, an investigation is an investigation, and this one took a slow toll on my nerves.

Throughout the ordeal, we had Atlanta Data Systems in our favor. ADS programmed policy comparison forms in strict compliance with every state's replacement regulations. In fact, the system reproduced the exact forms and instructions from every state insurance department. We prided ourselves on scrupulous record-keeping. Open and honest in the replacement business, we even provided policy comparisons in states where the law didn't require them. The fact that ADS – not our agents – prepared the required policy comparisons played in our favor during the investigation.

What a great irony – replacement regulations, cooked up to thwart the replacement process, actually gave A. L. Williams a "seal of approval." They improved our ability to replace cash value policies. A side-by-side policy comparison sold more term policies than our best agent ever did.

Barry Clause carried on his investigation for months. He noted that during his years in the North Carolina Insurance Department he had seen many incorrect replacement forms; he typically revoked 10 or 12 licenses per year, he said, from traditional agents for the improper use of replacement forms. But he determined A.L. Williams to be "an aggressive general agency" that was "more in compliance with replacement rules that the companies complaining against it." In fact, he said, "A.L. Williams and MILICO actually exceed regulatory and statutory requirements." The end result: Not one license revoked for improper replacement from our ranks.

The issues with North Carolina seemed settled. Or so we thought, until Barry Clause turned the investigation over to the North Carolina Attorney General. The charge? Determining if A.L. Williams operated as a pyramid – an illegal organization.

Barry put an entirely new A.L. Williams investigation into motion, this one far more frightening and unfamiliar than replacement.

A REGULATOR'S VIEW OF REPLACEMENT

"Traditional insurance companies see replacement as being 'improper, immoral and illegal.' Or as one agent put it, 'whole life is equivalent to motherhood.' Naturally an organization like A.L. Williams, which believes that replacement is often warranted, is going to have much criticism."

– BARRY CLAUSE, NORTH CAROLINA INSURANCE DEPARTMENT

MASSACHUSETTS

About that time, another regulatory problem cropped up. MILICO was domiciled in the state of Massachusetts. Now that it did most of its business underwriting life insurance for A.L. Williams, MILICO became a hot issue at the Massachusetts Insurance Department. Bob Turley had an up-and-coming leader there named Jim Gualtieri. As Jim's volume rose on replacement sales, so did complaints from the competition. In response, the Massachusetts insurance commissioner initiated a full-scale audit of MILICO and dispatched his chief investigator, Al Simoncini, to our home office in Atlanta. The goal? Find whatever proof it took to put us out of business.

Al came. Al stayed. A 280-pound cigar-chomping Italian, Al's mindset matched the industry's – A.L. Williams was a scam run by crooks out to steal people's cash values.

Every day, Al showed up at the home office with his crew. He plundered hundreds of files, sniffing around in every aspect of our business. State insurance departments around the country waited breathlessly for the outcome of his investigation, desperately hoping Al would find evidence to close us down.

Funniest thing happened: He couldn't find any.

After weeks of work, Al determined A.L. Williams was not a scam. Even better (or worse, depending on your viewpoint), we ran an outstanding company doing a great service for consumers. His research provoked a complete turnaround in his thinking; instead of hating A.L. Williams, Al Simoncini became a great crusader!

He returned to the Massachusetts Insurance Department. He reported A.L. Williams as a first-class organization run by great people, selling great products the right way. What a blow to our enemies in the industry! Al Simoncini, the tough-talking investigator sent to put us out of business, now stood with us – a 100 percent bona fide A.L. Williams convert.

Later, Al attended ALW Fast Start Schools and meetings in Massachusetts. There, he stood up as a representative of the insurance department and spoke with whole-hearted enthusiasm about the great job A.L. Williams did for consumers.

The world was beginning to believe.

MORE PROBLEMS

In the field, the sales force exploded. June month-end numbers came in: 4,000 apps sold in one month! We achieved Boe's predicted year-end numbers… in six months.

Great news. But, as we'd learned to expect, prosperity generated a whole new problem.

PennCorp hired TCC, the Austin-based technology company that sold us our Life System 70, to process our business, which included issuing twice-a-week paychecks to the field. TCC extracted policy and commission information from newly submitted business; this info went by satellite from our home office to Austin, Texas.

TCC's system processed the data, then sent it on to PennCorp's office in Santa Monica, which issued paychecks. Problems surfaced with lost policies and slow pay cycles. Sometimes, if the satellite transmission didn't work properly and Boe "couldn't get the cycle to crank," he and his staff would be at the office until midnight. Boe patiently explained it: 80 percent of submitted sales would go neatly "down the trough" for processing; the other 20 percent would slosh off the side and disappear into "a black hole in cyberspace." Terrible. Once again, administrative problems mired us down – even *with* our own home office!

We soon learned TCC's peak processing capacity was 4,000 apps a month. Somehow their software people neglected to tell us this pertinent bit of information. Understandable, really – no other insurance carrier had ever exceeded such a wildly high number. But, we had – in four months. We had the largest computer on the market, but TCC didn't have the processing power to "crank" it fast enough. Our sales force took the brunt of it – they had to deal with lost policies and disgruntled clients, or worse yet, no paychecks.

To further complicate our problems, Stanley Beyer and his right-hand man, Burt Borman, decided to send a red-headed Englishman named Les Moss to run MILICO. They wanted a PennCorp guy in place in Atlanta to protect their $100-million-dollar investment.

An old-school insurance guy, Les had no understanding of the A.L. Williams way of doing business. Worse, he had no interest in learning. Instead of letting Boe run the administration and work out the computer problems, he took over. Or tried to. Negative and arrogant, his presence immediately put an invisible wall between us and PennCorp.

Problem-solving slowed to a crawl. Stanley had sent the wrong guy for the job. Still, we'd signed the contract. We'd "married" PennCorp. Somehow, as partners, we had to learn to get along.

What made it doubly difficult were the production numbers. We had leaders all over the map on incredible growth spikes, and I had a slew of new RVPs to promote in July. Dennis Richardson stood out as the the biggest rising star. He had moved to Colorado in January 1980, opening that state for A.L. Williams. His Opportunity Meeting concept, which Hubert Humphrey copied with great success in Georgia and then Denver, brought in 150 or more recruits a month. In addition, Dennis had created a new "Sales Supervisor" position, between the entry level Sales Rep and more advanced District Leader, and attached a small override to it, still more incentive for part-timers. A dynamic speaker, Dennis earned his RVP promotion just 14 months after joining the company and now, along with Bobby Buisson and Tee Faircloth, had moved up to Senior Vice President.

COMMUNICATIONS

It grew ever more obvious that we needed better communication with the field force. Our sales agents hungered for printed materials that promoted our company principles, latest numbers, field success stories and home office news. We needed sales and marketing brochures to tell our story, to help agents at the kitchen table.

Frankly, it got annoying going on appointments and hearing the same old phrase: "We've never heard of A.L. Williams." Barbara King and her husband, Al, were friends and neighbors of ours in Snellville. I had an idea about Barbara. An executive secretary for several years at General Motors, Barbara quit to pursue a law degree. She had no experience in insurance, but she was sharp. I offered her the opportunity to launch our communications department.

Barbara came on board in May 1980 and formed what we called the Tucker-Norcross Publishing Company, operating out of our home office. Alone at first, Barbara quickly proved her ability to put in print what I wanted to say to the field. She designed a company magazine, flyers, posters and other print pieces. I also put her in charge of Leaders Bulletins, which for the first time ever could list production numbers pulled off the computer. For Trudy White and Angela, it meant no more twice-a-month phone calls to the field. Progress!

Two months later, we needed our own printer. We asked Mitch Slayton and his wife, Diane, relatives of Boe from Arkansas, to set up an in-house print shop for the sole purpose of printing A.L. Williams sales and marketing materials. They started in June 1980, in one room with a copier in a corner. Inside a month, Mitch and Diane, now named Greater Atlanta Printing (GAP), pumped out Barbara's new printed materials and communications from other departments with a small used multilith press. To distribute information as fast as possible, I put my brother, Don Williams, in charge of organizing a national distribution center. He'd worked in several departments in the home office by then and knew what to do. Soon we produced materials and put them in the hands of A.L. Williams agents on a regular basis.

All three departments came in handy as we prepared for our first RVP convention with PennCorp in August. We would hand out the first issue of our very own company magazine, The A.L. Williams Opportunity. The 16-page booklet featured full-color photos, and articles from Stanley Beyer, Angela and myself. It covered recent RVP promotions, key home office events, latest production numbers and other announcements. Barbara would also soon unveil The ALW Chronicle, a monthly newsletter that covered regional field promotions and events and printed photos contributed by ALW agents

> **Welcome to the A.L. Williams Opportunity**
>
> Welcome to America's fastest growing life insurance marketing organization. And welcome to a financial and service opportunity that might provide a whole new meaning to your life!
>
> You're soon going to hear more about A.L. Williams. Amazing, exciting facts about people just like yourself who have found new, rewarding careers serving the American Consumer. But before we bring you these facts, we'd like to share our philosophy with you...to explain the fundamental beliefs that motivate our Company and our Associates.
>
> **We Believe**
> **IN PART- TIME SALES REPRESENTATIVES**
> ...as the best way to provide complete training and practical experience without imposing the financial burden that can lead to high-pressure sales tactics born of desperation.
>
> **We Believe**
> **IN THE AMERICAN CONSUMER**
> ...as an intelligent money manager who will make the right decision when presented with all relevant facts regarding any purchase.
>
> **We Believe**
> **IN LIFE INSURANCE**
> ...as the only way to create an immediate estate when you haven't had time to accumulate cash.
>
> **We Believe**
> **IN THE LIFE INSURANCE INDUSTRY**
> ...as an old and honorable business that has contributed immeasurably to the growth of our nation and to the stability of the American family.
>
> **We Believe**
> **IN THE LIFE INSURANCE AGENT**
> ...as one of America's most important Professionals whose services for 200 years have assured a decent standard of living for those who live too long...and for the families of those who die too soon.
>
> **We Believe**
> **IN TERM LIFE INSURANCE**
> ...as the most practical way to acquire enough estate to fully provide for your loved ones if you die early.
>
> **We Believe**
> **IN ACCUMULATING CASH OUTSIDE OF LIFE INSURANCE**
> ...as the most efficient way to build for retirement at realistic interest rates in these inflationary times.
>
> **We Believe**
> **IN THE "THEORY OF DECREASING RESPONSIBILITY"**
> ...as the best approach to determining life insurance and cash accumulation needs, and assuring that enough life insurance is available while your family needs protection, and that enough cash is available when you need retirement income.
>
> **We Believe**
> **IN FAIR AND COMPLETE DISCLOSURE**
> ...as the only correct way to give the Consumer all relevant facts about life insurance.
>
> **We Believe**
> **IN DIFFERENCE OF OPINION**
> ...as the heart and soul of the American System in which philosophical adversaries can disagree totally, but still maintain respect for each other.
>
> **We Believe**
> **IN A.L. WILLIAMS**
> ...as the fastest growing life insurance marketing organization in the world, where success is based on service to the American Consumer and proper compensation for a job well done.
>
> BUT MOST OF ALL...
>
> **We Believe in YOU**
> ...and in your ability, regardless of your past experience, to become a successful, Professional Life Insurance Representative if you are willing to work, learn, and stick to the rules.
> THIS IS OUR PHILOSOPHY.
> We hope it will soon become YOUR philosophy too!

around the country.

Our communications machine – officially up and running. And not a moment too soon.

The first big test in our "marriage" with PennCorp loomed ahead.

MONTREAL

In August, we scheduled an RVP convention, a huge celebration with PennCorp, purposefully set in Hotel Windsor in Montreal, "the oldest hotel in North America." Our theme: "A.L. Williams is here forever! Let's go international!"

One of A.L. Williams' first sales brochures, circa 1980.

Full of historical sites and culture, Montreal seemed the perfect place to "think big" while strolling around clean, beautiful streets and parks, hearing people easily speak both French and English. Historic Hotel Windsor had been a favorite spot for royalty and celebrities from all over the world. *And now us*, I thought.

On the first evening, Angela and I hosted a huge banquet for all 88 RVPs, their Partners, and other guests. After a delightful dinner, I introduced a new estate plan for senior managers, unveiled *Opportunity* magazine and reported on company progress.

"We are way ahead of schedule," I told them proudly. "Our partnership with PennCorp has sealed our future. We have an exclusive contract. We have our own home office. There is nothing stopping us from conquering the world. Before long, we'll be doing business here in Canada."

We had a wonderful evening, full of high spirits and dreams for the future.

The next day, while the group toured "Old Montreal," Boe and I sat in a very tense meeting with Stanley Beyer and other PennCorp people. The news shocked us. "My actuaries have been researching the quality of business your sales force is writing," Stanley said, clearly upset. "Art, you lied to me. Your guys are out there writing bad business. Your persistency is terrible… we're losing millions of dollars. Our entire company is in jeopardy because of you."

I sat there, dumbfounded. Bad persistency? Losing millions? How could that be?

Our numbers looked good. Our company persistency hovered around 75 percent, meaning three out of four policies met the projected actuarial model and stayed on the books long enough to see a return. We'd *never* had a persistency problem!

I took this personally. I'd taught my team from the beginning that we only write policies for people who want them. No lies. No scams. No quick sales just to make a commission or win a contest. A.L. Williams stood for helping the consumer, not making a fast buck.

And we had safeguards in our system. Chargebacks had always been a strong deterrent to writing bad business. It might feel great to get that advance commission… but not if you had to give it back six months later when the policy fell off the books.

I looked at Boe and he shrugged, confused too. "I don't know, Stanley," I said. "We'll figure it out."

That afternoon, the group returned to the hotel for a business meeting. Without explaining why, I zeroed in on quality of business.

"This business is not about making money," I said, pounding the podium. "It's about doing what's right for families. It's about correcting an injustice. It's about writing the best policy you can for a family, one that will give them hope in the worst of circumstances… like losing a mom or dad. It's about recruiting people who are good people, who care about things like honesty and integrity. It's about running your business with the highest possible ethics. It's not just about building it big, it's about building it right!" I laid it on thick and loud and left no doubt about what I expected from our RVPs.

After the meeting, Stanley and I stayed up all night talking about persistency. Blindsided by the issue, I wanted Stanley to know how serious I was about solving it. Boe, meanwhile, phoned the home office, asking Dick Morgan, Dick Kinnard and Mike Adams for numbers and reports.

The rest of the convention went great. Angela hosted the first "official" Partners session with tremendous success. Stanley addressed the group with his usual style and elegance, focusing on all the positives, talking up future plans, and introducing Lee Myers, one of his top executives. We ended with a "grand finale" banquet at the Old Forte on St. Helen's Island, dining in the same lavish style and setting as French noblemen in 1691.

INSURANCE ACCOUNTING & PERSISTENCY

"For the sake of example, say that for every $100 of insurance premium an agent writes, the company pays out $300 in commissions and expenses. So you pay out $300 and take in $100. The pay-out part is known as the DAC – Deferred Acquisition Cost. The DAC goes down on the P&L sheet as an asset and is amortized over the expected life of the policy. If the policy is expected to be in force for 10 years, then every year $30 is written off the policy as an expense, until the entire $300 goes down to zero.

"Every policy has an expected life and amortization schedule. The problem comes in if the policy doesn't match the model and prematurely falls off the books. Then, the entire asset amount associated with it – the DAC – becomes an expense. Dropped policies show up as huge losses on the company's quarterly earnings report.

"A policy has to stay on the books for 5-7 years before it begins to make money. A premature policy drop switches the DAC from an asset to an expense the very day the policy is cancelled. Plus, ALW paid out millions of dollars every month in advance commissions. That's why it took huge amounts of upfront cash to operate A.L. Williams."

– TREACY BEYER,

PENNCORP EXECUTIVE

We sent the troops off on a high note. I told them we had some administrative problems we needed to solve with PennCorp. We had some state insurance departments unhappy with us. "But you know what?" I summarized. "That just comes with the territory when you're making history. You stir up some controversy when you take a stand. You've got to understand how great this thing is going to be for you and your family. It's going to be wonderful…*IF* we're good enough. *IF* we're strong enough. *IF* we're tough enough. *IF* we work hard enough. This business isn't for everybody. It's for those who want to win. We've already got some of you out there making $100,000 a year, $200,000 a year. We're going to have a club for you guys. But guess what? We want you making a million dollars a year! We're going to have a club for that, too. Some day we're going to beat Prudential. We're going to change the industry! That's what A.L. Williams is all about."

Our people charged out, ready to conquer the world.

NOVEMBER

I traveled the next two months on a 16-city tour of "Career Management Seminars," a two day managers meeting focused on reaching area leaders all over the country, coaching them on recruiting, training and compliance. I made sure every meeting emphasized the importance of writing good business. I pounded on persistency. The meetings spurred the business – we now regularly brought in 12,000 to 15,000 new recruits a month.

In the home office, Boe and his team doggedly analyzed new business, looking for streaks of bad persistency at every level – Rep, District, Division, RVP and SVP. A completely overloaded processing system hampered their efforts. The home office just kept getting pounded.

August, September, October – the number of new business apps climbed every month. Then came month-end November: a record-breaking 12,000 apps flowed through the door. Twelve thousand new policies in one month! Unreal. I was so proud of the field force, blowing and going like never before.

But we had choked the state-of-the-art Life System 70 with three times the capacity it was designed to handle. Nobody at PennCorp ever dreamed we would write this much business.

November 1980 Leaders Bulletin

An accounting problem with persistency… persisted. Stanley couldn't figure out if

PennCorp made money on us or not, eight months into the business. Les Moss, Boe and I stayed on the phone with Stanley and Lee Myers, answering questions about persistency, profitability, underwriting and processing. The power of our own home office came into play. With Financial Assurance and National Home Life, if a problem like lost apps came

up, we would have to get on the phone or travel out of state and work with unfamiliar people to solve the problem. Or we'd just have to take somebody's word for it – "Sorry, Art, we don't know what happened to those lost 100 apps but we did all we could."

Not any more. Even with Les Moss trying to manhandle the operations side, Boe made the rounds every day, checking the mail, counting new apps, working with the underwriters. He knew everybody on staff and what they did. If a problem came up, he got somebody on it. We were in the driver's seat. Stanley had to trust us… and it made him a little nuts. Boy, did I know that feeling. An interesting reversal, and I rather liked it.

DENNIS

With all the attention on persistency, one name consistently came to our attention – Dennis Richardson. According to several Texas leaders both in and out of Dennis' organization, Dennis ran such high recruiting and sales numbers for a reason: His Opportunity meetings were basically app-writing sessions.

According to our sources, Dennis would invite hundreds of people to his meetings, week after week, wow them with his charismatic personal story and presentation, then convince everyone "serious about joining A.L. Williams" to stay after the meeting. He gave a second talk specifically to that group – usually 80 percent of the original crowd –

then handed out an ALW hiring pack and a life insurance application. On the spot and under peer pressure, he forced them to sign up for both.

People typically bought themselves a $100,000 policy at the end of the meeting – no "Buy Term and Invest the Difference" presentation, no replacement, just the policy. Many in the audience were young – in their early 20s and unmarried – and classically bad candidates for life insurance.

Many of these spur-of-the-moment policies would lapse due to unpaid premiums – a natural outcome of trying to mass sell life insurance policies. It was just the wrong approach.

I'd been a little leery of the Opportunity Meeting concept from the beginning. It went against my warm market approach: Talking to friends of a new recruit in their home, personally going through the company presentation at the kitchen table and answering their questions, and then taking them to the Opp Meeting to show them the "bigness" of A.L. Williams. I worried that rushing people in off the street for a one-night Opp meeting would leave them confused, indifferent or misled about our crusade.

That appeared to be the case with Dennis Richardson's recruiting.

Age also concerned me. People in their late teens and 20s, typically still in college and unmarried, had no dependents or assets to protect. Why do they need life insurance? A waste of time to pursue them. The people who really needed what we offered were married, owned a home, had kids and regular income.

In addition, I'd always been conscientious about making sure people joined A.L. Williams for the right reasons. Far from a get-rich-quick scheme, I viewed "Buy Term and Invest the Difference" as a cause and a concept, a way of life. People joined A.L. Williams because they wanted to… not through peer pressure or because they were bullied into it.

Without pointing a finger, I regularly began to talk to Dennis on the phone, checking in with his numbers and the progress of his downlines, reminding him constantly that good quality business stood as a top priority in A.L. Williams.

I also talked to Dennis' upline, Jack Schulman, although Jack didn't express many concerns about Dennis and his approach to the business.

DALLAS

By December 1980, Boe and I felt strongly we had turned a corner with persistency.

From a field force standpoint, the Career Management Seminars had reached thousands of A.L. Williams Reps with a strong message about business ethics. Boe and I pinpointed several agents struggling with persistency and coached them, one on one. The Dennis Richardson issue appeared to be under control. On the administrative side, Boe determined that much of our persistency problem could be attributed to TCC's inability to handle the increasing flow of apps every month. In fact, we lost about one in five apps on a regular basis, a number I found atrocious.

On Sunday, December 7 – Pearl Harbor Day – we headed off to an RVP meeting in Dallas. We'd grown too big for companywide Fast Start Schools every six weeks, so I switched to leading RVP meetings on the same schedule. (A.L. Williams agents on the regional level put on their own Fast Start Schools.) For the Dallas meeting, I invited the top 25 RVPs to come in a day early for a special 6 p.m. banquet. I planned to announce at least 20 more RVP promotions. In one year, we'd gone from 32 RVPs to a whopping

115 RVPs; from 2,500 apps a month to 12,000. No insurance company had ever done what we were doing!

At 4 p.m., Boe and I took a conference call with Stanley. One second into the conversation, our smiles disappeared.

"The deal is off, Art," Stanley said firmly. "I've got a persistency report in my hand that shows we are losing *two million dollars a month* just to keep you in business. You are ruining our company, do you understand? I'm not spending another month on you guys. *No more commissions*. It's over."

Boe and I sat back, horrified. We'd worked for months to correct this problem. All our reports showed improvement. *How could it possibly be worse?*

In all the years I knew Boe, I saw him panic only once – this moment. He turned white as a sheet. I could tell he was thinking fast.

We knew Stanley had pressured his PennCorp people for a persistency report. We also knew the report couldn't be accurate because the computer system couldn't keep up. It couldn't process our business… much less put out a persistency report.

"Look Stanley, that report isn't right," Boe told Stanley. "It can't be. I'm not sure what the numbers are, but before you make the decision to cut us off, let us go back to Atlanta. We'll pull 5,000 apps and count them ourselves. Forget the computers. Let us do it by hand and see if we can come up with an accurate number for persistency. Just give us one more month, Stanley. One more month."

Boe clearly resorted to pleading. "I'll have to think about it," Stanley said, after a long pause, and hung up.

Boe got on the phone that instant with Mike Adams and Rick Slayton, another one of our computer whizzes. He told them to start pulling hard files on 5,000 life apps. By then, it was time for the banquet.

What a test. Boe looked positively ill. He sat down for dinner. Bill Orender began drilling him with questions about lost policies from one of his downlines. "There are some serious administrative problems going on, Boe," Bill said, bluntly. Boy, if he'd only known.

After the dinner, I stood up. I knew what I had to say.

"I want you to know last month we sold 12,000 apps," I told those top 25. "No company in the history of life insurance has ever sold that many policies in one month. But you know what? *We're probably going to be out of business*. The odds are against us to keep growing like this. All the state insurance departments are against us. All the other insurance companies want to put us out of business. All the newspapers want to write bad articles about us. Why? Because we're doing something right! Twelve thousand apps can't be wrong! This is the greatest company in the world. But we can only win if we're willing to pay the price. Are you willing? Are you tough enough to fight the battles, pay the price? YES? Then prove it!"

I went on at this fever pitch for two hours. We walked out, floating on high notes.

Tomorrow would be a different song altogether.

ROUGH

The next morning I started the meeting a little differently than usual.

I picked up a Coca-Cola bottle and threw it against the wall.

Immediately 115 sets of eyes fixed right where I wanted them: on me. Time for a locker room session. Time to knock some heads.

"I know we've got some administrative problems," I began at full volume. "Lost policies and slow paychecks and all that kind of crap. I know it. Boe knows it. We're working on it – I've told you that.

"We've got some big things going on right now and we're working very hard to fix all of it for you. I know it's a pain in the butt when you've got to go back to clients and tell them you lost their policy and all that. I know it, because we've been dealing with these kinds of problems for almost four years now. These are the kinds of problems you have when you're growing as fast as we are, when you're doing things no other company has ever done before."

1980 Company Logo

"But here's the thing." I paused and drew in a full breath. "One thing I will not tolerate is you guys out there screwing the consumer – screwing the reputation of this company – by writing bad business. We've got a persistency problem in this company. And I'm telling you RIGHT NOW, we are going to GET TO THE BOTTOM OF IT."

My blood boiled. Several guys had left their seats. They were bumping around, trying to plug in their tape recorders. It boiled a little faster.

RVPs liked to tape our sessions so they could listen to them again in their cars or offices. So usually I didn't mind. Today, I minded. Nobody was going to do anything but listen to me. Nobody was even getting out of a chair unless I said so. I slammed down my notebook. "Nobody tapes this meeting," I said, glaring out at the group.

Jay Fee, an RVP from Houston, didn't seem to be listening. He stood at the front of the room, distracted, still trying to plug in a tape recorder.

I walked fast over to Jay. I ripped the machine out of his hands. I grabbed the cassette, yanked out all the tape, slammed the whole mess on the floor. I spewed out a few foul words and stomped back up to the podium.

"Nobody tapes this meeting," I repeated. Total silence.

I started back on persistency and jumped down people's throats like never before. It was the riot act – not nice, not pretty. I held back nothing; I made no apologies.

Deep into this trip to the woodshed, I noticed a well-dressed gentleman at sitting by a door in the back of the room – Stanley Beyer.

Another test, I thought. *He's here to see if I'm serious about solving this persistency thing. Good. He ain't seen nuthin' yet.*

Mid-morning, I gave them a break. I stepped out in the hallway to find Jay Fee sitting at a table selling T-shirts that said "A.L. Williams changed my whole life." At another table, Jack Schulman hawked fake Rolex watches with an A.L. Williams logo in the middle. I clenched my teeth and thought hard.

After the break, I summoned Jay Fee and Jack Schulman up front. They stood awkwardly alone in front of their peers.

"We don't make money off A.L. Williams people by selling cheap crap... like fake watches and T-shirts," I thundered. "We're not in that kind of business. We make money by replacing expensive trash value policies with inexpensive A.L. Williams term. Period. I'm fining both of you DOUBLE whatever you got in that junk. When we get back to Atlanta, I'm probably going to fire you both."

Jack and Jay, red as lobsters, crawled back to their chairs.

I had even more. "Let me just tell you something else. I don't want to see any of you walking around wearing those big gold chains. Or wearing earrings. Or any other kind of jewelry crap like that. We don't sell cheap crap. We don't wear cheap crap. We don't hire people who wear cheap crap".

"THAT'S NOT THE KIND OF PEOPLE WE ATTRACT TO A.L. WILLIAMS. WE'RE A DIFFERENT KIND OF COMPANY, BUILT FOR A DIFFERENT KIND OF PERSON. We're here to right a wrong that's been done to American families... and we're here to build better lives for our own families."

This went on for a long while.

From time to time, I'd call on specific RVPs to stand up and ask me questions. We had microphones set up in the aisles.

Nobody wanted to ask me anything. My leaders looked down, leaned away from the mikes, slid down in their chairs, tried to disappear behind some bigger guy in front. When I called on them, though, they didn't dare ignore me. I asked them hard questions and twisted their answers around to suit my agenda. It was rough, old-fashioned, south Georgia locker room coaching. And I meant business.

At the end of two and a half days, people scrambled to get home. The brutal meeting, I hoped, would have a lasting effect. Stanley sat through every minute of my fire-breathing performance.

Only three people in that room – Stanley, Boe and I – knew how close we stood to being out of business.

NEW GUY

An idea had stayed on my mind for several weeks. Now, back from Dallas, it was time to act. Stanley needed tangible proof we meant to solve the persistency problem.

We also needed an organizational change. We were growing too big, too fast, for me and Boe alone to keep up.

"I want to bring Bob Miller into the home office to help out with the field force," I told Boe. "I want him to handle some of my work. We need another 'me', someone who can travel, do meetings, answer questions, teach our principles – just the same way I would. We're growing so dadgum fast I'm afraid our people aren't learning to build the right way.

"And, Boe" I added, "I want you to teach him the home office side of the business, too. We need another person to explain what's going on around here."

"Great idea," said Boe. "Let's bring him in."

Bob Miller was a perfect pick for the new position. I'd personally taught him all my tried and true sales and recruiting techniques. Totally "coachable," Bob built his Fort Lauderdale "scratch" office in textbook A.L. Williams fashion – the exact same way I built my organizations. His team continued to grow, and it maintained phenomenally high persistency, somewhere around 95 percent – the best in the company. Of his organization's first 525 sales, 512 still stayed on the books. No doubt about it, Bob was the guy.

Bob came into my office on Monday morning. I ran through a little presentation. I said, "I'm not sure what we're going to call this position. I'm not sure what or how I'm going to pay you in the long run. But if we make it as a company, and if you're up here helping us run the company, it seems to me you should be among our highest paid leaders. Right now, since I'm asking you to leave behind your base shop to move to Atlanta, I'll pay you $5,000 a month and expenses. Then we'll see how things work out. Do you think you could be ready to go to work here three weeks from today?"

Bob didn't disappoint.

"Art, Boe let me know you would make this offer. I've already talked it over with Jane. We're coming."

We shook hands. Bob Miller became, for lack of a better title, my in-house sales guy.

NEW POSITION

"It was a perfect day in December 1980, about 80 degrees. I walked out of my house and thought, I am never leaving Fort Lauderdale. It's the greatest place on earth to live. "The next day Art called and asked me to move to Atlanta for a new position. We put our house up for sale. It sold in five days. Our family moved to Snellville during Christmas break. The kids never missed a day of school. I showed up for work the first Monday in January 1981. We relocated in 21 days.

– BOB MILLER, IN-HOUSE

NATIONAL SALES DIRECTOR

DECISION

I planned to announce Bob's new position – quickly named "in-house National Sales Director" – after the first of the year. It would stir up a little controversy among the top field ranks, but they would deal with it.

Then one morning I walked into the office lobby to find Bobby Buisson waiting by the elevator. He looked miserable. Riding up to my office, he said, "Art, I'm dying out in the field. I want to be part of the home office. I've got to be in here where all the action is."

Unreal, this timing. Bobby knew nothing about Bob Miller coming in three weeks. He earned $450,000 a year, one of our top 10 field leaders. This couldn't be about money.

"Bobby, I don't know how I would compensate you," I said.

"Art, I don't care about the money," he said, an edge of desperation in his voice. "Don't pay me anything, just let me come in to the home office."

Sighing, I answered, "I don't know, Bobby, let me think about it."

Bobby's unhappiness did not completely surprise me.

He loved working with people, but remained uncomfortable with the field side of the business. I knew Bobby could be a huge asset in the home office – he would willingly travel, effectively speak to other organizations. He understood the crusade, had great loyalty, attitude and work ethic, and he knew how to "talk" A.L. Williams. We could use his help.

Still, bringing Bobby into the home office would complicate matters. It went all the way back to the long-ago decision I'd made at Waddell & Reed to promote Bobby to Division Manager over the better producer, Tee Faircloth.

Tee's wounds over that decision had never really healed, and he sometimes turned openly bitter, although he continued to work hard and do well all these years. To make matters worse, Tee had made a special visit to my office back in the summer to ask about opportunities. I'd told him then there were none. Now, that had changed.

So, hence my dilemma. I desperately needed help, and Bob Miller stood out as the one field guy to bring in. But, Bobby's Buisson's request threw a wrench in the plan. Now if I let Bobby come to the home office, politically I would also have to offer the position to Tee. No way around it. One of the company's top earners, Tee made $60,000 a month – significantly more than Bobby. An offer to Bobby but not Tee would absolutely devastate Tee, probably worse than before. I couldn't bear to do that to him again.

After a lot of agonizing thought, I offered the in-house National Sales Director position to both Bobby and Tee. But somehow, like the best laid plans of mice and men, it blew up on me.

Bobby already lived in Atlanta. He wouldn't leave behind a base shop so I offered him an office and expenses only. He agreed to start on January 1, along with Bob Miller.

I made the same offer to Tee, with a stipulation – he would have to move back to Atlanta to take the job.

Well, that made Tee furious. He'd been in Macon only six months and had no desire to relocate his family to Atlanta. He declined the offer. I understood the decision. By trying to be fair, I somehow sent to Tee just the opposite impression. Once again, it looked like I'd given something to Bobby that Tee deserved, and he took it hard.

The difficult, awkward situation would one day result in the loss of a top producer. And it needn't have. One in-house guy was all I wanted.

I should've stayed with my original plan.

YEAR-END

As 1980 drew to a close, we caught our breath. What a year! We changed carriers, opened our own home office (now operating with 250 employees), launched our own in-house publications department, unveiled our first company magazine, started our printing company that in six months pumped out more volume than 90 percent of all printing companies in the Atlanta area. We took our first company trip with PennCorp to Canada.

We processed 150,000 policy comparisons through ADS, and broke every conceivable record in the insurance industry – 12,000 apps in one month, 115 RVPs, $1.5 million paid in death claims – and more than quadrupled the amount of business we put on the books. Just three years in, we processed more business than 95 percent of the 2,000 life insurance companies operating in the United States and Canada.

Growing pains aside, we swept confidently into the 1980s. Our contract with PennCorp gave us rocket fuel. No other company in the marketplace competed like A.L. Williams!

Could 1981 possibly top 1980, our greatest growth year ever? Just how high could we really fly?

A.L. Williams in 1980

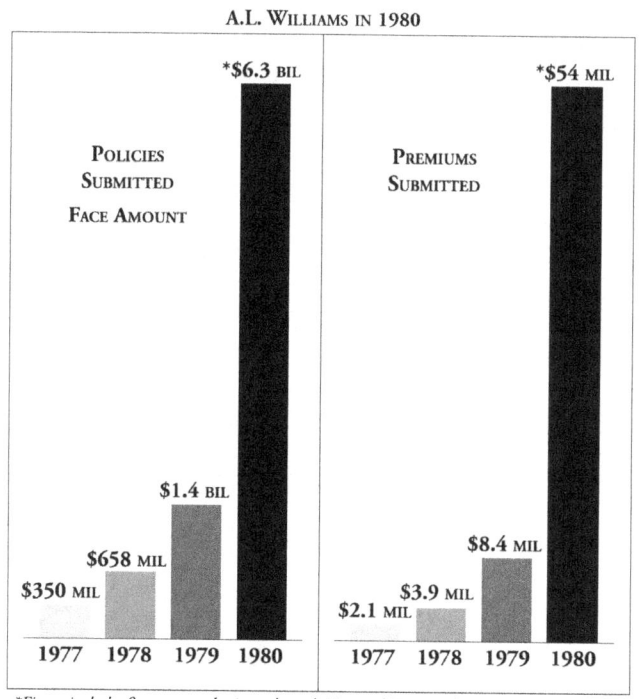

Policies Submitted Face Amount
- 1977: $350 MIL
- 1978: $658 MIL
- 1979: $1.4 BIL
- 1980: *$6.3 BIL

Premiums Submitted
- 1977: $2.1 MIL
- 1978: $3.9 MIL
- 1979: $8.4 MIL
- 1980: *$54 MIL

*Figure includes first quarter business through National Home Life

1980: RECORD-BREAKING YEAR OF GROWTH

January 32 RVPs

December 115 RVPs

March 2,500 apps

June 4,000 apps

November 12,000 apps

A.L.Williams Growth

18 Crossroads

By week two, January 1981, Boe and a team of home office analysts had worked through the manual audit of 5,000 new life applications. It took a long time to pull hard files on that many apps, even longer to go through each one, still longer to write down necessary numbers by hand, and even more time to analyze which policies stayed on the books and which fell off.

Finally, Boe had enough information for an accurate persistency report.

In a presentation to me and other key staff, with Stanley on the speakerphone, Boe announced the verdict: Our persistency was much better than Stanley's numbers... but not nearly as good as we'd projected.

Where was our lingering persistency problem? Some of it came out of administrative issues – part of growing pains, again – and Boe proved that with his report. But we had people problems, too – my area. I thought I knew how to solve the problem. Time to do it.

I called Dennis Richardson. I asked him to get all of his RVPs together in Denver for a mandatory meeting.

One of Dennis' downlines, a former Houston police officer named Neal Askew had been promoted to RVP at the rowdy Dallas meeting in December. Jerry Huston, a direct to Dennis who successfully copied his Opportunity Meeting format for mass recruiting, had recruited Neal the year before. Neal came full-time in May 1980 and immediately shot to the top of the Texas Leaders Bulletins. Neal discovered that all his police officer buddies owned the same whole life policies he did. A "Buy Term and Invest the Difference" crusader from the beginning, Neal took appointment after appointment, talking to police officers, state troopers and public safety workers in and around the Houston area. He educated them on the differences between whole life and term, sold dozens and dozens of policies and recruited like wildfire. He also tapped his wife Nita's warm market of schoolteachers with the same success. He did so well, so fast, that his first advance check seemed unreal – $5,563.01.

When the fat check came across my desk – a first-time check to a Sales Rep in Dennis Richardson's organization – I made a couple calls to underwriting. Jack Schulman confirmed that Neal Askew did business the right way, the A.L. Williams way, just at a very high volume.

In August 1980, I spoke at a special dinner in Houston at Dennis Richardson's request, promoting several of his new Division Managers in person, Neal Askew among them. A few minutes with Neal revealed his commitment and integrity. He'd been recruited at a Dennis style Opportunity Meeting, but Neal personally sold and recruited at the kitchen table, using follow-up appointments. By the time I promoted him to RVP in December, Neal's team numbered more than 200 licensed Reps. A rookie superstar, Neal earned nearly $100,000 in six months.

So we had guys like Neal Askew in Dennis' organization. But we also seemed to have persistency problems there.

When I met with Dennis and his team in Denver, I spelled it out pretty clearly.

"We're all together for a reason," I said bluntly. "We've got some problems with persistency in our company right now, and I just want to make sure we are all on the same page.

"Dennis, you came up with the Opportunity Meeting concept. In many ways, it's a great idea. A.L. Williams has gotten so big now and Opp Meetings offer a way for agents to bring in their new recruits.

NEAL ASKEW: FROM COP TO CRUSADER

"In March 1980, after my first Opportunity Meeting, I checked my life insurance policies. I had exactly what they were talking about – cash value. I had $85,000 on me, $5,000 on Nita and $10,000 on each of the kids. The kids had more than Nita, which made no sense. I put $250,000 term on me and $50,000 on Nita and added a child rider for the kids – for less than the $191 a month I was paying for the cash value policies. It made me so mad. I couldn't believe I'd owned that crap.

"I started casually asking other police officers if they owned a cash value policy from Ames & McClane, the insurance agency that handled the police department. Everybody answered yes. I thought, *maybe I ought to try this A.L. Williams thing*.

"In Texas at that time you could get a temporary insurance license in two weeks. I did that and started asking fellow officers if I could just look at their policies and maybe save them some money. Everybody was interested in that. We all worked extra jobs. I sold 71 policies in three weeks. My first advance check was $5,563.01. After seven weeks in the business, I earned $31,000. I made $24,000 a year as a sergeant with a master's degree. In less than two months, I put away more than a year's salary!

"In May, I quit and went full-time. Nita quit her teaching job. We knew it wouldn't be easy. It wasn't any get-rich-quick scheme. But I'd gotten really excited about the evils of cash value.

"My first death claim came pretty quick. Joe Zamaron, a friend of mine. I sold him a policy. Ames & McClane came in and talked him out of it. Then I went back and talked him out of theirs. He kept my policy. Three weeks later, Joe died in the line of duty. He left a pregnant wife and two kids. Instead of $30,000, his wife got $150,000.

"Before I found A.L. Williams, I loved my job and I thought it was what I'd do the rest of my life. But that case really hit home. I truly believed in the Crusade. I still do."

– NEAL ASKEW, RVP

"But there is a right way and a wrong way to do Opportunity Meetings. The right way is to introduce the A.L. Williams opportunity across the kitchen table first. *Then* bring the new person to the Opportunity Meeting. Show him the 'bigness' of A.L. Williams and the goodness of our crusade there.

"The wrong way is to bring people in off the street and make them buy a $100,000 policy at the end of their first-ever meeting.

"Our first responsibility in this business is to educate families on 'Buy Term and Invest the Difference.'

"*Educating* means sitting down with a *qualified couple* who's married, 25 or older with children, owns a home, has a job. Don't waste your time on college students or young singles – they can cause persistency issues!

"Educating means we take the time to go over our concepts, and give families a free analysis of their cash value policy. Educating means we come back on a second interview, before we ever try to sell them something. *That's* how we sell. In 14 years in this business, I've never once – ever – made a sale on the first appointment. Never!"

I confronted problem: Dennis Richardson and some of his downlines were shortcutting this honorable, tried-and-true system. Dennis just skipped the husband and wife at the kitchen table, skipped education and analysis. He grabbed for the green – cold, fast sales, no follow-up. The approach, horribly wrong, lay at the rotten core of our persistency problems. Dennis, for all his charm and talent, had made a fundamental error in judgment. He'd taught his leaders to circumvent the proven guidelines, to put themselves above the company, to think they were bigger and smarter than the rest of us. And the families that depended on our policies.

When I left Denver that day, I hoped Dennis and his team had heard my message. Dennis even pledged to change.

I wanted to believe him. But something told me to stay wary.

THE 10-YEAR CONTRACT

Our continuous "bull-by-the-horns" actions convinced Stanley we could correct the persistency problems. As growth continued to go skyward, it grew clear that the original $100 million contract, signed in September 1979 and designed to cover the cost of doing $100 million dollars of business, had been made obsolete.

THE COST OF DOING BUSINESS

- Average cost of putting a policy on the book = $3 for every $1 premium

- $250 = average policy premium

- 4,000 apps/mo. x $250 premium x 3 = $3,000,000 payout in commissions (June 1980)

- 12,000 apps/mo. x $250 x 3 = $9,000,000 payout (Nov. 1980)

- 18,000 apps/mos. x $250 x 3 = $13,500,000 payout (Jan. 1981)

- On average, our app count increased every month!

In the ten months we'd been in business with PennCorp, A.L. Williams delivered far more than originally promised. Starting with 2,500 apps in March 1980, Boe and I had projected 4,000 apps a month by yearend. Instead we'd produced that number by June… then tripled it to 12,000 in November. Near the end of January 1981, we had a shot at pulling in 18,000 apps. This month alone, it would take $13.5 million to pay the advance commissions to our sales force and cover the administrative costs of putting so many new policies on the books.

Incredibly, less than a year after our start with MILICO, we were out of money.

Once again, we stood at a crossroads with our insurance carrier. Familiar ground, of course. And with Financial Assurance and National Home Life, the only solution had been a forced change of carriers.

This time, I felt, would be different. The last few months had been touchy, but if I read Stanley right, he wasn't about to quit on us because of money problems.

I was dead right. In fact, Stanley embraced our cash flow shortage as "good news."

A true salesman, Stanley knew that most sales projections reflect nothing more than wishful thinking. Most companies say they'll grow X amount, but most never do. It *thrilled* Stanley that we'd grown beyond expectations. He made a commitment to find a way to finance us.

With our lawyers, Stanley, Boe and I began to hammer out a new contract. Stanley knew A.L. Williams had the momentum and the potential to become a real business giant in the next few years. Instead of a dollar cap, this time our contract would be based on time: 10 years. Stanley agreed to put his name on a contract that would obligate Penn-Corp to pay us billions in the next 10 years. It would require selling off a couple of Penn-Corp's small subsidiaries to finance us, but we'd face no limits on growth this time around. Stanley would pick up the tab on A.L. Williams, no matter how big we got.

FANC, FORERUNNER TO THE PUBLIC COMPANY

As we knocked out the 10-year contract, Boe and Stanley simultaneously began the early stages of negotiation for the creation of an A.L. Williams public company. A.L. Williams' consistent growth over four years clearly revealed its niche market. We operated with 25,000 licensed Reps in 47 states, the District of Columbia and Puerto Rico, with no hint of slowdown. The creation of a public company would accomplish two massive goals:

1. Generate an alternative cash source for the company.

2. Give the agents an opportunity to invest in the success of the company and create another incentive to build personal wealth.

In January, we formed a holding company called First American National Corporation. Under its umbrella, we added First American National Life Insurance Company. This company would eventually co-insure a portion of the insurance business written by A.L. Williams agents through MILICO.

Stanley also agreed to correct our computer problems. More computers, more employees, he'd pay for it. Administrative errors or malfunctions would no longer cause poor business performance or lost profits.

For his generosity, Stanley expected one thing in return: good persistency. Writing good quality business meant profits.

At the time of our original PennCorp agreement, we sold a 12-year deposit term product called "Triple-Dollar-12." The product's profit margins were based on actuarial tables estimating the probable length of time a policy remains in force. Putting a policy on the books cost $3 for every $1 of premium – a very high upfront cost. So, a policy had to stay on the books three to five years to "earn its keep." Our dip in persistency struck a hard blow to Stanley's bottom line.

Boe and I wanted to make up for the short fall.

Based on our production numbers and Stanley's profit losses, we believed an across-the-board 18 percent cut in commissions would recoup Stanley's losses. His response? Amazing.

"I don't want you to take a cut in commission," he said, shaking his head. "All I want is good persistency. If we're maintaining a 75 percent persistency level and meeting the profit margins on products like we're supposed to, then I want you to keep your money. Let's figure out a different way."

With actuaries, Boe and I came up with a new product, the Mod-11. The modified 11- year renewable term product would replace our current Triple-Dollar-12 product, sell for less and compete better in the marketplace.

The Triple-Dollar-12 required the client to pay the annual premium, then put down a "deposit" in the first year, usually around $1,000. If a client kept the policy for the full 12- year term, he got back a guaranteed tax-free "triple" return of $3,000. If the client dropped the policy any time in the first three years, he would lose the $1,000 deposit.

The Mod-11 varied in two important ways. First, in uniqueness – nobody else offered 11- year products. Second, the price – very competitive. It had a high first-year premium but super-low premiums for years 2-11 (see box). The premium structure also encouraged good persistency – no one wanted to pay that high first-year premium, then drop the policy. Why throw away $800? It also featured a flexible premium retirement annuity ride; families could buy in at premiums of $25 any time, with interest accruing from the first payment.

INTRODUCING THE MOD-11

Policy Year	Annual Premium*
1	$847
2 - 11	$224

*Based on $100,000 face amount, male, age 35. $25 annual policy fee.

With the new product, Boe and I agreed to take 18 points off the RVP commission contract, lowering it from 240 percent to 222 percent. But, as an incentive, if the RVP reached 80 percent persistency by year-end, his reward would be an 18 percent bonus. Bottom line, the RVP wouldn't receive a cut in commission, just a cut in advance. He got the full 240 percent at the end of the year… if he hit the persistency marks.

Stanley liked that idea, and he suggested we take it one step further.

"Let's reward people who produce *exceptional* persistency," he said with his usual zest. "If an RVP does 85 percent persistency, then he gets another 5 percent bonus. If he does 90 percent, he gets an extra 10 percent bonus. Nobody loses money on this deal if they maintain average persistency. Better than average, they'll make more money."

Boe and I were blown away. A change in pay structure designed to be a slap on the wrist to the sales force for persistency problems had transformed into an incredible solution.

There was one "catch" though. Behind the scenes, I had to make an undisclosed promise. From now on, I would bear personal liability for any and all financial losses incurred by the sales force.

If an agent stole money from a client, I was now on the hook to get the client's money back – even if I had to pay it *out of my own pocket*. If an agent didn't pay back charge-backs for some reason, I would. Roll-ups, debit balances, lawsuits – whatever the sales force could do to cost the company money, I became financially liable to cover those costs.

The personal liability issue was a confidential agreement between Stanley and me. Nobody else but Boe and Angela knew. Even though I now had a personal net worth of about $2 million – financially independent and debt-free – I signed on to take the risk. My reputation, my future, my finances – I put it all on the dotted line.

The moment we signed the 10-year contract, bad business became a very personal matter. But I knew in my heart we'd barely scratched the surface of all we would do.

THE PRESIDENTIAL

Our next RVP Meeting at the Presidential Hotel in Atlanta in February would be far different from our last ugly gathering in Dallas. This time, I wanted to ring all the good news to the rafters.

For two and a half days, I explained to 125 RVPs the outcome of our persistency research. Then I tore into the introduction of our new Mod-11 product with its revised pay structure and the year-end bonuses on the table for anyone who kept persistency numbers at and above the 80 percent level. Plus, there would be extra bonuses for leaders who could push their persistency even higher.

Next subject: The soon-to-be-signed 10-year contract with PennCorp.

"We sold 18,000 policies last month," I shouted. "Do you understand that no other insurance company in the history of the world has EVER sold that many new policies in one month?"

I heard some hurrahs.

"Do you know there isn't a computer system built anywhere that's big enough to process our business? Hey, we own the biggest, most sophisticated computer system in the world… and it can't even handle what you're doing!"

More yells.

"We've faced so many obstacles… and we just keep going. The competition is against us. Every state we try to do business in, the industry tries to stop us. The state insurance departments put us under some kind of investigation. Nobody wants to compete – they just want to shut us down. But guess what, we sold 18,000 apps last month!"

Wild cheers now!

"We are about to sign a 10-year contract with PennCorp, one of the biggest companies in financial services today. Stanley Beyer is committed to us exclusively for 10 years. He's going to spend *billions of dollars* on us in the next decade. We must be doing something right – Stanley loves us and the American consumer loves us! *Right?* We're on our way to becoming the biggest insurance company in the world!"

I rode the emotion coming from the room now. "In addition," I declared, "we are just months away from establishing our own broker/dealer firm. And, a seven-month production contest ends in March. In April, we'll take all qualifying RVPs to San Francisco and Hawaii for the next incentive trip!"

Pure magic, that meeting! Our hard-working people walked out of there ready to conquer the world.

On February 12, 1981, just two days after our company's fourth "birthday," Stanley and I signed the 10-year agreement, officially replacing the old $100 million contract.

How many crossroads had we faced in our short history? How many times had we almost gone out of business? This time, though, PennCorp and A.L. Williams tackled the problems together and solved them in a positive, constructive way. The signatures on that contract marked a true turning point in our company's history.

GONE

Before the RVP meeting at the Presidential, Neal Askew stopped by the home office to check on his RVP promotion. I'd promoted him in December 1980, but for some reason his paperwork hadn't processed. We ran a check; no mistake. Neal was still coded in the system as a Division Manager, which meant he still got paid as a DM. It meant big money. With a 60 percent override difference between DM and RVP, Neal's $80,000 to $100,000 in new business every month produced serious commissions.

So… Where was Neal's RVP promotion paperwork? Had Dennis Richardson, Neal's upline, somehow failed to turn it in?

I asked Dennis at the RVP meeting, and he seemed duly astonished. He claimed he'd turned in Neal's paperwork back in December and suggested the home office had lost it.

While new paperwork was prepared and processed, Neal estimated he lost about $60,000 in overrides. I had a nagging thought. Was this really all a mistake?

I asked around. Other downline RVPs reported similar experiences: Dennis would delay sending in their paperwork for 30 or 60 days, or until someone reminded him. He would blame the mistake on the home office, but it seemed he was giving himself an extra month or two to collect his downline's override income.

I also learned Dennis continued to recruit at the end of Opportunity meetings, breaking a pledge he'd made to me.

The problems with Dennis were tricky. We had no way to prove that Dennis failed to turn in promotion paperwork at the proper time. Plus, paperwork did get lost or misplaced in our hectic home office, though our staff worked very hard to make sure it didn't happen often.

One night Bob Miller, Bobby Buisson and I discussed the situation in Boe's office.

"I really don't want to fire him," I said. "Dennis is so gifted in this business. He's a pacesetter. He's done a lot for the company. But we can't let this go another month, if he's still doing what he was doing. It's just wrong. And it's bad business."

We left the office, but the situation nagged at me again. I called the team back, and we convened at Bobby's house, conveniently on the way home for all of us. Another concern bubbled to the surface. Dennis' downlines copied his shortcut system, and that was bad enough. Now I learned that other A.L. Williams leaders around the country experimented with the same one-meeting, sell-it-while-it's-hot recruitment model.

Why wouldn't he be imitated? Dennis had the largest organization in the company. Many looked at his fantastic growth and financial success and said hey, *why not*. Why not work less and make more?

I clearly saw that if we didn't act soon, our persistency problem could very well get away from us... for good.

"We just need to know if he's telling the truth or not," Bob Miller observed.

Boe spoke up. "Why don't I call and ask him?"

Boe had known Dennis since the National Home Life days. He picked up Bobby's phone in the living room and dialed Dennis in Houston. After some small talk, Boe asked Dennis straight up about his Opp Meetings: How were they running these days? Did he still use them to sell policies to new recruits? We sat silently. Boe grunted various responses. Finally he said, "Okay Dennis, talk to you later."

Boe put down the phone and threw up his hands.

"Yep, it's true," he said. "Dennis makes everyone buy a policy before they come to work with him. He told me all about his month-end numbers and his downlines. They *all* follow his system. He even wants to give a presentation about it at the next RVP meeting, Art. He hopes you'll 'see the light.'"

What a quiet room.

"That's all we need to know," I finally sighed, deeply grieved. "He's gone."

The next day, I called Dennis Richardson and fired him.

Dennis was the first leader to be fired in A.L. Williams, and one of our biggest. Tough. But once we knew the truth, we had no other choice. Dennis had many chances to change his behavior. Instead, he revealed his true character. He couldn't be trusted.

This first firing sent a message: A.L. Williams was a company based on doing what's right for people. Nothing less would be tolerated.

I also fired several of Dennis's downlines, including Jerry Huston, the guy who recruited Neal Askew. As word got out about the firings, a Richardson exodus began. Dennis quickly announced he would start his own financial services company, a sort of "mini" A.L. Williams. Many of his loyal downlines and their organizations began to leave with him. I called Neal Askew, one of Dennis' directs. He assured me he planned to stay. I reassigned Dennis' organization (what was left of it) to Neal.

We took a hit.

Eventually, about 90 percent of Dennis' organization (about 1,000 people) left with him. As advertised, he started his new company. The venture lasted about a year, then went under.

I anguished for Dennis. But he'd chosen to put himself above the team. His termination made it clear to everyone – you don't do that and come out a winner. No player is bigger than the team.

HAWAII

In April 1981, 155 SVPs, RVPs and home office leaders headed off to San Francisco. Barbara King led trip planning, and we called it a convention, though all of us knew an incentive trip when we took one.

For the first time in several years, I relaxed and enjoyed myself.

After San Francisco sight-seeing, plus a few meetings with much praise and recognition for all, we loaded half the RVPs – the top 75 – on a plane and flew to Honolulu. Our second A.L. Williams trip to Hawaii, and we played like kids in a candy store. Beautiful accommodations, gorgeous beaches, a real Hawaiian luau, endless amounts of delicious food – we couldn't get enough.

That meeting felt so special. Having worked together for many years now, some of us together all the way back to Waddell & Reed days or even ITT, we savored the rewards of all the long, hard years. What a comfort to spend "down time" with "best buddies." For the first time in a long time I felt at ease with the direction of the company.

The trip also softened the relationship between Tee Faircloth and me. Tee remained unhappy over the in-house National Sales Director spot. To get past that, and to ease my own guilt, I offered him the position again, expenses only. This time though, he could stay in Macon. To my great relief, Tee agreed. He would start June 1. *A clean slate*, I thought. I certainly had plenty of work for him.

The memory of that first trip to San Francisco and Hawaii would stay dear to my heart as one of the highlights of my A.L. Williams career. So many close friends. So much fun. Our company had the camaraderie of a family.

As the years went by, Angela and I gradually spent more and more time meeting young leaders, developing new relationships, selling them the dream. I enjoyed all of that, but looking back now, maybe it got out of balance. I allowed myself to be too open and accessible to new people.

Instead, I should've drawn back and spent time with my old-timer buddies, strengthening our relationships, selling them the dream, letting them know how special they were, giving them a bigger vision for the future. Not doing that certainly was a loss for me personally.

Deep relationships like that strengthen a person, body and soul. Perhaps it was a loss for the company, too.

NEW VOICE

Back In February 1973, a Senate Judiciary subcommittee in Washington, D.C., chaired by Senator Phil Hart of Michigan, held a series of hearings on the cash value life insurance industry.

At the time of the hearing, about 140 million Americans had some form of life insurance, a $235 billion asset industry. (Total life insurance in force at year-end 1971 – $1.6 trillion.) More than $789 billion of ordinary life insurance was in force and the industry's top five companies – Prudential, Metropolitan, Equitable, New York Life and John Hancock – shared 41 percent of this total and controlled nearly half of the assets of the entire industry, about 1,800 companies.

With the hearings, Joseph Belth, a life insurance professor at the School of Business at Indiana University in Bloomington, released a public statement about sales of life insurance. In 1973, he wrote:

"Cash value insurance is called 'permanent' insurance and term insurance is called 'temporary' in sales presentations. The fact is that only one-third of the 'permanent' insurance sold today will still be in force in twenty years. Mr. Chairman, let me reiterate: cash value polices – the type of policies that represent 72 percent of the $731 billion ordinary life insurance in force in 1970 – are a consumer fraud, not because they are inherently valueless but because purchasers are denied systematic and useful information about alternative plans available to protect their wives and children, and the price for that protection, while they are urged with all the colossal mind-bending skills at the company's and agent's disposal that Plan X is the best. It is very often the best for the agent and the company, but not for the customer."

I didn't know Joseph Belth in 1973, but reading that statement would lead one to lbelieve he advocated term insurance.

Public statements can be deceiving. In January 1974, Belth began publishing *The Insurance Forum*, a four-page newsletter covering insurance industry issues. In April 1981, Belth, after receiving "numerous inquiries about A.L. Williams from readers throughout the United States," published an in-depth article on us: "A.L. Williams: The Replacement Empire."

In it, Belth went into endless detail about the Mod-11 product and the annuity rider. He charted annual premiums and rates of return for both products and compared it to our ART (Annualized Renewable Term) product. He analyzed policy comparisons produced by ADS, going so far as to call home office executives Oliver Horsman and Bill Keane with questions on how we figured dividend calculations. His conclusions about A.L. Williams? Negative, of course.

By Belth's standards, our policy comparisons were too complicated and our product too expensive.

"From the buyer's point of view, the Mod-11 appears to be high-cost term insurance in relation to the ART," he wrote. "We believe buyers would be far better off to buy the ART policy with the annuity rider attached, rather than the Mod-11 policy with the annuity rider attached."

Realize now, that Belth was comparing an 11-year product to a one-year product. Eleven years of coverage versus one? Of course Mod-11 cost more!

Belth next took it on himself to condemn our business opportunity and use of part-timers. He wrote that A.L. Williams "displays some of the characteristics of a chain letter, and like a chain letter will sooner or later run out of prospective recruits and prospective customers. Until the operation runs its course, however, we fear that many people are going to be seriously hurt. Among those to be hurt are persons who replace policies that should not have been replaced, persons who buy high-cost term insurance when they should have purchased low-cost term insurance, and persons who enter the organization with high hopes that are dashed."

Ending the article, Belth stated his belief that "the sales activities of A.L. Williams are designed primarily for the purpose of channeling the cash values of existing life insurance policies directly into the commissions for members of the ALW organization. For this reason, it is our opinion that the ALW organization is engaged primarily in the churning of life insurance."

What a pile of it! Obvious from the beginning was one fact – Belth's bread had been buttered by the traditional industry. How was it possible to "channel" cash values into commissions? Our agents made replacement sales by the thousands because our educational approach and policy comparisons clearly showed clients how term would leave their families better off than whole life. That wasn't "churning," as he accused, but merely giving consumers the opportunity to make a better choice. We called it competition in an open marketplace. We called it the free enterprise system.

Belth saw just the opposite, of course. In months and years ahead, he wrote dozens of disparaging articles about A.L. Williams, creating a lucrative cottage industry for himself, using his industry-biased arguments against A.L. Williams to sell thousands of newsletters.

I never missed an opportunity to talk about Belth's latest rant, turning his "negatives" into positives for us. How could I resist playing up his comparison of A.L. Williams to a chain letter! His tedious carping only fueled our "warrior" mentality. We never slowed our efforts to do the right thing.

STATE WARS

In the state of Washington, a bill appeared in the House of Representatives that would make it illegal for an insurance company to pay commissions to agents with less than two years experience on any sale involving replacement of another company's life insurance policy.

Here we go again. The bill, prompted by heavy pressure from whole life agents all over Washington, was a thinly veiled attempt to stop the high rate of policy replacements made by A.L. Williams agents. When we heard about the bill in late April, it had been introduced and passed by the legislation just before close of session, leaving no time for hearings or discussion. A clear job of railroading. We asked local A.L. Williams agents to immediately go to the state house and lobby state representatives, which they did with gusto.

We also got some unexpected help from "the other side." Carl Ogren, a general agent for North Coast Life in Spokane, Washington, wrote a letter to Governor John Spellman regarding House Bill 144, Section 25, dated May 7, 1981, as follows:

Dear Governor Spellman:

House Bill 144, Section 25, will make it illegal for an insurance company to pay commissions to agents who have less than two years experience on any sale involving replacement of another company's life insurance policy. I strongly urge you to veto House Bill 144, Section 25.

This legislation is aimed primarily at A.L. Williams, Inc., of Atlanta, Georgia. A.L. Williams has designed a direct sales type mass marketing organization. Their approach is responsible for the wholesale replacement of many life insurance policies in our state. This replacement generally improved the insureds' position and impacted the previous agent's commission. As a result, many of the agents who have had policies replaced became upset and have attempted to propose this legislation to stop all replacement sales by new agents.

Since the A.L. Williams sales force is predominantly new agents, this legislation would significantly affect their marketing program. The A.L. Williams organization has resulted in a substantial number of complaints by agents to the Insurance Commissioner's office. I also understand very few complaints have been made by insurance buyers to the Commissioner.

I am not now nor have I ever been a member of the A.L. Williams organization; however, I have seen some of their marketing and they as a company are providing the insurance buying public with adequate and complete disclosure of their existing insurance programs and proposed insurance programs. They try to operate in full compliance with all existing regulations and laws.

I am opposed to the proposed legislation because (1) it restrains free trade in the state of Washington, (2) it is discriminatory, (3) it may adversely affect Washington insurance companies developing new products, and (4) publicized hearings were not held on this legislation…

The letter went on to explain that based on "some of the products owned by Washington families, improving the situation will definitely involve replacement and they should have that choice."

Mr. Ogren's points hit right on the money. In fact, his letter validated the war we'd been fighting against the industry for years. Whole life companies had no real interest in fair market competition. They could care less about giving the best product possible to the consumer. Instead, by whatever ploy they could to stop us, stall us, or better yet, make us quit, they wanted to stop replacement sales.

Fortunately, the Washington war didn't work. The Ogren letter, with our local efforts, hit their mark: Governor Spellman vetoed the bill in late May. In yet another state, the issue went away.

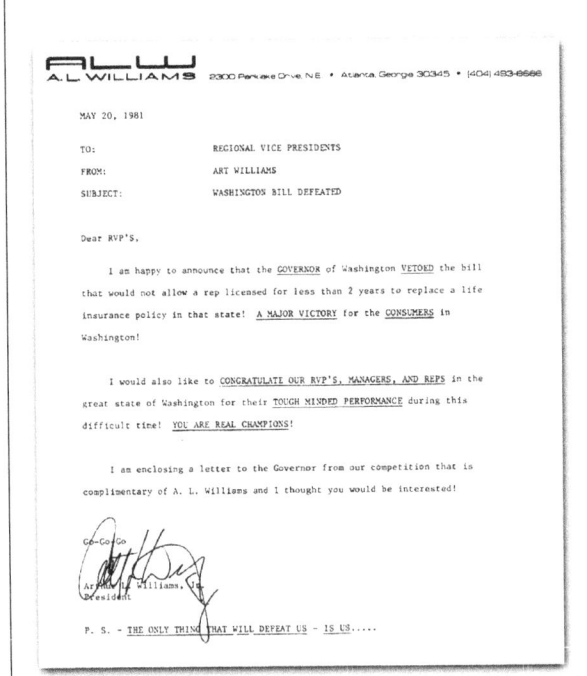

A replacement storm brewed up in Virginia, too, where in 1981, our A.L. Williams agents replaced poor-quality whole life policies by the thousands. The traditional companies – Metropolitan, Prudential, John Hancock and New York Life – took their complaints to Paul Penland, executive director of the Virginia Association of Life Underwriters. Penland scheduled a hearing in Richmond with the State Corporation Commission (a panel of three judges), with the intent of ordering a cease and desist against all replacements by A.L. Williams in Virginia. Penland describes the hearing day:

The room was full of high-powered general counsels and attorneys from all the major carriers. We all knew this was a testing ground, that if the Commission allowed a cease and desist against A.L. Williams in Virginia that it would pretty much happen in every state. That's what the big companies were hoping for – a ripple effect across the country. The session started at 9 o'clock, but by ten till 9 we realized nobody was there from A.L. Williams. We wondered if they wouldn't show and let this all go by default.

Just then, their senior counsel came through the door. He looked very young and confident. He introduced himself as Kevin King. I thought, well, he seems pretty happy-go-lucky. Today is going to be a tough day for him.

The hearing began. Mr. King asked the judges for permission to distribute information that might shorten the hearing. They agreed. He handed each judge a sheet of paper. He gave one to me, too. Columns filled the page. The first column listed names of policyholders. The next column listed their address – all Virginia clients. The third column listed the company name and original policy amount – $10,000 New York Life, $15,000 Prudential, $20,000 John Hancock. The next column listed the policy replacement by MILICO – $120,000, $150,000, $200,000 and so on. All the way down the page.

The last two columns showed the policyholders' date of death and the death claim paid by MILICO – $120,000, $150,000, $200,000 – all the way down the page.

The judges looked at the sheet and said, "Wait a minute. Are we here to talk about a cease and desist order against a company that is damaging the Virginia consumer?" I said, "Yes."

"But this paper shows a gentleman in Virginia had a $10,000 policy with New York Life that got replaced by a $100,000 policy with MILICO. Then he died six months ago and MILICO paid his family $100,000 in death claims. Did his family get hurt by this replacement?"

"Well, no," I said. The judges looked out at the room. "We've got no further business here."

As in Washington, the Virginia case stood as a great victory for A.L. Williams. Again, vindication! We worked for the best interests of the consumer, and the scoreboard told the story.

Still, the traditional industry had everything – everything – to lose. So they continued to come after us through political avenues… and also under the table. Rumors about A.L. Williams spread through state and local underwriters associations, the national organization of state insurance commissioners, industry publications, Joseph Belth and other university professors in similar positions. The life insurance industry opened wide an underground network of A.L. Williams conspiracy.

THE PYRAMID ORDEAL

Few rumors proved more persistent than the ones that grew out of the North Carolina Attorney General's pyramid investigation. A year after our replacement practices had been investigated – and completely cleared – by Barry Clause and his insurance department team, the pyramid investigation dragged on. Interestingly, at the request of Dick Morgan, Barry Clause left the North Carolina Insurance Department to work at A.L. Williams as head of our compliance and government relations department. Naturally, Barry proved a big help to Kevin King as he met over the pyramid charges with the Attorney General and his staff for many months.

Rufus Ligh Edmisten, the North Carolina Attorney General, carried a reputation among state insurance commissioners as a "pyramid expert." North Carolina had been home to Glen Turner's "Dare to Be Great," a company that really did operate as an illegal pyramid. Edmisten had just shut down Turner when A.L. Williams came on the scene.

As a multi-level marketing organization, unusual in life insurance, we did look like a pyramid in some ways. For example, our hierarchy system set no limits on how high an agent could advance in the company. Any qualified person could get licensed and achieve the highest override level based solely on sales and recruiting – and do so in any timeframe desired. But A.L. Williams' model and the pyramid model had two distinct differences.

- You could not buy a promotion at A.L. Williams. Everyone paid the same nominal sign-up fee and started at the same bottom rung commission level.

- An A.L. Williams agent did not have to buy a MILICO product to become an RVP.

To buy a MILICO policy, an agent paid the same price as any regular client. In other words, no built-in price inflation covered the cost of an RVP promotion. This stood in stark contrast to the "Dare To Be Great" scheme, which required new people to buy products to get into the company. Some even chose to spend thousands of dollars to "buy a promotion," then start at the upper levels of management.

As Kevin King, our legal counsel, noted: "Edmisten believed that if all our agents owned one of our MILICO policies, then we were a pyramid. But all our agents didn't own policies. The correct question was: Is there any reason to own the policy except to be a seller? They didn't ask that question. Many, many policyholders bought our products merely for a death benefit and not a job."

SECTION 14-291.2 OF THE NORTH CAROLINA STATUTE DEFINES A PYRAMID:

"'Pyramid distribution plan' means any program utilizing a pyramid or chain process by which a participant gives a valuable consideration for the opportunity to receive compensation or things of value in return for inducing other persons to become participants in the program…"

After months of meetings both at Raleigh and Atlanta, Kevin convinced the North Carolina Attorney General to spend an evening conducting a simple test. Kevin and his staff, alongside the Attorney General's staff, made a series of random phone calls to members of our sales force. They asked one question: Did they own a MILICO life insurance policy? The outcome of the test astounded the investigators. They learned that policy ownership was not a requirement to joining the company. What's more, they learned that the number of sales did not equal the number of recruits. Edmisten saw these facts as proof enough that A.L. Williams did not qualify as a pyramid. After a year and a half, Edmisten finally released a 17-page report concluding that A.L. Williams' published marketing plan did not violate North Carolina's pyramid law. The pyramid investigation closed.

What a relief to finally put that chapter behind us! Still the rumors of A.L. Williams, "illegal pyramid scheme," traveled the underground network. Like an urban legend, thousands of traditional agents repeated it as truth, all over the country for years to come.

ENDORSEMENT

We enjoyed some wins too, despite all these attacks.

Back in 1977, consumer advocate and term insurance expert Frank McIntosh publicly endorsed A.L. Williams and its "Buy Term and Invest the Difference" philosophy. He continued to support our cause.

Now in October 1981, we caught another endorsement, this time from a "big name" in the traditional insurance industry!

Head of his own organization, Arthur Milton was a nationally known insurance and financial authority, and the author of eight books on insurance and investing. His most recent book, *How Your Life Insurance Policies Rob You*, hit the bestseller lists and became a big favorite with our sales force.

Based in New York City, Milton had served in many leadership capacities over the years, including the Board of Directors of the General Insurance Brokers Association, the Board of Directors of the Atlantic Alumni of the Life Insurance Agency Management Association, and as an original sponsor of the College of Insurance in the state of New York. Five times Milton took honors as the life insurance industry's "Man of the Year," and he earned the "National Quality Award" for 35 consecutive years. He regularly spoke out on issues of consumer education and protection legislation and often took his remarks to the floor of the House of Representatives.

We met Arthur Milton at the grassroots. Back in the 1970s, when Boe ran his term insurance company in Texas, their paths crossed. One day in the home office, Greg Fitzpatrick called Bob Miller and excitedly told him about a guy he'd heard on a radio talk show "who sounds just like us." Bob mentioned the phone call and the name – "Arthur Milton" – to Boe… and his face lit up.

Boe called Arthur Milton that day. In a couple of weeks, we sat at a table over lunch with him in New York City. Arthur explained his main objective – "to make sure the consumer got the most insurance protection possible for his premium dollar." Bingo! We'd found an ally. He seemed equally as impressed with our organization and willingly agreed to publicly support our cause and our company. It began a long, rewarding relationship. In his endorsement letter, Milton wrote:

"For over 37 years, the life insurance industry has been very kind to me and I have developed an uncanny love for it. My concern for the low esteem that the American people hold for the life insurance industry and the average agent selling life insurance, plus my belief in the value of proper protection for the consumer, has led me to campaign vigorously for what I believe are critical changes needed in the industry's concepts and marketing methods.

"For these reasons, it was with special interest and curiosity that I spent several months researching the A.L. Williams organization. I was so happy and encouraged to learn that here is a marketing force dedicated to providing the consumer with a viable life insurance alternative. The kind of product you are selling, term insurance and tax deferred annuities, is, in my opinion, the only way to go for most people…

"A.L. Williams, you are to be admired for building, in a record period of time, the greatest and most productive sales operation that provides innovative insurance and a genuine service to the public. With much admiration, I look forward to watching the progress of your entire organization."

On November 3, 1981, Arthur Milton visited our home office for an afternoon reception with Atlanta-area RVPs. That evening, he addressed the sales force… to a standing ovation.

"One thing I know," he challenged the large group, "there are 150 million policyholders out there, waiting for you to help them 'get a dollar's value for a dollar spent' in the purchase of their life insurance needs. I know this organization didn't just happen. It happened because a man had a dream to serve the American people with the type of insurance they need and can afford, the type his organization will persevere in selling to them."

Milton's talk broke new ground. But we saw another innovation that night, too. For the first time ever, we videotaped an entire program. We'd sold audiotapes of talks and presentations by many top agents for a couple of years, but this was a first for video. Only a few days later, agents could buy Arthur's talk on videotape from our distribution center, along with copies of his book and endorsement letter. The videos sold fast. After that we taped nearly all our major meetings and events.

I began to think about the success of this medium. In fact, this videotape win would one day lead the way to our very own television studio – bigger and better than any other company's.

But I'm getting a little ahead of myself.

FANS

Work continued on setting up our own investment company, a subsidiary of The A.L. Williams Corporation (formerly First American National Corporation). Registration applications for the company, to be called First American National Securities (FANS), had been filed with the Securities & Exchange Commission (SEC), National Association of Securities Dealers (NASD), and in 47 states plus Puerto Rico. By July 1, 1981, FANS received its corporate charter and became a legal entity. The registration process finalized September 1.

Two weeks later, FANS announced its own training department, assisting A.L. Williams people all over the country with the necessary NASD licensing and sales training needed to become properly licensed securities agents. A certain percentage of the sales force already owned securities licenses, of course. But our own investment company and in-house training program would give many more agents the opportunity to sell both insurance and securities. We'd hit another huge milestone in our efforts to advance the total "Buy Term and Invest the Difference" crusade.

The road to founding FANS led over much the same ground A.L. Williams traveled. When we opened for business in 1977, I searched frantically for a company to meet our investment needs, finally landing a small financial services company in Atlanta called West America Financial Services. With ITT and Waddell & Reed, we could only sell their in-house investment products – mutual funds, and good ones… but certainly not the best. With West America, for the first time, we had the freedom to put together a fund portfolio that best met the needs of our market. We chose the "Tiffany" funds – the best performing mutual funds from top groups (Pioneer, Fidelity, Templeton, etc.). The days of selling lesser performing products were over.

West America originally had about 300 licensed representatives, primarily in four southern states. The company added six to 10 new reps every month. When we came on board, we immediately handed them 85 new securities licensed agents.

The company was thrilled. At first. As months went by, we added 30, 40, 50, 100, 200 securities licensed reps a month. Before long, West America found themselves in the same fix as Financial Assurance – we'd completely overloaded their administrative system!

On the plus side, West America made tons of money on our volume. Securities sales had a different commission structure than insurance, with 85-90 percent of the sale paid as commission to A.L. Williams agents. The rest went to West America – instant profit! Administratively, however, no one was smiling; they just couldn't keep up with the mas-

ALW Chronicle

The A.L. Williams Organization   Vol. I, No. III, Nov. '81

FANS, Inc. First Sale to ALW First Secretary

Billion Dollar Goal Reached... Monthly!

October establishes another new record for the A.L. Williams sales force. An unparalleled 18,130 new business applications were submitted during the month of October. This represents about a 12½% increase over the September totals. This new record is just another confirmation of the continuation of the increased momentum in business.

The face value of policy applications submitted has surpassed the billion dollar mark again for the month of October. This follows the billion dollar mark in face value on submittals set in September.

In 1977, when the A.L. Williams Organization was first established, Art in writers of term insurance. The face value of policy applications submitted is surpassing the billion dollar mark monthly. There is definitely a continuation of increased business momentum.

There are now over 200 Regional Vice Presidents all across the country and 2 outside the continental United States. The first giant step toward international growth has been made with Regional Vice Presidents located in Hawaii and Puerto Rico.

Tucker Norcross Publishing Company has doubled its staff in the past two months and has added the regular monthly publication of the **ALW Chronicle** to production, as well as the quarterly publication of the **A.L. Williams Opportunity**. They have entered the field of live video tape production.

For the past month, Atlanta Data Systems has processed over 6,000 pieces of incoming mail each week to produce approximately 26,000 runs a month. The national incoming return Watts lines are receiving over 500 calls a week to compile on average of 95.8 calls a day. Production is increasing and growing daily.

Greater Atlanta Printing just completed $150,000 in capital equip-

---

sive amounts of paperwork it took to license new agents and process sales.

So, enough. Three and a half years down the line, we took steps to launch our own investment company. Only time, manpower and money kept us from launching it sooner.

Ken Durham, an agent who'd started back in the early days of Waddell & Reed, emerged as the heart and soul behind the development of FANS. Multi-talented, Ken (the guy who imitated me so well) worked as a schoolteacher and band director before joining A.L. Williams full-time. In fact, he still directed Georgia Tech's band during marching season. Ken demonstrated a real head for securities, and he passionately believed in teaching clients – and our agents – how to invest their extra money in mutual funds. Through extensive travel, Ken led securities training sessions with RVPs and downlines, teaching them how to train their teams, and developing local instructors.

Ken symbolized the A.L. Williams philosophy – crusader first. He wanted to build the investment company so badly that he even worked for a few months without a salary. How many people would do that? Ken did. His passion, work ethic and zeal for investments helped FANS take off like gangbusters. Eventually, I promoted him to president of FANS.

On the home office side, I tapped Doug Hartline, one of our executives, to handle the technical/operations set-up of FANS. He teamed with Bill Keane and Mike Adams' ADS staff to design the specialized computer systems we needed to process the complicated investment sales, commissions and overrides, and maintain records. The securities business is even more regulated than insurance, if that's possible. Systems must follow all securities regulations to the letter. And Doug made sure ours complied.

On November 2, 1981, FANS officially made its first business transaction. Trudy White, my secretary, served as our first customer – Trudy, who believed in A.L. Williams so strongly that she'd left behind 20 years with Waddell & Reed to join us at our start, moving from Tallahassee to do it. She carried her A.L. Williams torch just as high as that first day and was "pleased as punch" to be FANS' opening-day investor.

The November 1981 cover story of The ALW Chronicle features Trudy White making the first mutual fund sale from FANS while Doug Hartline, left, and Art look on. A.L. Williams family.

YEAR-END

What a year 1981 proved to be – breathless progress, massive growth, staggering change. Our year-end numbers stunned all of us:

- $9.1 billion in face amount of policies submitted.
- $81 billion in premiums submitted.
- $6.5 million paid out in death claims – more than quadruple the 1980 death claims amount of $1.5 million.

Happy New Year! With our persistency problems behind us, and a new 10-year contract with PennCorp nailed down, it truly seemed like there was no ceiling on what we could do.

It can only be appropriate to give credit, once again, to the committed leaders in our sales force. Two special stories illustrate this.

We welcomed Bob Safford, the former agency president of National Home Life, into our A.L. Williams family. Prior to National Home, Bob had built his own insurance company and become a millionaire by age 28.

After the unexpected death of Art DeMoss, Bob took a well-deserved, year-long hiatus. In that time, he received several offers to run other life insurance companies but turned them down. All "traditional," he said – he no longer believed in their products.

After several "just staying in touch" calls from Boe, Bob joined A.L. Williams in December 1980. By September 1981, his team had broken so many records it was ridiculous.

Now here's the kicker: Bob was based in Philadelphia… and MILICO products weren't even licensed in Pennsylvania until mid-1981.

So Bob built his team with "greenies" from surrounding states for six months before he could even do business in his own state. He truly pioneered the Northeast region for A.L. Williams.

In Puerto Rico, another exciting story unfolded. José Rivera, an insurance representative for National Home Life and PennCorp before "landing" with A.L. Williams, built a business from scratch, too. Starting our contract March 1, 1981, he zoomed to Regional Vice President just seven months later – the first RVP promoted outside the continental United States.

Like Bob Safford, he overcame amazing obstacles to build a successful A.L. Williams business on the island. For one thing, Puerto Rico is small, just 111 x 39 miles, but José found himself competing against agents from 200 other life insurance companies. Also, local regulations did not allow insurance agents to approach or hire government workers, teachers or bank employees – prime candidates, of course, for the A.L. Williams part-time opportunity.

Despite the obstacles, José had managed by October to earn a monthly $15,000… and he never earned less. His organization numbered 2,500 licensed agents in a few short years.

"We are pioneers in Puerto Rico," José told me proudly. "Nobody was selling "Buy Term and Invest the Difference" until we entered the market. Now we are dominating it. Even our enemies respect us. They know that rather than defending company names, we are defending the interests of people."

The "Fabulous Five" Top Producing States Jan- Dec 1981

State	Face Amt Issued	# of Policies	Avg Face Amt
TX	$1,013,639,693	16,318	$62,118
FL	$629,108,413	11,590	$54,280
NC	$602,455,609	11,125	$54,153
GA	$546,238,149	9,160	$59,633
CA	$497,698,133	8,290	$60,039

BOB SAFFORD: FIRST 12 MONTHS IN A.L. WILLIAMS

- 639 sales
- $153,670 in premiums
- 249 recruits
- 56 Sales Supervisors
- 14 District Managers
- 8 Division Managers

NOTE: Bob couldn't produce business in his home state of Pennsylvania his first six months in business – because MILCO products weren't licensed there! Bob and his team still put huge numbers on the scoreboard.

"Immediate success? There is no such thing – unless you are willing to pay the price. To tell you the truth, I am so proud, so proud, so proud because I paid the price. I am not telling you that I was the best. I am telling you that I did my best. Being the best and doing your best – that is a different story."

– JOSÉ RIVERA SR.,

REGIONAL VICE PRESIDENT, PUERTO RICO

Every day, similar success stories from the field flooded the home office. Barbara King packed a new monthly newspaper, The *ALW Chronicle*, with those stories. It quickly became the company's most popular and widely read publication.

Sometimes, I didn't honestly believe things could get any better. But 1982 would prove me flat wrong.

1981 Company Structure

ALW - A.L. WILLIAMS

Life Insurance Sales - A.L. Williams Agency

Computer Services - Atlanta Data Systems

Printing - Greater Atlanta Printing

Publishing - Tucker-Norcross Publishing Company, Inc.

- - - - - - - - - - - - - - -

19 Going Public

January 1, 1982, the federal government under President Ronald Reagan passed new legislation on Individual Retirement Accounts (IRAs). This change hit the life insurance industry like a nuclear bomb. In fact, it struck just as powerfully as the FTC Report in exposing cash value life insurance as the ultimate rip-off.

The legislation allowed working people to invest up to $2,000 in an IRA… and write it off their income tax as a deduction. Couples with a non-working spouse could invest up to $2,250. Couples with both spouses working could invest up to $4,000 per year. Virtually every wage earner in the country – an estimated 50 million additional people – now qualified for an IRA.

Our company philosophy of replacing high-cost cash value policies with low-cost flexible term products automatically showed clients how to free up money for IRAs. People who never dreamed they could come up with a $2,000 contribution saw they could – by replacing their expensive cash value policy with an inexpensive term policy and saving "the difference" in an IRA.

But here's the "bottom line" blast: The federal government ruled that any investment qualified as an IRA – except cash value life insurance!

The IRA legislation, combined with the 1979 release of the FTC cost disclosure report, pounded the final nail into the coffin of traditional insurance. What timing! It gave us all we needed to shoot growth into the stratosphere.

THE POWER OF AN IRA

Example #1

Deposit = $2,000/year

IRA Investment

Year-40 value = $1,718,285

Example #2

Non-IRA Investment

15% personal tax bracket

Year-40 Value = $875,544

Example #3

Non-IRA Investment

28% personal tax bracket

Year-40 Value = $480,122

MOTHER

The weeks leading up to our first RVP meeting in 1982 had been trying. In December, Angela and I welcomed our children home from college, spoke at three regional conventions in Alabama, Tennessee and North Carolina, flew to New York for a reception at the United Nations with U.N. Ambassador Jeane Kirkpatrick, sent out 400 Christmas cards, attended three company Christmas parties, and held a reception in our home. A whirlwind.

In the midst of all the work, fun and holiday cheer, my mother was dying.

She'd been in decline for months, and now the end was near. Too soon for me, for all of us. Only recently had Mother enjoyed a more comfortable lifestyle. Losing her now just didn't seem fair.

Mother had been a widow for 15 years when she married a kind, elderly gentleman from Blakely. Eighteen years older than Mother, Mr. Maddox had been diagnosed with colon cancer several months before their wedding. Initially, Angela and I worried she would spend her second marriage nursing a new husband on a sick bed. In fact, it turned out just the opposite.

In the years after Daddy's death, Mother worked hard to stay afloat. Strong, an overcomer, she taught her boys to be tough, and she lived her own philosophy. She ran a successful antique business in Columbus during my brother Don's high school years. She also got her insurance license with A.L. Williams and made sales. After Don married and moved to Blakely to coach football, she moved back to Cairo where she continued to make sales for the company, sell antiques and do other odd jobs.

Angela and I always wanted to help her financially, to see her live a comfortable lifestyle free of worries. But before she married in 1978, we'd not had the means to do so. Teaching and coaching and then starting a business kept us from doing big things for her. Not that she would've accepted it – we helped pay Bill and Don's college costs, but Mother wanted no other help from us. Betty Williams had her dignity, and she wasn't about to take "handouts."

Mother was crazy about her three boys, our wives, our kids. She certainly loved A.L. Williams. It thrilled her that Don and Bill both worked with the company. She cheered for our success like she'd cheered at our ball games growing up.

Marrying Mr. Maddox changed her life for the better. A prominent landowner and founder of the local bank, he gave her the lifestyle we'd always wanted for her. His cancer in full remission, Mr. Maddox and Mother enjoyed two years of marital bliss, traveling and socializing. We were all so happy for them.

Then, in early 1981, Mother found out she had bladder cancer. At first, we thought she could beat it. Angela and I invited her and her husband to go with us on the company trips to San Francisco and Hawaii. But by then some really tough rounds of chemotherapy had made her too sick. She showed little improvement after that.

We buried Mother in Blakely on December 30, 1981. Her faithful husband stayed by her side until the end. So did Don, Bill and I, and our families. I knew Mother was a Christian. I knew she'd gone on to heaven. But still… We grieved, and said our farewells with heavy hearts.

My biggest fan, Mother had loved me through every part of my life. I'd wanted to give her much more, especially in those first years after Daddy died, when she seemed so burdened. I wanted her to live on and see the success of our company and the families involved in it. To see us all "be somebody," just like she'd raised us. Now she was gone at 59. Ironically, Mr. Maddox, her husband, would live another 20-plus years, almost to age 100.

We put together a wonderful funeral service for her. Many friends and family members spoke of her life and our memories. Meaningful... and emotional. When it comes to mamas, no day is ever the "right" day to say good-bye.

NATIONAL SALES DIRECTOR

I had to grieve on the run, of course. Back at the office, Boe and the staff churned full speed getting ready for the January RVP meeting. Now and then I would go to my office and shut the door for a few minutes. A friend for all seasons, Boe understood.

Recently, he'd presented a brilliant idea. Over dinner at our house one evening, Boe and his wife Myrna asked me to take half his compensation and put it toward creating a National Sales Director position. When Boe first started working for A.L. Williams, we'd set up his compensation package based not on a regular salary but on 2 percent renewals from the company, which meant his income lagged. While Boe earned a decent living, he didn't rank among the highest paid people in A.L. Williams. His request amazed me. We'd talked for months about wanting to create a field NSD position but funding always stalled the idea. At his own "expense," Boe came up with a solution.

I sat in awe. No one in the company had ever come to me and volunteered to give up half his income. In fact, nobody ever volunteered to give up any income. Period!

The timing of Boe's request was split-second perfect. Very quickly approaching our five-year anniversary on February 10, 1982, renewals were "ripe" and ready to explode, creating a "river" of new company income.

Understanding this, Boe wanted to make the necessary financial changes in his own compensation now, before the explosion. Otherwise, he would find himself in the uncomfortable position of being "overcompensated," and he didn't want that.

NATIONAL SALES DIRECTOR QUALIFICATIONS

1. A discretionary A.L. Williams appointment. Production is one of many requirements.

2. Must prove you are an A.L. Williams "great" in all areas. Great knowledge of the "A.L. Williams Way." Great loyalty. Willingness to pay an ever-greater price to see A.L. Williams succeed.

3. Production Requirements:

    a. Produce 25 first generation RVPs that each produce $30,000 first year premium in one month.

    b. Produce 15 first generation RVPs that each produce $30,000 first year premium in one month and have 75 total RVPs that each produce $30,000 in first year premium in one month (first, second and third generation RVPs).

    c. The first two RVPs that reach 50 total RVPs, each producing $30,000 in one month, and have 15 first generation RVPs will be considered for promotion.

NSD Responsibilities:

1. Act as The Company (A.L. Williams) in directing his or her entire hierarchy in all areas.

2. Hold meetings for all A.L. Williams people in his or her travels across the country.

3. Work with Art Williams and other National Sales Directors to prepare A.L. Williams for unlimited expansion and unlimited opportunity.

It compared to when I started the company and took a 25 percent override as compensation. As the company grew, my override steadily dropped... all the way down to 1 percent. Of course that 1 percent eventually produced many times more income than the 25 percent – the company had grown 100 times bigger!

As Boe and I began to develop the NSD program, we discussed how best to use this new block of money. We wanted our sales guys thinking "national." Right now they thought "regional." We needed a spur. It was time our leaders started thinking about taking *their own organizations national.* So, we designed the National Sales Director position to promote national expansion.

By meeting specific qualifications, every National Sales Director could earn compensation based on the *entire block of A.L. Williams business* – for the first time in our history! NSD bonuses would be completely separate from overrides and bonuses earned by their organization. We proposed that each NSD receive a monthly bonus of $15,000 – a total of $180,000 a year in extra income – for achieving a national level of production and performance. That, in turn, required producing a high number of RVPs.

We knew the temptation of dangling such a huge "carrot" – that was the idea. Some of the guys already earned $200,000, $300,000 and more in income. This bonus could double their income. The ability to override the entire company gave them a real chance to build financial security on a much higher level – a national level – an opportunity way beyond any we'd originally imagined. Historic.

Boe and I looked forward with great anticipation to the upcoming RVP meeting. We just couldn't keep the smiles off our faces.

JANUARY HIGHS

Starting on January 7, a Thursday afternoon, Boe and I launched into a three-day RVP meeting, our longest and most complex to date. In addition to talking about the new IRA legislation and our new Money Market Fund, we introduced an updated pay system and improvements to our recently announced Mod-15 product. We brought in home office and MILICO personnel to discuss administration, licensing, Atlanta Data Systems and regulatory updates. RVPs spoke throughout the meeting, our topics ranging from goal-setting to office management to "building it big."

To honor our upcoming five-year anniversary, Bob Miller and Bobby Buisson promoted the "Birthday Blitz," a series of 16 meetings to be conducted simultaneously at cities all over the country on February 12-13 by the company's top 80 RVPs.

We featured Stan Cottrell (a world-famous marathon runner we sponsored) as a keynote speaker. Stan held the record for the "run across America" – a 3,103 mile-run from New York City to San Francisco he managed to make in 48 days, 1 hour and 48 minutes. To promote our company, we sponsored him in an upcoming run across Georgia and on a 4,000-mile run of the Great Wall of China. Every mile of those events, he wore an A.L.

Williams T-shirt!

Stan's winning attitude made a perfect lead-in for announcing the new National Sales Director position. Boe stood up first, using overheads to explain the qualifications and compensation package. I stood to the side and watched faces.

At first, I saw furrowed brows and looks of confusion. Then, I witnessed a collective gasp as "the light" came on. What a magical moment! That announcement touched every person in the room. It opened the door to an even bigger future. Limits on growth? Eliminated!

We spent the rest of the meeting talking "NSD." All of a sudden, dozens and dozens of RVPs could envision moving to the next level, building their own A.L. Williams within A.L. Williams. Boe and I had hoped for enthusiasm like this.

Now leaders would decide: Was an additional $180,000 in annual income worth the work it took to produce lots of new RVPs and expand all over the country?

Time would tell. I had a feeling we wouldn't have to wait long.

ANNIVERSARY

As February 10 approached, A.L. Williams had been in business for five years. From seven RVPs and 85 Representatives in three states in 1977, we'd swelled to 300 RVPs, 50,000 licensed Reps, 800 offices in 47 states and an average of one RVP promotion a day. Yet it seemed we'd only just started.

Our licensing department, recently switched from MILICO to A.L. Williams, received about 1,000 new licensing applications a week.

ADS, our policy analysis company, had started with two employees in 500 square feet of space. Now, it employed 54 people in 12,000 square feet, operated seven days a week, and ran 28,000 comparisons a month.

Just two years before, MILICO opened with 45 employees in 7,000 square feet of office space. Now it had 400 employees with 35,000 square feet of space, and millions of dollars invested in high-end computer systems and equipment.

Another success story within the company, Greater Atlanta Printing, started with little more than Mitch and Diane Slayton and that little bitty printer stuck in a corner. A $30,000-a-month operation now, it ran full printing capabilities and 26 employees in its own location, ranking as one of the top 10 printers in Atlanta in paper use.

Our Tucker-Norcross Publishing Company started with one employee, Barbara King. Now TNP boasted eight employees with full design, art and publishing capabilities and a $50,000-a-month budget.

Both at home and in the field, an overarching sense of common purpose prevailed. We knew what we believed and we went after it. Sure, frustrations abounded. But as I often said, "Attitude is everything. Nobody wants to follow a negative, dull, disillusioned, frustrated, dad-gum crybaby." As a group, we understood leadership. Every day, A.L. Williams pursued its purpose – from the lowliest clerks to the highest leaders.

Nowhere did that camaraderie thrive more than in the Partners Organization. From a tentative start at the 1979 Sea Island Convention, it flourished into a full-blown grassroots movement. Thousands of Partners learned the A.L. Williams system through spouse sessions at all our major company events, regional Fast Start Schools, and local meetings held somewhere across the country every night of the week.

The volume of letters Angela received from spouses all over the country delighted and astounded her. Full of warmth and humor, the letters poured out personal struggles, sharing inspirational transformations from weak, negative Partners to strong, supportive ones. Angela excerpted many letters in her monthly column in The ALW Chronicle. The overall message rang out clear as a bell: We are all in this thing together!

FEBRUARY LOSS

As in every family, we took some blows, too.

On Sunday evening, February 7, 1982, we received terrible news. RVP Ron Wright and his wife, Marian, driving home from church in New Orleans, had been hit head-on by a drunk driver. The crash killed Ron and severely injured Marian. Within the hour, Boe and Myrna, Bobby and Red Buisson and their families met at our front door. We spent the next few hours in a state of shock, grieving, trying to understand.

It especially hurt Bobby, and for good reason. Ron had been one of his direct RVPs and a close friend.

Ron Wright, part of Bobby's Waddell & Reed base shop and one of A.L. Williams' original 85 founders, started his career as a Fuller brush salesman at age 19. Highly successful, he moved on to securities and then real estate. When the 1970s recession hit, he found himself in a tough situation – losing one fortune... and owing another. Refusing to succumb to bankruptcy, Ron joined A.L. Williams and went to work. His Louisiana team thrived in no time.

Just 44, Ron left behind a wife and three sons, ages 22, 20 and 17 – and a financial plan that would keep Marian financially secure the rest of her life. He did it right, the A.L. Williams way.

Marian asked me to speak at Ron's funeral. With a broken arm, nose and many broken bones in her face, Marian rested in intensive care. It would be months before she fully recovered.

At the funeral, packed with family, friends and A.L. Williams people, emotion washed over me. As soon as I stood up to speak, tears began to flow. Through sobs, I shared Ron's dramatic story. "The greatest thing a person can achieve in life is to do something meaningful and worthwhile, to be recognized among his peers as the best, a leader who can always be counted on, who makes the difference between victory and defeat." I paused to wipe my face, but went on, determined to share my heart.

"On February 7, Ron Wright retired 'on top.' He was the kind of team player who, when he graduates, you retire his jersey. He will be impossible to replace at A.L. Williams."

Ron's death was the first such loss in the company. It passed my understanding why such a great husband, father, friend and business leader had been taken so tragically in the prime of his life. Some things, I guess, we're just not meant to know.

FIRST OFFERING

From our first negotiations with PennCorp, Stanley held up a goal for us – the idea of creating a public company.

"This is something we can do together," he made a point of saying. Both Boe and Stanley had experience in creating successful public companies – Stanley with PennCorp and Boe with his former company in Texas. Stanley, a born salesman, intrinsically understood the value of giving the sales force a way to buy ownership in their own company. When a company is your own, you love it a little more.

Boe recognized the potential, too. He'd worked with Stanley and me on the concept since the persistency issue subsided. Boe proposed a genius idea – create the public company as a "reinsurance" company owned by the A.L. Williams agency. If our sales force could produce $84 million in annual premium, a staggering amount of business, then any business produced above and beyond that would be split 50/50 between MILICO and the A.L. Williams public company. Instead of MILICO selling a portion of premium to an outside reinsurance company, the most common procedure in the insurance world, our public company would act as its own reinsurance company, splitting both the costs and the profits of putting new business on the books – after passing the $84 million milestone, of course.

To our knowledge, an arrangement like Boe proposed had never been done before. But it made all kinds of sense, and Stanley heartily approved it. To Stanley, tying the success of the public company to a high production number made it fair, practical and appealing. If the sales force had a way to make money off the profits of the business, it would inspire them to write more business, number one, and write better business, number two. And if the sales force could actually reach the $84 million in business-on-the-books mark in one year, then they deserved the rewards of splitting profits with MILICO. Finally, higher earnings in the public company would drive up the stock price as well – a total win-win situation.

REINSURANCE

"Creating the A.L. Williams public company was my idea. I'd done a public company before and I knew how to do it. I also knew that reinsurance was a BIG thing. Art didn't early on; he later learned."

Setting the breakpoint at $84 million in premium was mentioned in the original $100 million contract with PennCorp and finalized in the 10-year contract. There is no way Stanley Beyer and PennCorp would've ever agreed to do what they did if they believed we were going to write that kind of premium. We asked to get 50 percent of it back after writing $84 million in one year. Do you understand how much more that would've been worth to their company? Nobody would've done that if they'd known. Nobody ever dreamed we were going to get this big and most agencies would never write $84 million in life insurance premium.

"It was a very shrewd business deal on our part. The whole key was getting the reinsurance contract to where we could buy the insurance. We would never have had a public company if we hadn't had that. Raising the money for the initial offering was really easy. People thought it would be hard but they found out it wasn't."

– BOE ADAMS

Looking back, I doubt Stanley ever really thought we would reach the $84 million. If he had, without question he would've pressed for a higher number.

We completed the first step of creating the First American National Corporation (FANC) as a legal holding company. The second step, filing a prospectus with the SEC, was also complete. The prospectus set the initial offering at $27 million, an amount we felt confident we could bring in, with two deadlines. Starting March 8, 1982, we had until June 30 to raise the minimum offering of $7 million. If we met that, we then had until

November 30 to raise the maximum offering of $27 million. In December, if all went well, we would be selling A.L. Williams public stock over the NASDAQ Stock Market.

Typically, companies hire investment banking firms to raise stock offerings. Pursuing the notion, I interviewed several on Wall Street who could do the job, including Merrill Lynch and Bear Stearns. Frankly, their commission fees spooked me. Even Stephens Inc., an investment bank in Little Rock, Arkansas, that Boe highly recommended – they helped Wal- Mart go public – wanted a whopping $3 million to raise the money. Every bone in my body said, "No way!" Boe agreed.

Boe and I told Stanley our decision. "We're not paying nobody nuthin' to sell this stock offering," I blurted. "We've got people. We're going to offer it to our own people. And we're not going to make them pay a commission."

Over the phone, Stanley said, "Art, that's fine. Just understand how hard people are going to laugh at you. This is not the normal way to do things. It'll be very tough to raise $27 million without some professional help."

I looked at Boe. He shrugged, a familiar twinkle in his eye.

"We'll see," I smiled. "We'll see."

INSIDER STOCK

We set aside 20 percent of the $7 million as "insider" stock, sold half price at $2.50 per share, and offered this to the Senior Vice Presidents and National Sales Directors. We offered stock in "rounds" of $10,000, with each member of the group having an opportunity to put in that amount per round, until all 280,000 shares sold.

Emotion ran high. People immediately geared into creative overdrive, coming up with ways to scrape together every penny possible for a stock purchase. Frank Dineen and Fred Marceaux put second mortgages on their homes, solely for buying shares. Bob Miller managed to scrape up $50,000. Bobby Buisson and Tee Faircloth "maxed out" at $167,000 each. Our leaders showed commitment like never before, flat-out putting their financial future on the line to invest in A.L. Williams. They knew in their gut what I did: This was a risk worth taking.

Another $4 million in common stock went up for sale at $5 per share. Just as I'd predicted, our sales force jumped on the bandwagon, blanketing their organizations and communities with prospectuses. At the home office, Bill Keane, FANC's executive vice president and treasurer, spent every day on the phone, talking non-stop to field people and policyholders about A.L. Williams. Share subscriptions rolled in.

SPRING SURGE

We hit another all-time high in March, with life apps surging to an incredible 21,446 and license requests peaking at nearly 7,000. New promotions dominated our April 1 RVP meeting – 21 new RVPs and two new SVPs, Kip Ridley and Mike Tuttle.

The most exciting promotion I gave – our first-ever field NSD promotion – was to Hubert Humphrey. He deserved it. In his four years with A.L. Williams, Hubert had produced 35 first-generation RVPs, 37 second-generation RVPs and four third-generation RVPs. He'd built in Georgia, built in Colorado, and returned to build again in Georgia. Simply a master at developing successful people, Hubert, in my opinion, became one of the greatest talents in the history of A.L. Williams.

Movie cameras rolled as Barbara King organized our first-ever A.L. Williams "major motion picture," to be debuted at our upcoming June convention in Boca Raton. Also from Barbara's newly structured "ALW Communication Center" came a carefully prepared marketing kit of sales and marketing materials.

How well many of us "old timers" remembered sitting down at a kitchen table with nothing but a pencil and a yellow legal pad! Now Barbara and her team gave us a complete "Success Pak" – an asset management presentation, recruiting and company image brochures, securities information, third-party materials, and a "Fast Trak" package for new Reps, with a training handbook and audiotapes from top leaders.

ALW ADOPTS NEW "LOGO"

One of the most exciting elements of the new marketing package is the design of a stimulating new emblem (logo) for A. L. Williams. Composed of bright yellow and orange tones, the logo conveys the warm, yet firey and enthusiastic spirit of ALW people.

Both the colors and the design of the logo symbolize elements of the ALW organization. It can't be reproduced in color in the Chronicle, so a black and grey version is used here to highlight the explanation of its meaning.

These lines (yellow in logo color) represent the ladder of success, the many levels of opportunity and achievement.

These bars (brown) represent the A. L. Williams opportunity. Everyone starts small, at the bottom rung. But each step up the ladder, your organization and your income gets bigger and better.

The outer bands (orange) represent the freedom, the flexibility to do your thing within the system.

Together the design symbolizes the levels of success, the growing opportunities and the freedom . . . in colors and style that come together to represent the dynamic A. L. Williams organization.

The new logo will be used on all A. L. Williams printed material, stationery and business cards, in video presentations, almost anywhere the A. L. Williams name appears.

The new ALW logo introduced April 1982

We also raised the curtain on a new logo, designed by a Chicago public relations firm. It would remain our company symbol for many years.

Days flew by.

In May, Angela, Boe, Myrna and I began a 14- city "Super Seminar" tour that zigzagged the country and filled our calendars till November. In May, we promoted 78 RVPs – the largest group ever in one month. A major incentive loomed – the upcoming RVP convention June 26-July 1, 1982, at the prestigious Boca Raton Hotel & Beach Club in Florida. Agents on the brink of becoming RVP pulled out all the stops to earn the right to attend this one.

The June 30 deadline for the $7 million initial stock offering approached fast, too. Subscriptions poured in daily, and good old Stanley Beyer confirmed his faith in A.L. Williams by purchasing $2.6 million in shares.

At this time, we officially renamed First American National Corporation the A.L. Williams Corporation. Once we went public in November, "ALWC" would become our NASDAQ trading symbol. The name change sent a much clearer message that our public company was being built by and for the A.L. Williams organization.

In the middle of this swirl, Stanley gave me a "suggestion."

In Houston for a Fast Start School, I took an unexpected call. "Art, I want you to buy $3 million dollars in stock," Stanley said with even greater passion than usual. "It's important for the relationship between PennCorp and A.L.Williams that you purchase that amount. We'll loan you the money."

Hmm. I have to tell you I had no real desire to go $3 million dollars in debt. Angela and I, 40 now, after years of taking on debt here and there to buy home office computers or grow office space or cover myriad needs of a growing company, finally felt a little financial breathing room. I didn't like owing a nickel to anybody. I couldn't fathom having a

$3 million dollar loan hanging over my head.

I argued with Stanley about it. "Look, I'd rather raise the money by offering more insider stock to a wider circle of field leaders, not just the NSDs and SVPs."

"No, Art, I won't let you do that," he said firmly. "I know from previous experience with our public company – that doesn't work. I'm really not offering you a choice here. If you want to do the public company, then you'll agree to buy the $3 million in shares. We need to know you are as committed to this deal as we are. And besides, you deserve this. You started this company. Trust me, it will be a good thing for you and your family in the long run."

Stanley was kindly passing on some hard-earned wisdom, and he turned out to be right about all of it. But he also wanted to "lock me up."

Even with our 10-year contract and my personal liability agreement, Stanley needed to make absolutely sure I wasn't going anywhere other than A.L. Williams.

So… I lost sleep over it, but I agreed to Stanley's proposal. My $3 million investment pushed us over the $7 million mark well before the June 30 deadline. We were securely on our way to creating the ALWC public company.

Though I didn't know it at the time, Stanley had another reason for tying me down. PennCorp was in the midst of merger talks with Dow Jones giant American Can. The outcome of their discussions would drastically affect us in the years ahead.

REVELATION

The sun shone brightly on A.L. Williams… With only one small dark cloud. His name? Tee Faircloth.

After serving several months as in-house National Sales Director, Tee asked to step down. To his way of thinking, reimbursement for "expenses only" did not provide adequate compensation for the effort he put out. He wanted the title of in-house NSD… and he wanted to override the entire company. "That's not going to happen," I told Tee firmly one day in my office.

"Well, that's crazy," he said. "I quit."

Truth be told, Tee made little effort to help the company on a national scale. In contrast to Bob and Bobby, received with open arms at meetings all over the country, Tee's appearances brought bitter complaints.

"Please don't send Tee Faircloth to any more of our meetings," I heard over and over in calls and letters, some of them from his own people. "All he does is criticize. He's down on everything."

Disappointing, to put it mildly, and for the thousandth time I regretted ever offering him the in-house position. I let him go back to leading his hierarchy as a "regular" National Sales Director.

Something nagged me, though. Tee always tilted toward negative; that was just sort of his personality. But now it felt like more than that; it felt downright destructive. Why? Income? His was huge – he ranked as the company's second highest earner behind Hubert. Hierarchy? He overrode some of the company's best producers. Something had changed. But what?

In June I got word of Tee meeting with Financial Assurance – the very same Financial Assurance that gave A.L. Williams its start in 1977. Joe Jack Merriman's son, Michael, now ran FAI. Tee visited Michael several times in Kansas City, even invited him to a couple of Fast Start Schools, "courting" him to underwrite Tee's own new insurance agency.

I got more information, confirming Tee's intent to leave A.L. Williams and start his own company. Finally, after looking into all the legal ramifications, I terminated Tee the day before the start of the Boca convention.

What a tragedy. Considering what lay ahead for A.L. Williams, Tee could've become fabulously wealthy. He held the title of "oldest recruit" in the company. Tee gave me Bobby Buisson's name way back in 1972. His organization included Hubert Humphrey, one of the most gifted builders in the company. Ronnie Barnes and Jack Schulman built huge organizations direct to him. Yet Tee had chosen a different path.

Immediately he started his own agency with "seven original RVPs" and Financial Assurance as the underwriter, just as I'd done with A.L. Williams five years before. And, like Dennis Richardson, he took several hundred people with him. Calling himself "the president for life," Tee launched headlong into building his new business.

It lasted less than a year.

For a second time, I felt forced to terminate a big company producer. I saw a great lesson here. Tee believed his own abilities made A.L. Williams great. In reality, it was the other way around.

To my knowledge, Tee never did as well financially as he did with A.L. Williams.

Even with Tee's loss and the hundreds of people he sucked away, A.L. Williams continued to grow. And not by a little, but by a lot.

No amount of adversity would slow this great team down now.

BOCA BOMBSHELLS

So, we convened at Boca Raton Resort & Club, one of the world's most exclusive resort destinations, with 537 RVPs and their spouses. I promised at least one "bombshell" a day and, buddy, that's what happened. I had surprises, too – for the first time as I walked the halls, I met unfamiliar faces. I didn't know the names of all the RVPs and their spouses! An aspect of big growth I never anticipated.

We shared updates about the public company and ALW stock subscriptions. We heard inspiring speeches by Stanley Beyer, Boe, many of our top RVPs and SVPs, and myself. Arthur Milton announced my appointment as "co-chairman of the Citizens Committee for the United States Mission to the United Nations," an appointment from U.N. ambassador Jeane Kirkpatrick. Angela's daily Partner sessions featured talks by Myrna Adams, Norma Humphrey, and others. The 30-minute film premier of "The Greatest Opportunity in America" drew rave reviews. Copies of the 16mm movie flew off the shelves at Barbara King's Communication Center booth, snapped up for use as a recruiting tool.

ADS broke big news, too – in-office computer systems would be available to qualifying RVPs. They could now produce policy proposals and comparison statements in their own offices. What progress!

Of all the bombshells, Awards Night drew the biggest buzz. I'd gone "all out" before, but this time? Outrageous. Hubert and Norma Humphrey – awarded the first-ever six-foot trophy for being "leaders who set new records and make us all dream bigger." Hubert, easily the company pace setter in building new RVPs, brought 50 new RVPs to Boca.

Most Valuable Players? Bob and Jane Miller, Bob and Pat Safford, Larry and Renee Weidel, and Ronnie Barnes lugged home door-sized plaques. Mike and Stephanie Tuttle and Kip and Carole Ridley (SVP of the Year), and Neal and Anita Askew (RVP of the Year) hauled out massive trophies, too.

Others awards – Most Outstanding Leadership, Big Jock Award, Comeback of the Year, President's Council, President's Award – had dozens of winners tripping up the stairs. Fifty-five "rookies" – guys like Tom Halpin, Chip Frost, Ed Heil, John Lennon, David Landrum, Mike Perry, José Rivera and Mike Sharpe – recognized for big-time star potential. And what fun… Nine "Torn Sweater" awards, including one to my old buddy, Lou Miller, from football coaching days. Lou, a recent recruit to our team after years of working in professional golf, laughed it off. He knew my ways!

1982 WALL OF FAME

These leaders, honored as the original Wall of Fame inductees, started a time honored tradition at A.L. Williams. Original oil portraits of each leader hung in the home office on behalf of their contribution.

Boe Adams

Hubert Humphrey

Ronnie Barnes

Bob Miller

Bobby Buisson

Bob Safford

Virginia Carter

Bob Turley

Rusty Crossland

Larry Weidel

Ron Wright

In an emotional moment, I presented Marian Wright with a gift and two checks – one from donations made by A.L. Williams people to the Ron Wright trust fund, and a second for commissions on sales made by Ron's organization. Still healing from her loss, Marian accepted graciously.

The biggest highlight? No doubt about it… The introduction of the A.L. Williams "Wall of Fame." To honor the people who'd made the most enduring commitment to our company, we'd commissioned 11 formal oil portraits, unveiled that night. The portraits would now hang in the conference room at the home office, a "constant acknowledgement of the pioneers who gave A.L. Williams a winning tradition."

Through the years, we added many more portraits to the Wall of Fame… and even created a separate "Wall of Fame" for Partners.

BILLION-DOLLAR MONTH

The July issue of A.M. Best's Management Report, an industry magazine, reported 1981 industry numbers: In two years, A.L. Williams vaulted from tenth place to fifth place in life insurance issued. The article singled us out, stating "A.L. Williams continued its meteoric rise in the life insurance firmament by issuing $3 billion more in 1981 than in 1980." To take fifth place, we sold $6.6 billion of insurance. Prudential? Still number one... but now we were breathing down their necks. In the last five-year period (1976-1981), A.L. Williams ranked number one in percentage gain in life insurance sales... with a mind-blowing 32,657 *percent increase*.

Then, our July 1982 numbers once again broke all previous production records – $1,003,869,000 of paid business put in force, with 15,100 policies and an average face amount of $66,481.

One billion in business in one month!

"When we founded A.L. Williams, I said we would be successful if we could pay for $1 billion in business in one year," I crowed to the sales force. "Now, after only five years in business, we are paying for that amount in *one month!*"

I asked Barbara King and her staff to prepare a quarter-page ad promoting July's billion-dollar month, which appeared in the *Wall Street Journal*, the *Atlanta Journal-Constitution* and the *Los Angeles Times*.

July saw 42 RVP promotions, August another 20. Angela and I enjoyed a late summer "Rendezvous on the Rhine" trip exclusively for the company's 26 SVPs and their spouses. A wonderful trip... and at every stop along the way, I pondered: "If Prudential is the number one producer of life insurance and we're number five... Then how do we get to number one?"

All at once I had it.

I loved to run A.L. Williams like a football team. Competition totally motivated our guys. So... Why not turn this thing into an all-out "ionship," just like in football?

Los Angeles Times - Thursday, September 23, 1982

The more I thought about it, the more I liked it: A.L. Williams could win the insurance industry's "National Championship."

We could be Number One – the #1 producer of life insurance in the industry. Now wouldn't that be something? It had always been my dream to beat Prudential. The competition would never know what hit them.

OPENING DAY

It came at us like a freight train – the public offering. We held our breath, counting down to November 30.

How many people told us we would never raise $27 million? How many people told us we could never reach that lofty total without an investment firm? It didn't matter now who said what – that day didn't reach the $27 million.

We reached $35 million – $8 million more than we needed, every penny scraped from the pockets and piggy banks of our sales force, clients and friends.

At that time, it was the largest self-underwritten stock offering in business history.

Poor Bill Keane. He got the arduous job of returning the $8 million dollar difference.

On December 1, Bill took the offering to NASDAQ. It opened for $5 a share.

FIRST PROSPECTUS

As executive vice president and treasurer of FANC, Bill Keane intricately involved himself in setting up the prospectus for the first public offering. According to Bill, the initial share price was set at $5 because "we felt our people could afford to purchase 1,000 or 1,500 shares at $5 per share. We thought it was a reasonable amount per share to raise the $27 million."

We chose NASDAQ over the New York Stock Exchange for two reasons. "NASDAQ had a minimum of $5 per share and their system operated on a bid-ask basis, which is what we wanted," Bill explained. "The NYSE required a higher share price and at that time we didn't have enough total shares outstanding to meet their start-up requirements."

We raised the initial offering amount of $27 million totally by referral – the largest private initial stock offering at the time. "I was on the phone 8-10 hours a day, talking to field people," Bill recalled. "We did it by word of mouth only – no underwriter. We didn't pay a nickel to raise the money. We had no problems whatsoever – we could've raised $50 million if we'd had to."

"Rejected" investors (those who had their money returned by Bill Keane), plus many others, took their money and bought ALWC shares over the counter. The first day on the market, our stock price shot from $5 to $8 per share. It moved to $12 a share the next day, and then to $16. By the end of the first week, it climbed to $27. In 90 days, it shot to $58 1/4 a share.

Our stock performance astonished the financial world. Once again, we experienced the blessing of perfect timing. After five years of stagnation, the stock market picked up speed again in late 1982. When our stock hit the market in December, the Dow Jones Industrial Average had just nosed over one thousand. Our stock immediately began to attract the best kind of attention. Peter Lynch, manager of Fidelity's fast-growing Magellan Fund, invited me to his Boston office. We spent hours discussing A.L. Williams. Peter, fascinated by our company story, purchased a huge block of shares through our secondary offering. Pioneer Funds bought shares, too, as well as other mutual fund companies.

In later years, Bill Keane and I made annual tours to meet with international investors – Scotland, England, France and Switzerland. We returned home through New York, Los Angeles, San Francisco and Austin to visit private U.S. investors, ending our trips in Little Rock at Stephens Inc. By then we'd hired Stephens as lead underwriter.

The A.L. Williams public company made millionaires of many who took the risk of investing in that initial offering.

Twenty years later, every $5 share was worth $600 – an amazing part of our story. Still, all our investments would've been nothing more than paper profit if we hadn't hit the $84 million mark.

We did that the very next year – 1983.

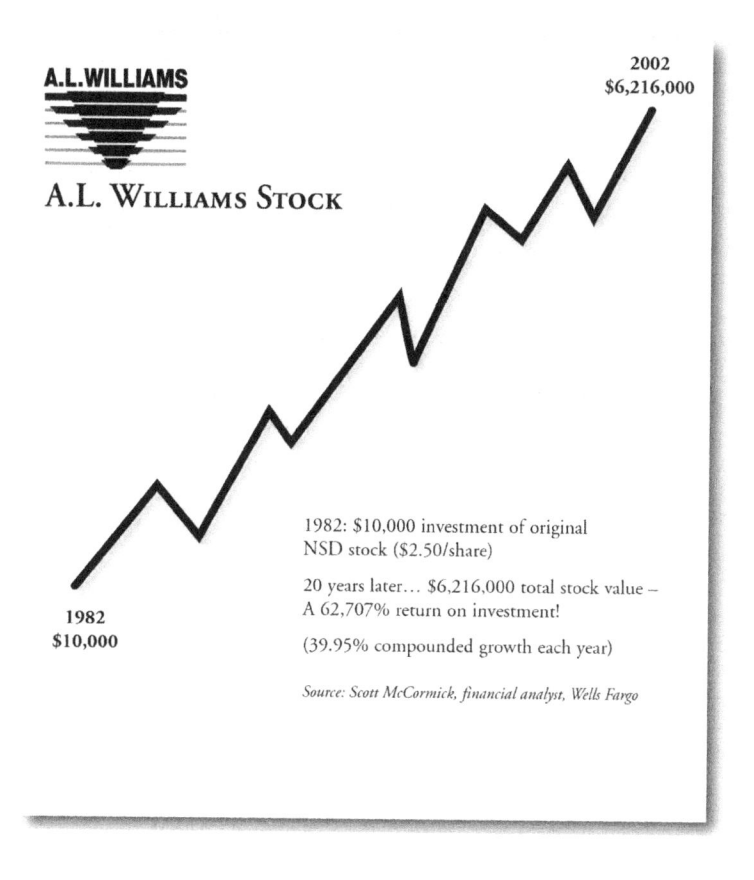

A.L. WILLIAMS

A.L. WILLIAMS STOCK

2002
$6,216,000

1982
$10,000

1982: $10,000 investment of original NSD stock ($2.50/share)

20 years later… $6,216,000 total stock value – A 62,707% return on investment!

(39.95% compounded growth each year)

Source: Scott McCormick, financial analyst, Wells Fargo

20 Big Time

As A.L. Williams blazed into 1983, two significant events pushed us into the national spotlight. The first one came almost by accident.

Lloyd Tomer, a Regional Vice President in Illinois, told a friend who worked for the Saturday Evening Post about his involvement with A.L. Williams. Lloyd's description of our company intrigued his friend so much that he passed the information along to editors, thinking the famous magazine might be interested in writing a story on us. Before long, the Post's editor, Cory SerVaas, arranged a meeting with Barbara King. Dr. SerVaas, a medical doctor, loved our concepts for promoting financial "health" with our family-friendly values. She agreed to do the story.

Barbara and her staff worked hard with a Post writer to create an article that correctly captured A.L. Williams. Frankly, the story caused some nerves at the home office. After all, so many negative and erroneous articles had been written about our company. Would this be one more printed attack on our "oddball" system of using part-time agents to sell insurance? Would we be forced once again to read about a so-called "pyramid" run by an ex-high school football coach with no business experience?

We were all in for a pleasant surprise. At our December 1982 RVP meeting in Atlanta, Dr. SerVaas made a special appearance to unveil the March 1983 Saturday Evening Post cover story – an illustrated portrait of yours truly along with the headline, "A 'Dadgummit' Georgia Football Coach Tackles the Insurance Industry."

The eight-page article featured lots of color photos and covered the A.L. Williams saga, starting with my coaching career and unlikely entrance into the insurance world. It also highlighted the careers of some top producers like Bob Turley, Virginia Carter and Greg Fitzpatrick. It also thoroughly (and accurately) explained our three-step sales process.

Holding up the proposed cover at the meeting, I gleefully announced to the RVPs, "Our competition can no longer ignore A.L. Williams. Imagine their surprise when they go to the newsstands to buy their favorite magazine… and who do they see? Me, that guy who's been causing them so much trouble!"

Landing on the cover of the Saturday Evening Post, one of the country's oldest and most respected magazines (five million readers!) gave us our first big national media exposure. For the first time, a credible publication took the time to rightly explain our concepts, system and the competitive advantage we held in the marketplace. The Post understood what we did for consumers, captured it and endorsed it. No amount of advertising dollars could have purchased the kind of prestige and influence generated by that article.

Dr. SerVaas graciously gave us permission to sell reprints, but I don't really think she knew what she was getting into. Even the Post's seasoned publishing executives couldn't believe it when orders for 87,000 copies flooded into their Indianapolis offices. Within days, copies of the article sat on kitchen tables in thousands of homes and offices all over the country.

The March issue hit the newsstands in early February. In Albuquerque for a Fast Start School, I noticed it in the hotel gift shop.

It caught me totally off-guard. Seeing it for the first time on the magazine rack…with my face on the front… Startling! A few minutes later, I was full bore into my speech when someone ran up on stage holding a copy. The whole room erupted. Twelve hundred people started jumping up and down, cheering and clapping. It took 10 minutes before they calmed down.

That excitement reached far beyond New Mexico.

The next day, A.L.Williams stock doubled.

ULTIMATERM

Our theme for the RVP convention in Las Vegas in May – "Reach for the Stars" – could not have been more appropriate. Nine hundred RVPs and 1,700 ALW offices now stretched across the U.S. and Puerto Rico. Four more National Sales Directors – Ronnie Barnes, Rusty Crossland, Bob Turley and Larry Weidel – stepped up. And we had a new product series – "UltimaTerm."

UltimaTerm – "the ultimate" in term insurance – quickly generated overwhelming response from the field… and for good reason. Our most comprehensive and competitive product series to date, UltimaTerm configured as a 15-year modified premium base policy with add-on riders. It offered a great way for clients to pile on extra protection for very little cost. Built-in persistency safeguards also kept prices down while rewarding the sales force for writing good business. UltimaTerm? A win-win-win for client, agent and company.

We priced UltimaTerm to compete with super-cheap products like non-smoker ART and association group insurance. Easy price comparisons and the extra savings on insurance costs opened the door for higher volumes of "invest the difference" sales, as well.

Not surprisingly, sales took off like wildfire. By the end of the year, our average policy face amount climbed from $65,000 to $125,000. The average industry policy? A mere $13,310, according to the 1982 Life Insurance Fact Book.

We never introduced a new product that didn't improve on the previous one. In designing UltimaTerm, we made a giant step toward having the most competitive product on the market. Still, to my thinking, UltimaTerm wasn't quite "it." I wanted a level-term policy – one to replace the higher first-year premium with a level premium… and thus allow us to truly dominate the marketplace.

We came close with UltimaTerm. The day would soon arrive, though, when we would really "have it all" in the product arena.

Until then, UltimaTerm played its part. It served the family well… and pushed our production numbers into the ozone.

AMERICAN CAN

As much as the industry wanted to depict us as some sloppy, fly-by-night operation, we simply proved otherwise. *The Saturday Evening Post* story triggered more company profiles in financial publications like *Barron's*, *Wall Street Journal*, *BusinessWeek* and the *Atlanta Business Chronicle*, plus dozens of other publications.

Someone else had noticed us, too. For months, Stanley Beyer had quietly held negotiations with a huge Dow Jones company called American Can.

Founded in 1901, American Can was an old-line East Coast corporation in Greenwich, Connecticut. For decades it ranked as the number one can maker in the world, one of the 30 blue chip companies in the Dow Jones industrial average. Its CEO, Bill Woodside, realized cans were fast being replaced by plastic. He wisely wanted to move American Can's holdings away from the dying manufacturing industry toward financial services. Recently, he'd purchased a life insurance holding company, Associated Madison, from Gerald Tsai Jr., a top Wall Street executive. Woodside then hired Tsai to head his new financial services division.

American Can, loaded with cash, stood ready to buy. Shopping the industry, Woodside and Tsai noticed a general state of stagnation. Nobody seemed to be growing. Suddenly Santa Monica-based PennCorp popped on their radar. That company was on fire. Why?

Numbers revealed PennCorp's subsidiary, MILICO, underwrote Atlanta-based A.L. Williams, the fastest-growing life insurance agency in the country. For six straight years, A.L. Williams had done nothing but shoot straight up. Digging deeper, they discovered a simple 100 percent "Buy Term and Invest the Difference" financial concept coupled with a part-time sales force fueled the company's success. Something clicked. The insurance industry, quite frankly, reminded Tsai and Woodside of the dying can business. Here, though, an aggressive young company had honed a sharp competitive edge. This unique system for marketing life insurance to consumers could possibly revolutionize the outdated whole life insurance industry.

"AMUSED AND AMAZED"

"As the new guy on the block, we specialize in making mincemeat out of all the big major life companies. Frankly I have been both amused and a little bit amazed at the life industry's reaction to A.L. Williams. I experienced the same thing as an old-line producer of cans when new companies, unburdened by old plants and investments and with no unions, competed with us."

– WILLIAM WOODSIDE, AMERICAN CAN CEO,

NATIONAL UNDERWRITER MAGAZINE, JULY 16, 1983

To Woodside and Tsai, the controversial side to A.L. Williams didn't matter one bit. This "everyman" upstart stood on the threshold of becoming the largest writer of life insurance and mutual funds in the country… maybe even the world.

Eager to reposition American Can as a leader in financial services, A.L. Williams looked like just the rising star the two men sought. They knew we needed lots of operating capital, but their pockets bulged. They could relieve Stanley and PennCorp of the financial burden we generated and open new doors of expansion for all of us.

PennCorp and American Can signed the merger agreement in September 1982. Almost immediately, they announced an extension of the A.L. Williams contract to the year 2000, overriding the 10-year contract Stanley and I signed the year before.

"The importance of this event cannot be underestimated," I told the sales force, pumping them up. "Our contract with American Can extends to 2000 – the next century. Our future is secure! They've given us the stability and financial strength to support our greatest sales efforts, and we're fixing to explode all across the country like you can't believe! Folks, if you are ready to 'be somebody,' now is the time. Don't get left on the sidelines. We're entering a *new era* at A.L. Williams."

True enough. We had officially "gone public." Now people knew us. Companies knew us. A.L. Williams was fast becoming a household name.

GUNSLINGER

At American Can, Gerry Tsai approved of our performance as a "large modern marketing force." Working from his quiet Manhattan office, he got busy building up the financial services side of Can's business. He spent $1 billion acquiring other financial services companies. First, Transport Life Insurance out of Fort Worth; then an investment management firm he renamed American Capital Research & Management. He purchased it as a way to add highly rated mutual funds to our list of "invest the difference" products. Only a few months into the job, Gerry's division produced 60 percent of American Can's operating earnings. He received a well-earned promotion to vice chairman.

Near retirement, Bill Woodside would soon recommend to the board of directors that Gerry Tsai succeed him as chairman and CEO – a good thing for A.L. Williams.

What a pair! Gerry Tsai, a sophisticated Wall Street player, and Art Williams, an old football coach from South Georgia. Our lives seemed as different as night and day… yet deep down we shared something. Both mavericks, we enjoyed taking on "the establishment."

Gerry grew up in Shanghai, raised by a father who worked for Ford Motor Company and a mother who was a born trader and speculator. Immigrating to America in 1947 at age 17, he earned a bachelor's and master's degree in economics from Boston University in just two years. In 1952, Boston's Fidelity Management & Research Company hired him as a stock analyst, and a few years later he convinced Fidelity founder Edward Crosby Johnson II to let him launch the new Fidelity Capital Fund.

Breaking firm tradition, Gerry turned it into an openly speculative public growth fund. Avoiding typical blue chips like U.S. Steel, he keyed on fringe stocks he calculated to be on the verge of explosive growth, companies like Polaroid and Xerox. He created a system for rapidly buying huge blocks of shares on the upswing, then just as quickly selling them off at the first sign of a market dip. His "gunslinger" trading style risked much… but it paid off big.

By the mid 1960s, Gerry personified the famous "go-go" trading style that would forever mark the decade. His knack for picking hot stocks, based on his own complex set of market indicators, inspired a long list of imitators and earned him a place in history as a Wall Street golden boy.

In 1965, he left Fidelity and Boston to create his own Manhattan Fund in New York. It officially opened February 15, 1966. Gerry, expecting to raise $50 million at the most, stunned Wall Street by receiving a record-setting $270 million. Two years later, at the top of the market, he sold his mutual fund company to C.N.A. Financial. He stayed on as executive in charge of acquisitions, retiring for good as a fund manager.

In 1973, he left C.N.A. to start his own brokerage firm, later acquiring National Benefit Life, a direct mail insurance company, and Associated Madison. This twisting road led him to American Can, PennCorp and then to A.L. Williams.

In the next few years, Gerry continued his makeover of American Can. He sold off its paper, packaging and manufacturing holdings. He eventually purchased prestigious Smith Barney at the height of the market in 1987, and renamed the entire company Primerica to better reflect its financial services focus.

Gerry Tsai, shrewd and brilliant, became one of the few on Wall Street to successfully transition from fund manager to boardroom executive. To his credit, he perceived the value of A.L. Williams and willingly bet his future on ours. Gerry, with all his experience and superstar status, contributed a major push into the big time for A.L. Williams.

COMMON SENSE

Momentum began to build following the release of the March Saturday Evening Post cover story and the merger. On the road constantly with Super Seminars and Fast Start Schools, Boe, Bob, Bobby and I saw energy and passion that simply blew us away. Everywhere, the sales force loved UltimaTerm. They loved the Post article. They loved the crusade. They sold and recruited through the roof.

In April, our A.L. Williams Corporation board of directors approved the first stock split (5 for 2). Bob Safford earned his promotion to National Sales Director. And Hubert Humphrey became the first agent to be paid $100,000 in one month.

"Gerry Tsai bought PennCorp to show the diversification of American Can. Gerry saw A.L. Williams as the biggest thing in PennCorp and he liked that. He didn't have any idea what we did, technically. He didn't know too much about the insurance industry. He had some people around him who did. His main thing was building up the stock. Gerry was some kind of smart – the smartest man I ever dealt with. You could get out of him what you wanted in a minute. I really liked him... But I knew from the beginning he was in it for the short-term."

– BOE ADAMS

In May, we held two landmark meetings: our first annual stockholders meeting in Atlanta, and our first trek to Las Vegas for the year's RVP convention.

At both meetings, I trumpeted our good news and rolled out our newest challenge: *Beat Prudential.*

"Every major financial company thinks they're going to control the market and be the first one-stop-shop for financial needs," I announced. "Sears bought Dean Witter, they think it's going to be them. Prudential is the world's largest life insurer, and now they have Bache. They think it's going to be them. Well, guess what? By the end of 1984, it's going to be us. We are absolutely on target to become the number one writer of individual life insurance and investments in the world. It's time to step up to the plate... and *beat Pru!*"

"Beat Pru!"

It became a steady drumbeat as we sped through a summer where amazing things seemed to happen every day. In June, we shattered another record, placing $2.01 billion life insurance in force by selling 19,116 policies with an average face amount of $105,000.

MILICO, now operating with 500 employees and spending $2.5 million a month administering A.L. Williams' business, moved into a much-needed 60,000 square-foot multi-million-dollar data center, thanks to the commitment and support of PennCorp and American Can. Our achievements ran on and on.

One idea from that incredible year gratified me in a special way.

Not long before, G. Scott Reynolds, the author of *The Mortality Merchants*, passed away. Scott, a strong supporter of A.L. Williams and a consumer advocate a little ahead of his time, had become a good friend. Written in 1968, his pro-term insurance book read like a breeze and our sales force had purchased thousands of copies over the years, opening it countless times with clients and prospects. We also used Norman Dacey's industry exposé, *What's Wrong With Your Life Insurance*, the most thorough book on whole life vs. term insurance ever written (although extremely technical and difficult to follow).

These books pointed out a glaring gap: Where did Middle America find a good book on financial planning? *Nowhere!* An up-to-date, consumer-oriented guide that explained how to buy the right kind of life insurance, invest money in an IRA, or plan for the future simply did not exist.

Back in my coaching days, I learned to keep a scratch pad by my bed because I'd often wake up in the middle of the night with ideas for new football plays. If I didn't write them down then, I would forget them by morning.

One fateful night in June that habit came in handy. I sat bolt upright in bed. "Art, you dummy! Why are you waiting for someone else to write on a book on financial concepts? We are the experts – why don't we write it?"

Suddenly my mind was crystal clear. I knew exactly what to do. Grabbing the scratch pad I started writing.

First off, this "book" needed to be a magazine. People will read a magazine before they'll read a book, I reasoned. Second, the language should be short, simple and to the point, so the reader can grasp the concepts fast. We should have a few graphs and pictures, but only simple ones. (People hate to look at charts they don't understand.) And last, the cover should be bright red, to catch readers' attention.

Next, I scribbled down all the chapter titles and a book title, "2 + 2 = 4: A Simple Plan For Financial Independence."

The 1985 cover, listing Art's 10 steps to financial freedom.

I could hardly sleep. Pure inspiration was scrawled on that scratch pad, I just *knew* it.

The next morning I tore off to the office. I called an emergency meeting with Boe, Bob, Bobby, Barbara King and a few others. I pulled up the grease board, scratched out "inspiration" in big letters and proceeded to share my midnight epiphany.

"We are onto something dadgum big here," I said, practically jumping up and down. "We *are* the experts. We can use this book to educate just about *anyone* on how to plan a financial future! This is the consumer guide that's missing in the marketplace right now.

Let's give Middle America one more reason to turn to A.L. Williams for the answers – because we've got 'em!"

Reaction? Half the group said, "Yeah, great idea." The other half thought it was stupid!

We put it into production that day. The boss is the boss, after all.

The biggest beef turned out to be the title – nobody liked the "2 + 2 = 4" idea, and I could see their point. A little clumsy. So we all thought and thought, and then one day it hit me: *common sense*.

A.L. Williams, the "common sense" company. Our financial principles? Plain "common sense." Nothing complicated about them. People just learn and apply them and they work, regardless of age, income or past financial experience. Perfect. *Common Sense: A Simple Plan For Financial Independence* became the name of the little red magazine that outlined a 10-step plan to achieve that goal.

Common Sense hit our second-annual trip to Boca Raton in August as bombshell #1. What a meeting! Normally closed for the off-season, Boca's resort management agreed to open up the place just for A.L. Williams. Some 1,500 turned-on ALW "term-ites" snatched up *Common Sense* copies at the convention, and sales took off from there. By year-end we'd sold more than 1 million copies. At Greater Atlanta Printing, our in-house printing company, Mitch Slayton could hardly run the presses fast enough. By 1985, we'd sold 6 million copies, translated it into Spanish and sold thousands of Spanish versions.

As time passed, demand for the book continued to accelerate. By 1988, we published 200,000 copies a month, with a grand total of 16 million copies in print throughout the United States, Puerto Rico and Canada. A phenomenon! Common Sense turned into the biggest seller on financial independence up to that time… all because of a little "night vision," a handy scratch pad and a willing staff.

EUROPE

We designed a little common sense into the year's incentive trip, too – back-to-back excursions. With Barbara's planning, our top 80 producers – our "giants" – first joined the other contest winners at Boca for a few luxurious days of fun and meetings. From there we spirited this group off to England and Scotland for 10 merry old days of five-star treatment.

It seemed we made news these days anywhere in the world – the BBC filmed one leg of our trip, on perfectly restored Pullman railroad cars, as we rolled through England on our way to Edinburgh. One of Queen Elizabeth's chefs came aboard to prepare our meals. The food? Fabulous. We truly ate like kings and queens on that glorious ride.

REACH FOR THE STARS

Oh yes, the good times rolled!

In August 1983, our A.L. Williams Corporation board of directors declared a "five-for-four" stock split, effective September 16. ALWC joined the 75 new stock issues less than three years old to make the first annual *OTC Review's* list of "Top 500 OTC Companies."

That same month, FANS' discount brokerage firm began to offer general investment services to the public. FANS clients could now buy or sell common and preferred stocks, options or bonds, and set up retirement accounts like IRAs and Keoghs, saving the high cost of investment advice. The discount brokerage, another important outlet for reaching families, operated as part of the A.L. Williams Corporation.

Also in that busy September, A.L. Williams received its first write-up in an industry trade magazine – The National Underwriter. Stock analyst and industry watchdog Thomas Meakin called and asked to spend an afternoon visiting our home office in Atlanta. He followed with an in-depth – and remarkably positive – article for that well-known publication. Some comments:

"Art Williams comes across as a combination of positive thinker W. Clement Stone, and fabled agency builder Charles E. Becker. Add to this a touch of Billy Graham and you have an approximate profile of Arthur L. Williams, Jr.

"Art Williams' sales force has been criticized for being 'inadequately trained,' unprofessional,' and 'incompetent.' Oh, really! This 'ragtag' sales force is now selling more than $2,000,000,000 (that's right, more than $2 billion) in new face amount term life insurance a month. Art Williams feels that they could be selling more than $4,000,000,000 (that's right, $4 billion) a month sometime next year. Sounds incredible but the average face amount per policy is now circa $125,000 and there are how many sales associates? (I've lost count!) It could happen.

"The industry's big gripe with A.L. Williams is not that record amounts of term insurance are being sold, but that whole life policies are replaced in the process. Well, let's not lose too much sleep over this contention. Superb senior analyst, Robert H. Branche of Shearson/American Express, and Frederick V. Hill of Moseley, Hallgarten, commented on this point. 'There's a lot of whole life out there that should be replaced. If companies refuse to rewrite those low return policies, they are fair game for Williams and the 'Universalists.' Amen."

Meakin's article ruffled the feathers of our critics – especially Joseph Belth, who accused us of soliciting Mr. Meakin to write the article and even paying his expenses. Nonsense, of course. Kevin King, our chief counsel, wrote a series of eloquent rebuttals to Belth's belly-aching. In one editorial, Kevin nailed him: "We wonder who Mr. Belth is concerned about – the whole life companies and his reprint customers… or the consumer?"

The hits just kept coming. In October, we broke our monthly sales record again, placing $3,722,138,600 billion of life insurance in force. *Un-dang-believable*! Just last July 1982, we'd set the record with $1 billion. Now, only a little over a year later, we were closing in on the $4 billion mark.

The booming business, as you can imagine, cut like a two-edged sword. Great for our sales force and for public relations, our volume absolutely overloaded operations, the processing side of our business.

For three years now, PennCorp executive Leslie Moss led MILICO… but that company needed a change. Les, a nice enough guy, nonetheless held to an old-insurance traditional management style. It didn't work with A.L. Williams, where nothing – nothing – was typical or traditional. Standard 9-5 working hours didn't mean a lot to us. Taking care of field support did, and if that meant working overtime, or sometimes even around the clock, then that's what had to happened. Nothing should slow down the sales force.

Les did not understand this. He kept a white-knuckled grip on MILICO's purse strings and waited for weeks to solve a problem. While we pumped $3 billion worth of business a month through MILICO's offices and begged for more employees, supplies, equipment and materials, Les drummed fingers in his office, waiting to see if our growth was "for real." Even approving new purchases and new hires had to pass through Les, causing the whole process to come to a grinding halt. Les just couldn't convince himself to spend money on us. His mentality kept an invisible wall between A.L. Williams and MILICO and shot tensions through the roof.

But things had changed for Les now. PennCorp had a boss all of a sudden. And American Can liked the way we did things. We wielded a lot more leverage than before. Treacy Beyer, one of PennCorp's top executives, since 1980 had shuttled between Santa Monica and Atlanta as Stanley's middle man. Ivy League educated and a Rhode Scholar, Treacy understood perfectly how vital it was to stay ahead of the growth curve and keep supplies flowing to the field.

For months, I'd wanted Les replaced with Treacy. *Now* the time had come to make my move. On one visit to Atlanta, I asked Treacy if he'd consider a role as MILICO's chief operating officer.

"It would mean relocating to Atlanta," I said, thinking this might be a sticking point. Treacy and his wife, Darcy, loved Santa Monica, where Darcy excelled as a successful real estate agent. To my utter delight, Treacy expressed enthusiasm for such a move. Trump card in my back pocket, I flew to Santa Monica. I expected a showdown.

In Stanley's luxurious office, I spelled it out. "Stanley, I'm telling you right now, Les Moss is an obstacle to progress, and he's got to go. I've come out here to tell you because you are my friend. You've done some wonderful things for our company, and I owe you that. But if you tell me you can't do anything about Les Moss, I'm on the airplane. It's sitting at the airport right now waiting for me and I'm headed for New York to tell Gerry Tsai."

Stanley folded his hands on the desk and frowned. "What do you want to do, Art?"

"I'd like to replace Les Moss," I said.

"With who?"

"Treacy Beyer."

Stanley frowned. "Treacy wouldn't leave California."

"Ask him."

Stanley buzzed Burt Borman into his office. Burt's amusing lack of people skills came in handy. When Stanley explained I wanted to replace Les Moss with Treacy Beyer, Burt went on a tirade.

"Art, you're crazy as hell if you think we're going to let you take over that home office. Do you think we're idiots? We run MILICO, not you. Stanley, you can't let any General Agent walk in and tell us how to run our business. This is a bad situation here. Bad! You can't let Art Williams give you non-negotiable demands. We'll end up with a complete loss of control. Is that what you want?" On and on he went.

"Listen, Burt," I said coolly. "My friendship with Stanley is the only reason I came out here. You sold this company to Gerry Tsai. I'm just paying you a courtesy call. If you won't make this decision, I'm getting in my airplane right now and flying to New York. I'll tell Gerry just what I've told all of you for three years – this guy is killing us down here."

I took a deep breath, angry. "So Burt, y'all can make a decision now. We can keep our relationship together, where you can keep running A.L. Williams from your standpoint. Or we'll just bypass your butt and go straight to New York. It's up to you. But you ought to know that I'm solving this problem today."

Burt slammed his fist down.

"Well, you can go to hell, Art. No way we're going to let you do this. I don't give a damn if you get on that airplane or not."

"Fine."

I got up and headed for the door. I had my hand on the handle when I heard Stanley say,

"Oh no, no, no, no, wait Art, come back here." That's when I knew it was going to happen.

Stanley called in Treacy, to ask if he'd move to Atlanta, trying to smooth the situation. Stanley and Burt fully expected him to say no, of course.

When Treacy said yes to the position and the move, Stanley expertly contained his shock.

Burt stormed out of the room.

Stanley, Treacy and I spent the rest of the afternoon working out details. By the end of 1983, Treacy was in place as head of MILICO… in Atlanta.

Darcy went house hunting.

With Treacy, we experienced a united home office for the first time ever. No longer two companies at odds, we were totally focused on serving the sales force. The invisible wall collapsed. Treacy understood the big picture – A.L. Williams was profitable, able to deliver, and hot as a firecracker. The more he helped us grow, the more money PennCorp would make. Treacy boned up in Boe's office, studying our needs and solving problems. When he wasn't busy there, he traveled, talking directly to field leaders, asking what they needed to succeed. His approach made all the difference in the world.

The change may not have happened without Stanley. He agreed to it over Burt's strong objections, knowing he released a corner of power to us. He also knew the decision was in our best interest – and his. American Can relied heavily on our success; it only made sense to give us what we needed.

Still, it took backbone on Stanley's part. I would be forever grateful.

A.L. WILLIAMS – 1983

- $23.7 billion face amount of insurance placed in force – #1 term company in the world

- Average policy size – $120,000

- Average monthly death benefit payout – $1.5 million

- $30 million in death benefits paid out 1980-1983
- 10,000 securities sales made each month
- $75,000,000 invested through mutual funds each month
- 80,000 licensed insurance representatives; licensing 5,000 new agents per month
- 8,000 securities licensed representatives; licensing 2,000 new reps per month
- 2,000 RVPs with 200 RVPs promoted monthly
- $1.4 million paid out in persistency bonuses
- 91 inductees into new "$100,000 Club" with Super Bowl rings
- 400,000+ clients

"I WANT PRU BAD"

As 1983 swept to a close, three more field leaders rose to National Sales Director: Mike Tuttle, Neal Askew and Kip Ridley. Our year-end numbers seemed pulled from blue sky.

I always told the field "the scoreboard tells the story." Our unique beliefs had sparked a revolution and driven us to the forefront of a staid old industry. Approaching our seventh birthday, we ranked as the number one producer of term insurance in the nation, breaking all previous production records. By the end of 1984, I hoped to become the number one producer of individual insurance *in the world*.

And so, the time had come.

After talking it up all year, we officially launched an all-out campaign to be National Champions… in insurance.

"Beat Pru" became our battle cry for 1984.

I tossed out hundreds of "I Want Pru Bad!" T-shirts to our leaders at the December 1983 RVP meeting at the Hyatt Regency in Atlanta. Like a drumbeat, "Beat Pru" echoed around that vast meeting hall.

I knew we could. Everything was in place for us to harness our ever-mounting momentum and put more insurance sales on the scoreboard than Prudential – the biggest of all insurance companies.

21 National Champs

Of course, nothing is easy.

By year-end 1983, as we got bigger and did more business, we tromped harder than ever on the toes of the traditional industry. Licensed now in 49 states (all states except New York, with a completely different regulatory system) A.L. Williams faced 49 insurance departments with 49 insurance commissioners. We dealt with 49 sets of rules, regulators, investigators and legislatures. All of them, in my opinion, worked with a bias toward the traditional insurance companies because, quite simply, the traditional insurance companies financed the system.

For seven years now, the industry had been unable to solve a growing problem – us. Our contrary concepts and beliefs and unrelenting sales had profound effects on state insurance departments. Sleepy clerical departments used to processing maybe 30 licensing applications in a month, now flooded over with 200, 300, even 500 apps a month.

The replacement issue snarled their bureaucracy, too. A typical insurance department used two or three investigators, who handled maybe five or six complaints a month. With A.L. Williams openly replacing thousands of whole life policies, state insurance departments suddenly held a fire hose – 300 or 400 complaints a month. No wonder the insurance departments hated us – we buried them with work and covered them with complaints. (From the industry, not the families we insured!)

The truth? No state insurance department ever welcomed us onto the scene. Not one. We never enjoyed a situation like, "Well, Arkansas thinks A.L. Williams is okay for families there, so Louisiana does, too. Come on in!" Never happened. I can't honestly point to one peaceful day in our business life when we didn't have some issue churning with state regulators. We entered a cold, hostile environment, and in all the years of A.L. Williams that never changed.

In a nutshell, we succeeded against all odds – state insurance commissioners all lined up with the powerful insurance companies out to protect their whole life financial pipeline. We exposed the ancient industry lies and replaced whole life policies with term. The industry, clinging to its own propaganda, called us crooks and fought back any way it could.

With insurance regulators on their side, the competition came at us in myriad back-door attacks. For example…

Tougher licensing requirements. In Georgia in 1967, I bought a temporary six-month insurance license for $10. I could sell life insurance for six months before taking my state licensing exam. Before long, the state eliminated temporary licenses altogether. Licensing fees increased 5-10 fold.

Mandatory education requirements. Continuing education requirements, almost non-existent in the early days, became mandatory and more elaborate as time went on. The industry wanted to make licensing part-time agents a lot tougher.

Replacement notification. Every state insurance department devised some kind of law that required a written policy comparison before a whole life policy could be replaced with a term policy. This requirement was not only ridiculous, but unconstitutional. Except for life insurance, no other business in the marketplace had to consult its competition before making a sale.

Early on in A.L. Williams, we battled at least 15 insurance departments over the validity of deposit term. As we moved away from that product toward UltimaTerm and other modified term products, the battles didn't slow down. They just changed focus, although replacement always stayed at the root of the resistance.

KANSAS

While small skirmishes over minor adjustments to minor regulations continued constantly, a couple of cases turned major. For example…

Fletcher Bell, the Kansas insurance commissioner, a tough industry old-timer, openly disliked us. Other state commissioners eyed him closely, hoping he would succeed where other states had failed. In 1981, Bell contacted us, concerned with the large number of temporary insurance licenses being issued through his department to our guys. He launched an investigation into our licensing procedures and, for good measure, initiated a formal review of all our advertising materials.

The investigation, with many twists and turns, dragged on for months. Kevin King, Barry Clause, and other A.L. Williams staffers made numerous trips to Topeka, working hard to resolve the issues. We hired outside lawyers to help. At one point, lawyers from St. Louis, Atlanta, Chicago, Los Angeles and Topeka worked on the case.

Finally, in 1982, the department issued a consent order, listing allegations of our wrongdoings, our agreement to improve in these areas and our agreement to pay a fine – $13,500.

After a year-long investigation, what did the Kansas department identify as "wrongdoings"? Mere semantics. A couple of our brochures failed to name MILICO as our underwriter. Another brochure stated it contained the entire FTC Report (hundreds of pages) when it really listed only a summary – a serious "misrepresentation," they complained.

That was it! I was livid. This investigation took no issue with our concepts or sales approach or what product best served families. The carp was over minor wording on a few brochures. A $13,500 fine for that?

Well, spit fire. My approach stood: *"We're not settling nothing. No fines* – ever." We'd never paid a fine before and we weren't about to start now.

I flew to Topeka to meet Fletcher Bell. A savvy politician, Bell welcomed me warmly. We sat down. I told him my personal story, explained our concepts and crusade. Took plenty of time, too. He seemed to listen. Then he started to talk.

"Art, I've enjoyed getting to know you," Bell said pleasantly. "But I'm tired of all this controversy. The department takes phone calls every day from people getting their business replaced by you. They're upset. We're upset. It's time to settle all this down."

He paused. Then, smiling, he said, "Art, I can tell you're a great guy. That's why I have no doubt in my mind – you'll want to join the life underwriters association. Let them meet you. Let's work this all out."

Whoa! This guy spent a year investigating A.L. Williams to put us out of business… and now he thought I'd just "play nice" and join the establishment? He didn't know me very well.

I looked him straight in the eye. "Mr. Bell, I will never join the life underwriters association. As far as I'm concerned, those people are the enemy. They screw the consumer with a ripoff product. I don't know what that means to you, but it means a lot to me. Our people are out correcting an injustice. As long as whole life agents sell cash value, we'll be after them. Don't expect this war to cool down, Mr. Bell. In fact, it's only going to get hotter."

In the end, however, we were forced to pay the $13,500 fine. Irritating? Yes. But I felt like I'd made my point with Kansas. A.L. Williams stood for the good of the American family. Not the industry. That would never change. And never again would we pay such a fine.

TEXAS

A year later, in 1983, another battle emerged. The Texas state legislature passed a law that no insurance company could license more than 350 new recruits a year. The bill was obviously aimed at A.L. Williams; no other company even came close to that number. As the bill sat on the Governor's desk, awaiting his signature, other types of insurance companies – property and casualty, accident and health – realized the bill would affect their businesses and protested the limitations. Under pressure, the Governor rejected the bill, the issue dropped.

As often happened, the industry's vain attempts to limit us limited them, as well!

RUMOR MILLS

Long after cases in North Carolina, Texas, Kansas and Mississippi settled in our favor, the bustling, buzzing "conspiracy" network of traditional agents and underwriter associations repeated their own twisted versions. Time and truth did not matter. For years, clients heard we were:

- a pyramid scheme

- a cult

- banned from doing business in Mississippi

- outlawed in Kansas

- outlawed in Texas

- outlawed in all 50 states

- a bunch of crooks

- going out of business in six months

Quotes from letters:

"The main problem is that the founder, A.L. Williams, is in jail for fraud."

- - - - - - -

"...I am also attaching a copy of an article from the Better Business Bureau of St. Louis concerning the questionable practices of A.L. Williams and Associates."

- - - - - - -

If anything got in print, like the consent order from Kansas, a million copies circulated through the network overnight. And stayed in circulation.

One strange incident involved a small Better Business Bureau located outside St. Louis. Its president issued an article vehemently advising people not to do business with A.L. Williams. For some reason, his article ended up in the hands of every whole life agent from coast to coast – and every whole life agent began to use it with clients.

I couldn't understand the article. Our agents did business in that area, sure. But why such hostility? The piece seemed to carry extra weight because of its Better Business Bureau affiliation.

Then the truth came out. The president of that little bureau? A whole life agent... doing his part to bring down A.L. Williams. He used his "title" to authoritatively issue a warning and broadcast it nationally.

Another Better Business Bureau in Chattanooga, Tennessee, did something similar. An ad in the local paper read, "Warning! Don't Do Business with A.L. Williams!" with a phone number to call for information. I dispatched local NSD Ronnie Barnes and a lawyer to their office. It took the threat of a lawsuit to stop the ad.

How disappointing! The Better Business Bureau advertised its reputation as a consumer protection organization "with a proven record of honesty and integrity." It reality, it represented little more than a group of "member" businesses trying to eliminate competition from non-members.

Boy, did that sound familiar.

DOUBLE WHAMMY

Regulatory attacks weren't the end of our distractions. We poked a stick in the other eye of the entrenched insurance industry by releasing *Common Sense*. Nothing (so far) compared to the maelstrom we provoked by printing that book.

The industry reacted so strongly for two big reasons. First, we put our philosophy in writing, spelling out the "three nevers" of buying life insurance:

1. *Never* buy any kind of cash value or whole life insurance, including universal life.

2. *Never* buy a life insurance policy that pays dividends.

3. *Never* buy life insurance as an investment.

Talk about fightin' words! Nobody had ever dared to put those words in black and white. Our 80,000 agents made 25,000-30,000 sales a month… and that little red magazine stayed with most of them, the perfect leave-behind piece. *Common Sense* was sweeping the country.

The industry's second big belly-ache – the page on policy comparisons. Shortly after we introduced UltimaTerm, I came up with an idea for a comparison flyer. On a piece of paper, I wrote down eight or nine of the most recognized policies from top traditional companies, like Prudential and New York Life. I included a couple of term products and listed their premiums side-by-side with UltimaTerm's.

That chart told the tale. If a client could buy our level UltimaTerm policy for just $5,400 spread over the 15-year life of the policy… and get $200,000 coverage… why in the world would anyone buy a whole life policy and spend $33,000 for the same coverage? Or worse yet, an endowment policy that cost $50,000?

I showed my hand-written policy comparison to Boe, Treacy Beyer, Kevin King and Steve Silverman, a PennCorp lawyer from Santa Monica.

"I want to use this," I said, as they ogled the numbers. "If we can get this chart to our families at the kitchen table, cash value will be practically indefensible."

Steve Silverman, a 15-year veteran of the insurance industry, spoke up. "This is brilliant. You're comparing the biggest policies from the biggest insurers in the world. Nobody has ever done this kind of premium comparison before."

I nodded. "Right. So how do we get it done?"

"First, we have to figure out how to equally compare the premiums," Steve said. "Some are level; others are not. The comparisons must meet regulatory guidelines. It will be tricky. All the traditional people will say it can't be done, of course."

"Good," I said. "Do it."

Over the next few weeks, Steve quietly assembled an independent team of consulting actuaries and regulatory lawyers – people who worked in the industry but weren't "owned" by it. Their great challenge would be to "level the playing field." Insurance companies configured every policy type differently, and every policy within a policy type had its own separate pricing schedules and rates. UltimaTerm, a 15-year modified term product, was a totally different animal than a whole life policy from Prudential or a universal life policy from Life of Virginia, or even a whole life policy from Northwestern Mutual. And all those policies varied from a Metropolitan endowment policy or a New York Life 20-Pay policy. Somehow the actuaries would have to come up with a credible way to equalize the price comparison.

COMMON SENSE COMMENTS FROM FIELD LEADERS

"We don't ask clients to read COMMON SENSE, we tell them to read it. Once they do, it's like an atom bomb going off in their heads. Sometimes we give a quiz on certain sections, like the magic of compound interest. I'm planning to distribute a thousand copies a month."

– RVP RAY ZINK, LYNCHWOOD, WA

"This book is unique in financial planning books. I'm getting the best response from the 'Start A Family Tradition' section. Some people get so excited reading COMMON SENSE that by the time we go back for the second app, the sale is already made. They

tell me after reading it they finally understand financial planning."

– RVP DOUG HARTMAN, ANAHEIM, CA

"This book is like having a machine gun in the days of cowboys and Indians. It's the best thing yet, the most incredible piece of sales literature ever."

– RVP MIKE DOYLE, SOUTH PORTLAND, MAINE

The UltraTerm brochure would name specific policies from specific insurers, so Steve also hired libel counsel from the New York Times. No one relished being sued for making false product statements.

The brochure turned into a huge undertaking, costing well into six figures. But Stanley and Steve strongly felt strongly the outcome would justify the outlay. Together, we were creating something new: *price competition*. Before A.L. Williams, nobody in the insurance industry competed on price.

We looked at many, many versions of the brochure, all scrutinized by dozens of actuaries, lawyers and executives. *Common Sense* hit the street about this time. We wanted the UltimaTerm comparison chart in the insurance section, but it still lacked final approval, so we ran a generic version – no policy names or insurers, just price comparisons – instead. That page alone triggered a fresh firestorm of controversy.

Finally, a couple of months later, we put in the finishing edits and approvals. The fourpage UltimaTerm brochure – one page of policy comparisons and three pages of footnotes – required a massive three-ring companion binder filled with actuarial calculations, statistics, analyses, corrections, approvals and attorney letters of opinion. We'd built a masterpiece of regulatory compliance.

We printed up thousands of glossy-paper copies and introduced the brochure at the next RVP meeting, explaining it fully.

"'This brochure is not a leave-behind piece like *Common Sense*,' I coached from the podium. "It is a teaching tool. Use it at the kitchen table. Point your client to the type of policy he owns. Show how much it's really costing him. Every policy on here is one the biggest sellers from the biggest companies out there, like Prudential, New York Life and Metropolitan.

Nothing like this brochure has ever been done before. You hold a piece of history in your hand!"

What powerful weapons! Armed with the UltimaTerm brochure, *Common Sense* and "Buy Term and Invest the Difference," the field charged… and every state insurance department went on high alert. If A.L. Williams hadn't given traditional agents enough to snipe about before, now we had something to make them scream hysterically. Suddenly, everywhere they looked, a customer carried a thin red magazine telling people not to buy "any kind of cash value or whole life insurance, including universal life." Or he waved a four-page product brochure comparing apples-to-apples costs on major policies.

The news horrified whole life. Devastated whole life. A.L. Williams had delivered a double whammy to the industry. Sales and recruiting soared in the field, and we hosed down the backlash fires in the home office.

UltimaTerm Beats Term Life, Universal Life & Whole Life!

15-year cost for life insurance – Male, Age 30
Death benefit – $200,000

Policy	Insurance Company	15-Year Average Annual Premium
1. UltimaTerm	MILICO	$363
2. 5-year Renewable & Convertible Term	State Farm	$473 (non-smoker) $633 (smoker)
3. Annual Renewable Term	Transamerica-Occidental	$508 (non-smoker) $792 (smoker)
4. Universal Life	Life of Virginia	$886 (non-smoker) $1,246 (smoker)
5. Whole Life	Northwestern Mutual	$1,706
6. Whole Life	Prudential	$2,183
7. Endowment at 65	Metropolitan	$3,368
8. 20-Pay Life	New York Life	$3,727

REGULATORS

Thousands of traditional agents and underwriter associations declared *Common Sense* pure evil and swamped 49 insurance departments with phone calls. They questioned every chart. They screamed for more footnotes. They demanded sources and proof that our numbers weren't cooked or exaggerated. War spilled into the open now, and conflicts over *Common Sense* would rage for the next seven years, prompting a few adjustments… and many reprintings.

The UltimaTerm brochure did little to calm this regulatory turmoil. It did create more job security for Steve Silverman and Kevin King, who on behalf of PennCorp and A.L. Williams respectively, eventually made the rounds to 35 state capitols, armed with that enormous three-ring binder of back-up material. Some local problem with an agent (or other issue) might prompt the visit, but in the end regulators always wanted to talk about the UltimaTerm brochure. Traditional insurance agents gave them so much heat about it, they had to know more.

A premature win in Texas helped us. Texas allowed pre-approval of insurance advertising material, which Steve and Kevin obtained early on from Texas's state commissioner. That "seal of approval" went a long way with other state insurance departments worried that our brochure was not appropriate to use in their state.

BEAT PRU? IMPOSSIBLE!

"Art took a bold leadership position with the "Beat Pru" campaign and I didn't agree with him at first. When I looked at our 1983 numbers it was a huge stretch to think we could double them in 1984 to beat Prudential. My logical mathematical mind said that can't happen.

"When I told Art he said, 'Bob, you don't know how to promote nothin'.' His attitude was, 'Balls to the wall, we're going to beat Prudential!' From the beginning his enthusiasm and belief got us all on board. We started challenging people to beat Prudential. It was huge."

– IN-HOUSE NSD BOB MILLER

In general, regulators loved to tell Steve and Kevin "you can't do this." Patting the binder, they happily responded, "We can and we did!" Some states threatened to bring proceedings against us over the brochure. None ever did. The piece was "bomb proof." Steve Silverman later grinned that the entire experience had been the "most fun" he'd ever had inside the law.

THE RACE

In the middle of this increasingly hostile environment, our "Beat Pru!" drumbeat grew deafening as 1984 got underway.

Prudential – the largest insurer on the planet. Our goal? Put more coverage – more individual face amount – in force in 1984 than them.

David calling out Goliath.

"Beat Pru!"

The idea bordered on outrageous… but why let that stop us? If we beat Prudential in 1984, great. If we didn't? So what. We'd have enough forward momentum to whip them in 1985. Call it a "shoot-for-the-stars-hit-the-moon" approach. Either outcome made us a winner.

Boe, Bob Miller and Bobby Buisson jumped on board. We went over-the-top aggressive, talking up the "Beat Pru" campaign at every meeting we held. "This season," we hammered, "we're playing for the National Championship!"

We had just declared war on a very large, very visible enemy. Our people picked up on it quick. Clever and creative, they passed out their own "I Want Pru Bad" T-shirts and flyers. They held meetings and contests, mobilizing their downlines and their downline's downlines. With Ultim Term and Common Sense to help them sell and recruit, we launched a January-April company contest rewarding the top 350 earners with a nine-day June incentive trip to Hawaii. It looked like gasoline poured on a bonfire.

In March 1984, I announced more incentives:

• A "Rockbusters" contest from May 15-October 15 would allow 625 producers to qualify for a 5-day trip to Boca in December.

• RVP meetings would now "regionalize" in three sets of meetings held in 18 cities across the country. RVPs, SVPs and NSDs had to attend one meeting in every series.

• A 10 percent commission increase on Mod-15 and UltimaTerm base products and a 10 percent cash flow increase on product sales would pay on first year premium and advances. (For RVPs, this equals an average override boost of $128 per sale.)

• Increase in renewals paid through six generations.

• Re-emphasis on building 7-10 RVPs and financial independence.

At the next regional RVP meeting, I wasted no time pumping up the field force. "Timing is so important in business, and everything has come together for A.L. Williams at just the right time," I said proudly. "Everything, and I mean everything, is in place for A.L. Williams to DOMINATE the largest industry in the world. The opportunities available right now are very rare and very, very special. It's critical we realize this kind of opportunity doesn't come around very often. For most people, it's only once in a lifetime.

What a shame it would be to look back 10 years from now and say, 'Oh, if only I'd realized.' Don't miss this chance to do something truly great with your life."

By the end of June, we'd written nearly as much business in six months as the entire year of 1983. Reaching the $17 billion premium amount at the halfway mark kept us hungry and hopeful. To beat Prudential, we had to produce at least $37 billion, which boiled down to putting another $20 billion on the scoreboard. Six months seemed like plenty of time... except that July and August were always notoriously slow and December a total write-off. It meant we had three good months – September, October and November – to produce the huge amount of business needed to beat Pru.

POLITICS

In June, Angela and I stepped off the rocket for a special event – a visit to the White House.

Back in 1980, A.L. Williams entered the world of politics, uniting behind Reagan's first bid for the presidency. After four years of Jimmy Carter, even a fellow Georgian like me knew nobody wanted to re-elect the guy. In my opinion, he'd been a sorry governor... and an even sorrier president.

Electing Reagan seemed to me of utmost importance. The more I learned about his political philosophy and what he wanted for the country, the more he became a candidate I could totally support.

Under my leadership, A.L. Williams mobilized first in Georgia and then across the country, campaigning heavily for Reagan, raising money for his campaign, rallying local voters to the polls. I know without a doubt our efforts helped move Reagan into office. Once there, Reagan didn't let us down. He cut taxes, changed the IRA contribution laws to benefit working families, got interest rates back under control, and, in general, gunned the country's economy back into motion.

In Reagan's first four years in office, A.L. Williams people expanded political involvement at the local, state and even national level. Now, we supported political action groups in every state. A.L. Williams agents worked wherever they lived to put people into office who could understand and support our cause – especially state insurance commissioners. In Georgia, we worked hard for the election of Republicans to the U.S. House of Representatives, including Newt Gingrich, who went on to become Speaker of the House.

Our grassroots efforts made us major players in the "Reagan Revolution." Our efforts did not go unnoticed.

President Reagan invited Angela and me to visit him in June. The power of his presence immediately struck us. He seemed to fill up the whole room as he stepped over to greet us with a smile and handshake. Our meeting was brief but memorable. He thanked us for being major personal donors to his campaign. He asked for an update on A.L. Williams. After a photo, we left. I told Angela later that the Reagan meeting reminded me of one with Coach Bear Bryant. Each man captured a room just by walking into it. Both exuded indescribable, inspiring, indomitable charisma.

FALL PUSH

Our incessant growth had us bursting at the seams. Already we needed more home office space.

We worked with Richard Bowers, the same guy who had helped us find the Northlake offices, and pinned down a tract of land in Duluth, a suburb 20 miles north of downtown Atlanta. While it would take several months to complete the office park, we could soon look forward to 150,000 square feet of badly needed office space compared to our now cramped quarters in Tucker.

Later that summer, I left for a month-long stay at a Pritikin health spa in Santa Monica. With all the marathon work hours, I'd put on some unwanted weight. Now at age 42, my father's death from a heart attack at 48 came to mind more often than I liked to admit. Time to find a place to crash for a while, lose the extra pounds and get my diet and exercise program back on track. Pritikin offered a great heart-conscious weight-loss program.

During that month away, I worked with Dona McConnell, our top writer at the home office, to finish a book about our company's leadership and people management principles. Like *Common Sense*, I set out to create a simple, easy-to-read guide that our agents would actually pick up and read. Unlike Common Sense, we came up with this book's title in one day: *Pushing Up People*.

Dona and I spent lots of hours on the phone, talking through the principles and faxing drafts back and forth. We came up with a slim, 180-page paperback that outlined 20 principles for mastering the art of "pushing up people" – teaching people how to succeed. A short, two- or three-page essay covered each principle, explaining exactly how to apply it, using examples from my years with Coach Taylor, football and A.L. Williams. A reader could pick it up and learn a principal in five minutes every day. When the book came out in October, that's exactly what people did.

THE 20 PRINCIPLES OF *Pushing Up People*

1. Everybody Wants to "Be Somebody"
2. Treat People "Good"
3. Build Personal Relationships
4. The Secret – Praise & Recognition
5. Spouses – The Forgotten Power
6. Freedom With Responsibility
7. Stand For Something
8. Total Commitment: First Step to Greatness
9. Become a Crusader
10. Develop a Positive Attitude
11. You Get What You Expect
12. Get Your Priorities Straight
13. Know Where You're Going
14. Don't Be Afraid to Fail
15. You've Got to Pay the Price

16. Do It First

17. Build With Quality

18. Always Move Ahead

19. Remember the Giving Principle

20. Never Give Up

I wanted *Pushing Up People* to really capture our core goodness, our "coach approach" to teaching people success. One example, generated from my early days with Coach Taylor: You can get more out of players if you focus on their strengths instead of their weaknesses. Coach Taylor was a master at praising and recognizing success – *any* success, no matter how small. He held county-wide track meets and gave away dozens of ribbons to kids, many just for participation. But, alongside the praise, Coach Taylor taught an unbelievable work ethic. If a kid wanted the big goodies, like a starting position or a college scholarship, he had to do a lot more than show up; he had to work his tail off. He had to perform. When he did, Coach Taylor's words of praise often meant more than any prize.

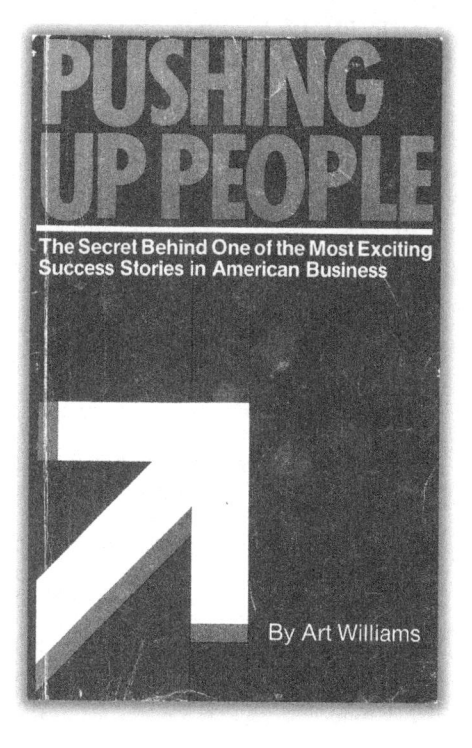

That simple philosophy of "treating people good" formed the foundation of A.L. Williams. I credit that philosophy as a main reason we'd become one of the fastest growing companies in American business. People flourished in our environment because we emphasized the positive instead of the negative. Our system rewarded people who built and promoted leaders. An RVP didn't become a $100,000 earner by personal production; he had to coach leaders under him to produce. He had to invest time and energy in teaching new Reps the right way to sell and recruit.

We offered folks the total opposite of the corporate approach, where bosses do whatever they can to keep employees "under the thumb." Instead of hoarding company success secrets, I taught them – over and over, at every meeting we held – and they went down the line from there.

If you wanted to be a big winner in A.L. Williams, it happened one way: teach and motivate your downlines to be big winners, too. You want more, you give more – the A.L. Williams way. Through that selfless style of leadership, we created a business empire.

So many books on leadership and management are just theory... and so complex that people don't take the time to read them. Not *Pushing Up People*. It became our company "bible." Every new recruit got a copy, usually as a gift from his upline. Every full-timer carried a copy in his or her briefcase. Though not meant for clients, copies ended up in their hands, too. People wanted to read it. The universal concepts applied to any leadership situation – coaching, teaching, parenting, Boy Scouts, Sunday School, business, you name it.

Pushing Up People captured the true spirit of leadership at A.L. Williams.

Pushing Up People, A.L. Williams' timeless classic is still widely read today.

COUNTDOWN

Summer burned into fall. The A.L. Williams sales force pushed production like never before. Competing agents, underwriters associations, regulators and state legislatures had done everything they could to hold us back – pass laws, bring lawsuits, write negative articles, spread lies. Nothing slowed us down. We had a "mad-on" with Prudential. We championed the cause of term insurance.

And, in spite of the hostility, it began to look like we just might take on the biggest giant in the land… and win. As the year waned and the numbers poured in, Boe and I gasped in amazement.

Historically, July and August, vacation months, show lower sales numbers. Not this year. September held strong. October surged – a whopping $4.15 billion in new business on the books, a new record over October 1983's spike of $3.7 billion.

Then came a staggering November… 211 RVP promotions, 12,000 new recruits, 41,871 life apps… and a new A.L. Williams agency record: ***$6 billion in production!***

Boe tallied our year-end numbers. He and I wore out a pencil, writing and re-writ-

	Recruits	RVP Promotions	Life Apps
July	6,747	134	28,615
August	11,076	134	31,575
September	9,277	126	29,601
October	9,955	183	38,378

ing. Finally, by the looks of it, we'd sold enough to put us into the industry's number one spot. (December numbers count on the next year's totals.)

We needed to be sure. I sent Richard Cain, a compliance department employee (and a former insurance department deputy – the same one who summoned me to Atlanta for "twisting" way back in 1970), downtown to the state insurance department to look up yearend numbers for all life insurance companies.

Final year-end production totals for insurance companies aren't officially released until March of the following year (when annual reports come out), but I knew the unofficial numbers on hand would be very close to a final number. Before we went to the December Boca RVP meeting with 1,200 fired-up termites and their spouses, I wanted to make sure we could truly celebrate.

I wanted to know if we were National Champions.

As a former insurance department deputy, Richard knew just where to find the numbers. He seemed a little reluctant at first... until I told him this was the least he could do after being so mean to us all those years. He grinned and brought back an answer.

The numbers told the story: MILICO, with the A.L. Williams agency, topped the life insurance industry for 1984 with $38.3 billion business in force! Prudential? A sort-of close number two with $34.1 billion. New York Life lagged a distant number three with $24.3 billion.

Victory! We won the National Championship!

A.L. WILLIAMS – 1984

Oh what fun! We swept into Boca on a cloud – 1,200 top producers and their spouses! For two joyous weeks, we feasted, we shouted, we gave out 6-foot trophies and door-sized plaques and a thousand other awards. Total celebration! We delivered inspiring speeches and dropped balloons from the ceiling. We were number one! Why not break out full football uniforms for all the NSDs, "suit up" and run out on stage for a pep rally? Many Partners dressed as cheerleaders and jumped up and down, cheering the number one team. What a moment! I will never forget seeing Virginia Carter decked out in a full set of pads, pulling that helmet over her hair-do, grinning ear to ear.

We all beamed. We'd won the biggest National Championship in the largest industry in the world!

We beat Prudential! We roared and cheered like kids again.

It's not all that often in life you really have something to celebrate. As a football coach, the time we beat Waycross stands out – one of those times we beat a team I thought would kill us. I'll carry that win to my grave, something I'm so proud of.

But this win? A different level completely. I'd been in the insurance business 17 years now. We'd climbed mountains. This win was monumental. Life-changing. Important to every person at A.L. Williams.

Until now, I think we'd held our collective breath and kept our heads down, afraid to quit working, hoping somehow this thing would fly. I'd always felt in my gut we would make it... but we faced so many crises, so many turning points.

This time, we had done something nobody could argue with, nobody could take away. Winning a National Championship? Truly a worthy celebration!

Those days at Boca seemed magical, a dream. We shared a real happiness, a profound sense of achievement. All together at a marvelous resort at Christmastime... and we'd just beaten the number-one team in our industry in the world. What a memory.

WINNING

That convention kicked us into the golden era of A.L. Williams. From Boca '84 on, our guys waved that championship banner over competing agents every day: "We are National Champs! *We* beat Prudential!"

The confidence of our people went through the roof. We all felt better. I talked differently. The sales force talked differently. Even Boe, the ultimate visionary, talked differently. We spoke with confidence before, but it always sounded like the voice of the little country team trying to come in and beat the big 5-A city team at the state championship.

This time, we had the bragging rights. We had proven ourselves big-time winners.

I could see a new chest-beating look in faces. "Hey, want to make fun of us? Come on. There's only one number one insurance company and it's not Prudential!"

What a message we sent to insurance commissioners, regulators, competitors: Reckon with us. We write huge amounts of business in every state. We pay death claims that replace shameful little $5,000 policies with life-saving $100,000 policies. We are credible. We'd beaten Goliath to prove it.

I think, bottom line, you need an enemy. You grow stronger and faster with an enemy than without one.

It's something you learn in coaching. Every Friday night, you line up kneecap to kneecap against someone in the "wrong-colored jersey." All week long you focus and prepare, then you go out, play by the rules, bust your butt and do everything you can to beat that "enemy." You breed a focused, winning-oriented mentality.

In 1984, we suited up to beat our "enemy." We worked our tails off all year long. When the game ended, our team tore down the goal posts.

National Champs! The celebration didn't end in Boca. It kicked off a seven-year winning streak... and nothing was ever the same for A.L. Williams and our people again.

1984 SCOREBOARD

1984 SCOREBOARD

A.L. WILLIAMS
$38.3
BILLION

PRUDENTIAL
$34.1
BILLION

INDIVIDUAL INSURANCE ISSUED!

PART VI - Golden Era

"Folks, we're only here for a flicker.

I look back and I still feel 16. Seems like just yesterday I was in grammar school, high school, college. I don't know why I am the way I am, but my butt's always burnin'. I want to amount to something. I want to make a difference with my life. When they get ready to click out my lights one last time, I want to look back and say, 'Art, you were okay. You did pretty good.'"

– ART WILLIAMS,

"THE A.L. WILLIAMS DREAM" VIDEO

22 Momentum

A.L.Williams stepped boldly into 1985 as the world's largest marketer of insurance. Not just term insurance – *all* individual life insurance put in force, topping some 2,000 life insurance companies. This agency success meant our public company, the A.L. Williams Corporation (ALWC), also thrived.

In January, I took Bill Keane, ALWC's CFO and executive vice president, and several other executives on a 13-city international tour to drum up interest – and funds – for our second public stock offering. We met with institutional investors and portfolio managers in London, Glasgow, Edinburgh, Boston, Minneapolis, New York, San Francisco, Dallas, Houston, Los Angeles, Atlanta and Little Rock. In every city, I happily passed out copies of *Pushing Up People*.

Stephens Inc., Bear Stearns and Robinson Humphrey-American Express managed this second offering, and it far exceeded our expectations. Seventy investment firms agreed to serve in the underwriting group, resulting in a sale of 3,162,500 shares (a million more than we planned) and $23.5 million in capital. Several European companies purchased shares, making A.L. Williams an "international" company.

The new capital would fund the future co-insurance of life insurance and annuities business from ALWC's subsidiary, A.L. Williams Life Insurance Company (ALWLIC). With our MILICO co-insurance agreement, ALWLIC now had a total of $10.4 billion of insurance in force at year-end 1984, up from $3.8 billion at year-end 1983 (an incredible 174 percent increase). Assets now totaled $106 million; nearly *double* total assets at year-end 1983.

First American National Securities (FANS), our broker/dealer, and ALWC's other subsidiary, also boomed, with a total of 10,500 securities licensed agents – making us one of the largest securities sales forces in the country.

Most impressive? Its growth in sales –154,000 in 1984 for an enormous 151 percent increase over 1983. FANS became the industry's number one seller of securities products for Pioneer Group, Fidelity Destiny and Oppenheimer and hit number four in American Capital sales. Its discount brokerage, completing its first full year of operation in 1984, also did well – impressive considering the NASD's stringent licensing and continuing education requirements for any agent with a securities license.

Feeding off agency growth, ALWC brought in $9.8 million in income. After-tax earnings per share increased from $0.37 to $0.46, with shareholders' equity totaling $49.5 million.

Not bad for just under four years of business.

ABLAZE

Late in February, I received a call from the office of Paula Hawkins, a United States Senator from Florida.

Paula was a first-term Republican Senator, elected in the Reagan landslide of 1980, very popular with Floridians. On the phone, her staff explained Paula had received so many letters from people praising *Common Sense* that she'd read it. By that time, *Common Sense* had sold close to 10 million copies, and A.L. Williams had become the largest producer of insurance in the world, making a national impact. Paula enjoyed reading *Common Sense* so much that she placed a public commendation of the book into the Congressional Record on February 20, 1985.

On March 5, Angela and I flew to Washington, D.C., and met Paula for lunch in the Senate dining room. She presented us with a copy of the Congressional Record with her commendation. Her remarks still fill me with pride.

Mrs. Hawkins. Mr. President, in 2 years it will be the 50th anniversary of the enactment of the laws that established our Social Security system which commenced in 1939. Today, we face serious questions about the system's operations and solvency.

…It is the goal of all Americans to be financially secure, particularly in their old age… Unfortunately, too many Americans rely on the Social Security program to provide their income in their retirement years.

…I want to commend the efforts [of] Arthur Lynch Williams, Jr., for helping all of us address these concerns…. in a simple, straightforward book entitled "Common Sense."

…[Mr. Williams] believes in consumer education and presents some simple guidelines on how each person can build… financial security using basic tools of financial planning…

…He reviews many strategies for achieving security, including individual retirement accounts, maximum life insurance at minimum premiums, mutual funds, money market funds, and tax-deferred annuities…

…I am glad to see enterprising people like Mr. Williams foster common sense attitudes and offer us the benefit of his thinking and experience to help all of us look to ourselves and not the Government for our future financial security.

Senator Hawkins' commendation galvanized our sales force. They talked it up everywhere. Our next printing of *Common Sense* included a copy of the Congressional Record on a back page.

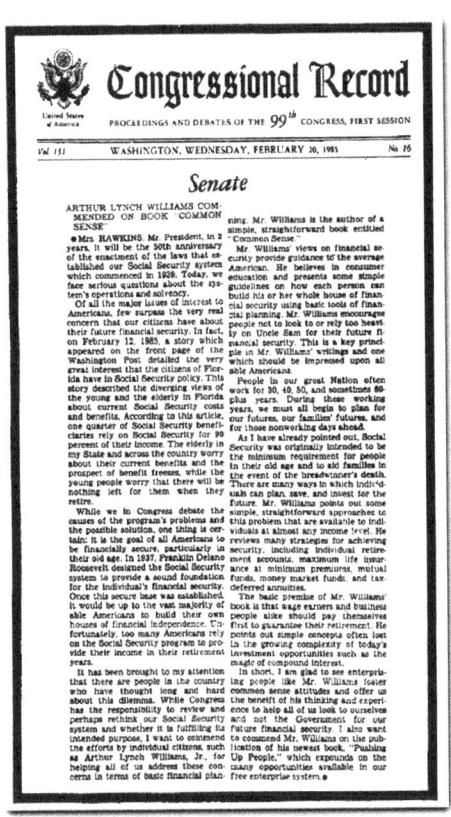

Copy of the *Congressional Record*

Of course, our competition didn't like this "endorsement" one bit. Once the Florida Association of Life Underwriters association got wind of it, they put the heat on Paula, chastising her bold stand and circulating a bulletin to its members that blazed, "Paula, Paula, how could you?" At the home office, we just shook our heads. Par for the course.

A couple of weeks later, insurance companies released their official 1984 financial statements, confirming our "National Championship" win.

We celebrated all over again – T-shirts, banners and buttons shouted our victory slogan: "We're Number One!" I had the publications department do up a big poster that said, "Great News! The Ball Game is Over!" and it listed the final numbers for A.L. Williams, Prudential and the other "Top 5" companies. We also created a "1984 National Champs" ad featuring a football player and the Congressional Record commendation and published it in newspapers all over the country.

Talk about dumping gas on a fire. Calling ourselves "National Champs" really stirred up our competitors. They didn't like it one bit. We heard it over and over from the losing teams: *"There is no such thing as a national championship in life insurance."* Well, there was now!

Every chance we got, we "talked up" being National Champs.

The entrenched industry handled it this way. In one article, some underwriter wrote, "Besides, we won anyway. We brought in three times the premium. A.L. Williams isn't even keeping score right." A very revealing comment. See, we measured our "National Champs" win on the policy face amount (and by now our average policy size topped $120,000). We measured the quantity of protection we put in place for the families we served.

Our competitors measured how much premium they'd written… or rather how much money they'd taken out of the pockets of consumers.

No matter. The sales force momentum of 1984 made us a giant locomotive that picked up steam in 1985. Faster and faster we went. By March month-end, we were on pace to outdo even our 1984 numbers.

Everything prospered, everywhere. From the ALW Distribution Center, my brother Don informed us that 415,500 copies of *Common Sense* went out in March – with 215,000 copies sold in the last week alone.

Then there was FANS – sales, licenses and new cash climbed by more than 50 percent in the first quarter. Could we see exponential growth?

As Boe put it, we had "broken the code" on production.

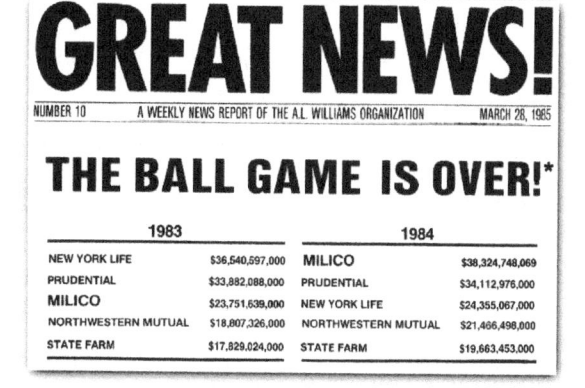

GREAT NEWS!

THE BALL GAME IS OVER!*

NUMBER 10   A WEEKLY NEWS REPORT OF THE A.L. WILLIAMS ORGANIZATION   MARCH 28, 1985

1983		1984	
NEW YORK LIFE	$36,540,597,000	MILICO	$38,324,748,069
PRUDENTIAL	$33,882,088,000	PRUDENTIAL	$34,112,976,000
MILICO	$23,751,639,000	NEW YORK LIFE	$24,355,067,000
NORTHWESTERN MUTUAL	$18,807,326,000	NORTHWESTERN MUTUAL	$21,466,498,000
STATE FARM	$17,829,024,000	STATE FARM	$19,663,453,000

GREAT NEWS!

A.L. Williams sales force and FANS

ACAPULCO

Mary Durham had worked at A.L. Williams for many years now (her husband, Ken Durham, traveled and trained the FANS sales force). Mary did not have any prior travel agency experience, but like so many of our A.L. Williams employees, she had an unbelievable work ethic, top-notch organizational skills and a passion for helping our sales force succeed. Barbara eased her into meeting planning in 1981, and together they planned the

227

first Boca meeting in 1982. In 1984, Mary stepped up to take the reins of our Meetings & Conventions department and in-house travel agency. She went on to plan hundreds of spectacular events for our people. Any time, for any company trip, meeting or convention, any size or format, Mary and her staff owned the details – from initial site inspection to the return flight.

(Just an aside. Mary, like Barbara and so many other staff members in every department, learned the fine art of flexibility. Part of my coaching style of leadership. I called a play. If it didn't work, I called another one – immediately. I'll never forget one RVP meeting. I had Mary book it in Atlanta for 300 people. Two days before the meeting, I upped the attendance to 3,000! I think she still has gray hair over that one. Our home office staff learned to expect instant change… and to roll with the punches. What a group.)

This year, I asked Mary to check out the Acapulco Princess. I had a reason. Back in 1970, the first contest I won with ITT Financial Services took Angela and me to the Acapulco Princess, along with 25 or 30 other couples. Pulling up in front of that magnificent resort made my eyes turn big as baseballs. The 15-story hotel, built to look like an Aztec pyramid, sat in a sea of lush tropical flowers, swans and flamingos, flowing fountains and Mayan artwork. The open-air lobby featured fountains of fire and water, and you could step through it to see the Pacific Ocean. A playground for millionaires and Hollywood movie stars, the Princess radiated romance and intrigue. One story held that Howard Hughes rented the penthouse for the last few months of his life.

Now, 15 years later, I would return to the Acapulco Princess… with my company. We would pack out the entire facility for three weeks – *with nearly 4,000 people!*

By now, A.L. Williams meetings had become an art form. In addition to free time, we scheduled general sessions, NSD workshops, FANS workshops, Partners sessions, and of course, the gala awards night. We'd grown so much that large hierarchies reserved ballrooms and did their own evenings of recognition.

In recent months we'd added an organization called Marriage & Family Resources, led by pastor Jim Powers, a personal friend and former Campus Crusade for Christ staff member. Jim offered optional workshops at our meetings with a wealth of materials on family and marriage. Helping our families succeed in these two areas of life mattered to me and Angela very much. We knew people struggled to keep life balanced. Jim's involvement offered a new way to reach out with support.

We'd added optional Sunday morning worship services, too. Initially conducted by qualified field leaders, the services included worship music and sermons. Eventually, they grew more sophisticated, featuring top musicians Babbie Mason and Michael Tate, and renowned speakers Chuck Colson, Beverly LaHaye, Jerry Falwell, Pat Robertson and Dennis Rainey. Many people told us their lives changed by attending a company worship service.

The Acapulco meetings let us celebrate in lavish style… but not without headaches. Language differences and health issues made for some comic moments… and some not so comic ones. Getting the hotel people to set up our audio/visual equipment or move boxes or do anything at all required fistfuls of cash. Trying to get our awards and T-shirts pushed through customs proved a tremendous hassle. Finally, we had to pay off the Mexican customs officials… and even then one-third of our boxes got stolen – hundreds of T-shirts, many prepared for specific award categories and winners.

Annoying? Sure. But we couldn't help laughing when a couple of days later we noticed locals walking around Acapulco wearing our A.L. Williams T-shirts… and observed street vendors selling some of our awards. All part of the drama and adventure that made being a part of A.L. Williams so much fun.

OPEN HOUSE

Shortly after our return from Mexico, Angela hosted her first-ever Partners Open House at our home. Her companywide invitation to Partners brought 500 spouses to see us, from hierarchies everywhere.

The Partners Open House turned out to be such a smash success that Angela made it an annual event. The tour grew to include the homes of other top local ALW leaders and some of our home office executives, as well.

Just like everything else in A.L. Williams, this whole concept caught on. Eventually, what started as a quiet day tour of our home in 1985, turned by 1989 into a three-day mini convention for 5,000 Partners at the Atlanta Civic Center. Our Partners enjoyed a great weekend getaway, which included motivation and education, as meetings and workshops filled the agenda.

As we knew well by this point, nobody motivates agents better than spouses.

OFF TO THE BALL

As hard as we worked, we celebrated. Those years deserved to be special – and we made sure of it.

We barely had time to catch our breath from Mexico before we tore off on another huge excursion – this time a 10-day incentive trip to Germany and Austria for the elite company producers, around 400 couples. Starting in Munich, we enjoyed three great days of sightseeing. From there, we boarded a train to Salzburg, Austria. The train had 20 cars, every one of them filled with our people. Angela and I boarded the last car, and we spent about 20 minutes talking with that group, getting to know them. As the train chugged through the Alps, we moved up to the next car. By the time we pulled into Salzburg hours later, we finished up our visit with the last group in the front car.

I suppose some people would call that "working," but Angela and I felt it was more like visiting family. The spectacular scenery outside the windows impressed, but not more than the conversations we enjoyed inside.

From Salzburg, we went on to Vienna where we toured castles, cathedrals, museums and art galleries. The food tasted wonderful and live music filled the air. Vienna is the music capital of the world, thanks to its adopted son, Mozart. Orchestras played in the plazas every evening; it made that beautiful city even more enchanting.

During our days in Vienna, we all took waltzing lessons, too – because we were going to a ball!

For our last evening in Vienna, we rented the Hofsburg Imperial Palace, a massive 700- year old castle once the winter home of Austrian royalty. The Hofsburg holds high revere in Vienna and rarely rents out to American companies. It was a real coup that we obtained permission to hold an event there. So, in honor of our A.L. Williams "Grand Ball" at this extraordinary historic venue, we asked our entire group to "dress accordingly" – black-tie tuxedos for the men and formal ball gowns for the ladies.

"Now won't it be interesting to see a bunch of old coaches and schoolteachers dressed up like that!" I chided the group early on. "I'm not sure some of us even know what a tux is!"

To take us from our hotel to the Hofsburg, in the center of Vienna, we arranged for the top 100 people to ride in horse-drawn carriages. Behind them, the remaining 700 people rode in sleek Mercedes limousines.

Angela and I sat in the first carriage. That line-up of 25 carriages and 100 limos seemed to stretch for miles. How thrilling to watch the couples step out, dressed like kings and queens, grinning from ear to ear, ready for the ball. Even those "old coaches" (like me) looked pretty dadgum good.

A.L. WILLIAMS SALES FORCE

	MARCH 1984	MARCH 1985	PERCENT INCREASE
Avg Face Amt	$122,000	$150,000	23 %
Recruits	6,854	17,138	150 %
Paid Business	$2.53 billion	$5.39 billion	113 %
Sales	30,351	47,059	54 %
RVP promotions	126	398	215 %

	Jan	Feb	March
Net cash	$10.6 million	$15.1 million	$23 million
Death claims	$109 million	$70 million	$115 million

FIRST AMERICAN NATIONAL SECURITIES (FANS) – 1985

	Jan	Feb	March
Sales	14,358	16,070	23,648
Total Licenses	10,543	11,263	11,808
New Cash	$26 million	$27.7 million	$42 million

As we looked over the group, everyone seemed to be in place and ready to go… except Nick and Becky Alise, the couple selected to ride in our carriage. Nick and Becky were "rising star" leaders in Bob and Jane Miller's Florida hierarchy. We'd rewarded their hard-earned success by asking them to ride in the first carriage with us.

Still, as we sat and waited for them, we wondered if they could tell time. Minutes ticked by. The horses began to stomp and fidget. Dresses rustled and a few people murmured they were getting too warm in the late afternoon sunshine.

More time passed. No Nick and Becky. A staff member ran to call their room from the lobby. No answer. Someone pounded on their door. No response.

Still more time passed. Baffled, we looked at each other. "They're going to make us late for the ball," I grumbled.

Then, suddenly, the hotel door burst open. Out flew Nick and Becky. Racing down the steps, they practically fell into the carriage, breathless and apologetic.

"What in the world were you doing?" I blurted to Nick. "You're holding up the whole train here!"

Becky's face turned blood red and Nick chuckled, "Art, you told us to treat this trip like a honeymoon and, well… *that's what we were doing!*"

Angela and I looked at each other… and burst out laughing. Poor Becky slid down in her seat, trying to hide in her gown. "Becky is embarrassed but I told her, oh don't worry about it. Art won't mind if we're late for *that* reason!" Nick grinned.

Angela and I roared even louder. We all doubled up and howled… all the way to the palace.

At the Hofsburg, we disembarked, carriage by carriage, car by car, and walked up a mountain of stairs to the grand ballroom. A vision I will never forget it – all our ladies in their beautiful gowns, on the arms of their handsome men, floating up that enormous ancient stairway.

The fairy tale was just beginning. Inside the ballroom, we sat down to a spectacular concert by the Vienna Boys Choir. Then a man dressed in formal attire and a white wig proceeded to the front of the room with a huge staff. Slowly – one, two, three times – he pounded the staff on the floor, announcing the first course of the meal. Six more times, he made such an appearance. Elegant waiters expertly swarmed over us after each announcement, bringing mouth-watering courses.

PRAYER

"Art prayed before that meal at the Hofsburg and I'll never forget it. I've heard him pray many times but that night it was long and deeply moving. He prayed about what a blessing our company was to our families and how thankful he was to God for so richly blessing it. It was so specific it seemed like he had prepared for it but I found out later that he had not. He was just sharing from the depths of his heart."

– IN-HOUSE SNSD BOB MILLER

When we could eat no more, the orchestra struck up a waltz. Angela and I stood to dance first. Now, I must admit, dancing is not really "my thing." But our dancing lessons paid off. Soon other couples joined us and we filled the floor. Waltz after waltz, we whirled and swirled, laughing and stepping in three-quarter time, enjoying the "spell" of that magical place and our moment in it.

Oh, what an unforgettable night of romance! Dreams really do come true. We stood on top of the world that special night in Vienna. The stars were ours for the taking.

THE A.L. WILLIAMS WAY

Eventually, the dream ended. After floating home from Austria, we all plunged headfirst into preparations for our upcoming convention in Las Vegas. I got to work with writer Dona McConnell, Barbara King and the entire publications staff to create a 300-page fundamentals manual for the sales force – *The A.L. Williams Way*. The book covered every aspect of building a successful business within A.L. Williams – our company philosophy, RVP responsibilities, recruiting, running a base shop, organizing meetings and events, field training, leadership attitudes, money management, people management and Partners. Each topic took just one page of text, making *The A.L. Williams Way* a concise, neatly organized manual of all the issues and philosophies every person in A.L. Williams, from new Representative up to National Sales Director, needed to know by heart.

We once covered the same information in the old days of Fast Start Schools. Back then, I devoted the first 45 minutes of every Friday night session just to talking about the "goodness" of A.L. Williams, and the value of "Buy Term and Invest the Difference." I always told new recruits, "You win with your heart, not your head. If money is why you are here tonight, if money is what excites you most about A.L. Williams, then you've already lost." Those first 45 minutes were all about capturing hearts. Read a rate card? Give a presentation? Any old person can learn to do that. But capturing the heart? *That's* the hard part.

In his last speech, Vince Lombardi held his audience breathless when he said, "The secret to success in business can be said in one word: 'heartpower.' Capture the heart, and you've captured the person. Get people to fall in love with your company."

That is why we started Fast Start Schools – to make people "fall in love" with A.L. Williams. That's why, early on, I spent hundreds of hours talking personally with leaders like Bobby Buisson, Bob Turley, Rusty Crossland, Virginia Carter, Frank Dineen and Bill Orender. I'd explain over and over that the difference between a $100,000 a year salesperson and a $5,000 a year salesperson is one thing – *the way he feels about what he does*. I wanted everyone in the company to feel good, in his heart, about us. That was "the spirit of A.L. Williams." Now, of course, growth pushed us to educate in different ways. Thus, *The A.L. Williams Way* – all the concepts and philosophies that made our company tick inside and out, in writing.

At our convention (the Aladdin Theater in Las Vegas in September), I planned to go through *The A.L. Williams Way* page by page, concept by concept. I envisioned reliving the exciting old Friday nights of Fast Start Schools.

CLOSE CALL

The night before the convention, Kevin King knocked on the door of my hotel suite. "Art, I've got something to tell you and I think you better sit down," he said. "We just got hit with a $500,000 verdict in Huntsville."

I felt my face flush red-hot. The case, very familiar to me, had been going on for weeks. Will Worthington, an RVP in Huntsville, Alabama, had scuffled with his office manager. In Will's version of the story, the office manager attacked him after a heated exchange, and Will defended himself. The fistfight ended quickly, and even though the office manager didn't seem hurt badly, Will, apologizing profusely, took him to the hospital emergency room. Believing their conflict could not be reconciled, Will relieved the office manager of his duties. The man then hired a lawyer and sued Will for wrongful termination. The case came to trial in Huntsville.

Kevin King describes what happened next:

"Being busy with many issues, I asked another lawyer in our legal department to hire a local lawyer to handle this lawsuit. The lawyer took the case, but the suit turned out to not be about wrongful termination. Wrongful firing is not a big deal unless it involves race, religion or gender. This case had none of those elements, so we weren't worried about it. But the local lawyer was unprepared for what happened.

"The plaintiff's lawyer decided to put the whole company on trial. Without warning, he brought out a poster-sized photograph of the office manager, taken the night of the fight, showing his face all bloody and bruised. The lawyer held up the picture to the jury and said, 'Look! These A.L. Williams people are part of an evil empire, a pyramid. They pound the stuffing out of their people if they don't do what they're told.'

"That picture stunned our lawyer. The office manager looked like he'd been beaten to a pulp. The jury awarded him a $500,000 settlement."

Kevin went on. "Art, the lawyer who represented Will didn't do a very good job, in my opinion. We should've known about this poster-sized picture ahead of time. What happened is the plaintiff's lawyer turned this case into an attack against A.L. Williams."

This news stopped me cold. The case was a real pickle, and here's why. If we paid the $500,000 without a challenge, it would set a legal precedent that A.L. Williams accepted the jury's judgment, that our company was a pyramid. That would open the floodgates to a thousand copycat lawsuits all over the country. For an anxious second, I saw the whole company going up in smoke.

"Kevin, you told me not to worry about going to Huntsville because this case wouldn't be a problem. *Half a million dollars!* Do you understand? *This could wreck A.L. Williams!*"

Kevin sagged in his chair, looking guilty for not personally handling the case.

During the conversation, people entered my room. Boe and Myrna Adams, Bob and Jane Miller, Bobby and Red Buisson and several staff members stood around listening, a little uncomfortable.

I called the group into a huddle. "We're not leaving this room until we come up with some way to resolve this situation," I stated flatly. "We don't have half a million dollars to pay this fine."

Boe, in his usual reassuring way, answered. "Art," he said, "don't worry about the money. The money really isn't the issue. We can figure out a way to pay this kind of fine. We're going to get sued from time to time, that's just business. But maybe we need to solve a bigger problem here and upgrade the legal department. Sounds like we didn't hire the right people to represent us and we got taken to the cleaners. Let's hire some better lawyers."

Kevin spoke up. "Art, I think we can appeal the case. The fine is outrageous and the opposing lawyer really inflamed the jury with his rhetoric. He was out of line. We just need to find a better lawyer to handle the case."

Kevin was right. Appealing the verdict – that was the way to go. Only slightly relieved, I broke up the meeting, and we all headed over to the Aladdin Theater.

Somehow we got through that convention. As usual we covered the world. In addition to rolling out *The A.L. Williams Way*, we introduced plans to launch our own in-house television studio. We announced our imminent expansion into Canada. We threw a great meeting in spite of this latest crisis… even though from time to time I felt like the world's greatest actor.

Back in Atlanta, I called a friend of mine, George T. Smith. My Sunday school teacher back in Cairo, George now sat on the Georgia state supreme court. He listened to my explanation of the lawsuit and the $500,000 verdict. "Art, there is something not right with this case," he said. "You need to appeal, and I know the best guy to handle it."

He contacted a lawyer friend who immediately agreed to take the case.

That week, Kevin hired an experienced trial attorney named Dick Young and put him to work on the Worthington case. Dick went to Montgomery, hired the lawyer George

233

recommended, and filed an appeal on the grounds of inflammatory rhetoric.

THE WILL WORTHINGTON CASE

"The danger of a half million dollar verdict was that the competition – Prudential, Met Life, whoever – would take that verdict and come into the consumer's home after we'd replaced the policy and say, 'You don't want to do business with this company. Look at what this court in Alabama ruled.' So, even though the issues weren't terribly important in this case, we just couldn't afford to lose it because of what the competition would do with it.

"Cases like this were all 'bet the company.' They were high-risk, high-profile litigations that challenged the very legality and methodology of the ALW business model. Therefore, if we lost the case, that meant a precedent now existed. Competing companies and agents then could use the case against us all over the country. Very high risk. Very important to win every case.

– DICK YOUNG,

ALW CHIEF TRIAL COUNSEL

We had a shot, on those grounds. In the first trial, the plaintiff's lawyer had told the jury in no uncertain terms that they needed to "stick it to that rich guy, Art Williams," stating seditiously that I was such a heartless individual I didn't care enough about the case to bother coming to little 'ole Huntsville to testify. He had twisted the case completely away from wrongful termination into a blunt solicitation for money from me.

Dick hired several more lawyers to prepare for the appeal. When the case appeared before the Alabama state supreme court, they came out blazing. The court reversed the verdict and threw the whole thing out. We didn't pay one penny.

	1979 Projection for 1985	Actual 1985 Numbers
RVPs	120	7,471
Division Managers	1,250	3,524
District Managers	2,500	9,965
Reps	50,000	93,960
# of Sales	250,000	366,151
Face Amount	$18,250,000,000	$39,650,569,337
Annual Premium	$87,500,000	$235,068,942
Advance Commission	$175,000,000	$178,342,371

To celebrate, I gave the lawyers a $100,000 "victory" bonus and Will Worthington a heavyweight championship boxing belt. That's how strongly I felt about winning that case.

Right after that, Kevin and Dick hired a crack team of trial lawyers, and we never got caught flat-footed again. Dick Young, a real stickler for pre-trial planning and strategy, contributed enormously to our legal team. Over the years, various parties sued us for millions and millions. We paid only one fine ($13,500 to the Kansas insurance department) and never lost a court case.

Not one.

$100 BILLION BREAKTHROUGH

Going into the final quarter of 1985, our entire home office staff busied for the move into our new A.L. Williams International Headquarters in Duluth. On September 7, 1985, we held groundbreaking ceremonies at the new location. In addition to expanded office quarters, a new 40,000 square-foot Data Center would now hold our massive records managements operation and company mailroom (with our own Zip Code). After eight years of growth, we'd found ourselves flung out over several office parks, in eight buildings. One campus, one modern, convenient facility, would improve our administrative efficiency.

Preparing for a sales force presentation in my spacious new office, I found an old projection sheet from our 1979 convention. I couldn't believe the numbers. Back then, we "thought big" but it was nothing compared to now.

It looked like another championship year.

Then came another record-breaking milestone: Between March 1980 and November 1985, the A.L. Williams sales force placed a smashing $100 billion of business in force. *$100 billion worth of new life insurance* put on the books! Only nine other companies in the history of the life insurance industry had ever accomplished this. Most companies never reach the $1 billion mark. We had produced 100 times that amount in just under six years – in the oldest, largest industry in America. We celebrated with a full-page ad in the *Wall Street Journal*.

Amazingly, we'd accomplished this feat (and won 850,000 policyholders) without the help of television advertisements, a national media campaign, or a fancy public relations firm. We just reached out to families across the kitchen table and showed them a better way to protect their lives.

GOING INTERNATIONAL

International opportunity now beckoned. We began to seriously investigate the possibility of expanding our business into Canada. Puerto Rico (thanks to the efforts of NSD José Rivera), and Guam (thanks to Hawaii-based NSD Ed Heil, who introduced the A.L. Williams opportunity there) and the U.S. Virgin Islands operations did well already. But those locations were all U.S. territories, not technically "international."

Many agents had Canadian friends or family members interested in A.L. Williams, and they wanted the chance to take our opportunity north of the border. With our growing momentum, it looked like the perfect time.

In 1984, Boe sent Dick Morgan to Toronto to meet with the province's insurance superintendent and investigate Ontario's current insurance climate. Dick, a veteran insurance man, took a good look at all ten Canadian provinces. He saw major potential.

"Boe asked me to investigate Canada," Dick recalls. "I visited the Ontario insurance department, got familiar with their operation. I explored the other provinces, too. When I came back, I told Boe the market looked right. The Canadian public was underinsured and under-employed. I saw no reason why A.L. Williams couldn't be successful there."

When Canadian politicians realized the size and scope of A.L. Williams, they got excited about getting our business into Canada. They could see we'd create a huge number of jobs and boost the economy. They promised to roll out the red carpet if we came.

Looking at Dick's research, Boe and I agreed with his assessment: expanding into Canada looked like a easy run into the end zone. Twenty-five million people lived in Canada, a huge market. The traditional insurance industry sold tons of cash value life insurance; Canadian families were vastly underinsured. "Buy Term and Invest the Difference" and our business opportunity would be attractive there. Canadians wanted better jobs… and more of them.

In the spring of '85, Boe and I assigned Dick the task of organizing the Canada roll-out. Our plan: Launch by fall.

As in the U.S., each province in Canada had its own insurance department. We opted to start operations in Ontario, the largest province, then move to other provinces.

The first hurdle would be to establish the Canadian equivalent of our A.L. Williams agency and complete the lengthy process of licensing products. Our product sales would be underwritten by Pennsylvania Life Insurance Company, a subsidiary of American Can already operating in Canada for 15 years. Our agents would obtain their individual licenses as the larger administrative processes neared completion.

Recruiting and hiring part-time insurance agents posed a small problem. According to our Canadian legal representatives, the provinces had no part-time agents and did not promote part-time employment. Still, no regulations on the books prohibited it. What great news! It looked as if we could do business in Canada much as we did in the U.S.

As the legal aspects of expansion into a foreign country gradually began to fall into place, we began to consider who could successfully take A.L. Williams "international" in the crucial months ahead.

To my thinking, we needed somebody up there who could be the Art Williams *and* the Boe Adams of Canada… and Dick Morgan fit the bill. A skilled administrator, Dick had 20 years in the life insurance industry, successfully running operations at National Home Life and MILICO. Boe moved Dick all over the company – underwriting, quality assurance, licensing, government relations, securities – and for good reason. Dick knew how to get the job done.

He understood sales, too. In fact, Dick shared my passion for "Buy Term and Invest the Difference" and helping families. He and his wife, Betty, lived out the ALW financial principles of buying term insurance, saving and investing for the future. Even better, Dick was a people person. He could "talk A.L. Williams" as good as anybody. In fact, he relished opportunities to talk about A.L. Williams.

Launching Canada would be Dick's legacy – his chance to open up a "virgin" country, to build a home office and a sales force from scratch. Boe and I knew Dick was "the guy" – that special kind of leader who could make this thing go.

Clearly, we had a ton of faith in the guy.

"Before I left," Dick recalls, "I asked Boe, 'What about money?' He handed me a check for $100,000. 'Just let me know when you need more,' he said. And off I went. That was the extent of our business plan. It was probably not the Harvard business school version of what to do, but oh was it fun."

Right before Thanksgiving, Dick and Betty Morgan, along with Glenn and Karen Williams, and several other home office workers moved to Toronto, found some office space in a warehouse and set up shop.

Glenn Williams, a couple of years out of college, started part-time in A.L. Williams, then joined the FANS inquiry department in 1983. Licensed to sell securities, Glenn worked as one of the original account executives in the discount brokerage arm of FANS. He'd been indispensable in starting that business from scratch. His strong securities background made Glenn a perfect match with Dick's insurance expertise.

When Dick and Glenn opened the office doors, people from the U.S. crowded up to cross the border. But, not just anyone could do business in Canada.

Maybe we all had a slight misconception. We assumed Canada, this big friendly vague area to the north, wouldn't really require us to treat it like a foreign country. *Wrong.*

Any U.S. citizen needed work visas and immigration approval to begin earning income in Canada. Those weren't always easy to get. After all, Canada had unemployed people; the government didn't like issuing visas so foreigners could come in and take jobs. In addition, we still lacked approval for some insurance products and our agency licensing. Bottom line, agents did not yet have authority to make sales.

Did that stop them from trying? Oh no. They'd drive up to the border, get rebuffed, go home, then try again in a few days. One guy tried three times to cross the border… with a mattress strapped to the top of his car!

Twenty-eight RVPs from various parts of the United States moved to Toronto, at least temporarily, to start organizations. Hubert Humphrey, our sales force's first million-dollar earner, led the pioneer charge. A master at "selling the dream," Hubert had already worked in Canada off and on for months. His 800 Canadian recruits waited in the wings for the final paperwork to clear to begin selling and recruiting.

In the final weeks of 1985, Dick Morgan met with Ontario's insurance department to finalize the deal.

Convinced now that A.L. Williams would create jobs for Canadians, not take them away, the immigration department began to approve work visas. As December gave way to January 1986, it seemed moving into Canada would be as easy as moving from Georgia into Florida. Any day now, we would be fully approved to start business.

Then, out of the blue, Ontario's superintendent of insurance hit us with a bombshell: The sale of insurance by part-time insurance agents was now prohibited. Insurance sales agents must be full-time in the business. And, they could not be simultaneously employed in another trade or profession.

The news knocked us sideways. Until now, every signal from Ontario government officials had been thumbs-up. We'd spent hundreds of thousands of dollars renting office space and putting our people in place. Dozens of A.L. Williams leaders had relocated on their own nickel. Some had already recruited new Canadian teams.

Now this. I shouldn't have been surprised. Once again, the traditional life insurance industry had "gotten to" the local politicians and regulators. Our same old battle. It just followed us to Canada.

As usual, the regulation took aim specifically at A.L. Williams. Competing companies, well aware of our U.S. reputation as a "replacement" company," put pressure on key Canadian authorities to slow us down in the most effective way they knew: Taking away our part-time option.

For a little while, we feared their line of attack might work. The change panicked many of our transplanted RVPs. Living on a shoestring, they'd patiently waited for the green light to release their teams and begin making sales. Now, not only did approval stay delayed… it would not allow recruitment of part-timers if it ever did release.

I understood their frustration. But we had no time to waste on frustration. Quickly, I flew to Toronto for a meeting with the Canadian staff and RVPs.

"Word has come down from the regulators that Ontario won't allow part-time agents. Now that's a tough lick," I started out. "But understand – we're pioneers opening up new territory. It's not supposed to be easy. Let me remind you. We haven't done all we've done in A.L. Williams by giving up or giving in. A.L. Williams is a company of destiny. We will find a way to make this work."

Right then and there, we figured out the part-time issue. Our strategy? Hire the nonworking spouse of a married couple as a full-time agent. That spouse would get licensed and start making sales. The working spouse would learn the business alongside the licensed spouse, go on appointments, attend Fast Start Schools, get licensed, too. We would basically recruit couples instead of just one spouse. Partnership at its finest! This approach to recruiting gave us a legitimate way to follow the regulations and still offer Canadian families the same great opportunity we offered our families in the States.

Game plan in place, we prepared to forge ahead. Midway through January, we got the okay from the Ontario insurance department to begin selling. Finally, after a year of planning and waiting, A.L. Williams opened for business in Canada!

The next six months in Canada? A roller coaster ride! Our Canadian and American teams rushed to recruit and build new organizations. The weather? Cold. The culture? Diverse. Some RVPs threw in the towel and came home, but many more stayed and made a success of this once-in-a-lifetime opportunity.

Dick Morgan tells a funny story about opening that first office. His wife, Betty, and Glenn Williams' wife, Karen, set up the licensing department. "One day, a man named David Francis walked in and said to them, 'I want to sign up,'" he shares. "They looked up and said, 'What?' This guy said, 'I know all about A.L. Williams and I want to sign up.' Filling out his app, Betty asked him to spell 'licensing' because Canadians spell it differently than Americans. David still laughs about joining an insurance company that didn't know how to spell licensing. An attorney, David ended up being one of our top leaders. What about that? Nobody even recruited him. He just volunteered!"

By the end of the year, we did business in all Canadian provinces, except French-speaking Quebec. That one took a bit longer, but not much – just a matter of getting all our materials translated into French and approved by the Quebec insurance department. People said it couldn't be done. We did it.

TRIAL & SUCCESS

From the beginning, we made the Canada operation "family," including the northern team in everything we did in the States. Our conventions, our Super Seminars with 20,000 people, our contests and fabulous incentive trips – it just blew their minds. They couldn't get enough! Total support and commitment from the U.S. helped them to answer the challenges and keep building.

And buddy, we saw challenges. Override problems and currency differences quickly surfaced. At first, Canadian officials didn't want to approve the release of override commissions to U.S. agents. Our lawyers got it ironed out. But the difference in the U.S. dollar versus the Canadian dollar created another problem. Commissions are based on percentage, not actual dollar amounts. A U.S. RVP, receiving the usual 20 percent override on a sale made by a Canadian downline agent, got a shock – his check came to only $80 instead of the expected $120. Commissions went up and down every day, too, based on the currency value.

Federal income tax? Another complication. Both the Canadian and the U.S. governments wanted our agents to pay income tax on overrides – double taxation! Our lawyers eventually worked that one out, too, though it meant everybody on both sides of the border had to be extra careful with record keeping.

In true A.L. Williams style, none of these obstacles slowed us down. Our people once again did what they do best – work the system. With the same pioneering zeal as our "original 85," they opened the eyes of Canadians to the wisdom of "Buy Term and Invest the Difference" and replaced thousands of whole life policies with term. The crusade, reborn, recruited thousands, built new teams, opened offices all over Canada.

One success story stood out. Randy Nelson, a Georgia RVP direct to Hubert Humphrey, exchanged business cards with a Canadian travel agent, Nasir Sidikki, on the Acapulco trip the previous summer. Nasir, intrigued by the A.L. Williams opportunity, made a special visit to the Atlanta home office to meet Hubert and Bobby Buisson. By January 1986, Nasir held the distinct honor of becoming Canada's first recruit… and the first there to buy an A.L. Williams insurance policy. Randy went on to build an outstanding, productive organization.

By the end of 1986, we'd put $665 million of paid business on the books – this by a tiny, 750-person sales force. By the end of 1987, that climbed to $1.9 billion in new business, out-writing top rival London Life… and making us the number one producer of life insurance in Canada after only two years of business. It took us six years in the United States, but only two in Canada. In spite of all the obstacles, we stood at the summit in a vast country… even without our bread-and-butter part-time opportunity.

LEADERSHIP

Nobody deserves more credit than the man we selected as Canada's fearless leader, Dick Morgan. He, along with Glenn Williams and some key personnel, created an atmosphere that mirrored our U.S. bedrock philosophy of "the salesperson is king."

At the Canadian "head office," staffers understood that their jobs depended on the success of the sales force. Dick lived it. He made it a goal to spend most of his time in the field, traveling from office to office, province to province, speaking at Fast Start Schools, meeting face to face with as many Canadian ALW agents (and their spouses) as possible.

Ever practical, Dick chose the slow month of January to visit all the province insurance departments. What "luck." In Canada in January, no other insurance company representatives cared (or dared) to travel. With insurance superintendents as his captive audience, Dick used that fish-in-a-barrel opportunity to build rapport and sell them on "Buy Term and Invest the Difference." It went so well he made it a habit to go every year in January. Regulators grew to count on his appearance – and look forward to it – in that cold, snowy month. Dick's friendliness, strong motivational abilities and years of government relations experience combined for a powerful, positive impact on the regulators.

"I would sit down with them and explain they had an under-insured population," Dick says. "I spelled out our 'Buy Term and Invest the Difference' philosophy. Regulators found it hard to argue against that philosophy. They realized that the insurance industry strongly opposed us, but they didn't take any non-political stands. Ultimately, they came to respect us and what we did for the consumer."

Leadership is everything. Dick likes to credit the A.L. Williams system for the success of Canada, but systems only work when the right people run them. A.L. Williams simply couldn't have picked a better person than Dick Morgan to be our leader in Canada.

CANADA – FACE AMOUNT ISSUED

1986	$665 million
1987	$1.9 billion
1988	$4 billion
1989	$5.5 billion

A.L. Williams – #1 Producer of Life Insurance second year in Canada

23 Common Sense

The December 2, 1985 issue of *Forbes* magazine listed the A.L. Williams Corporation as one of the top 100 new stock issues of the past 10 years. Their analysis of our public company included these interesting facts:

• *Forbes* ranked ALWC 23rd out of 1,920 companies brought public at more than $1 a share since 1975.

• The new issues were selected based on their performance against Standard & Poor's 500. ALWC outdid the index by 289 percent.

• Based on its initial offering price of $5 a share in 1982, a $100 investment in ALWC would return $813 by December 1985 – just three years after opening.

• ALWC – the only company in the top 83 to self-underwrite its initial offering.

The *Forbes* article came like a cherry on top of our sweetest year so far. As 1985 slipped into 1986 and year-end numbers began to come in, our success surpassed all expectations.

The momentum that swept us to victory in 1984 continued to surge all 12 months of 1985: A.L. Williams and MILICO had placed in force an incredible *$65.5 billion* of individual life insurance. Once again, we claimed the number one spot – the National Champions of the life insurance industry – *for the second consecutive year!* We smashed more records to do it. In December 1985 alone, we put $7.4 billion in new business on the books in one month, breaking our old November 1984 record of $6 billion.

The news didn't stop there. Our $65.5 billion production figures set an all-time industry record – no other insurance company had ever written so much new business in one year. We had beaten the number two and number three companies *combined*. Prudential finished the year with $29.9 billion and Northwestern Mutual with $23.1 billion. Together, their combined total – $53 billion – fell a full $12 billion under our total.

Just to make sure Prudential couldn't claim to be number one in any area, we totaled their productions in ordinary life, group life, credit life and industrial life – stuff we didn't even sell – and that figure added up to $63.6 billion. Even throwing in all that stuff, we still beat them.

Unbelievable!

It meant thrilling news for the public company and our shareholders. As holding company for two subsidiaries – the A.L. Williams Life Insurance Company (ALWLIC) and First American National Securities Inc. (FANS) – the A.L. Williams Corporation now ranked as a mature performer in the financial services industry. The coinsurance agreement Boe had so deftly devised with MILICO back in 1982 continued to reap results – ALWLIC now coinsured 35 percent of all new business written by MILICO. Consequently, ALWLIC's total face amount of insurance in force by year-end 1985 topped $19.8 billion – a figure that put ALWLIC in the top 4 percent of 2,000 insurance companies in total amount of individual insurance in force. Not bad for a five-year old!

The FANS side produced staggering results, too. By year-end 1985, our securities subsidiary had become the nation's third largest securities sales force, with 14,400 registered agents. Our motivated reps put an estimated $630 million of contributions under the mutual fund management of other firms, recording a 44 percent increase in total sales. FANS ranked number one in the sale of Pioneer Group; number two in the sale of American Capital funds.

ALWC earnings? Wow! Assets at the end of the year totaled $207.9 million, compared to $116.5 million at year-end 1984. Year-end shareholder equity nearly doubled – a 1985 total of $90.7 million, compared to $49.5 million at year-end 1984.

The glory came with a price. As always, growth kept demand high for more capital – we faced expenses for advance commissions to the sales force, plus maintaining legal reserves for all policies currently in force.

In the past, the A.L. Williams Corporation had met its capital requirements through the initial 1982 stock offering and our second offering in January 1985. Now we'd gone a step further and developed financial agreements with a consortium of banks. The banks agreed to buy a certain amount of "receivables" (a percentage of the advance commissions paid by MILICO to the sales force) in return for cash. This amounted to a $60 million-dollar line of credit, giving us the constant cash flow required to pay out millions of dollars each month in sales force commissions. Assembling the consortium (Banc Boston, Chase Manhattan Bank of New York, the First National Bank of Minneapolis, the First National Bank of Boston) Treacy Beyer displayed his brilliant ability to build strong relationships with some of the largest and most prestigious banking institutions in the country.

Their cash in hand, we turned our energies again to growing at the same blistering pace.

PRODUCT BOMBSHELL

January 1986 found Boe and I totally immersed in analyzing year-end numbers. Our jump from $38.3 billion new business in force in '84 to $65.5 billion in '85 represented a 51 percent growth increase. Our average policy face amount stood at a staggering $147,000, up from the '84 average of $125,000. Based on historical performance and the fact that our momentum remained in high gear, I saw no reason why we shouldn't set even higher goals for the agency.

"Let's come out and tell the sales force we're shooting for $90 billion on the books this year," I told Boe. "I think that's completely doable, don't you?"

"Absolutely," Boe agreed. "Especially with what what's on the table here. We've got a great year ahead."

For weeks now, Boe and I, along with input from Treacy, Bob and Bobby, and Bob Whitney, our chief actuary, and his staff, had been immersed in our own kind of Manhattan Project – developing an unprecedented new product.

I was so excited I could barely sleep at night. We had in the pipeline the biggest bombshell in the history of term life business – a 20-year level term product guaranteed to age 100. A *permanent term product with no extra first-year premium* – a 100 percent consumer-oriented product.

To understand the revolutionary impact this product would soon make on the marketplace requires a little background.

Truth be told, I'd dreamed of this since my days at ITT Financial.

INSPIRED INNOVATION

Through the years, we took aggressive steps to always lower the cost bar for consumers and raise the competition bar for our industry. Back in 1972, full-time with ITT, my sales team sold a decreasing term product – a good product that fit well with our "Theory of Decreasing Responsibility" philosophy. (That theory illustrates how the best plan for most consumers is to buy low-cost, high-coverage term in the early years of heavy financial responsibility while at the same time investing systematically in a solid, long-term savings program for retirement years.)

After switching to Waddell & Reed in 1973, we sold an even better product – Annual Renewable Term (ART). As you may remember, Waddell & Reed's ART product was the best term life program in the United States at the time – so competitive we just crushed the competition with it. ART's only drawback? Starvation. The average commission per ART sale averaged just $99, with $8 overrides. How could we work out there, training the field, for eight bucks? No way we could build a lasting sales force on that kind of income! Not enough hours in the day. Then came the switch to deposit term.

Averaged over 10 years, a deposit term policy cost about the same as an ART. The difference was its extra first-year premium. For the first time, agents collected an additional amount – $1,000 – to sell the policy. The product benefits were huge – the client earned back double his money, $2,000 for a $1,000 investment (a 7.2 percent tax-free return), at the end of 10 years. The product proved a tougher sell for the agent. Instead of collecting $20 a month for an ART, he had to convince the client to part with an extra $83 a month for the first year of the policy to cover the "deposit."

Still, selling it really wasn't that hard. You just explained to the family that the $1,000 was their "guarantee" to keep the policy the full 10 years. As a reward, they doubled their money back. When an agent sold it like that, a family never had a problem with deposit term.

The $1,000 deposit, remember, helped solve our early persistency problems. Good to keep policies on the books, good for commissions. (Instead of a $99 commission for an ART policy, the deposit term product delivered a $550 commission.) Deposit term proved a product we could build on.

Then Bill Adkins at Financial Assurance helped us develop a new "variable" deposit term product, based on a client's age.

EXAMPLE: A 25-year old client would pay a $250 deposit instead of $1,000; a 35-year old client would pay $500; and a 50-year old client would pay the full $1,000.

This improvement gave us a "friendlier" edge at the kitchen table. Later on, Bill and I developed a "Triple Dollar 12" deposit term product, a 12-year level term policy even more competitive than the 10-year. This great policy gave clients a triple return on their deposit – a $3,000 (9.6 percent tax-free) return on a $1,000 upfront investment. We continued to sell this product with National Home Life.

Then, with MILICO in 1981, we innovated again with the Modified 11-year product, a better product for the consumer, always our number one goal. Ferociously competitive at the kitchen table, too. And, maybe best of all, Mod-11 confused the competition.

While many insurance companies sold a 5-year term or a 10-year term, no one sold an 11- year product! Our competition couldn't figure out how to attack it. It usually took a ponderous company like Prudential about a year and a half to publish sales materials geared to compete with our products. By then we'd come out with something different...

...Like Mod-15, which we rolled out a couple years later. It was even more competitive than Mod-11. Then, in 1983, we introduced UltimaTerm, an updated version of Mod-15 – the most outstanding, attractive, competitive product we'd ever configured.

Until now.

For 12 years, I'd yearned to return to the "dream world" of ART, where we would never again charge that higher first-year cost.

Now, 1986, my dream was about to come true. We had our fingers on the trigger of a new permanent 20-year level term product, guaranteed to age 100. No "extra" first-year premium. Named "Common Sense Term," this dazzler would do it all – carry a family through those early years of having babies and paying a mortgage and, at the end of the 20-year term, give the family a choice to either renew for another 20 years... or let it go to decreasing term.

The elimination of the extra first-year premium made Common Sense Term the cheapest product in the marketplace sold by any sales force. The beautiful thing was that Boe, Bob Whitney and I had inversely structured rates based on face amount – the higher the face amount, the lower the rates. A family would benefit more from a face amount of $150,000, $200,000, or up; so we made it cheaper, per thousand, at the higher amounts.

Higher face amount gave the agent an incentive. To earn the same commission he earned selling a $120,000 Mod-15 UltimaTerm policy, for example, the agent now had to sell a $150,000 CST policy. The rates and incentives went hand in hand.

So. Here it was. At last, a better product for the family – at a lower cost – with incentives to the sales forces to do an even better job for the family.

The best part to me – the part that absolutely *thrilled me to pieces* – was finally eliminating of that extra first-year premium. CST absolutely stood out – our most perfect product since ART.

Now it really struck me. It was more than possible that all our sales force growth and momentum would look like child's play compared to what was ahead. How could other companies compete with what we were about to unleash? They just didn't have the system in place to distribute good term products... even if they had one to sell.

What a moment. Common Sense Term! I was so happy I was giddy.

MAJOR BOMBSHELLS

At a jam-packed SVP meeting in March 1986, I confirmed – with a big grin – our second consecutive National Championship win. The crowd went wild as I explained again how we'd beaten, no *pounded*, the number two and number three companies, Prudential and New York Life. Beaten both *combined*.

The place roared. I had better news than that though. "As great as that is, I'm about to tell you something that will blow these numbers out of the water," I shouted. "I'm so proud to announce this I can't stand it.

"We're about to roll out the most revolutionary product in the history of life insurance – a 20-year level term product to age 100 that eliminates the extra first-year annual premium. This new product has been a dream of mine for 12 years. It's so fantastic it will practically sell itself!"

Enthusiasm racing, Boe and I spent several hours explaining CST. When introduced, the new product would be available in three categories: smoker, non-smoker and, for the first time, preferred non-smoker. A 1985 in-house study had revealed that 70 percent of our clients didn't smoke. A non-smoker policy and now a preferred non-smoker policy gave us yet another advantage at the kitchen table. Some families might see up to $100,000 more in coverage for the same price as a smoker policy, depending on age.

Timing our rollout remained an issue. CST was currently being reviewed and approved by 49 state regulators. On track for nation-wide release by October 1, Boe and I had made an unprecedented but "common sense" decision. We would roll out CST state by state, with some states likely to be approved as early as June.

The staggered introduction would create a slowdown in sales among agents in unapproved states, so we offered an "exchange privilege" to families who bought an ALW/MILICO policy within six months of CST approval in their state. They could pay a small fee and convert their policy to the less expensive Common Sense Term.

"To my knowledge, this is the first time any company in the entire life insurance industry has offered this privilege to its clients," I told the SVPs. "The competition will never know what hit 'em!"

I dropped one more bombshell: A major reduction in NSD promotion guidelines. Currently, we had 26 ALW leaders in the top field position of National Sales Director, including in-house NSDs Bob Miller and Bobby Buisson. We named just two NSDs in 1985 (Dennis Schechter in New Jersey and Lafayette Walker in California), and two more in 1986 (Monty Holm in Nevada and Gary Payne in Colorado). Time to ratchet up the competition.

"The day that A.L. Williams recruits one person whose opportunity is not better than it was for me or anyone else is the day this company begins to die," I told the SVPs. "We've put your future in your hands with these new guidelines. It doesn't depend on anybody else. In the past, a promotion took months. If you want to go out there and blow and go now, you can earn one in half the time. CST will electrify your business!

"This company is going past big-time! We need more great leaders at the top. I predict 30 new NSDs this year. Who's it gonna be? You?"

Once again the place erupted.

We had one more change – a streamlined "Pathway to RVP" to make promotions from Representative to RVP easier. We wanted movement at all promotion levels during the CST rollout. It would speed our massive forward momentum. It would also lock in, or improve, our persistency. We were setting out to write $90 billion worth of new business this year. Why not make it the highest quality possible? We wanted every member of the field force to be in total business-building mode. Our goal, as always: Reward the builder.

Already a blowout, we had one more good-news bomb to drop on our SVP meeting. It was almost as amazing as Common Sense Term. Soon, we would launch our own in-house satellite television network, ALW-TV.

ALW-TV

Our sales force now numbered close to 140,000. Our Canada expansion presented vast new amounts of real estate to cover. Communications, a constant need, poured out of the home office every week. Mostly paper, fax or phone messages, this river of information concerned me.

From my earliest days of building a sales force, I knew how vital it was to see people personally and to speak to them personally on a regular basis. Sometimes, we could. Regular meetings and conventions kept our leaders and their organizations connected to an extent. Since 1980, Barbara King, head of communications, had improvised many ways to keep the sales force "in the know."

WEEKLY BLUE BAGS. Twice a week, printed materials on company meetings, contest updates, compliance changes, production information and other changes went out to RVP offices, along with paychecks, in an oversized blue nylon postage-paid envelope – the "blue bag." The blue bag served as our company's "pony express;" the RVPs returned it full of licensing apps, life insurance apps, and paperwork.

PUBLICATIONS. Our publications department pumped out tons (literally) of sales materials – flyers, brochures, posters, booklets, flip charts, etc., to the sales force.

TAPE OF THE MONTH. Our audio "Tape of the Month" series addressed field issues. RVPs listened to the recordings in their cars, driving to and from work or appointments. They passed them on to new recruits or other downlines.

ANNUAL INCENTIVE TRIPS AND CONVENTIONS. Incentive trips brought together contest winners for unforgettable meetings at unforgettable locations. We celebrated our greatest achievements and goals here.

REGIONAL SUPER SEMINARS. Regional "Super Seminars" in cities all over the U.S. and now Canada featured top ALW leaders in large venues, typically to 10,000 – 15,000 people. A great forum for mass communication and training.

LOCAL MEETINGS. ALW leaders sponsored their own regional meetings all over the country. Occasionally, they trekked to Atlanta for meetings.

All these vehicles moved the ball, motivated the team. Still, I believed in being with people in person. It absolutely offered the best way to communicate the "A.L. Williams Way" of building a business, more valuable than any other form of communication.

Yet, not even flying to meetings in my own airplane could add more hours to a day. At a point, it became no longer possible to get everywhere and see everyone. An average of 10,000 new recruits flooded in each month. We licensed 5,000 new agents and promoted 175 RVPs every month. We needed a new way to mass communicate. We needed it fast.

Barbara checked into video conferencing, the vogue technology at the time. Basically, it came down to just two-way TV, allowing people at two locations to see and hear each other simultaneously. Research revealed the expense of set-up wouldn't justify it.

Then something new came to our attention: satellite television.

Interestingly enough, the information came from our own company "family." Gerry Tsai, recently promoted CEO of American Can, had purchased Satellite Conference Network, a company that created satellite television networks for businesses. Reza Jafari, an Iranian entrepreneur who established the Tehran national television network a few years before, headed up the business.

It was hot. Companies like General Motors and Home Depot wanted the technology for the same reasons we did. A television studio with a satellite dish that linked to a satellite could beam hours of programming into any A.L. Williams office in North America. We could create and transmit hours of programming... and "personally" visit each RVP office every day! *Unbelievable.* Satellite TV looked like a winner.

On November 15, 1985, we signed a contract with Satellite Conference Network. It began the $5 million process of creating "ALW-TV"... and the Common Sense Network.

GETTING READY

Barbara worked with Reza and his staff to put many tasks in motion. First off, we needed a television studio. Smack in the middle of moving to our new Duluth headquarters, we had the luck of good timing once again. We jumped on an empty 10,000 square-foot building on campus and transformed it into a full-blown television station, complete with a soundproof studio large enough to hold a stage and audience, control room, recording booth, cameras and equipment, offices and storage.

We contracted with Scientific-Atlanta to build a satellite dish outside the studio. The gigantic, unwieldy contraption had to be built at their facility, then assembled piece by piece at A.L. Williams. While this went on, Barbara began signing up qualified RVPs for satellite dish installations at their offices. As always, competition drove reward incentives: RVPs had to show a $40,000 annual cash flow (or a $75,000 annual cash flow for two "clustering" RVPs). Every RVP bought his own equipment and paid the monthly service charge. By January 1986, 350 dishes fixed their faces on our satellite – dishes all across the country, with another 200 in the works. A.L. Williams and the television communications age surged ever closer.

Next, staff decisions. For several years, we'd worked off and on with a Chicago consulting firm on promotional videos for the sales force. The videos were well produced and useful... but costly. Now, with our own studio, we needed no outside vendors... just a high-quality staff inside. A staff able to turn projects on a dime.

With my blessing, Barbara put Yvonne Tyson in charge of the television studio. Hired in 1982 as a still photographer for the publications department, Yvonne moved into video production as the years went by. Like Dick Morgan in Canada, Yvonne made every position her life's passion.

This one, too. She immediately began hiring camera operators, producers, scriptwriters, directors and technicians. Our plan to launch with five hours of programming a day, five days a week, demanded thousands of decisions.

We set the primary purpose of ALW-TV as a tool to train, educate and motivate our sales force. We'd program this powerful new medium with an ambitious line-up: breaking news (or "emergency meetings," as I called them), insurance product training, FANS and securities training, company and compliance updates, agent profiles, production rankings and contest updates. But our centerpiece would be the "Monday Morning Managers Meetings," a two-hour program, every Monday at noon, focused entirely on the fundamentals of building a successful A.L. Williams business.

We scheduled our first broadcast for Monday, April 28, 1986. Exactly one week before, on Monday, April 21, I called a press conference at the Waldorf-Astoria in New York City and announced to the world that A.L. Williams would launch "ALW-TV, the Common Sense Network, the largest privately-owned satellite television network in the world."

The glamorous hotel setting equaled the scale of the announcement. Other big companies – Coca-Cola, Ford, Wal-Mart, Home Depot – used satellite networks. But the sheer audacious size of our operation set us on a higher plane.

By our first broadcast, 500 offices would link to the network. Another 500 would come online in 1987. Many *towns* didn't have that kind of network, never mind other businesses.

And that was just the beginning. The system could hold unlimited satellites.

Just as our "Buy Term and Invest the Difference" concept had cattle-prodded a sluggish, sullen industry back to life, our television innovation now upped the ante on how a company could educate, inform and motivate a vibrant, growing sales force. Again, insurance saw progress on a huge, historical scale… and A.L. Williams led the way.

LIGHTS, CAMERA, ACTION

A beehive of activity surrounded final preparation of the TV studio. Inside, carpenters and technicians worked around the clock, finishing the on-camera stage areas and nearby control room. Outside, Scientific-Atlanta engineers completed the colossal satellite dish that would beam our programming into outer space. All over North America, RVP offices tuned and tinkered with their satellite dishes to get them properly installed and working.

At the home office, Boe and I and the TV crew made preparations for the two-hour premiere of the "Monday Morning Managers Meeting." We did a couple of trial runs in front of the cameras. A good thing, too – I felt so happy I wanted to jump up and down… In fact, I did. Several times.

Finally, Monday came. As the time drew near 12 noon, I took my place in front of a freshly-built podium, completed just hours before. Studio ready, cameramen in place, the director stood close by, listening to his headset.

"Stand by cameras…" he said. "Stand by audio. Stand by talent. Stand by mics. Stand by Art…"

I was so pumped up, I could've turned a handspring. Just offstage, I could see Angela and Boe, both beaming, thrilled too. Bob Miller and Bobby Buisson sat in the audience, grinning. The entire studio crackled with energy and anticipation.

The director started the countdown. "Ten seconds to live. Nine. Eight. Seven…" I re-stacked my notes. The cameramen stared into their viewers.

"Three…"

Silent now, he held up two fingers… then one… then pointed at me. My cue. I was on! The first-ever program for the ALW-TV Common Sense Network suddenly beamed on air to 500 offices and thousands of our people…

LIVE!

"I'm not a movie star, folks, I'm just a dadgum coach!" I said, grinning, as the audience clapped and cheered. "Welcome to the world's largest privately owned satellite television network! This is one of the greatest days in the history of A.L. Williams – and it's all for you!"

I took off from there. I explained the story of how ALW-TV came into being, crediting tremendous efforts by Barbara, Yvonne and the staff. I moved on to contest updates for the upcoming summer trips to Boca and Hawaii. I gave other news. Standing in front of those cameras seemed like the most natural thing in the world. I talked A.L. Williams for an hour straight.

Next, Boe came up and updated the roll-out on Common Sense Term. Top producers Hubert Humphrey, Neal Askew and Ronnie Barnes each took a turn at the podium, sharing their tips for winning big. I clapped Bob Safford on the back for claiming his spot as the third A.L. Williams leader to cash flow $1 million in 12 months.

A second hour flew by. Too fast. It all seemed a blur when I closed out the show saying, "Remember this, folks. The Common Sense Network isn't going to win for you. All the programs we offer won't make you financially independent. YOU are the key to winning. YOU are the key to becoming financially independent. The purpose of this network is not to glamorize A.L. Williams, but to teach, train and motivate you to win big for your family. See you next week!"

Poof! Like that.... we went off the air.

What a blast! That show started something truly life changing for the sales force, our leaders and for me. The "Monday Morning Managers Meeting" became a Monday morning tradition, for years to come.

Additional programming filled our airwaves, too.

Ken Durham's "Securities Spectrum," a one hour program for our securities licensed agents, offered invaluable advice on how to sell FANS' recommended list of mutual funds. Angela's monthly "Partners Perspective" addressed the many roles of Partners. These shows, and others, streamed our top-producing agents and their spouses into the studio for live or pre-taped segments. We had great, personable talent in the sales force and we regularly featured speaker favorites like Bob Miller, Bobby Buisson and others on ALW-TV, sharing "secrets" on recruiting, team building, and every other business topic. RVPs with satellite dishes taped these shows and used them again and again for meetings and training. Our broadcasting proved a marvelous resource… and as the weeks went by, we got better and better at using it.

TERM-ITES GATHER FOR HISTORY-MAKING PREMIERE

On Monday, April 28, 1986, thousands of A.L.Williams term-ites gathered in front of their TVs to see history in the making. Art's "Monday Morning Managers Meeting" got rave reviews, as did the rest of the premieres. Here's what some top SVPs say about the new Common Sense Network:

Steve Sharpe – *"They worked on our satellite dish until 2 a.m. Sunday night, but it was up and working for Art's first managers meeting. The show really renewed the crusading feeling. It put us back in touch with the things that have made A.L. Williams great. What the TV is doing for the crusade and the downline guys will be phenomenal!"*

Jon Lavin – *"For our people to be able to plug in every day for this kind of motivation will send our organization into orbit! We've been resold the dream. Our team feels like they are part of something great!"*

Jim Minor – *"We crammed 300 people into a room for the premiere. It was hot and uncomfortable…and totally worth it! Our people are more excited than ever!"*

– THE ALW CHRONICLE, MAY 1986

One example: Not long into my ALW-TV "career," my daughter April came to work at the studio, learning TV production from the ground up. A few months later, she took the dubious honor of cutting her directorial teeth on my show.

I thought things were working out great. But it didn't take April long to notice that two hours seemed like an eternity for people watching. By 1 o'clock, most squirmed in their seats. Me? I didn't notice; I could talk shop for *hours*.

One day, April came to my office. "Daddy, two hours is too long," she said. "You are wearing these people's butts out. You need to cut the Monday show down to an hour." She said it with such certainty that I agreed without a single "but."

After that, the Monday show ran smoother, faster. Easier to keep the energy high with one hour instead of two, I often saved "bombshell" announcements for the last few minutes, building anticipation to the end with teasers on how "the best was still to come."

Our initial idea of 25 hours of original programming proved too exhausting and too ambitious. Nobody in the field had time to watch that much TV anyway.

In the end, Yvonne and crew put together a more manageable schedule – two hours on Monday, Wednesday and Friday, with the Monday show as the main focus.

Like everything else at A.L. Williams, we did television "our way." Why follow someone else's format? Or copy some slick corporate production style? We ran our network pretty much the opposite of other corporate networks out there, and that's why it worked for us so well. *Know your audience!* We weren't afraid to experiment with content and format. If a show worked, we kept it. If it didn't we changed it, fixed it, or scrapped it.

Most importantly, we never stopped being ourselves. TV can be an intimidating medium. Many corporate networks produced their programs with hired actors, scripts and Teleprompters. We quickly learned that wouldn't work for us. None of us were "professional." None of us planned on becoming so. Our TV crew accepted early on that they would have to adapt to us; we were not going to adapt to them – even if we could. When we dropped the marker while writing on the board, oh well. When we mispronounced a word, or someone tripped a bit walking onto the stage, so what? We just kept going. We didn't have time for re-takes. We didn't have to time to be perfect. We didn't want to be. The message mattered most. Get that clear, and we were happy. It made us real and watchable.

ALW-TV became an incredible blessing. Broadcasting from our Atlanta studio instantly, every week, allowed us to super accelerate growth in the U.S. and Canada. But, as the years went by, it became a bit of a curse, too. I often treated that Monday show like a locker room. I'd pound that podium and speak my mind. If a field agent made some grievous error the previous week, I'd get on there and blast him. I wanted everyone to learn from it. I'm a coach. That's my personality. But sometimes people mistook my rant as negative carping. Well… sometimes, they were right.

And, looking back, I often shared too much. Field problems. Office problems. Legal problems. Why bother? I should've kept those issues to myself. Better to have spent that precious time selling the dream.

PUBLICITY

In April, we notched another company first.

FANS' securities sales led A.L. Williams' insurance sales – 56,000 securities apps compared to 53,000 insurance apps. That set an all-time record, too.

At the beginning of the year, Ken Durham and I set a goal for FANS to reach $1 billion in cash sales. We also issued a decree – every insurance client should have a chance to invest in an IRA with a mutual fund. March numbers suggested we were on track to achieve our goals.

"We're going to do to the securities business what we did to the insurance business," I told the sales force on ALW-TV. "Many people will look at these numbers and say it happened because of IRA season. But I don't think these numbers will go down. A mutual fund with a good track record completely destroys universal life, dividends, whole life – anything associated with cash values. Remember, an IRA is the greatest investment in America, and a mutual fund is the greatest investment *vehicle* in America."

Our FANS sales force now numbered 17,000 – up from 12,000 just a year prior – a 38 percent increase. Likewise, our total initial sales for April 1986 now stood at 55,181 – a 112 percent increase over 26,076 sales in April 1985 – staggering numbers.

To our delight, we also saw a little positive media. On May 11, 1986, the New York Times printed a profile on A.L. Williams – "Crusading for Term Life Insurance" – that accurately captured our business philosophies and current state of growth. My favorite part of the article honed in on Prudential and the soon-to-launch Common Sense Term:

[Art Williams] is, as he puts it, "on a crusade for term insurance." His own conversion began 19 years ago, when his father died, leaving a whole-life policy that failed to support the family.

Today, his strong view about traditional life insurers – combined with the mounting number of policies his army of zealous agents has sold to customers wooed from other companies – have stirred up antipathy among many in the industry.

"It is a parasitical organization," said George Exner, vice president for district agencies at the Prudential Insurance Company, who point out, accurately, that most A.L. Williams policies are sold not to first-time life insurance buyers, but to those who hold cash-value policies issued by other companies.

Mr. Williams seems to relish going after this market. "Our business is the replacement business," he said, adding that he has just instituted a 20-year, fixed-rate policy to lure more of his rivals' customers. "With the new policy, our competition won't be able to match it in price. We're fixin' to knock their butts off like you wouldn't believe."

A positive July article in *TIME* magazine, called "Terms of Enrichment" also gave a nice nod to our non-conventional approach to life insurance:

Williams' astonishing success in an $820-billion-a-year industry stems from a fervent, evangelistic selling style with a single-minded concentration on one product: inexpensive term insurance. This kind of no-frills policy makes a payout only when the insured dies. For that reason, term-insurance premiums may be only 20 percent of what customers pay for the more common, whole-life and universal-life policies, which still make up about 89 percent of the U.S. market.

...Williams hammers home the gospel of term insurance through a door-to-door sales force of 140,000 spread across 49 states and Canada. The sellers are linked by a $5 million private satellite TV network, over which the stocky, balding Williams delivers daily pep talks. Nearly all of the employees are part-timers, and many hold other jobs, as teachers, firemen and even mayors. He claims that by using part-time agents his company spends 75 percent less than competitors on everything from desks and chairs to phones and plants.

...more and more people seem convinced that term insurance offers the most protection for the least money. Williams expects the amount of new coverage that he sells this year to surge by 38 percent, to $90 billion, and he predicts $120 billion for 1987. He boasts, "We are positioned to dominate the largest industry in America for the next 20 to 25 years." At the rate he is going, that may not be much of an exaggeration.

The articles made for great talks at summer meetings in Boca and Hawaii. But these write-ups were soon dwarfed by a massive event in October that put us smack in the national spotlight.

VICTORY '86

Politics grew increasingly important to me as the years passed. Our company's soaring growth paralleled with Reagan's era as President of the United States. An coincidence? I don't think so. Among other things, Reagan's domestic policies strongly promoted the value of the free enterprise system, entrepreneurship, and systematic saving via IRAs.

When Reagan took the presidency from Jimmy Carter in January 1981, the top income tax bracket bled 71 percent. Reagan managed to drop it to 40 percent. He understood the worth of the business owner, small or large, and he worked long and hard to rejuvenate the economy after Carter's dismal failings.

Reagan also believed in the power of the individual. "Entrepreneurs and their small enterprises are responsible for almost all the economic growth in the United States," he liked to say. So closely did his philosophies of hope and opportunity mirror ours that it felt almost like we were in sync with a national movement. In fact, Reagan knew about A.L. Williams and he believed in what we were doing.

With Reagan finishing out his second term, I moved on to support lower level campaigns, including personal friend Pat Swindall, who'd won Georgia's 4th district congressional seat for the 1984 election, and Newt Gingrich, another Georgia Representative to the U.S. House of Representatives.

Still, somewhat of a newcomer in political circles, it surprised me when the Georgia GOP called and asked me to chair a "Victory '86" rally in early October. The evening event would be held at the Omni Coliseum in downtown Atlanta. The featured speaker? None other than President Reagan, coming to campaign for Republican Senator Mack Mattingly, up for re-election in November. It would be Reagan's last visit to Georgia for the year.

The rally would take place a few days before our SVP convention, already scheduled at the Atlanta Civic Center. Mary Durham and I instantly moved up the convention dates to coincide with the rally. If I was going to host this thing then, dadgum it, we would throw the biggest and best rally the President had ever seen. We would pack the Omni to the rafters with A.L. Williams people. This meeting would be the memory of a lifetime.

The day drew nearer. I had every staff member at in the executive office on the phone lining up people to attend the free rally scheduled for 7 p.m. on Wednesday, October 8. My plan was to get as many Georgia school kids there as possible, too – school groups, Boy Scouts, church groups – and give them this special chance to see the President in person. At least 5,000 of our RVPs and home office employees would pack out the rest of the seats. (Maybe leaving a few for government officials, local politicians and top GOP donors!)

Then, two days before the rally, Kevin King, our rally contact person, took a call from the Secret Service.

"Let me review the President's schedule with you," said the curt voice on the other end of the phone. "The President will arrive at Dobbins Air Force Base at 1:23 p.m. At 1:25, he'll enter his limousine. At 1:46, he'll arrive at the Omni, and at 1:52 he'll be introduced. At 1:54, he will speak."

Kevin said, "Well, excuse me, but our event starts at 7 p.m."

The voice said, "Let's review the President's schedule. The President will arrive at Dobbins Air Force Base at 1:23 p.m. At..."

Kevin stopped him. "We'll take care of it," he said.

We found out later the rally had moved up so President Reagan could make a meeting that evening with Russian President Mikhail Gorbachev in Reykjavik, Iceland.

The time change meant no school children would attend the event. So I jumped on ALW-TV for an "emergency announcement" and urged any member of our sales force to attend, if possible.

On Thursday, Angela and I rode by limousine to Dobbins Air Force Base. We stood waiting as the President disembarked from Air Force One (at 1:23 p.m.). As before, Reagan exuded a commanding presence.

What a thrill to meet him again and shake his hand.

We spent a few minutes at the airport with him, visiting. He remembered Angela and me from our White House visit. I caught him up to speed on A.L. Williams' latest achievements. He looked clearly pleased to hear our progress and asked a question or two. A.L. Williams, he said, was the kind of company making America strong again.

We arrived at the Omni in separate cars. Secret Service men – lots of them – escorted us back stage. Red, white and blue garlands and banners fluttered everywhere. High school bands and gospel choirs performed and people packed the place to the rafters. Squinting into the arena, it almost looked like most faces in that crowd belonged to A.L. Williams people.

Someone introduced me. I went out on stage to start the rally. The place went nuts. Yep, those were our people out there all right!

In typical A.L. Williams style, the crowd started stomping and chanting.

"*Who's a stud?* He's a stud! *Who's a stud?* He's a stud!"

I tried to talk, but the roar intensified. Finally, I shouted into the microphone, "You know what?"

The crowd boomed back, "*Whaaat?*"

"We just put together the largest political rally in the history of Georgia! Is that awesome... or is that awesome!" The crowd howled twice as loud.

I went on.

"I was talking to the President. I told him how we beat the number two and number three companies combined in production last year. Two of the most famous companies in the world, Prudential and Northwestern Mutual – and we beat them combined! And we did that by selling only term insurance – the best term products with the best value for the consumer. I said, 'Mr. President, I don't know of any company that's doing anything as meaningful for the American consumer as A.L. Williams is doing right now.' And you know what?"

"*Whaaat?*" came the roar.

"He said, 'I think you're right!'" A splendid moment.

I introduced President Reagan. As he came out on stage, the jubilation soared. The bands struck up "Hail to the Chief." Some 2,500 balloons and 600 pounds of confetti streamed gloriously out of the ceiling. He stepped up to the podium, and the crowd began to chant again.

"*Who's a stud? He's a stud!*"

They yelled it again, over and over. Reagan stood with his hands raised, graciously trying to quiet the crowd. He shot me a look, eyes twinkling. Then he shook his head and laughed out loud. He got the biggest kick out that cheer.

Finally, the crowd quieted, and he went on to give a great speech.

I was so proud of our people. We turned a last-minute rally into a nationally covered historical event everyone would remember for a lifetime.

REAGAN... WHO?

"Darcy and I were sitting down in front with a group of wealthy Georgia Republicans. They'd never heard of Art Williams. When Art came on stage, the place went crazy. This older man and his wife sitting next to us were totally confused. They kept asking us, "What is going on? Who is this man?" It was humorous. They thought Reagan was supposed to be the star of the show."

– TREACY BEYER

"ATTITUDE IS EVERYTHING"

That evening at the Atlanta Civic Center, we kicked off our two-and-a-half day SVP convention. The stage, decked out in red, white and blue bunting from the rally, awaited. Adrenaline pumping, I bounded to the podium. What an extraordinary day!

But tonight, we had serious business to conduct. I couldn't wait to get at it. Recently, Boe and I made a major change in compensation that resulted in a 60 percent cut in the first generation override. It pushed RVPs and above to build bigger base shops. Some leaders had veered from that role; this change would financially nudge them back. Hand-in-hand with the recently raised standards in persistency, both changes encouraged a stronger building mentality.

Both changes drew criticism. Well, part of my job as "head coach" was to push the team, and that's what I did. We desired our people to be successful; that often required tough standards. And change.

"In the last six months everything that I ever thought I wanted A.L. Williams to be has happened," I started. "But some of you have come to Atlanta really down in the dauber. It is not possible for some of you sitting out there to win in A.L. Williams with your current attitudes.

"Tonight, I want to shake you out of that attitude. Over the next couple of days, I want to show you a bunch of stuff that I know will help you get straight.

"Now, I'm going to be pretty tough. Folks, if you are not totally consumed with this wonderful moment in A.L. Williams, if you are not more proud to be a leader of A.L. Williams, more excited about the future, more determined to win than right now, then listen up. We never promised it would be a bed of roses. We promised it was going to be a pain in the butt. We promised we were going to have disappointment after disappointment. But if you have not made up your mind to jump into A.L. Williams, participate in this thing, and share in these magnificent rewards that are going out to you, then you are in a very small minority. Some of us in this company will go off and leave you behind.

"You know the difference between the fence-sitters and the people who will take home big recognition here tonight? *Attitude.*

"Attitude is everything. In some of the best people in A.L. Williams today, I don't see a lot of talent. I don't see a lot of difference in these National Sales Directors sitting up here and a lot of you sitting out there, in terms of ability.

"The one thing I see in the NSDs is they don't quit. Ever. Back when we went from Mod-11 to Mod-15, you had to average maybe a $120,000 policy to make the same money you made on a $60,000 policy. I saw these people continue to work. Every time there was a change or an adjustment, the winners just kept trucking. That's the difference.

"Tonight I'm going to pull rank on you a little bit. You need to understand – I am the *head coach of this company.* I got letters from some of you recently that said, 'Art, I've lost trust in you.' Folks, that don't matter. Understand – there's never been another company in American business history that's done more for the consumer or delivered more for its people than A.L. Williams. I don't have to prove a thing to you.

"Do you know any football team out there where the players go to the head coach and say, 'Coach, I don't know if I like you. Coach, I don't know if I trust you.'

"No! You don't play football that way! You darn sure don't win that way. See, here's how it works – the players have to *prove themselves to the coach.*

"At A.L. Williams we have a philosophy. I have a very specific way I want A.L. Williams to be built. If you challenge that, then you'll come out a loser. When I decided to cut your first-generation override by 60 percent, if you did not hate Art Williams for a minute, then you probably wouldn't be human. I understand that. But I took that money and put it in a pool. And if you go out there and do a good job – not a great job, but a good job – you'll make 300 percent to 400 percent more money.

"I think some of you don't want to go back into the base shop. You're too comfortable. Understand – you are only hurting yourself and your own family. Sales are going straight up. Some of you, though, will be left behind.

"Remember, your number one goal is to build a company within a company. I said that in 1977. Look at everything your NSD has done and duplicate it. If you think like that, there are no limits for you. You can go out and make $5 million or $50 million.

"Number two, your personal goal is to become financially independent. I said in 1977 that I wanted A.L. Williams to be known as the company that produced more financially independent people than any other company has or ever will. That's important to me.

"Number three. Your best game plan? Keep building a big base shop and keep producing successful first-generation RVPs! That's what you want your people to do, no exceptions. If you keep producing first-generation RVPs until you have 3 or 5 or 7 or 10 or 12, then you will more than meet your financial goals.

"With all that in mind, let me ask you something. How committed are you? This company can do 15 good things for you, then one uncomfortable thing, and that one thing causes you to quit. So again I ask – how committed are you? How bad do you want to win? Can you stay positive when it's tough? Can you stay positive when you don't get a promotion? Or take a 60 percent cut in commission? Will you work for a huge reward?

"This is the way I choose to run A.L. Williams. If we're not growing, we're dying. These compensation changes are designed to pay the producers – to take it away from the duds and give it to the studs. If you go out and build a big base shop you are flat going to make a fortune."

By the end of the night, I felt something happen… The rock budged. That may sound crazy, but I sensed a profound shift in the deepest regions of people's hearts – a swing toward better personal decisions, toward greater responsibility for families, businesses and teams.

Do I have proof? As Common Sense Term continued to roll out through the states, sales held steady… and then began to rise.

Clearly, the staggered release of CST and major adjustments in persistency and compensation had caused a slowdown. That happens when changes come thick and fast.

But now, as the year wound down, sales and recruiting jumped back on track. Momentum picked up steam again. That tremendous accomplishment proved something to me – the leaders in A.L. Williams were real. They "got it." They understood what I had tried so hard to tell them.

Our people fought for the right reasons and for the right people – their families, their clients and their company.

I prized that far more than whether or not our year-end numbers hit $90 billion.

24 New Era

By March 1987, we had the facts: A.L. Williams won its third straight National Championship in the life insurance industry, putting $71.1 billion in new business in force. We even broke our own production record for the second straight year. In what was fast becoming a company tradition, we handily beat the number two and three companies combined – Prudential with $30.9 billion and Northwestern Mutual with $26.1 billion.

The good numbers felt especially significant with all the changes we'd weathered in 1986. And timely, too – 1987 marked 10 years in business for A.L. Williams.

We did a couple of ALW-TV programs to commemorate our anniversary in February, including a special reminiscence with the six remaining "original RVPs" – Bobby Buisson, Bob Turley, Rusty Crossland, Frank Dineen, Virginia Carter and Fred Marceaux. We saved most of the celebration, though, for a very special April RVP convention in New Orleans themed "A.L. Williams: Ten Years of Greatness."

"After ten tough, challenging, rewarding and very successful years, we truly are in our moment of greatness. The opportunity could not be better than it is right now," I announced to 12,000 top leaders and managers on opening night. "Our international support system is finally in place. We are positioned to explode to the top of American business."

As I listed our 1986 accomplishments, a sense of pride electrified the convention center:

- Third straight year as National Champions – 1984, 1985, 1986.

- Licensed insurance sales force of 150,000 – the largest insurance sales force in the industry.

- 66 National Sales Directors with annual average cash flow of $400,000.

- More than 1 million policy owners.

- Lowest cost of the top 50 life insurance companies in the industry.

In terms of our past, present and future, our "present" already boasted a new milestone.

In April, A.L. Williams and MILICO surpassed $200 billion new business in force since 1980 – an incredible record. We'd accomplished this in seven short years, outworking hundreds of companies in business for decades.

Our parent company, led by Gerry Tsai, renamed itself Primerica to reflect its increasing trend toward financial services. Recently, Gerry had purchased New York-based brokerage and investment house Smith Barney for $750 million.

"I have only one obligation – one responsibility – and that is to give you the support you so richly deserve," Gerry declared at our convention. "I will devote my energy and my resources to help this company grow, so we can be very proud of each other in the years ahead."

With the fireworks, we set off the usual bombshells. We rolled out a new product called Common Sense Decreasing Term to age 65. Complementing our 20-year level term product, we designed CSDT specifically to meet the needs of older clients, as a rider for additional mortgage protection or as a standalone policy. As usual, we structured it to be the most competitive product of its kind on the market. I couldn't wait to see how fast the sales force would take it to families.

A second bombshell – a new mutual fund group appropriately named Common Sense Trust. The new funds (a growth fund, growth & income fund, and a government fund), were created by an agreement between First American National Securities (FANS) and American Capital Asset Management, a subsidiary of American Capital Management & Research (one of our sister companies). To handle the business influx CST would surely generate, we put together a new customer service department: Common Sense Shareholder Services. A good thing we did, as we soon found out.

Effective April 1, 1987, Boe and I devised a 9 percent commission bonus increase for the RVP and SVP bonus pools. As we intended, the pools, totaling $50 million, rewarded RVP leaders and above who produced consistent monthly premium in their base shops and met the company persistency requirements. RVPs could even "double dip" in both the RVP pool and the "Builders" pool by upping their numbers. Some earned monthly bonuses as high as $20,000.

	Life Insurance Policies In Force	ALW Market Share
USA	142.5 million	
A.L. Williams	1,135,138	.796 of one percent
Canada	14.0 million	
A.L. Williams	3,427	.02 of one percent

At year-end 1985, Prudential had 18,693,599 policies in force, for a market share of 13 percent.
(Source: 1986 Life Insurance Fact Book)

The four-day meeting spotlighted the achievements of old-timers and new stars alike. Then we turned to the future. We would be moving into other areas of financial services – home mortgages, accident & health, property & casualty. Fine and good. But even with our world record-breaking sales numbers, we had barely even scratched the surface of the life insurance market. Our ultimate goal was 10 percent of the market. Right now, we garnered just under 1 percent!

Our opportunity to grab market share beckoned. According to Prudential's 1986 annual statement, that company issued 887,879 policies… but 1,563,784 polices terminated. Similarly, New York Life issued 302,616 polices… with 597,603 policy terminations – nearly double. Even more startling, Metropolitan issued 310,179 policies… with a whopping 1,138,515 policy terminations. Think of it! Met Life lost four policies to every one its agents put on the books! And get this – a public survey performed by ACLI, an insurance industry statistical service, revealed that only 1 percent of those surveyed thought that whole life cost more than term!

Was something wrong? We'd spent 10 years building a massive sales force. We'd put $200 billion worth of new insurance on the books. Still, families bought expensive cash value policies… then ended up dropping them. Obviously, the crying need for our "Buy Term and Invest the Difference" crusade was just as strong, just as wide open, just as needed as the day we started.

In a new recruiting video, "The A.L. Williams Dream," I laid out our great opportunity:

"Cash value life insurance is the biggest rip-off that's ever been sold to the American consumer. Their number one product is universal life – the most dishonest life insurance product on the market today. Folks, we do what's right. You can be proud of the money you make at A.L. Williams. You make money by doing a good job for people, saving them money and providing a great service."

Business surged through every level of leadership, from the newest Representative to the most experienced National Sales Director. On a 10-city Super Seminar tour that summer, we sensed the increasing excitement.

The numbers told the story: the Common Sense Trust family of mutual funds brought in $225 million in its first four months of sales. Even when the stock market crashed on October 19, 1987, falling an unprecedented 23 percent all over the world with no warning, FANS continued strong, ending the year with a total mutual fund sales volume of $1.6 billion. Since July, MILICO had processed an average of 65,000 life apps per month (October spiked at 76,368).

An NSD cruise in early December celebrated the promotion of 82 new National Sales Directors – 75 the last four months of the year. Five NSDs – Bobby Buisson, Hubert Humphrey, Mike Sharpe, Ronnie Barnes and Bob Safford – moved into the million dollar earner category. Thirteen NSDs earned $500,000+, with 100 more earning $100,000 and up.

That wasn't all. When 1987 ended, the insurance scoreboard said it again: $81.4 billion new business in force.

For the fourth consecutive year, A.L. Williams had won the individual life insurance National Championship, out-producing Prudential ($26.5 billion), New York Life ($40.4 billion) and Met Life ($14.3 billion) combined. We had surpassed our own '86 record by $10 billion.

Our golden era at A.L. Williams emerged in grand style.

1988

1988 began with a fresh slate of 10 Super Seminars spanning North America for the next 12 months. For the first, in January, we packed out the San Francisco Civic Center with 7,000 fired-up term-ites.

Meanwhile, significant change was in the works for A.L. Williams on the corporate level.

With Gerry Tsai and his executive team, Boe and I decided to merge the A.L. Williams Corporation with MILICO, now a subsidiary of Primerica. MILICO was an old buddy, of course, our sole underwriter for the past eight years and our partner in co-insuring the massive amounts of term life insurance sold by our sales force.

Since MILICO was the larger company, merging it with the A.L. Williams Corporation would require a "reverse acquisition." This meant ALWC would give up more than 50 percent of its stock ownership to Primerica for the deal. This good move would free up several hundred million dollars in new capital to pay administrative and underwriting costs, which remained as extensive as ever. The deal would also give our sales force a boost in stock profit, if we negotiated correctly. In short, this new arrangement would allow the A.L. Williams agency to grow at its scorching pace without having to borrow money to cover expenses.

Since it involved our public company, the transaction required shareholder approval. Peter Lynch, manager of the prestigious Magellan Fund and one of our major shareholders, expressed concern over the potential transaction when he first heard it. Peter did not want to see our public company merge into a bigger company without adequate compensation. Using Peter's wise advice, we continued negotiations with Primerica with an eye to closing the deal by year-end. The months went by; soon other corporate developments gave us much more to think about.

DIVERSIFICATION

Back in the early days of PennCorp, Stanley Beyer and I always disagreed on one issue – product diversification. Stanley felt strongly we should take advantage of our huge customer base by adding new product lines. He constantly pressured me to ask the A.L. Williams agents to sell auto and homeowners insurance, mortgages and other financial services products. I always said no.

True, we held a captive audience. Yes, we added thousands of clients every month. But I saw no need to sell more products. I wanted the sales force focused on one thing – "Buy Term and Invest the Difference." We hadn't even come close to saturating the insurance market. Our investment side did phenomenally well, certainly, but it hardly dominated the industry. We had a long way to grow in our two chosen fields.

Finally, in 1988, with our sales force close to 200,000, I felt more comfortable with selling other products.

In March, we launched ALW Home Mortgages, Inc., a mortgage banking operation. Our sales force offered home mortgages at competitive rates by telephone and mail. We then resold the mortgages to mortgage wholesalers, removing us from payment collection, loan defaults and interest rate risks.

A few months later, we introduced a couple of accident & health products – a Common Sense Hospital Plan and a Common Sense Disability Income Plan – to help families meet financial needs in the face of serious injury or illness.

These products were okay. But it was hard for me to get excited about them. They filled a niche market, but they weren't revolutionary or cutting-edge. To my thinking, we needed to come out with the best product on the market, whatever market that might be.

For a couple of years, I'd been attracted to property & casualty insurance. Clients asked us over and over about automobile and homeowners insurance. I decided to check into it.

What I discovered got my juices flowing. P&C insurance, like traditional life insurance, was sold the old-school way, through fully licensed agents who worked for long-established companies like State Farm, Travelers and Allstate. Just as A.L. Williams had rattled the life insurance industry by selling term insurance with part-time agents, we could shake up this tired P&C market.

Here was my idea. Why require our sales guys to get a P&C license? We could have a system that allowed "qualified" A.L. Williams clients – either insurance or investment clients with our company – to call an 800 number and talk to a P&C representative. Doing business that way, we would eliminate the agent's commission. It could save the consumer 15-20 percent on auto and homeowners – hundreds, possibly thousands, of dollars.

Since our guys would not be licensed, the sales force would not get a direct commission on any sales. But they would be helping families find another way to save money on two other types of insurance, auto and homeowners insurance. It would tie them even more securely to our A.L. Williams family.

I also wanted to add a one- or two-point profit margin, then plow the money back into compensation for the sales force – in bonus pools, incentive trips and such. The sales model would simultaneously eliminate a time-consuming licensing process and give us another powerful way to create loyal customers. Removing sales commission would save our A.L. Williams clients mega-bucks… and without question start another war with competitors like Travelers, Allstate and the rest.

It would launch a whole new crusade! I could already smell the gunpowder in the air!

Surprisingly, Boe rejected my idea. He felt strongly that our sales force should have a fully licensed P&C person in every A.L. Williams office. That way we could sell our clients a good P&C product and make the full commissions. Since Boe and I disagreed in this rare instance, I dropped the idea. I could always bring it up again at a more opportune time.

[Just a side note: A few years later, Warren Buffet did the 800 number no-sales-commission concept with Geico, which became the biggest P&C company in the world.]

MORE POLITICS

Since the Reagan rally in Atlanta in 1986, my name popped up frequently in political circles, often even as a possible candidate for Georgia governor.

While I entertained no such ambition, my commitment to politics on a personal level and through A.L. Williams remained firm… a good portion, I'll admit, out of sheer necessity.

Since A.L. Williams and even before, back to my days as a part-time and full-time insurance agent, the state-level politics so blatantly propped up by the traditional insurance industry proved abhorrent to me. As a general rule, I couldn't stand politicians. Too many had no backbone. Too many just wanted the perks that came along with being in office.

But as A.L. Williams began to grow and face direct challenges to our products and philosophy, we had to step up and fight. Our crusade for families was right, and the battle to give them better term products was righteous.

Thankfully, our company attracted people unafraid to work for causes. As A.L. Williams spread state by state, our agents with connections to people in office worked hard to influence local and state elections.

By the mid-80s, in addition to political action committees in every state, we employed Washington lobbyists to fight for us at the national level. Haley Barbour, Republican (who later become the head the Republican National Committee and governor of Mississippi) and Don Fierce, our Democrat.

Back in Georgia, A.L. Williams became deeply involved in positioning Tim Ryles, an Atlanta-based consumer rights expert and frequent guest speaker at our Super Seminars, to become Georgia's next Insurance Commissioner. Tim's eventual election would be a major triumph, considering the hostile political environment we had encountered just 10 years before. Now we would have our own man in that position.

Even more important for A.L. Williams would be Zell Miller, Georgia's lieutenant governor, a rising political figure who often and freely voiced his public support for A.L. Williams. An outspoken proponent of the free enterprise system, Zell would soon become governor, and then U.S. senator. So the political landscape was changing dramatically for A.L. Williams. Our tireless efforts for eight years finally started to pay off.

One major political victory just occurred. The replacement regulations, so long in place, that required our agent to notify a competing agent about a policy replacement and provide a complicated policy comparison and dividend breakdown – all that rigamarole…. Now, incredibly – *eliminated*. The new procedure: our agent sent a simple one-page notice to the client family, asking them to review and compare other policies they might own, and determine if a replacement might be in their own best interest. This regulation shift spread rapidly to other states.

It was a quiet concession to A.L. Williams, an acknowledgement that this ridiculous regulation had produced absolutely no effect on us. In fact, it had helped us grow. The industry finally just gave up and took it off the books.

On the personal front, my wealth, success and outspoken devotion to conservative family values served as a drawing card to political affiliation. In recent years, I'd met Jerry Falwell, head of the Moral Majority and founder of Liberty University in Lynchburg, Virginia. We became good friends and he invited me to speak at the 1987 National Religious Broadcasters Convention in Washington, DC. I delivered there the most famous rendition of my "Do It" speech, a speech that became synonymous with "Art Williams" over the years.

I also met televangelist Pat Robertson, when he asked me to be a guest on his television talk show, The 700 Club. The financial principles outlined in *Common Sense* intrigued Pat, and the day I appeared as a guest we offered a free copy of the book to anyone who called the program. We gave away thousands. I personally supported Pat in his 1988 bid to become the Republican candidate for President, a bid he lost in the primaries to Vice President George H.W. Bush.

Supporting political candidates required me to walk a fine line. Head of a 200,000 member sales force with the world's largest private satellite TV network at my disposal, I could easily have used all that power for personal political gain. Legally it was not wrong… but to me, personally, it was. My political beliefs tended toward the conservative Christian right, but others in the company held different views. Some were atheists. Some were liberals. Some voted Republican, others voted Democrat. Our company really represented America. Different viewpoints? Acceptable. Expected.

THE "DO IT" SPEECH

Excerpts, National Religious Broadcasters Convention, February 1987

Leadership is everything. You show me anything in these United States that wins and I'll show you a leader at work. You show me a successful church, Boy Scout troop, club, football team, business, I'll show you something run by a leader.

At one time in my life I thought you had to be smart to win. I used to work with these smart people that dressed so pretty and talked so pretty and used these big words. They just intimidated me and I said, "Art, you can't ever be that good. Why don't you just throw in the towel and go on back and coach football for a living?"

And I found out two things about smart people. I think it's almost impossible for a smart person to win in business in America today, because I found smart people spend their whole lifetime figuring things out.

They're always trying to figure out an easier way and a quicker way. And another thing I found out about smart people is they just don't get around to doing nothin'.

And see, somebody like Art Williams, everybody said, "Well, he can't do it. Somebody like that can't do it."

But he does it.

See, folks, I want you to know almost everybody in America almost does enough to win. They almost get there. They almost are over the hump. They almost have it going.

Almost is a way of life to almost everybody in America.

But the winners do it. What do they do? They do whatever it takes to get the job done.

They do it – and do it – and do it – and do it – and do it – until the job gets done.

And then they talk about how great it is to be somebody they're proud of. They talk about how great it is to finally have achieved something unique – how glad they are that they didn't quit like everybody else – how wonderful it is to finally make a difference with their life.

We need leaders in America who can "Do It."

A perfect example. That summer, the 1988 presidential election going full tilt, we chose to make our presence known at both parties' national conventions in a strictly promotional way. In July, we welcomed the Democratic National Convention to Atlanta with a huge billboard just outside the Georgia World Congress Center. In August, we joined Coca-Cola to host a reception at the Republican National Convention in New Orleans. We didn't do it as a political statement. We simply wanted the nation to see our maturity as a company that in 11 short years had earned its stripes in one of the toughest industries in the world.

Politics aside, the A.L. Williams machine continued to roll. Halfway through 1988, our average monthly app count stood at 75,000. In February, apps spiked to 83,800... only to be outdone in March with 93,400. This year, we'd set a stretch goal of $100 billion new business in force at year-end. Right now, we had a shot.

But on the national scene, the securities sector still reeled from the October '87 stock market crash. Many investors had simply fled the market. Mutual fund sales volume dropped a precipitous 50 percent from the previous year. Investment firms laid off brokers by the thousands.

All this was bad news for Gerry Tsai, who had purchased Smith Barney at a pricey $750 million at the height of a bull market. While A.L. Williams continued to surge, Smith Barney was now worth half its sale price. Primerica would probably see some changes.

AIRPORT MEETING

In late June, A.L. Williams was enjoying its annual convention at Boca Raton. Out of the blue, Boe received a call from Gerry Tsai.

"Gerry wants us to go meet a guy named Sandy Weill," Boe told me, hanging up the phone.

"I'll call for the plane," I said. Early that afternoon, Boe and I flew to Peachtree-DeKalb Airport, a busy small-plane airfield in the middle of Atlanta. In a little conference room, we met with Sandy Weill, the CEO and chairman of Commercial Credit, a Baltimore-based consumer lending company. We didn't know a lot about Sandy, except that he was a self-made man. He started out as a nobody and worked himself up the Wall Street ladder through sheer hard work, smarts and determination. We liked the familiar sound of that.

The meeting lasted a couple of hours. In that time, Sandy explained his keen interest in purchasing Primerica. Having been in the brokerage business most of his career, his goal now was to build a financial services empire. After purchasing a struggling Commercial Credit from Control Data in 1986 and staging a major turnaround, he wanted to move up.

Primerica, with its connection to the A.L. Williams & Associates Agency and Smith Barney, offered Sandy a prime opportunity to do just that.

But, Sandy stated firmly, there would be a condition.

"Based on the numbers I've seen, A.L. Williams is the most important part of Primerica," Sandy said. "You account for one-third of the profits. You have a sales force of 200,000. Your potential is really off the charts. I'm not interested in pursuing this purchase without your support."

Boe and I spent time telling Sandy our philosophy and where we wanted to take the company in the years ahead, emphasizing our desire to add product lines and expand internationally. Sandy was clearly intrigued. When we parted ways that day, I told him, "Look, if you can work out a deal with Gerry, we're fine with it."

Flying back to Boca, Boe and I talked excitedly. Meeting Sandy Weill had been a total positive. It looked like Primerica stood on the verge of making some big moves and as far as we could tell, they were all good for A.L. Williams.

ALL YOU CAN DO

As summer progressed, every day seemed to get a little more exciting. Thousands attended our Super Seminars at every location. From San Francisco in January, we'd traveled to St. Louis, Toronto, Salt Lake City and Baltimore. We'd hit five more cities before year-end.

Super Seminars often opened with "Rockbusters," an upbeat music video created by our television staff. Set to the theme song from the movie "Ghostbusters," it showed an animated Rock of Gibraltar, (Prudential's logo), continually blasted and pulverized as the soundtrack boomed, "Who ya gonna call? ROCKBUSTERS!" The crowd flipped over that video, singing and stomping along, pushing the meeting adrenaline extra high.

The atmosphere reached its electrifying peak at the Los Angeles Super Seminar in July. The Forum, home of the Los Angeles Lakers, jammed with 15,000 "term-ites."

Friday evening, I dropped a bombshell.

"Did you know Benjamin Franklin never said nothin' compared to what I'm fixing to tell you tonight?" I yelled.

The crowd thundered.

"I'm about to tell you 16 words guaranteed to make you wealthy. This is going to save you thousands and thousands of hours of agony and frustration."

I paused for effect.

"All right, you ready? The whole ball game, guaranteed to make you a superstar?"

The crowd roared again.

"Here it is: *All you can do is all you can do... But all you can do is enough!*"

As the place went wild with standing, stomping, cheering, clapping ALW agents, I unveiled the first A.L. Williams book to be published outside our company, aptly titled *All You Can Do Is All You Can Do, But All You Can Do Is Enough*.

The book detailed A.L. Williams' rise to glory in the insurance industry, plus the success stories of many top agents, all tied together by the business-building principles that worked so well for all of us. Designed for the entrepreneurial-motivational-self-help crowd, the book played up our time-tested philosophies of learning how to win in life – especially if you are "average and ordinary."

"It's been twenty years since I first entered the business world as a part-time representative for a company that sold term insurance and investments," I wrote in the introduction. "During that time I discovered some amazing things that I want to share with other people like me. I discovered that you don't have to have extraordinary abilities to succeed. You can be the most common person in the world and still do something uncommon with your life."

That weekend, we sold 7,000 autographed copies in two hours.

The book idea had come from Sam Moore, a friend of mine, owner and president of Thomas Nelson, a Christian publishing company in Nashville. Sam, also an "inner circle" friend of Jerry Falwell, he heard my "Do It" speech at the National Religious Broadcasters convention the year before. Ever since, Sam had urged me to put what he called my unique style of "motivation and inspiration" down on paper.

"You know, Art, you ought to do another book and let me publish it on the national market," he suggested several times. "You've really got something to say."

In January, after careful consideration, I agreed, but with a caveat. I didn't want my name on some fluffy, empty-headed self-help book.

I told Sam, "If I'm going to do a book I don't want it to be some pie-in-the-sky thing that makes people think winning is easy. Because it's not. And I don't want it to be a book about succeeding just in business. This has to be about succeeding in life. That's what I always taught my football teams and it's what I've always taught the A.L. Williams salespeople. This is not just business, this is your life. You can't separate the two."

Now, we had a book that fit the bill, created in collaboration with Angela, Barbara King, Dona McConnell, my writer of previous books, and two other top writers in our publications department, Arden Feiman and Tammy Savage. I decided to donate all profits to Family & Marriage Resources as a way to help that important organization continue its mission. Every day they helped thousands of A.L. Williams families stay on that tricky track of balancing family life with building an A.L. Williams business. Their efforts meant the world to Angela and me. Giving back was my heartfelt way of saying "thank you" and "keep going."

Barbara King and her staff did a bang-up job of marketing and it didn't take long for *All You Can Do* to make its mark. By August, after the initial 150,000 hardcover run, it made the *New York Times* best-seller list. By September, with 400,000 hardcover copies in print, it ranked No. 1 on Waldenbooks bestseller list and No. 1 on the "demand list" at Ingram Book Company, the nation's largest book wholesaler. By December, paperback rights had been snapped up by Fawcett Books, audiotape rights by Random House and foreign rights by nine countries. A million and a half paperbacks sold before all was said and done.

PRIMERICA

All summer, Sandy Weill continued to pursue Primerica, often sending his CFO, Jamie Dimon, and several other key executives to "check us out" at the home office or company events. Plainly, they liked what they saw. I think they especially loved the sales force enthusiasm and the high-spirited mood of our meetings, all of which must have been in stark contrast with the merger negotiations. Attending our third-quarter NSD meeting, Sandy confessed anger and disappointment over Gerry Tsai's exit demands during breakfast one morning. Just as they moved to seal the deal, Gerry revealed, hidden in the severance agreements, costly "golden parachutes" for himself and 10 of his top executives. The extra $60 million almost killed the deal. Why? Primerica, with annual sales of $3.8 billion and 22,000 employees, was four times as large as Commercial Credit, with its $912 million in annual sales and 3,700 employees. Swinging the sale was complicated enough, without throwing in the pricey pay-off.

I just listened as Sandy vented, silently thankful to be uninvolved.

A couple of weeks later, on August 29, Sandy Weill finalized the deal with Primerica, golden parachutes and all. It would be several months before I learned that the deals Gerry Tsai had made on his own behalf were "peanuts" compared to the deal Sandy made for himself at Primerica. At A.L. Williams, we viewed our new parent company and its CEO as a total positive.

To officially introduce Sandy to our sales force, I extended a special invitation to him to attend our Super Seminar in Detroit on October 28. It would be his first big A.L. Williams meeting, and I wanted him to make a speech. Sandy agreed, if we would send him some tapes of past meetings. He wanted to get a flavor for our seminars, he said, which he'd heard resembled old-fashioned revivals. Barbara King sent off a package to help him prepare.

In Detroit, we packed the huge Pistons basketball arena to the ceiling. Folks knew of Sandy's appearance, and the crowd was even rowdier than usual. "Rockbusters" blared from two giant video screens when we escorted Sandy to the front row of the auditorium. The song phased out, and I ran out on stage, wearing my favorite blue T-shirt with the words "Do It!" in letters about a foot high.

"How bad do you want to be somebody?" I yelled.

"*Bad!*" the crowd screamed back.

I went on. "I'm so excited today I just can't stand it! This company is on FIRE – ain't that right?"

"*Right!*" came the staccato return.

"We're one of the greatest success stories in American business, ain't that right?"

"*Right!*"

"But you know what?"

"*What?*"

"They ain't seen nothin' yet! We're fixin' to the blow the minds of the competition like never before. Now ain't that right?"

"*Right!*"

We went through our usual routine, in perfect sync. Then I turned the subject to Sandy Weill.

"I'm about to introduce you to someone who is a giant in the financial services industry. He's the former head of American Express. He owns Commercial Credit. Now he's fixin' to take over Primerica and become the CEO of our parent company! The reputation this guy brings to the table is just unbelievable. We thought things were good before – now they're going to be a thousand times better. Help me welcome Sandy Weill!"

Sandy openly confessed his dislike of public speaking, and as he walked on stage, sweat rolled down his neck and speech notes trembled in his hands. But he was smiling, and I grabbed him for a bear hug.

The crowd leaped to its feet, stomping and chanting, "*Who's a STUD? You're a STUD!*"

Total bedlam with pom-poms, noisemakers and balloons.

Sandy stepped to the podium and tried to quiet them, nervously glancing at me for help.

Finally, the noise subsided and he began to speak. A few sentences in, Sandy hesitantly

inserted that magic phrase: "You know what?"

The crowd jumped on it. "*Whaaat??*" they roared back.

Startled, Sandy looked up. He hadn't expected that. But he tried it again, a little louder this time.

"You know what?"

Again came the booming reply: "*WHAAT??*"

This time, he grinned from ear to ear and went on with his speech. At the end, the crowd gave him a standing ovation. Sandy beamed, ecstatic, as he left to go back to New York. His first visit with the sales force? A home run. Sandy Weill was absolutely in love with A.L. Williams.

A grand moment. Unfortunately, such days of happiness would be numbered for Sandy and me.

BOMBSHELLS & MERGERS

The first weekend in November 1988, our top leaders and their Partners gathered at Pebble Beach in Carmel, California, for the fourth and final NSD meeting of the year. Thirty-seven newly promoted NSDs had joined the ranks and a new position, Senior National Sales Director, with its own set of builder-stretching guidelines, created a whole new buzz about moving up. Hubert Humphrey, in his typical pacesetter style, already met the guidelines. Several others waited on the cusp.

Boe and I announced four new commission bombshells to increase field cash flow – temporarily reduced RVP promotion qualifications, a 15 percent increase in the RVP base shop contract, a 100 percent increase in the RVP bonus pools, and a huge increase in firstyear overrides for first- through third-generation RVPs.

The guideline changes would strengthen the company at the Regional Vice President level by enticing Regional Managers – the highest paid part-time position – to go ahead and make the leap to full-time.

We meant the cash flow increases to create a bonanza for the folks willing to work and build and grow with the company. A bit of danger lurked in the changes though. They eliminated renewals, which had always served as a kind of forced savings program. Now all commissions would be paid upfront.

"This will cause serious problems for people who can't or won't manage their money," I reminded the group. "As SNSDs and NSDs, we must set the example. Remember, it's your personal responsibility to keep your family on track to financial independence. Be sure to take that back to your organizations. These changes should make some folks take a long, hard look at the way they manage monthly cash flow. The people who do it right are going to win like never before!"

A couple of special guests also created a stir. Angela and I had asked Sandy and Joan Weill to attend the Pebble Beach meeting, an invitation they accepted with delight. NSD meetings, smaller and more intimate, were a good way for Sandy and Joan to get to know our top leaders, something Sandy had expressed a desire to do.

Just like Angela and me, Sandy and Joan had married young and had their children right way. They adored a son, Marc, and a daughter, Jessica, along with their grandchildren. After 33 years of marriage, Sandy still called Joan his closest confidante; he often asked her opinion on business decisions, just like I did all the time with Angela. Clearly the Weills valued marriage and family as we did, and our warm "family" atmosphere drew them in.

One night before dinner, we scheduled a "grip and grin" photo session – Sandy and Joan and the NSDs. With 150 couples to shoot, we worried about time… and sheer exhaustion. Angela and I decided to put the Weills in a quiet room with the photographer and gave Bob and Jane Miller the job of bringing in one couple at a time, with strict instructions to keep on schedule.

Bob and Jane were gracious, thoughtful hosts, sharing backgrounds and personal stories about every couple as they stepped into the room. The information gave Sandy and Joan a springboard for easy conversation throughout the event. They loved putting the names with the faces and hearing the stories of how various people came to be part of

A.L. Williams.

After that meeting, I reflected. Every encounter with Sandy seemed to go better than the last. I felt we'd found a real person, a real friend. Instinctively, I never trusted politicians or Wall Street executives. But I felt Sandy was different. He made no secret of the fact that he loved A.L. Williams and that somehow we would be a major player in reaching his goal of building the world's largest financial services empire.

I should've trusted my instinct.

Still, things seemed fine. On November 30, at the annual A.L. Williams Corporation shareholders meeting in Atlanta, shareholders approved the stock swap for merging MILICO into ALWC as a wholly-owned subsidiary. For a 100 percent interest in MILICO, Primerica received 44.58 million shares of newly issued common stock, increasing its holdings in ALWC from 17.4 percent to 69.8 percent, and making it the largest stockholder.

The transaction tripled ALWC's total assets to $1.5 billion and the company's net worth shot from $156 million to $755 million, freeing up much-needed capital to fund our diversification into accident and health, credit cards and, soon, property and casualty.

Angela's December 1988 issue of Partners Press of captured our Pebble Beach meeting with Sandy & Joan Weill.

ALWC common stock continued to trade publicly on NASDAQ.

"This is a historic day," I told shareholders. "There has not been one moment in the last 11 years I have owned this business where I have felt as good as I do now. I think we are good enough to take the stock to $100 or $200 per share. We have a chance to build a new Coca-Cola or IBM."

Shareholders accepted my resignation as chairman and CEO of the A.L. Williams Corporation and approved my replacement, Treacy Beyer. I gave up leadership for structural reasons – it was a conflict of interest for me to be owner of the general agency, A.L. Williams and Associates, and chairman of the corporation that negotiated with the agency.

Treacy, president of MILICO since 1987, would fill the role perfectly. Bill Keane, our top financial executive, became president.

Now, I'd put my total energies into building, motivating and leading the sales force.

On December 15, shareholders of Primerica and Commercial Credit approved the $1.7 billion merger of those companies. Officially, Sandy Weill took the name "Primerica" for his newly joined company.

A.L. Williams had truly entered a new era. No longer could the industry pass us off as a "ragtag army" of unprofessional nobodies. Our 225,000 licensed representatives made up the biggest sales force and the largest writer of individual life insurance in the world. We were the "franchise player" in the grand plans of Sandy Weill, a Wall Street legend with dreams of creating a financial services giant. With A.L. Williams producing 35 percent of Primerica's profits, why wouldn't we feel good about things?

The numbers at year-end simply took our breath away: $92.3 billion in individual life insurance issued by the A.L. Williams-MILICO team in 1988. Ninety-two billion! For the fifth consecutive year, we topped the life insurance industry, beating our biggest competitors New York Life ($46.3 billion) and Prudential ($36.2 billion) combined… and they weren't even close. We'd even eclipsed our own record from the previous year by nearly $11 billion.

It looked like nothing – nothing – could ever slow us down.

25 Dynasty

On opening day of 1989... numbers amazed even us. We led the nation in new individual life insurance for the fifth consecutive year, issuing $92.3 billion in face amount of coverage in 1988 – more than any other life insurer in the nation. Our sales force in Canada added $4 billion to that number, bringing our international company total to $97 billion. The Canada numbers reflected an amazing 149 percent increase over their $1.9 billion in new business put in force in 1987, just one year before.

The A.L. Williams Corporation boasted $1.7 billion in assets and $800 million in net worth. Our largest subsidiary, MILICO, ended the year with $257.9 billion of total individual face amount in force – more than any other insurer in the United States.

Our public company (69.8 percent majority-owned by Primerica, a diversified financial services giant with $16 billion in assets and $1.26 billion in income) now ranked among the FORTUNE Top 50 Diversified Financial Companies, and one of the 30 Dow Jones Industrial Average companies. Our sales force numbered 225,000 licensed insurance representatives, and 35,000 of them also held licenses to sell securities. Despite the 1987 stock market downturn, our FANS sales force held strong as the number one producer of American Capital and Pioneer mutual funds in 1988. The asset growth of our Common Sense Trust proprietary funds rose 113 percent by year-end, from $373 million to $796 million.

Our sales force spanned 49 states, Canada, the U.S. Virgin Islands, Puerto Rico and Guam. Our world's largest satellite television network now beamed programming three times a week into 1,000 offices. On average, every month, we brought in 13,000 new recruits, received 71,000 life apps, and paid out $40 million to $60 million in commissions to the sales force.

Diversification into mortgages, more investment products, accident & health products and, soon, home and auto insurance, was going well.

Boe and I continually examined what it would take to expand into European markets. In the last 12 months I had met with insurance companies in London and Paris and found strong opportunity. Also, I took a call from John Amos, CEO of American Family Life Assurance Company (Aflac), in Columbus, Georgia. John and his two brothers, Paul and Bill Amos, founded Aflac in a little one-room office back in 1955, over the years building their company into the biggest marketer of cancer insurance in the world. Significantly, in 1974, Aflac became the only American company in history licensed to sell life insurance products in Japan.

John, familiar with our success, proposed a joint venture. "Art, you and your team are the greatest marketers out there and I have an exclusive contract to market life insurance in Japan. We really ought to put together a deal. The opportunity there is wide open. This could be huge for both of us."

Intrigued, I whole-heartedly and sent Treacy to Columbus to discuss the possibilities. With most of Japan's workers caught in its system of lifetime employment with one company, our be-your-own-boss approach would offer a breath of fresh air. Amway made its system work there; it seemed logical we could, too. On his return, Treacy acknowledged that it was feasible to consider Japan a "new frontier" for our sales force, but one that would be extremely complicated, based on their insurance laws and regulations. Also, it would take a good bit of financing to launch, even with Aflac.

Until we worked out the money issue, the opportunity would stay "back burner" for now... along with European expansion.

On February 6, 1989, another dream came true: We began trading our common stock on the New York Stock Exchange! Bill Keane had achieved his long-time goal of switching ALWC from trading on NASDAQ to the "Big Board." Not every public company earned such an honor. We had, due to Bill's efforts, and our stock's extraordinary track record of growth – a five-year growth rate of more than 50 percent per year.

As it happened, the switch came on the eve of our 12th anniversary bash at the home office, the celebration of our fifth consecutive National Championship. I decided to send Treacy Beyer, Bill Keane, Barbara King, Bob Miller and Bobby Buisson to Wall Street for the big "opening day" kick-off on the famous trading floor. Thrilled to be the "hot shots" who got to ring the bell, they snapped pictures with the NYSE president as the ticker tape rolled across the Big Board for the first time, listing our NYSE ticker symbol: ALW.

A prestigious event, for sure, but I felt just as happy to skip it. A trip to New York would only be a distraction right now. Too many big, powerful, wonderful things were happening at A.L. Williams and I chomped at the bit to do more: International expansion. Diversification. More products. More commissions. More promotions. Extra trips. Added incentives.

Boe and I loved to sit and dream, and we'd come up with a million good ideas. New territories – England or Japan – especially fascinated us. We'd made it happen in Canada. But how would we get enough financing to do all we wanted? How would we expand our support system to handle all the new business sure to be generated? How would we stay out in front of this growing juggernaut called A.L. Williams, keep more and more troops motivated, writing good business, moving in the right direction?

There might not be an easy answer. But maybe there was a solution.

BIG TALKS

Not long into February, Boe walked into my office with an interesting proposal: Sandy, he said, wanted to buy out the remaining 30.2 percent of stock in the A.L. Williams Corporation. He wanted our public company as a wholly owned subsidiary of Primerica.

I sat at my desk looking over some RVP promotions letters I needed to sign.

"That makes sense," I told Boe, "since Primerica is already the majority shareholder. Sounds like a good move for our stockholders. Guess we can talk it over with the board of directors."

"Right," said Boe. He paused. "There's more. Sandy wants to buy the agency, too."

My head shot up. "No way. That won't ever happen."

Boe sat down. "Art, we need to look at the big picture. I think Sandy is someone we can really work with on a deal like this. He's a good businessman. He likes our ideas."

"True," I nodded. Boe went on. "And we have issues to address at some point. We've got to put some kind of plan in place in case something happens to you, right? A lot of people depend on this company for their livelihoods – the agents and their families, and home office people, too. If something happened to you, the stock would drop, all the people who invested their futures in our stock would be devastated. The agency would probably have to be sold. We could all lose everything we've worked for. We need to have a plan to make sure this company is here for people fifty or a hundred years from now. Sandy's offer could be the right thing."

"We'll talk about it, Boe, but I have no desire to sell the agency," I said firmly. "I love the fact that we sell for another company, but we're still independent. I don't want to retire. I don't ever want to work for some big corporation again. That's the reason I left Waddell & Reed back in 1977 in the first place. I don't ever want to sell A.L. Williams."

And I didn't. But Boe was right. We had reached a point where a responsible and caring leader had to contemplate possibilities.

For a couple of years now, Boe and I had talked privately about what would happen to A.L. Williams if I died suddenly. We really did need a way to protect all we'd built. We needed to position the agency to outlive me, outlive all of us.

Now and then, people threw out those "what if" questions. I'd always answer confidently: "Boe and Angela would run the company."

The subject had come up again last summer, while we flew on the plane to a Super Seminar. I repeated the comment and this time, Angela burst out, "Art, that's ridiculous! Boe and I can't run this company. As much as I love and respect Boe, he would not work for me, and I could probably not work for him. I'm your wife, for Pete's sake. I might be fairly good at what I do for the company, but I can't do what you do. That would be like telling me to go fly this airplane. It's not a viable plan. We need something better."

And Boe agreed. So, for a few months now, he'd been talking seriously about slowing down, maybe even retiring in two or three years. I was 47. Boe, 53. We'd both been working at an unbelievable pace for 12 years now. Boe was getting a little tired. It was hard for me to think about not having Boe there to run the business, although I'd always planned for Treacy to replace Boe if something happened to him.

We both acknowledged another issue, too – my health. The elephant in the room. Longevity did not run in my family. Lost my dad at 48 to a heart attack, an uncle at 43. I was nearly 48. Worse, back in 1987, I began suffering unexplained fainting spells. The first time I blacked out, I was at home, talking on the phone to Boe. Angela found me slumped over my desk.

Tests with heart specialists at renowned Emory Clinic in Atlanta showed no heart blockages. The doctors sent me home without a satisfactory diagnosis.

All seemed fine. Until three weeks later. In the middle of an executive meeting in my office, all of a sudden I reared back in my chair and passed out, stiff as a board. My breathing appeared to have stopped.

Bob Miller and Dick Kinnard, both with some emergency medical training, laid me on the floor and unsuccessfully tried to wake me up. I began to turn gray, and they were afraid I'd swallowed my tongue. Dick tried frantically to pry open my jaw with a pen, but every muscle in my body had locked up. He broke his pen trying.

A minute passed. Still, I appeared not to breathe. Frantic, Barbara called the ambulance – she thought I must be dead, or close to it. Then finally my whole body went limp and I woke up in a cold sweat, totally exhausted, as if I'd just run a marathon. But I was breathing normally again.

The ambulance blaring into the parking lot alarmed the entire home office complex. Somehow Barbara managed to divert attention, and I got into the ambulance without the staff seeing me. We rushed off to the hospital.

I felt terrible, causing such a fuss. But obviously something was wrong. A lengthy battery of tests at Emory revealed a very sluggish heartbeat, "typical of an over-conditioned athlete." My pulse would slow way down almost to the point of stopping, making me pass out. A pacemaker would fix the problem, doctors said, so they rigged me up, connecting a wire to the bottom chamber of my heart.

Weeks went by. Several more fainting spells occurred. The doctors made adjustments in the "pace" of the pacemaker. Finally, the episodes stopped.

My family history of heart problems had reared its ugly head. My own sense of good health felt compromised. Angela worried about the stress. Barbara worried that publicity on my office "episode" would cause the stock to collapse. "It's risky to have the fate of this whole company depend on one man," she'd say to me from time to time. In fact, the rest of the executive team picked up that theme and repeated it over and over in the following months.

And it was true. My health, my age and the urgent need to create a permanency for the future – all these issues called for attention.

Sandy's offer sat on the table. Time to talk… even if I wasn't exactly thrilled about it.

SOLUTION

At the home office, I began to spend marathon hours discussing the possible sale of the agency with Boe, Treacy, Barbara, Kevin, Bob and Bobby – my most trusted advisors. Angela often sat in our meetings, too.

Boe described a double whammy scenario for the sales force. "If Art died right now, the family would take over the agency. Then every advisor in the world would tell Angela to sell the agency…And that's what would happen," Boe said. "We would lose our leader and be forced to sell. Two huge transitions like that could destroy the company. And that could wreck the families in our sales force, their stock holdings and their business opportunities.

"Sandy Weill is prepared to buy the agency. I think if we make that transaction now, while Art is still alive and managing it, the transition goes seamlessly. Art would stay here and head the sales force, keep the whole thing going. Then, if Art died, we would already be in a position to maintain the operation. The stock would remain stable. Our field leaders would continue to do business. Life would go on. I think that's what Sandy means to offer us."

Both the scenario and the solution made sense. An agency sale would secure the future for everybody; we would also then have the money and support to expand globally, to diversify. I would still lead the sales force, live my passion. Nothing would change that much… unless I died. Even if that happened, the agency would go on. The sales force would continue, doing what they already knew how to do, building security for the families they served… and their own families.

The more we talked, the more I accepted the idea. Still I couldn't bring myself to say yes, even for all the right reasons. Wasn't there some other way? Did I really have to sell my beloved company?

The weeks passed. Sandy and I talked directly now. We envisioned all Primerica could do for A.L. Williams. Sandy dreamed big, too – he planned to build a financial services empire through cross-selling. Right now, he could tap two major markets: Smith Barney, with brokerage and money management services, appealed to high-income clients. Commercial Credit's loan programs drew lower income clients. Now, A.L. Williams would fold in the vast, valuable middle-income market.

By merging, Sandy would use the A.L. Williams sales force to market products from his other companies to our two million clients. Imagine how many mortgages, accident & health, property & casualty, debt consolidations and money management products we could put on the books!

His dream fit well with mine… especially when we agreed to stay focused on the key role of our two main products – term insurance and mutual funds. After all, it was success with those products that brought us to the big dance in the first place.

To compensate me, Sandy explained he would purchase the agency outright – for an upfront price of $75 million. I would continue to get my commission income over the length of a 20-year consulting contract. I would stay in place as head of the sales force.

Then, with the financial backing of Primerica, A.L. Williams would open up new territories in Europe and the Far East and diversify into new product arenas. A.L. Williams would be free to grow just as big as we wanted it.

How could I lose? How could our agents and executives lose? I believed Sandy. The more time we spent together, the more I believed in what we would do together.

Back in the days of PennCorp, Stanley Beyer kept close tabs on our numbers, but he wasn't involved on a day-to day-basis. Gerry Tsai, even less so; Gerry gave us what we needed and let us run the show.

Sandy was different. He wanted to know everything. He spent time learning everything he could about A.L. Williams. He liked our philosophies – building a company with part-time agents, keeping our salespeople "king," "Buy Term and Invest the Difference" and "pushing up people." He and Joan seemed to love our people. They could never hear enough success stories – stories of how families' lives changed, thanks to our products and opportunity.

In the many hours we spent together, I felt like Sandy and I really got to know each other. I felt our relationship surpassed "just business." We were friends. When Sandy came to Atlanta or I went to New York, we spent many hours together in meetings, talking over lunch, throwing around plans and ideas, dreaming about the future of our great companies.

I felt we were really in sync. I felt we shared the vision of where we wanted to go and what we wanted to do. I felt we were all in this together.

VEGAS MAGIC

In April, we headed off to Las Vegas for our annual convention, this time attended by 20,000 RVPs and Regional Managers. I so looked forward to the meeting. This year's theme, "The Magic Is Back," seemed perfect for the Las Vegas Convention Center – an awesome place the size of two football fields.

The view of all those people? *Breathtaking.* Video screens hung strategically around the facility, allowing everyone to see events on the 120-foot-wide stage. We featured a special speaker – Sandy Weill. We proudly offered 200 home office and NSD exhibits, marriage and family workshops, messages from me, Angela, Treacy, Boe and many top field leaders, hundreds of awards and handouts.

Yvonne Tyson, head of the ALW-TV crew filming the entire convention, promised a grand extravaganza on opening night, complete with lasers, smoke, dancing and drama. But I doubt Yvonne had any idea the kind of "drama" the night would actually create.

I stood offstage, waiting to go on after the opening number. A formal evening, I wore a white dinner jacket and black bow tie. Some Las Vegas-type dancers warmed up in back, but I didn't pay much attention. The A.L. Williams Band (under Ken Durham's direction) and Chorus (under SVP Rita Huckle's direction) performed with their usual gusto and I thought over my speech.

Then the gala kick-off show... kicked off! I heard a snappy tune – our very own custom-created "The Magic Is Back" theme song. The big screens showed inspirational video footage of well-known A.L. Williams greats and lasers shot colorful beams across the auditorium. When the song ended, I would make my grand entrance through a tunnel of laser lights and dry ice.

Suddenly I snapped to attention.

Out in the middle of the color and clamor, I saw those dancers from backstage. They twirled and jumped... and when their skirts flared I could see they wore barely anything underneath. I was shocked. Shocked and *embarrassed.* And the longer I watched, the madder I got.

I marched over to Yvonne, stage-directing on the side, and gave her a choice, scorching piece of my mind.

"What is this crap?" I yelled. "Those women are out there dancing without any pants on!

What is the matter with you? That's not A.L. Williams!"

Yvonne, flustered and shocked herself, tried to explain. "I don't *know* what happened! They were wearing pants when they practiced!"

I stormed off, leaving her in tears. I had a mind to stomp out on stage and shut the whole thing down, but somehow I held myself in check until the debacle hit its last wailing note. Buddy, you better believe I seized the stage then.

Striding out, I gripped the podium with white knuckles.

"Folks, I don't know what you think when you see something like what you just saw up here on stage," I said in a loud, terrible voice. *"But this ain't no damn show."*

I paused. The smoke and the lights and the Vegas mood vanished. Twenty thousand people sat in that vast auditorium... *Total silence.*

I looked down at the front row. Angela sat there, along with Boe and Myrna, the Beyers, and Sandy Weill. Their eyes stretched wide. They'd never seen anything quite like this before.

"This... is... your... *LIFE*," I said, pounding the podium with each word. "We are NOT here to put on a trashy show for you. We are here to *HELP YOU*."

I stopped again, so mad I could hardly talk. I couldn't believe a spectacle so inappropriate had just taken place at an A.L. Williams convention. "If you think what you just saw here tonight is what A.L. Williams is all about, then you can just go home. *Now.*"

The mood in the auditorium had shifted 180 degrees from the start of the night, but the hard switch had been necessary. No way I wanted our leaders in that room to walk away thinking that girly show was "okay by me."

I made my point. The moment passed. I went on with my regular speech.

"I'll probably never say anything more important to you than what I'm going to say tonight. If you came to Las Vegas to visit with friends, have a second honeymoon, or get away from the pressures at work, that's great. I want you to do some of that.

"But here's the real reason we're all here. It's to see that the *magic is back* at A.L. Williams.

"I believe A.L. Williams is at a turning point – *a moment of greatness*. We are in a position to build a historic company! We've built a company that's produced more millionaires, more families making over $50,000, over $100,000, than any other company in America and Canada. We're the number one company in the largest industry in the world!"

The crowd thundered.

"Our new compensation program is working well. Last month in March, 17 people cash flowed over $100,000 – in one month. Six people cash flowed over $200,000 – in one month. One leader even cash flowed over $300,000 – in one month. Now let me ask: *You think I ain't proud?*"

The crowd boomed again.

"Yes, the *magic is back*. But listen! That don't guarantee you nothin'. The company can't get so good that you can take a dud and make him a stud. A company can't win for you."

I held up my thumb and forefinger with a hair's breadth between them. "This is the difference between winning and losing. This much is the magic!

"As I reflect over the past 12 years, I recall many moments of greatness. The 10-year contract with PennCorp. The building of the home office complex. Beating Prudential. The MILICO merger. The New York Stock Exchange. Each was a triumph... but *the best is yet to come!*"

"When I look at the future of this company and what we've got going, I'm absolutely at the peak of my confidence in our ability to fight, compete and win. I believe with everything in me that we're going to win. And at the top of my list of reasons why I have so much confidence? Boe Adams, Treacy Beyer and the management team they are developing under them in A.L. Williams."

In a surprise presentation, I then dedicated the convention to Boe and Myrna Adams and Treacy and Darcy Beyer, honoring their contributions to A.L. Williams.

Convention Dazzle

"Art's speech at the beginning of the Las Vegas convention was a great example of Art being Art. He knew the meeting got off in the wrong direction and he totally turned it around. His speech set the tone for the rest of the meeting.

At the SNSD reception later that night, Sandy pulled me aside and said, "That Art Williams is a genius!" I didn't know what he meant. He said, "He staged that whole thing! He put those dancers up there so he could make that speech! He totally took control of the meeting."

I was stunned. "Sandy, Art didn't know anything about the dancers. That was just his reaction," I told him. But Sandy went on talking about Art's genius ability to stage such stunts and capture the crowd. He didn't understand what had really happened."

– IN-HOUSE NSD BOB MILLER

Then I dropped a bombshell announcement. "You think this year's convention is great, 20,000 people here in Las Vegas? Well… just wait till next year. We planning it next March at the Super Dome in New Orleans with 40,000 people – double this event!"

Cheers rocketed around the auditorium.

Sandy made a brief speech after mine. "I have to give credit to Art and his leadership abilities. Who else could get 20,000 serious-minded people to travel to Las Vegas to think about careers and bettering themselves? I don't think I could!" He grinned as the crowd responded. "Can you imagine another business leader in this country who talks about the family, who encompasses the spouse as a part of the company? Art doesn't just say it… He means it, and he makes it work.

"Art and I share a fundamental belief," Sandy went on. "We believe you should not take away from the best to support the underachievers. This is how the company has grown, and how it should continue to grow. You are winners, dedicated to your families, dedicated to delivering a quality product. Over time, we'll develop products to help you grow even more."

Sandy finished with a promise. "We have no model to follow. We are creating our own model. The next ten years will be awesome."

APPROVAL

Back in Atlanta, merger talks continued. The people I trusted most all firmly agreed that selling the agency to Sandy was the best and right thing to do. The A.L. Williams board of directors – Bill Keane, Barbara, Kevin King and myself, plus outside directors Marvin Arrington, an Atlanta City Council member; Johnnie Caldwell, former Georgia insurance commissioner; Jim Miller, president of Atlanta-based Fidelity National Bank; and Lee Myers, former COO of PennCorp – also discussed the merger. They leaned strongly in the direction of selling, too.

The final decision hung over me, a sword of Damocles. My head said "sell." My heart said "don't." I feared our loss of independence. I welcomed resources and support.

One issue stood above all the rest – how to preserve the company forever. Selling the agency to Sandy, the company would be in good shape to continue on, even if something happened to me. Merging solved this issue, the biggest problem of all. And nobody – not one person – spoke against it. Everyone I trusted counseled in favor of the sale.

I came to a decision. There simply was no alternative.

I would sell "A.L. Williams & Associates," a.k.a. the General Agency, to Primerica. I would receive an initial cash payment of $75 million, plus my normal commissions, and continue on as a consultant and head of the sales force for the next 20 years. Primerica would buy the remaining 30 percent of the A.L. Williams public company and merge it into Primerica. We would consummate the two deals before year-end.

A decision had to be made. Still, in my heart of hearts, I felt no peace. The right thing to do for the company didn't feel like right thing for me.

Sandy had asked me to speak in early June at a Smith Barney meeting in Point Clear, the site of our first A.L. Williams convention. After my presentation, I headed up to Sandy's room. "Sandy, I've thought about this a lot," I began. "This is the toughest thing I've ever had to decide. In fact, I started off thinking there was no way I'd ever sell the agency. But I believe now it's the right thing to do for the future of the company."

I took a deep breath.

"I've decided that I can trust you. I will sell the company to you. I'm going to tell Boe to get with you. Let's get this thing done."

Sandy beamed. "I think we have a great future ahead of us, Art," he crowed. I said I agreed.

I called Boe to tell him the news. He practically jumped through the phone.

"Art, I could just kiss you!" he shouted.

"Yeah," I managed to smile. "Well, I'm glad you can't!"

On Friday, June 9, I joined Sandy from his New York office to conference call with the Inner Circle, 75 of our top-performing, handpicked leaders. I explained the good news of Primerica buying out the remainder of the public company. It would probably result in a windfall for ALW stockholders, I told them.

Then I went to the big news.

"Sandy has also offered to buy the sales force. When we first discussed it, I was completely against it. But now, after months of weighing all the advantages and disadvantages, I think it is the right thing to do."

I felt a lump in my throat, as the words I thought I'd never say came out. "You all know I've had heart

Primerica Corp.

Firm Proposes Stock Swap For Rest of A.L. Williams

Primerica Corp. proposed to acquire through a stock swap the minority stake it doesn't own in A.L. Williams Corp. The transaction has an indicated value of about $390 million.

In a related development, A.L. Williams agreed in principle to acquire closely held A.L. Williams & Associates Inc. for $75 million and further payments of unspecified amounts.

A.L. Williams Corp., Duluth, Ga., underwrites insurance and other financial products. A.L. Williams & Associates is a general agency whose 200,000-member sales force sells the products and services of A.L. Williams Corp. Primerica, a Greenwich, Conn., financial-services company, holds a 69.8% stake in A.L. Williams.

Officials of the concerns said that they wanted to consolidate the business ties among the three companies and that the transaction will lead to stronger products and services.

Under the Primerica proposal, Primerica would swap eight-tenths of a Primerica common share for each of the approximately 20.4 million A.L. Williams shares outstanding, or 29.2%, held by public shareholders.

The Wall Street Journal, Monday, June 12, 1989

problems. I've got a pacemaker. My dad died at 48 from a heart attack.

"For a couple of years now, it has been a deep concern of mine that without some kind of plan in place to preserve the future of the company if my life ended... that your futures and the future of our company could be devastated. Merging the sales force with Primerica means A.L. Williams goes on, no matter what.

"I've had everyone on the home office executive team look at this proposal from every angle. We've talked for months, talked till we're all blue in the face, and we all concur. It's still in the planning stages, but I have agreed to sell the A.L. Williams agency to Sandy Weill and Primerica.

"I will continue on as head of the sales force, just like now. With Primerica's support behind us, we can really build a team that will dominate financial services for decades. Sandy is a proven leader. I'm so excited about the future and what we will be able to do."

Not unexpectedly, field reaction came back very mixed. Rumors of a possible merger with Primerica had swirled for weeks. Now, the news confirmed, the idea of selling the sales force shocked and upset some. The worst fear? A.L. Williams, as part of a traditional corporation, would lose its independence.

"I totally understand your fears," I told people. "I've had them, too. I've always liked us being independent.

"But the bottom line is... I don't see any alternative. Our relationship with Sandy and Primerica gives us the permanence that we need. *You* need. Now we have new financing, and a chance to really move into new markets and open new territories. And if anything happens to me... then your business and your stock investments are protected. That's what this merger is all about – you."

By Saturday, June 10, news of the merger and the stock buy-out hit the media. In a prepared statement, Sandy announced, "The proposed agreements demonstrate Primerica's commitment to the continued growth and success of the A.L. Williams sales force. With a permanent relationship with this powerful distribution network, under Art Williams's direction, as well as a commonality of shareholder interests to serve, we will have an even stronger base from which to capitalize on the dynamic potential of this unique organization."

The proposed agreement still had to pass approval of directors at Primerica and A.L. Williams Corporation. The stock buy-out also needed board approval, plus a green light from ALW shareholders and regulators. An investment banker would be appointed to review the fairness of the merger proposal. All these reviews were normal, standard operating merger procedures.

The home office seemed openly pleased and excited about the developments. Some field leaders, though, expressed unhappiness. I believed that with time and talking, we could smooth out their issues. The grand vision of all we could do with Primerica's support would make believers of our "doubting Thomases."

I put the decision behind me. Time to move on.

THE ANALYSTS OBSERVE

"Arthur L. Williams Jr. agreed Friday to sell his A.L. Williams insurance agency to A.L. Williams Corp., a subsidiary of Primerica Corp., which already owns 69.8 percent of the Duluth-based insurance company...

"Analysts who follow A.L. Williams Corp. said they were not surprised that Primerica wants to buy the rest of the corporation, or that Mr. Williams decided to sell his agency.

"I think Art Williams probably feels that over the long term, to continue the continuity, they [the corporation and agency] needed to be incorporated," said Thomas G. Richter, senior vice president of the Robinson-Humphrey Co. Inc. in Atlanta.

"I think he always felt that way. It was just a matter of when to do it."

"Frank W. Anderson, an analyst with Stephens Inc. in Little Rock, Ark., said A.L. Williams Corp contributes more than 40 percent of Primerica earnings, so it is not surprising that the financial services conglomerate with executive offices in New York wanted to buy the rest of the company."

– EXCERPTS FROM ATLANTA JOURNAL-CONSTITUTION,

JUNE 10, 1989, "WILLIAMS SELLING HIS INSURANCE

AGENCY TO UNIT OF PRIMERICA."

CEASEFIRE

Kevin King and his legal team stayed busy with a couple of big regulatory cases – one with the Tennessee insurance department, the other with California. Both cases as always, blatantly generated by the competition, required some top-notch research and defense skills from our lawyers, but they really amounted to "much ado about nothing." A.L. Williams won both cases.

Here's what happened.

On May 1, 1989, with no prior notice to A.L. Williams or MILICO, Tennessee's insurance commissioner issued a "cease and desist" order prohibiting A.L. Williams from advertising or selling life insurance policies in correlation with the sale of mutual funds. Note the key words – "in correlation with."

Tennessee insurance department regulations prohibited the sale of correlated sales – life insurance products and mutual funds, bound and sold together. A correlated sale took place when a customer bought a life insurance policy and then immediately borrowed from its cash value to buy mutual fund shares. Or the customer could purchase mutual fund shares and then borrow against those shares to buy life insurance. In other

Tennessee Department Indicts MILICO/A.L. Williams

By Joseph C. Razza Jr., CLU
LAN Senior Editor

Tennessee's Department of Commerce and Insurance ordered Massachusetts Indemnity and Life Insurance Company (MILICO) and A.L. Williams Insurance Services (ALW) to cease and desist engaging in the correlated sales of life insurance policies and mutual funds or other securities because they had not complied with the department's rules. The cease-and-desist order was issued on May 1, 1989.

However, on May 11, the commissioner gave ALW temporary authority to resume the correlated sales of insurance and securities, with the further order that ALW would supply the department with all advertising and promotional materials its agents are using in Tennessee.

In a separate development, the Tennessee insurance department issued a "Report of Investigation" relating to MILICO and ALW, which was prepared by Lewis F. Elrod, supervisor of investigations. According

to the report, which runs 108 pages, the department received complaints alleging that MILICO and ALW violated "unfair trade practices laws, advertising regulations and the correlated sale of mutual funds and life insurance regulations."

The report says that the investigation reveals that MILICO and ALW "have apparently established a system of deliberate evasion and violation of the insurance code and regulations in the state of Tennessee through the use of deceptions that

Continued on page 40

July 1989 / LAN 25

words, the customer purchased two products with the same dollars. You can see why the regulators prohibited the practice.

Now, Tennessee had issued a "cease and desist" order against us for correlated sales. Funny thing though... A.L. Williams marketed no such product. Our insurance-licensed ALW agents sold MILICO life insurance policies. Our securities licensed ALW agents sold mutual funds. We had some agents licensed to sell both... but they never sold those two products as a bundle, and money from one was never borrowed to purchase the other. Strangely, we'd been ordered to stop doing something we'd never done in the first place.

The headline in this article, which appeared in the July 1989 issue of LAN (Life Association News), a publication put out by the NALU (National Association of Life Underwriters), shows how far the competition willingly pushed to discredit A.L. Williams. No indictment came out of the Tennessee case.

A.L. Williams and MILICO were never indicted for anything.

Other than the headline, the word 'indict' does not appear in the article.

Much ado about nothing, right? Not to the industry. A "cease and desist" order against A.L. Williams made big news. Our enemies gleefully twisted the order to suggest that A.L. Williams had been "banned from doing business in Tennessee." Headlines said this very thing in many papers. Even the Tennessee Insurance Department tried to distort our "Buy Term and Invest the Difference" marketing approach into a violation of the correlated sales prohibition. All nonsense, of course. But it started yet another war between "us and them."

Competing agents piled on, pressuring the insurance department to take action against us. Once the traditional industry realized they couldn't get us on correlated sales, they brazenly switched their strategy to attacking our sales practices, following a badly biased report issued with the heavy influence of competing agents and the Tennessee Association of Life Underwriters. When they realized that wouldn't work either, they charged us with violating state advertising laws, claiming our sales materials were "untruthful or misleading." Here was a new ploy, copied from the California Insurance Department, based on a showdown case currently pending in San Francisco.

We settled the Tennessee case about a year later by dropping the use of one brochure and making minor wording changes in a couple of other pieces. Unfortunately for the competition, all the negative publicity and legal fuss generated by proponents of the case only served to get our name in front of a wider audience. Our sales and growth in Tennessee never even slowed down.

The case with the California Department of Insurance began in May 1988. At the request of the California Association of Life Underwriters (CALU) and a Prudential agent in San Francisco, California insurance commissioner Roxani Gillespie filed a complaint against A.L. Williams and MILICO for the use of a booklet written by consumerist Arthur Milton.

Arthur's 1984 booklet, *Why A.L. Williams is Right For the Consumer*, unabashedly advocated the purchase of term insurance, specifically our products, over whole life policies. Our agents had used the practical, 24-page piece very successfully at the kitchen table.

Commissioner Gillespie charged that the booklet contained false and misleading information about life insurance in statements like "the new Universal Life Products are nothing more than the latest sham," and "you lose your cash values if you die."

The case centered around one question: Did the Arthur Milton booklet contain misrepresentations? Or was it merely Mr. Milton's written opinion on life insurance and therefore appropriate for consumers? Simple questions… but figuring out answers cost us $600,000 in legal fees and expenses, before the case concluded.

The trial began March 1989. As usual, we involved our people. Kevin asked local NSD, Doug Cain, to make sure our agents filled all the seats in the courtroom, a hundred seats or so, first thing every morning. This pre-emptive strike left no room for the competition's supporters. Their positive presence, Kevin said, made all the difference in the world.

"It always helps to put faces on people and to humanize the issues," Kevin explained later. "It was good for the judge and witnesses on both sides of the case to see the full support of our agents all four days of the trial."

TRENCH WARFARE: LIFE UNDERWRITERS ASSOCIATIONS VS. A.L. WILLIAMS

By Kevin King

1. NALU – NATIONAL ASSOCIATION OF LIFE UNDERWRITERS

NALU, a 139,000-member organization with 1,000+ member associations representing hundreds of insurance companies across the United States, actively discredited A.L. Williams through numerous tactics. It routinely placed anti-A.L. Williams articles in its many association newsletters and magazines, passed out 500,000+ copies of anti-A.L. Williams brochures, and distributed anti-ALW videos entitled "Rhetoric or Reality" and "What've You Got To Lose."

In one brochure, NALU quoted the research of a "Dr. Arthur L. Williams of Penn State" (a different person) that said "few term policies are in effect 20 years after they are bought " – a deliberate attempt to mislead consumers into thinking that (the real) Art Williams didn't believe in his own type of product.

NALU often discussed the "A.L. Williams problem" at its group meetings and conventions. The 1988 NALU convention featured anti-Williams crusader Bob Michael and his seminar "Winning Strategies v. A.L. Williams," which compared Art Williams to Adolph Hitler and Jim Jones. Its president during this time period, Alan Press actively pursued A.L. Williams in a monthly industry column.

2. CALU – CALIFORNIA ASSOCIATION OF LIFE UNDERWRITERS

After Commissioner Gillespie filed the Accusation with the California Insurance Department in May 1988, CALU distributed copies of the Accusation (and related materials) to any agent or association outside of California – upon request, free of charge. The trial began March 1989. On July 28, 1989, Judge Judson announced his recommendation that no disciplinary action be taken against A.L. Williams, and dismissed the complaint due to lack of sufficient merit. The August 1989 "CALU Update" newsletter, however, sent a different message. It described the Accusation in detail, but failed to mention the total exoneration by Judge Judson, leaving the reader to think A.L. Williams still risked losing its license in California. The newsletter mass distributed to agents and associations throughout the country.

3. RIVERSIDE COUNTY ALU (CALIFORNIA)

On January 8, 1988, the Riverside County ALU held a day-long seminar called "Sack the Coach," featuring Ken Young, another outspoken anti-Williams critic. The five goals of the program were: (1) conserve your business, (2) insulate your clients from A.L. Williams, (3) get back to lost clients to conserve business, (4) provide knowledge for combating replacement, and (5) make money on ALW clients.

Hired frequently by Prudential, Ken Young led many anti-Williams seminars and sold an "I Got Art Kit" through his company, "A.R.M.S." (Anti Replacement Method Services).

4. MINNESOTA ALU

On December 5, 1988, the Minnesota Association of Life Underwriters conducted a seminar called "Winning Against Williams," featuring ALW critic Bob Michael.

5. LOUISIANA ALU

In Louisiana, on June 27, 1989, LALU president, Sandra O'Keefe, publicly urged the State Insurance Department to investigate ALW and MILICO. She requested that the public and LALU agents forward complaints to her office.

On July 7, 1989, LALU sent out press releases to the Louisiana media, stating the same request. Many Louisiana newspapers carried the press release as a "story," creating the impression throughout the state that A.L. Williams had engaged in improper conduct. (See article below.) No investigation took place.

6. TEXAS ALU

In August and September 1989, TALU sent out notices, letters and newspaper advertisements disguised as stories, describing a routine market conduct examination of A.L. Williams and MILICO as an "investigation of misrepresentation, defamation and non-payment of claims." The hype created the impression that specific acts of wrongdoing by A.L. Williams and/or MILICO had caused the State of Texas to react with this examination. (In truth, Texas conducts 70-80 market conduct examinations a year. This regular examination did not single out ALW/MILICO.)

The Texas State Department of Insurance censured TALU on August 31, 1989, for this mischaracterization. Nevertheless, on September 7, 1989, TALU sent out a press release alleging "misrepresentation," "defamation," and "non-payment of claims" in regards to A.L. Williams. As a result, "stories" and advertisements about the so-called "investigation" appeared in local newspapers, further entrenching the perception that A.L. Williams engaged in serious improper conduct.

SUMMARY

Much of this subversive activity, tho not all, came to a halt following the dismissal of the California case in September 1989. However, lies about A.L. Williams, such as… outlawed in all 50 states, banned from doing business in Tennessee, banned from doing business in California, doesn't pay its death claims, is an illegal pyramid, and so on… continued to circulate as "truth" among certain circles for many years.

LALU newspaper article:

> **LALU president calls for A.L. Williams investigation**
>
> Sandra H. O'Keefe, recently elected first woman president of the Louisiana Association of Life Underwriters (LALU), says she is asking Insurance Commissioner Doug Green to look into the actions of A.L. Williams agents' operations in Louisiana, due to the number of complaints from the organization membership and from consumers.
>
> O'Keefe cited Tennessee's recent investigation that condemns many of the A.L. Williams firm's marketing practices there, according to Thomas M. Angel, LALU public relations chairman.
>
> "As professional insurance agents we are extremely concerned about the marketing methods used to sell life insurance by certain groups of agents," she said. "Because of possible conflict of interest, it would be impossible for us to do an objective analysis such as was done in Tennessee.
>
> "Therefore, we have called on the commissioner's office to investigate the marketing practices of this specific organization. If the A.L. Williams sales practices in Louisiana are anything like those in Tennessee — and we believe they are — then an investigation is certainlyb called for to protect the insurance buyers of the state," she said.
>
> O'Keefe became the 45th president of LALU since it was founded in 1955. The statewide, non-profit organization totals some 3,000 members.

A July 1989 article from a Louisiana paper "reported" Lousiana's new ALU president calling for an "investigation" into alleged wrongdoing by A.L. Williams and MILICO. Neither the wrongdoing, nor the investigation, ever took place.

Our people packed the courtroom, and several saw themselves well quoted on television during the highly publicized battle. It took six months, but Judge Judson finally reached a stunning recommendation: All action against A.L. Williams and MILICO should be terminated without discipline.

In his recommendation, the judge found two instances of misrepresentation in the booklet. The two items related to the inappropriate use of information from A.M. Best, an independent statistical firm. However, he determined the violations to be neither material nor meaningful. Judge Judson recommended that no disciplinary action be taken against A.L. Williams, and that the entire complaint be dismissed, citing the legal doctrine "de minimum non curat lex" – "the law does not concern itself with trifles."

His ruling went to Commissioner Gillespie, who followed his recommendation and completely dismissed the complaint.

What a thrilling victory! Total exoneration. Again the outcome clearly revealed the root problem as our competition, not the regulators. We'd won yet another battle over competition in the marketplace – a war between two very different products and two opposing philosophies. It still remained the choice of a family to decide what type of insurance best suited its needs.

The dismissal sent one more strong message to the competition. For 22 years, we'd fought regulators and the competition – since that day back in May 1967 when I'd been called to Richard Cain's deputy commissioner office at the Georgia insurance department and asked if I'd replaced a whole life policy with term. From that moment on, we'd been at war with our competitors. Beyond all doubt, this case proved they couldn't beat us in a courtroom. They would have to come up with better products to beat us at the kitchen table.

For all practical purposes, the regulatory and legal war ended with the California case.

A.L. Williams and our unbeatable "Buy Term and Invest the Difference" crusade had won.

BOMBSHELLS

On Monday, July 31, just three days after Judge Judson's dismissal of the California case, I jumped on ALW-TV with major announcements.

"First off, I want to tell you the news from California. The industry took its final and best shot… and lost big. This is a real victory and I'm so proud of our company and our people who worked so hard out there in California."

The studio exploded in cheers. (Think of the streets of America on VJ Day, and you have an idea.) The war was *over*. What a milestone in our company history.

I went on to talk about some exciting events to come. Several months back, I'd announced an NSD-only convention to Australia… at a cost of $3 million dollars. I'd now decided to use the money to recognize more leaders. Instead of that trip, I wanted now to bring every new NSD and his or her Partner to "Little River," our Madison plantation home, for a special three-day weekend with Angela and me.

I added another incentive for NSDs, too – six NSD meetings per year, just for winners of special NSD-only contests. This "NSD Elite Team" would enjoy two-day, all-expenses-paid meetings with top company leadership.

"These will be old-fashioned, get-down-and-get-after-it meetings," I declared. "We are going to focus on leadership – an intense kind of leadership training you can pass to your downline leaders. This will build leaders from the ground up."

Finally, I announced that my Inner Circle of top field leaders would no longer be "permanent." Inner Circle members would attend meetings and conference calls based solely on their "ability to perform right now."

"Eventually, I want 100 people on my Inner Circle. But I promise you, I will always put my 'eleven best people on the field,'" I stated.

Then I spelled out the "six strengths in a leader" I wanted on my "first team."

- **Loyalty**

- **A positive life – not just a positive attitude**

- **Creativity in leadership**

- **Super intensity**

- **A 'team first' attitude**

- **A mindset of A.L. Williams as more important than just a job**

"That's my starting team. That's who I want," I said. "I will announce rotating members at meetings and conference calls. I urge you to use these six strengths when you choose your inner circle, too. Who is performing magnificently right now, regardless of level? Who is not performing at 100 percent maximum right now? Coasting? Resting on laurels? That's over. This is a new level of competition!"

I sent two messages to the sales force:

1. A.L. Williams will pay builders a "bonanza" in the next 10-15 years.

2. Extreme competition had returned to the company.

True to form, the wake-up call did the trick – our August month-end numbers spiked off the charts. Life apps blew past my 100,000 goal to a whopping 107,546 – the highest monthly count in company history!

The competitive edge had returned to A.L. Williams, one-thousand-fold.

A GIANT EMERGES

On October 31, the A.L. Williams Corporation held a special shareholders meeting at the home office. Shareholders voted unanimously to approve Primerica's proposal to buy out the remaining 30.2 percent of A.L. Williams shares. Primerica's stockholders did the same.

Since the merger announcement in June, a few of our prominent shareholders, like Peter Lynch, expressed a thought that the value of the stock swap offered by Primerica was too low. In response, Primerica bumped up the exchange ratio from 80 percent to 82 percent. Salomon Brothers, the investment firm hired to handle the fairness analysis, established the price as sufficient. (The exchange ratio was just a mathematical way to even out the stock price, making ours equal to theirs.)

The adjustment rewarded our stockholders with an instant 22 percent "raise" in price. For every 100 shares, stockholders earned an extra $625. It's not often that a stock price jumps 22 percent in one day. An incredible windfall and reward passed to our A.L. Williams families who had invested their hard-earned dollars in our public company.

On November 1, 1989, in Sandy's Primerica boardroom in New York, Sandy and I signed the official paperwork. The entire transaction – the buyout of the public company and the sale of the A.L. Williams sales force – was complete.

Afterward, Sandy looked at me and asked, "Well, Art, how does it feel? The pressure is off now. I'm so happy for you."

I smiled. We shook hands and chatted. But inside, his comment made my stomach twist.

I never once viewed this deal as a "pressure's off" kind of thing. I'd signed those papers for one reason – to protect the company. I didn't plan on slowing down or getting out.

In fact, I'd picked up the pace. In addition to the upcoming RVP/RM convention in New Orleans in March, I'd launched a huge cycle of "Become a Builder" contests. Starting in May, we would treat 1,800 qualified winners to incentive trips to one of five spectacular locations – San Francisco, Hawaii, Boca Raton, Bermuda and Europe. We were about to spend $10 million rewarding those builders. I meant for next year, 1990, to be our greatest year ever at A.L. Williams.

Later that month, at our NSD meeting in Palm Springs, we unveiled a new company logo to signify the start of this "new era" in company history.

"Everything we accomplished in the past 12 years has been fantastic, but today, I believe the best is yet to come," I declared from the podium. I wore a red T-shirt emblazoned with the new logo. "The next five to 10 years will be A.L. Williams' greatest."

As 1989 swept into 1990, year-end numbers blew us all away. Again, the sales force broke its own "world record" for face amount of individual life insurance placed in force, issuing *$93.4 billion* in new business on the books. Canada issued $5.5 billion, bringing our company total to an astounding *$98.9 billion!*

Even more marvelous, we smashed the $300 billion barrier for cumulative individual life insurance put in force since March 1980. MILICO's total now stood at *$301.1 billion.*

These business milestones stood alone, achieved by no other life insurance company

– and we'd done it in ten years.

Announcing this news on the Monday ALW-TV broadcast, I could hardly contain myself. "Sometimes when you are building a championship team, you have to take a step back in order to take a giant leap forward. Think of all we did in finalizing the merger with Primerica and positioning a new compensation system. If we ever had a year we could've backslid a little, it was 1989. But we didn't! We continued our unbelievable growth, just as we have every year since 1977. Folks, we did $93.4 billion in a reorganization year! We beat the second and third companies combined *again*! Now that's the way to end a decade!"

Something else I just couldn't wait to announce – our 1989 average death claim was $112,000, compared to Prudential's $3,000 and Metropolitan's $4,000.

"This would be a sad world without A.L. Williams," I told our people with real emotion. I remembered my own family when Daddy died. "I'm so proud of the way we've built this company – with people who understand that our Crusade is right and good. I'm so proud we took on the largest industry. We've changed lives… and we really have changed the world… one family at a time."

We kicked off a new decade in the Superdome in New Orleans. On Wednesday, March 7, 1990, an unprecedented 40,000 A.L. Williams people streamed into the city from all over North America. We filled up nearly every hotel and motel in a 30-mile radius. That afternoon, at a special NSD meeting at the Hyatt Regency, I passed out neon yellow jackets and caps to all the NSDs. (NSD Partners got neon pink jackets and caps.)

"I want you to stand out all week long," I told them. "You are the leaders of this company, the present and the future. I want people to stop in the streets of New Orleans to ask you why you are wearing these jackets… and I want you to tell them *you earned it!*"

All day Wednesday and Thursday, A.L. Williams people passed through registration. We offered a slate of 60 workshops conducted by dozens of field leaders and home office execs on every important business subject. Workshops filled up immediately. For the first time ever, the size of the Superdome allowed us to hold all general sessions at one location, with no separate Partners sessions or breakout meetings elsewhere. That meant all attendees would hear all the speeches. And what a star-studded line-up we offered:

- **Gerald Ford, 38th president of the United States; honorary member of Primerica board of directors**

- **Joe Gibbs, head coach, Washington Redskins, three-time Super Bowl champion**

- **John Templeton, founder, Templeton Growth Fund**

- **Sam Rutigliano, head football coach, Cleveland Browns**

- **Rev. Jerry Falwell, founder and chancellor, Liberty University**

- **Max Cleland, Georgia Secretary of State**

Thursday evening, Opening Night kicked off with a spectacular parade featuring 5,000 participants – winners of the "Become a Builder" contest, NSDs, and the Inner Circle. Olympic style, each group made a grand entrance dressed in tuxedos and evening gowns, waving flags. After an inspirational, patriotic performance by the ALW Band &

Chorus, Angela and I made our grand entrance.

Just beforehand, standing backstage on the massive red, white and blue set that stretched across the floor of the Superdome, I looked out at the crowd.

Forty thousand people.

A lot of people… even in a huge stadium. Company leaders filled those seats – NSDs, SVPs, RVPs and Regional Managers – not greenies. I sucked in my breath.

"This is it," I thought, as the music swelled and laser lights flashed and sparkled. "This is the moment we've all worked so hard for, all these years." Tears of joy welled in my eyes. I gazed at something extraordinary… A gathering most leaders only dream will ever happen for their company.

It was happening for A.L. Williams. Truly, a company of destiny.

Angela and I walked out on stage, hand in hand, for our introduction. It felt like a dream. The whole Superdome glittered with flashing lights and smiling faces.

As I stepped to the podium to make my speech, I'd never felt so good, so strong. The crowd rose to its feet, thundering, chanting, clapping. This was Waycross and Prudential and Primerica – every win along the way combined.

The people there could feel it, too – an electricity that zipped through every mind, every heart. A sense of greatness achieved… and the anticipation of greater things yet to come.

"Every now and then, if you're lucky, you have an opportunity to participate in a once-in-a-lifetime event," I proclaimed from the podium.

"Tonight, we are participating in history. This A.L. Williams event may be the largest meeting ever held by one single company.

"Tonight, in New Orleans, in the Superdome, in this historic meeting, I'm announcing our theme for 1990." The stage backdrop, which displayed the A.L. Williams logo, electronically "flipped" to reveal the new 1990 theme and logo: "Be Proud, Be Tough, Attack!"

The crowd roared. I yelled, "You know what?"

"*What?*" echoed back 40,000 voices.

"This is the sixth consecutive year we've won the National Championship!" At that moment, spotlights beamed on a huge red banner above the

The New Orleans RVP/RM convention, held March 8-11, 1990, at the Superdome, featured special guests and a new ALW logo.

289

crowd that read: National Champions 1984, 1985, 1986, 1987, 1988, 1989.

"I'm so proud of you I can't stand it! All my life I've wanted to be somebody. I've wanted to make a difference, wanted people to look at me and say, 'Art, you're special, you're different.'

"I've always believed the difference between winning and losing is this much. To win you've got to have an edge. I think part of this edge is you have to be proud. So proud it just oozes out of your body. If you just like something you'll never be great at it.

"I *love* A.L. Williams. I love everything about it. I'm proud of all the things we stand for. I'm so proud we took on the largest industry in the world. In any city, town or village in Canada and the U.S., you can go into any insurance company's office and ask about A.L. Williams and they will squirm and turn red. They know we are the undisputed leader! You think I ain't proud?

The crowd boomed.

"Our competition was big and powerful and they used their influence against us when we were small, nothing but a peanut. But we were proud! And we didn't quit. Think how bad it would be for the American family, the Canadian family, if A.L. Williams didn't exist. Think if we'd quit!"

"You know the biggest reason why people fail in this business? They quit too soon. To win, you've got to fight the fight, six, eight, ten years. It's tough to win in the big leagues. But you know what? A.L. Williams was built for people who grew up hungry, who want to be somebody – the two-percenters.

"To win in the free enterprise system, you have to do what's right. You have to be honest. Tell the truth. Not cut corners. At the same time you have to be tough. Most people think you can't be good and tough at the same time. Bull. You have to stand for something. Our concepts are good for the consumer. This isn't just a job to us. It's not just a way to make money. We're on a crusade!

"Tonight, I'm issuing a call to arms. We can't become too pretty, too comfortable. We can't feel too good or too important. Today, the market is bigger than when we started in 1977. Our compensation, our products, our support – they're better than ever.

"But you know what? Products are not the key; neither is compensation. You don't win with support. Folks, you are the key.

"There are no guarantees in the free enterprise system. We have a chance to build a company the magnitude of Coca-Cola. We can become famous all over the world. We can do great things. Or…" I paused.

"We can become comfortable, lose our edge and become like any mediocre company with a mediocre future.

"The enemy is not Prudential or the NALU. The enemy is us! It's our attitudes, our dreams, our goals! The enemy is complacency, the willingness to accept being good when we can truly be *great*.

"So what about you? Are you comfortable? Can your family count on you? Are you proud, tough, willing to attack? Think about it. The bottom line – A.L. Williams fails if you fail! It succeeds… if you succeed!"

That night – that entire New Orleans meeting – symbolized the pinnacle of all we'd achieved in A.L. Williams, all that was to come.

I didn't know it then, but the New Orleans convention would be my last as leader and founder of the sales force. The road with A.L. Williams was about to split and, unbelievably, I would go a different way.

The months to come would be the hardest and darkest days of my life. But through it all, one truth sustained me: Every waking moment since February 10, 1977, I'd lovingly and relentlessly devoted everything I had to build A.L. Williams into a great company. Now "my baby" was in the hands of someone else.

26 A Hard Good-Bye

On July 20, 1990, I made a sudden, unexpected farewell announcement to the A.L. Williams sales force.

The problems stemmed from dealings with a former ALW sales agent, Randy Stelk. In 1987, we fired Stelk from A.L. Williams for "rebating," a severe ethical violation. After Stelk left A.L. Williams, he formed his own company called Amerishare and began to violate his non-compete agreement by recruiting and soliciting A.L. Williams agents and clients. A 1989 injunction, ordering him to "cease and desist" his illegal activity, did little good.

We fought back hard. A.L. Williams consisted of good people with good morals. But we were warriors. If you were looking for a fight, then you better bring your lunch, because we would fight you all day, all night, and the next day.

Stelk, through some personal connection and influence, convinced the U.S. Attorney in Jacksonville to open an investigation against A.L. Williams on the pretext that we were a "big" company trying to put a "little" company out of business.

At Sandy's request, I stepped down to take "a leave of absence" until the Jacksonville investigation was over. That's what I was told.

The irony ran deep. Over the course of our history, A.L. Williams had been investigated dozens of times. And we *always* won. This time, Sandy had taken over the company and he had his own lawyers – and just one of my lawyers – fight the investigation. Sadly, I was not allowed to be involved. I could only watch from the sidelines, forced to remain silent.

For the next few months, attorneys worked diligently to provide information to stop the investigation. We were the victim, but it took time to prove.

After three months, battling the case, the truth emerged. The U.S. Attorney in Jacksonville offered a settlement with no fines. It didn't happen. Sandy said no.

Not until October 1992 was the case dismissed entirely.

Those two years of "limbo" put me into an emotional tailspin. My bitterness grew deep and even self-destructive at times.

HITTING BOTTOM

Within eighteen months of my departure, the sales force plunged from 225,000 licensed agents to 70,000. And stayed there.

Boe left the company for good, Treacy moved up to interim leader for a few months. In the years that followed, Sandy sent in a series of corporate leaders to get the sales force back on track. It proved to be a terrible, turbulent time for the company. The constant changes devastated both the sales force and the home office staff.

The hardest part? I couldn't fight back. Legally, my hands were tied. I could do nothing to help the company I so dearly loved. I was excluded completely. Talk about a cruel irony: I had sold A.L. Williams to make sure it would last forever. Now it looked as if I'd ruined it.

Seeing the company I'd so much of poured my life into almost destroyed... almost destroyed me. I tumbled into depression, a bottomless sadness for me, for everyone.

To add even more sorrow, my brother, Bill, died of a heart attack at 45, just a few months after I left the company. He died as suddenly as my father had, at almost the same age. He left his wife, Patsy, and their two beautiful children. It was a ray in the gloom that Bill's term policy and investments left them in good financial shape. My brother's diligence in following our company's principles saved his family.

In 1993, Primerica asked me to come back and speak at a convention in Atlanta and I did. But that was the end of it. By then, I got the picture – returning to the company in any capacity would not be possible.

Sandy and I could never work together again.

We built companies two different ways. Sandy was not capable of building a company the way we built A.L. Williams; I was not capable of building a company the way Sandy built his.

Sandy believed in wearing a suit, having lunch and playing golf with his competition, and avoiding negative publicity.

I believed in wearing a T-shirt with "I Want Pru Bad" on the front, relentlessly "getting after" the competition, and lots of controversy.

Sandy focused on driving up the stock price. I focused on winning a cause and pushing up people.

Polar-opposite approaches to business. They both worked... but not together. Oil and water.

Looking back, regarding Sandy, I think I got it wrong. Convinced that Sandy believed in me and supported my vision for taking A.L. Williams global, I overlooked deeper issues. In reality, I can see now that Sandy had different goals, different reasons for purchasing A.L. Williams. They didn't dovetail with mine.

As a Monday morning quarterback, I now believe Sandy meant all along to take over leadership of the company – without me.

A couple of clues.

In late November 1988, the A.L. Williams board of directors – Jim Miller, Lee Myers, Johnnie Caldwell and Marvin Arrington – met in a downtown Atlanta hotel to approve the 70 percent majority sale of ALWC to Primerica. Sandy and I sat in another room, waiting for what I thought would be a quick decision.

Instead, the directors deliberated for hours.

Understandably, Sandy got nervous. "Art, what is going on?" he asked. "I thought you said this was a done deal."

"I thought so, too," I said, exasperated. "They just keep asking for more time." Sandy crossed his arms. We waited again.

Finally, the directors called me in. Their comment surprised me. "Art, are you sure you want to sell the public company to Primerica? We question whether you and Sandy can work together."

"Look, I've thoroughly analyzed this decision," I told them, again. "I am totally positive Sandy and I can work together. Can we wrap this up?"

After a little more discussion, they signed their approval. The deal went through.

Years later, I learned those four men placed a bet that Sandy and I wouldn't last eight months. Prophetic, I guess. Eight months after I sold the agency to Sandy, I was asked to leave.

I failed to notice something else, too. Dated December 4, 1989, this *BusinessWeek* article appeared just a month after the agency sale.

- - - - - - - -

[Sandy] Weill is aware of A.L. Williams' reputation. He says that its "image will improve" but declines to give more details. Analysts speculate that Weill will try to reduce the influence of Arthur L. Williams Jr., the insurance company's founder. Williams, who has no official title, is paid an undisclosed percentage of all commissions generated by A.L. Williams agents – a very lucrative arrangement for him. He motivates his salespeople with emotional pep talks, reaching back to his roots as a Columbus (Ga.) high school football coach. Williams has made enemies over the years in the industry.

Weill admits the role of Williams, a top Primerica shareholder, could change. "What he did in one period may not be what he's doing in the future," Weill says. Whether A.L. Williams can earn the profits Primerica wants may hinge on Weill's ability to keep Art Williams happy, while cutting his impact on the company.

"The Battalion that Will Press Primerica's Sales Attack,"

– BusinessWeek, December 4, 1989

- - - - - - - -

Hindsight… always 20-20.

MOVING FORWARD

The two years following my departure from A.L. Williams stand as the hardest of my life.

Deeply worried, I stopped eating and sleeping. I lost a lot of weight. Then the pattern reversed; I began eating too much and gained extra weight. Nothing helped. Initially, I found no solace in family or friends. Every day seemed like a year. At our home on Amelia Island, I spent days walking the beach, mourning the loss of A.L. Williams. Angela walked with me every step of the way, always my faithful partner.

Truth was, I didn't know how to go on. I felt sick, hopeless. My main purpose in life? Gone.

During this time, people reached out to me in special ways. Boe Adams stood by me, one of my greatest encouragers and supporters. Frank Dineen, always a good buddy, called me every day, just to talk… and listen. Jim Powers, head of our Family & Marriage Resources organization, called often to comfort.

Even though people in the company were told not to communicate with me, hundreds of calls and letters flooded in, filled with love and concern.

Jerry Falwell kept in touch as well. Over the years, many well-known Christian speakers had graced the pulpit of his Thomas Road Baptist Church in Lynchburg, Virginia. I asked Jerry to send me copies of what he considered the most outstanding sermons.

Jerry took my request seriously. Instead of just "a few," he sent me 365 sermons – one for every day of the year. When the box arrived, I tore into it like a starved man on a deserted island. I listened to all the sermons, over and over, sometimes three or four a day. I read my Bible every day, too, saturating my mind in God's Word.

Slowly, new thoughts emerged. Since my days in Cairo, many times it seemed things just worked out in my favor. Analyzing it all, I knew I'd depended too often on my own strength. Facing this final crisis with A.L. Williams, realization hit hard: Life was not about me, or my gifts. It was about *God's faithfulness*.

Over the years, I had seen His faithfulness in A.L. Williams. Time after time, His hand of providence guided us to victory over insurmountable odds. His blessings overflowed to our people. So many lives changed for the better, thanks to His working through the auspices of the company.

Remembering God's faithfulness to our family kept me going. I counted my blessings.

I couldn't imagine a better spouse than Angela. We'd lived our marriage as a team. I couldn't imagine two more wonderful children than Art and April. God continually blessed our relationships, keeping us close through the years. It made me proud as a daddy when Art followed in my footsteps and coached high school football, before launching his own successful business. It was an answer to prayer that our children both chose wonderful, ideally suited spouses. Interestingly, April married Mark DeMoss, Art DeMoss' son.

In the darkest pit of those awful years, more beautiful grandbabies began to arrive, filling us with indescribable joy.

That one blessing soared above the rest. *Time with family*. I was able to invest my time and energy in seven marvelous grandchildren – something that would not have been possible, at least not in this way, if I'd stayed at the company.

Through their little lives, the light returned to mine. God's faithfulness continued to flow. Little by little, purpose returned to my weary bones. Life was worth living again.

It's like King Solomon says in Ecclesiastes 3:1: "To everything there is a season, a time for every purpose under heaven."

In the end, I gave up my grief to accept, in humility, a hard, but deeply valuable lesson – God had a plan. And it was much bigger than me.

Gradually, life came full circle.

27 Legacy

Life came full circle for the company, too. As years pass, I see more of "the plan" unfolding. Known since 1991 as Primerica Financial Services, the company finally got back on track and is doing great. In 2000, two "true sons" of A.L. Williams – John Addison and Rick Williams – became co-leaders of the sales force. Today, under their leadership, the sale force once again numbers more than 100,000+ licensed agents and reclaimed its "title" as the largest financial services sales force in the world.

In 2004, the company issued 400,000 new life apps and a face amount of $91.4 billion – the biggest year since 1989.

On the global scene, the business opportunity expanded successfully into the United Kingdom and Spain, with new sales forces now in place in those countries. At year-end 2005, the total face amount in force now numbers $581 billion – more than half a trillion dollars. The company paid also out an incredible $703 million in death claims. Diversification? Also successful, with $4.2 billion in total investment sales and $5.2 billion in consolidation loans.

Because PFS is part of the Citigroup empire – the largest financial services company in the world – global expansion and diversification have increased the size and scope of the original opportunity. The company's future is truly secure.

The life insurance industry's future, however, is not!

VINDICATION

When we entered the market in 1977, that industry controlled 60 percent of U.S. assets, *and* the regulators *and* the politicians.

Their story today? Very different. Their glass house shows some serious cracks.

In 1995, Prudential Securities paid out $1.5 billion in fines to settle more than 100,000 investor claims.

In 1996, a task force of insurance regulators in 29 states, led by the New Jersey Department of Banking and Insurance, discovered that Prudential insurance agents improperly pressured clients to replace their life insurance policies with more expensive policies in order to generate commissions, a practice known as "churning." Prudential paid $410 million in lawsuit settlements and a record $35.3 million in regulator fines and clients reimbursements as a result of the findings.

Prudential wasn't alone. In 1994, Metropolitan Life agreed to pay $20 million in fines and $76 million in policyholder refunds to settle allegations it improperly marketed life insurance policies as retirement or savings plans.

In 1995, New York Life agreed to a national class action settlement in a dispute over dividends that cost the company $65 million.

Unbelievable! The very thing we were accused of doing for 20 years was actually going on in the companies trying their hardest to put us out of business.

(Remember... Even though the industry controlled the regulators, the largest fine

A.L. Williams ever paid turned out to be $13,500 – over a sales brochure. No fines ever for consumer complaints.)

THE INDUSTRY SPEAKS

Bottom line? *The industry is changing*. It must. It can no longer conduct "business as usual" and expect success.

The scoreboard tells the story.

In 1977, there were 2,000 life insurance companies in operation. By 2003? Only 69 life insurance companies sold new life insurance! Only 39 companies recruited even one new life insurance salesperson.

In 1977, whole life dominated 86 percent of all life insurance sales. Over the last 26 years, whole life sales dropped to less than 20 percent.

Today, only 2.7 percent of consumer dollars go toward life insurance protection. Where is the rest? In mutual funds and annuities – separate savings and investment vehicles – not bundled products like cash value or universal life.

In 1977, the entire industry boasted 257,000 agents. By 2003, the number had shrunk to 177,000 agents – a loss of 80,000. (If you recall, the A.L. Williams sales force numbered 225,000 in 1989. Unbelievable! A.L. Williams had more licensed agents than the entire industry *combined!*)

In 2003, the entire insurance industry recruited 29,968 agents. (Compare this to A.L. Williams' 240,000 new recruits per year.)

Where do all these numbers come from? The industry itself. In 2003, an elite life insurance group called "Task Force for the Future" released a report stating the following damaging facts:

- **The industry has lost its capacity to build "face-to-face distribution."**

- **The "value relevance" of permanent life insurance is becoming "marginalized."**

- **Individual term insurance is the industry's dominant product.**

- **The current distribution system is failing.**

Want another shock? The report revealed that regulators now seek to protect the consumer. How about that! All those years of being an *industry* "protector"... *Now* it dawns on them to care about consumers!

Two more "kickers." In today's insurance environment, 89 percent of all new agents are out of business within four years. And... between 1977 and 2003, the traditional industry lost *41,000,000* (that's million) policies.

What do these facts show? One, today's families are better educated about life insurance products. And two, the traditional industry regularly fails to meet their needs.

I believe A.L. Williams played the major role in instigating these epic changes.

DYNASTY

Not long before he died, Arthur Milton (consumer expert and five-time life insurance industry "Man of the Year") shared these observations about A.L. Williams:

"When it came to offering the American consumer what they needed most, A.L. Williams did it best. Their 'Buy Term and Invest the Difference' concept was right. Unlike other companies that sold whatever product made the company and the agent the most money, A.L. Williams sold term insurance only, the cheapest (and purest) form of death protection.

"Their approach was right, too. A.L. Williams' idea of marketing life insurance through the recruitment of an army of part-time agents was revolutionary. The combination of those two concepts brought to the marketplace a better product at a better price – the free enterprise system at its best. It worked well. Even now, no other life insurance company in the history of the industry has ever developed a sales organization as large as A.L. Williams.

"Just as history looks on Henry Ford as the innovator who put America on wheels through mass production of the automobile, I think history will look on Art Williams as the revolutionary who created a distribution system to sell the right kind of insurance and investments to the general public. That accomplishment, to me, is one that not only changed a deeply troubled industry, but empowered 'average and ordinary' people to achieve the heights of financial well-being."

In 1977, "Team A.L. Williams" set out to do the impossible. Together, we desired to change an industry and improve our lives at the same time. Mission accomplished. Today, consumers *know* about term insurance. It's the dominant insurance product on the market.

One last point. Every year, sporting events crown new champions. But few teams dominate the competition for years at a time. Teams like... The New York Yankees – 39 World Series appearances, 26 wins. No other Major League Baseball team even touches those numbers. The Green Bay Packers – five championships in seven years, victories in the first two Super Bowls. Coach Vince Lombardi took a last-place team and transformed it into a football juggernaut. The UCLA Bruins – a record-setting 10 NCAA championships under Coach John Wooden. The Boston Celtics' 16 NBA championships – the most of any basketball franchise.

These teams emerged from obscurity to become sports dynasties. Their competition knew them, respected them, even feared them.

A.L. Williams achieved a similar feat in business. Born a "peanut" with 85 people on February 10, 1977, we grew to such size and scope that every insurance company (all 2,000 of them) and every insurance agent (250,000) across the United States, Canada and Puerto Rico knew us. It didn't matter if it was Los Angeles, a city of 15 million, or a little town like

Cairo, Georgia, with 10,000 people – you could walk into any insurance office anywhere and ask if they'd heard of A.L. Williams. The answer? A red-faced, teeth-gritted, vein-popping yes.

The competition knew us *well*.

In 2004, John Roig, a former coach and one of A.L. Williams' great leaders, sat down for a haircut in his favorite barbershop, a place he'd patronized for 20 years. The barber finished his work, pulled off the apron and said, "John, I want you to meet this gentleman. He just moved here to Fort Lauderdale. He's in the same business you are."

The man in the next chair stood up and stuck out a hand. "Glad to meet you, John," he said. "I'm with Life of Virginia. Who are you with?" John stood up, too. He looked at the outstretched hand but didn't take it. "I'm with your worst nightmare," he said.

Without hesitation, the man blurted, "You don't mean A.L. Williams!"

Thirteen long years had passed since A.L. Williams' name change to Primerica Financial Services.

The competition *still* knows us well.

You think A.L. Williams didn't start a revolution? You think our educational approach to families, letting them decide between two totally opposite products, wasn't effective? You think we didn't trigger a disturbing, monumental, irreversible shift away from "business as usual"?

You think I ain't proud?

We created A.L. Williams to correct an injustice. We dared to be different. Our goals? Impossible. But we did it... We brought a tyrannical industry to its knees... and destroyed the concept of cash value. What a legacy.

FINANCIAL INDEPENDENCE

Our greatest legacy, however, surpasses even that. Company records and accomplishments... changing an industry... all of those amazing feats pale in comparison to what we did for people.

Although we'll never know the exact number, thousands and thousands of families across the United States and Canada followed our "common sense" financial concepts and changed their financial destiny forever. Agents, clients, or both – people who learned to choose the right life insurance, save the difference systematically in mutual funds, IRAs and 401(k)s, and take charge of their finances.

We paid out *billions* in death claims, helping families. We paid out billions in commissions, offering people an unbelievable opportunity to change their present lives, and even future generations. Many people came into the business and never made big incomes... but they did become financially independent, just by following our company's financial principles.

I think of people like SNSD Randall and Mary Walker. Randall farmed and ran a paper route, Mary worked as a schoolteacher. His first year as RVP in 1978, Randall made $136,000 and never looked back. He went on to build a huge organization, become one of the top leaders in the company, and a multi-millionaire. In December 2005, Randall passed away from complications with cancer, but his personal legacy lives on. Mary and their children are financially secure, thanks to Randall's diligent saving and investing.

I think of people like SNSD Frances Avrett. When her husband became ill, Frances bought a greenhouse business to support him and their five children. She worked long, hard hours for very little income – about $18,000. In the early '80s, she dropped everything to master A.L. Williams. Today, Frances is a millionaire, debt free, one of the company's most respected leaders.

I think of people like NSD Mike Perry, a former coach who earned less than $20,000. In a recent letter, Mike shared that his annual income is now $300,000 and their net worth... $1.7 million.

Today, dozens, perhaps hundreds, of people enjoy another kind of legacy: Their children involved in their businesses! Leaders like Virginia Carter, Bill Orender, Greg Fitzpatrick, John Roig, Ann Baxter, Nick Alise, Dick Walker, Ed Randle, David Landrum, Gary Howard and Kip Ridley to name just a few, are building their own "next generation" of leaders with their children – kids who literally grew up in A.L. Williams! Two great examples: When Bob Turley retired, he put his son, Terry, in charge of running his business. When José Rivera in Puerto Rico decided to step down, he did the same with his son, José Jr.

In the face of loss, other family situations occurred. When Donnie Riggs died, his son, Donnie Jr., took over the business. Lawrence and Todd Walker did as well, when their father, Lafayette Walker, passed away. Two wives of A.L. Williams leaders – Mary Walker and Patti Schechter – assumed hierarchy leadership when their husbands (Randall Walker and Dennis Schechter) died.

What a dream come true for families to be able to build their own businesses and then pass them on to spouses, sons or daughters, even grandchildren. That's the power of business ownership.

Thousands of people benefited from company stock investment. Many of our salespeople had never owned a share of stock in their lives, until they purchased A.L. Williams stock. Linda Hapner, Bob Miller's office secretary, for example. In 1982, she invested $1,000 in ALWC stock – and retired with $200,000.

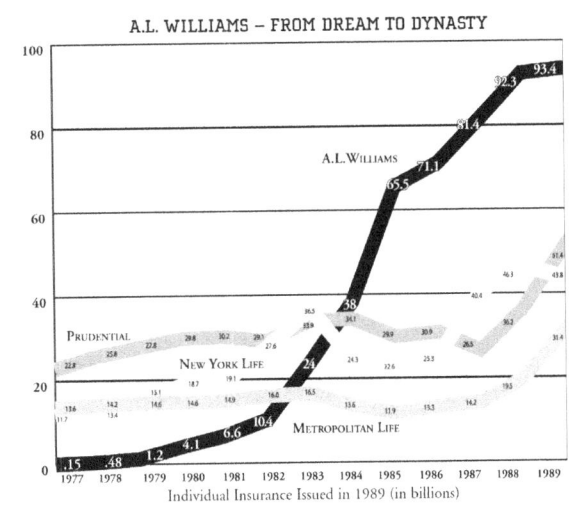

Another good one: Mike Perry's mother, a homemaker whose husband never earned more than $25,000 a year, invested $3,500 in ALWC stock. Today, that sum is worth $300,000 – and she earns $10,800 in annual dividends.

A $10,000 investment in original company stock now equals $6 million. Many families made that risky but wise investment.

From the beginning, A.L. Williams emphasized making and saving money, with the ultimate goal of financial independence.

In 2005, Primerica produced 5,000 leaders earning $50,000 or more annually; 2,000 leaders earned $100,000 and up; 200 leaders topped $500,000. Sixty leaders now cash flow one million dollars or more.

An impressive record! Achieving financial independence still remains a primary goal for Primerica's families today.

The legacy also encompasses lives changed on the inside. I can't give any statistics or facts, only observations. But I think it's probably impossible to go through what we did without coming out better for it. Ask any person from A.L. Williams, or in Primerica today, and see what kind of answer you get.

But here's what I see… A legacy of people who live their lives with more wisdom, confidence, discipline and fulfillment. They know how to work with perseverance to reach their goals, whatever they may be. They go about their days more positive, more encouraging to others around them. They live with passion. They fight for principles and worthy causes without quitting. They choose to serve others, help others, because it's the right thing to do. They know from experience the deep satisfaction that results from living that kind of lifestyle.

I think many would call themselves better leaders. They enjoy better marriages and closer families. They keep their priorities in order – God first, family second, business third.

Now please don't misunderstand. I'm not saying everybody's life is perfect. Nothing is perfect. But I am saying it's *better*. I know I've changed for the better in many ways. I've seen similar transformations in hundreds of others.

A.L. Williams leaves a legacy of great and special people who still model these principles – the same principles Coach Taylor preached to me and all his boys, back in Cairo.

1. **Do what's right.**

2. **Do your best.**

3. **Treat others the way you want to be treated.**

And that's it – our finest legacy of all… Our people.

THE SCOREBOARD TELLS THE STORY…

A.L. Williams: #1 in Every Important Category

#1 in Consumer Concept: We sold term insurance 100 percent of the time, compared to the 13-percent industry average. The typical cost of our term product – $210 for $100,000 of coverage, compared to the typical industry cash value product of $1,272 for same amount ($100,000) of coverage.

#1 in Lowest Cost to Consumer: Averaging all products sold to the consumer, our cost was $3.33 per $1,000. New York Life – $16.17; Prudential – $18.17.

#1 in Average Size Death Claim: Our average death claim: $95,131. Compare to Prudential's at $4,500. Industry average: $6,000.

#1 in Efficiency: We spent less money marketing our product, passing savings to the consumer. Example: In advertising, per policy issued, we spent $0.04 to Prudential's $41.54 to New York Life's $68.50. In office expenses, per policy issued, we spent $149.23 to Prudential's $1,383.64.

#1 in Life Insurance Sales: For seven straight years, we out-produced ALL other life insurance companies. In 1988, we produced $92.3 billion, compared to #2 New York Life at $46.4 billion and #3 Prudential at $36.3 billion. We beat their combined totals of $82.7 billion.

#1 in Total Business In Force: In 12 short years of business, A.L. Williams became the industry's "first and only" $300+ billion company, compared to Prudential's $245 billion and New York Life's $208 billion in cumulative face amount, after decades of doing business.

#1 in Mutual Fund Sales: Largest investment sales force in the world. We helped our clients invest billions of their savings in the best investment vehicle available – mutual funds with IRAs and 401(k)s – an unbeatable combination.

#1 in Size of Sales Force: 225,000 licensed men and women in our sales force. Prudential – a distant second with 40,000.

#1 in Educating the Consumer: Our financial guide book, Common Sense, sold over 16 million copies.

#1 as an Investment: After 20 years, an original 1982 investment of $10,000 in A.L. Williams stock was worth more than $6,000,000 – an annual return of 39.95 percent.

#1 Business TV Network: Largest business television network in the world – bigger than Coke, Ford, Wal-Mart – bigger than "all of them!"

Epilogue: Looking Back

"How do you define winning? I've always said it's the person looking back at you in the mirror. You and you alone know whether or not you really won. You can fool everybody else for a while, but you can't fool yourself. When I look in the mirror, I'm proud of what we did and I'm proud of the way we did it. I look back on A.L. Williams and I wouldn't change nothin.'"

Three days before Coach Taylor died, his wife called. She asked me to come see him and I did.

Coach Taylor was in the last stages of cancer, bedridden, breathing through an oxygen mask. But the day I came, he got out of bed, shaved and sat in a chair for what would be our last visit. I will never forget that day. I spent most of the time telling him how special he was, how he'd changed my life and so many others. Tommy Taylor had been my one true hero, a lifelong role model.

But he had something to tell me, too: his regrets.

I saw the anguish in his eyes. He looked at me and said, "Art, when you get to the end of your life, you have two thoughts. One is how fast time flies. The years between 50 and 60 just flew by in a flash. But the years between 60 and 70 – they were gone in a blink of an eye. The second thought is now I'm 73. My life is over. And… I have so many regrets."

His words just tore me up.

He was so near the end, within days, maybe even hours of dying. If there was ever one person in the world who didn't need any regrets, it was Coach Taylor. I spent our last two hours together telling him so. He lived the most selfless life of anyone I've ever known. He worked two full-time jobs his whole life – recreation director and high school coach. He never made much money. He coached simply because he loved it. He loved the kids.

There's an old Chinese proverb that says, "If your vision is for a year, plant wheat. If your vision is for ten years, plant a tree. If your vision is for a lifetime, plant a person."

Coach Taylor planted hundreds of people, and they in turn planted hundreds of people, who planted hundreds of people. His legacy lives on and on and on.

As a fellow Christian, I knew Coach Taylor was saved. When he died, no one questioned where he'd be spending eternity. I spoke at his funeral. I shared again what he meant to me and to so many others. I miss him so much.

Now I have entered the "fourth quarter" of my life. Coach Taylor and his words of that last afternoon stick in my mind.

What are my joys, my regrets? Every speech I made in A.L. Williams, I talked about how we are "only here for a flicker." We have just a few short years on this earth to make a difference.

When I set out to write this book I had two purposes. One, to record the history of

A.L. Williams, to put down on paper how we fought "The Crusade" and won. I wanted to make sure my grandchildren and their children and their children understand how hard A.L. Williams worked to make the world a little better for them.

Two, I wanted an opportunity to share some of my thoughts from the last few years, to talk straight from my heart, to explain what went right, what went wrong. It will be the first time I've talked publicly about these issues. Think it's time I did.

THE BIG REGRET: SELLING THE COMPANY

For twenty-three years, I called thousands of plays as head coach of A.L. Williams. Some good, some bad. But the all-time worst call for me, personally? Selling A.L. Williams.

My number one goal in selling A.L. Williams was to make it "permanent." Primerica (now Citigroup) offered all the right stuff: stability, unlimited growth capacity, skilled leadership, boundless capital. Endless conversations revealed Sandy's desires: build A.L. Williams into an international powerhouse. Everybody I trusted said "sell." Convinced, I said *let's do it*.

Something nagged at me in the depths of my heart. I pushed it away.

I realize now what it was. I forgot how much I hated corporate America. I forgot the way they treated sales people – the most important people in a company. That reason alone – corporate America – nullified the other dozens of good reasons to sell.

We didn't build A.L. Williams to fit that mold. Think I've mentioned that before. In the sale, my compensation was spread over a 20-year period. Why? I planned to be "on the job" for 20 years. That was *my* plan! But I ignored a contract loophole. Primerica had to pay me... *but they did not have to keep me*.

"Who would want A.L. Williams without Art Williams? Wouldn't you want Walt Disney if you were buying his company?" My thinking? It simply never occurred to me that Primerica might want to run A.L. Williams without me. Or that my season as leader would end before I planned.

Strangely, I didn't realize what others did: Leadership changes... Company culture changes... *Inevitable*.

It's like buying a house. What do you do first? Change it! New colors, carpet, cabinets. You don't ask the former owners for permission. Who cares if they don't like it?

Same with business. Call it naiveté or stupidity, I believed Sandy and Primerica liked everything about A.L. Williams. I believed "corporate America" would remain safely at bay, far outside our fortress walls. *Wrong*.

Because I didn't understand, and certainly did not expect it, being asked to leave the company became the most painful thing I've faced in my life. But the truth is Sandy bought the company – the 225,000-member distribution system, that is. He paid a lot of money for it. He owned the right to run it his way.

I get it now.

WHAT IF?

One more expectation I held at sale time: A.L. Williams would carry its sweeping success international.

That didn't happen immediately, like I planned.

In my toughest moments, I wonder… what if? A.L. Williams grew for 23 straight years *without one down year*. If we'd continued at that 1990 pace, how big would we be now? 500,000? 1,000,000? I don't know.

What if… We'd launched "aggressive diversification" into other areas of financial services where consumers were being "ripped off " – other types of insurance, banking, discount brokerages, mortgages? Endless possibilities! More "enemies," more wars, more clients, more fun… and a bunch more income for our people!

What if… We'd expanded into Europe and the Far East? How widespread could A.L. Williams be today? All that momentum… All that potential… Stopped cold in 1990. Thousands of people… gone.

What if I had not sold A.L. Williams? The question still haunts me. I can't help but wonder.

But, you know what? Part of the glory of "head coach" is getting to call the final shot, for better or worse. I made the call to sell A.L. Williams. Overall, it was best for the company. However, I deeply regret it hurt and disappointed so many of my A.L. Williams teammates. My departure certainly didn't go as planned. I wish I'd done better.

I apologize to all the A.L. Williams people.

CHOICES & REGRETS

Life is full of tests. I know I've failed many tests in my life. I didn't always make the right decisions. I made glaring errors and suffered the consequences for them. Some of my teammates didn't make the right choices when under fire. None of us is perfect. We all make choices we regret. And life isn't always fair.

Sandy enjoyed being a Wall Street "darling" because of his phenomenal ability to grow Citigroup into an international giant. Yet, as he approached the end of his career, Sandy was forced to endure several investigations and huge negative publicity. His company paid out more

than $5 billion in fines and settlements. I'm sure he wishes he'd done some things differently.

Not long ago, I read an article in the Miami Herald about my old nemesis, Randy Stelk. After Amerishare, he started another company, Future First Financial Group. Authorities arrested Stelk and his co-workers in Florida, in May 2003, for fraudulently diverting millions of dollars of investor funds. He was charged with one count of aggravated white-collar crime, one count of racketeering, one count of securities fraud and three counts of grand theft in excess of $100,000. Each count carries a potential 30-year prison sentence.

According to the article, Stelk currently is out on a $10 million bond, awaiting trial.

What a tragedy.

When we fired Stelk in 1987, my attorneys strongly advised me to revoke his insurance license. The justified action would've prevented him from ever selling insurance and investments again. But, after careful consideration, I chose not to. Randy and his wife had three kids.

Their tearful appeals tore at my heart. Taking his license would've ruined his livelihood.

Now looking back, I wish I had. Sure, it would've caused hardship for Stelk at the time. But in the end, removing him from the industry would've saved our company years of headaches. And, even more importantly, perhaps it would've saved him and his family from the far greater calamity he faces today.

OVERCOMING BITTERNESS & REGRETS

Remember this story? Second season at Kendrick High. Ninth game. Our guys head to head with another undefeated team – the "game of the week." Late in the fourth quarter, we scored a touchdown. Score: 7-6. A two-point conversion would win the ball game.

I called timeout, told the offense to run fullback-over-strong-tackle. Something inside of me kept saying, *Art, fake that and run a bootleg*. But the other play, our bread and butter play, always came through. I decided to go with it. So we ran off-tackle... and the other team stopped us.

I should've run a bootleg. I felt it in my gut. But I didn't call it. We finished the season with nine wins and one loss. One play – one lousy yard – separated us from an undefeated season. I had to live a whole year, one whole year, thinking about that one bad call.

That feeling symbolizes the regret I held for my last call as head coach of A.L. Williams. I made thousands of calls in that role... but I ended my career by making the wrong call. I felt it in my gut, but I didn't listen. Instead of one football season, I lived many years with that heartache.

Regret over that decision and bitterness at being asked to leave overwhelmed me at times. I almost let it ruin me. What a waste.

If there's one lesson I've learned since stepping away, it's that bitterness can ruin you. It's been a war of its own kind – one I don't fight nearly as well. Beating Prudential? A piece of cake compared to this.

A real turning point came when I chose to stop feeding the bitterness and move on. I confessed my guilt, anger and disappointment to the Lord. I initiated contact with close friends and let them know how sorry I was for selling the company.

Then, and only then, did I sense real forgiveness and peace – the healing salve I so desperately desired.

David writes in Psalm 136:16 that the Lord is in charge of each of our days. He promises His grace to get through them – without bitterness. I knew my challenge: To apply my faith to these difficult circumstances.

I forgave people who criticized me, questioned my motives and decisions.

I forgave Sandy.

After a long struggle, I forgave myself as well.

The Lord, in His faithfulness, continues to show me how to live "right." The journey goes on. I'm just an old tough-butt coach, you know. I'm so thankful for His love and patience.

I'm thankful for other positives, too. Just as I had to go on with my life, so did many others. To my utter delight and amazement, thousands of former A.L. Williams leaders took our financial and leadership concepts and built other entrepreneurial businesses – in all walks of life, in every type of industry, in communities everywhere.

Other old teammates initiated ministries, charities and foundations. They now lead thriving organizations that reach countless people in need – all over the world.

Their far-reaching impact, effort and creativity touch me deeply. These fine people represent A.L. Williams. The spirit that was… and is… our company. A heritage of goodness that sweeps on… Bigger. Better. Wider. Stronger. More than I ever dreamed.

I'm so proud of that I can't stand it.

ONE LAST THING…

This past year, thanks to the miracles of modern medicine, I recovered from open-heart surgery. At 64, I've now lived longer than any other male in the Williams family. Although I don't know how many more years the Lord will grant me, I want to end well.

When one chapter in your life ends, another begins. I'm grateful for every opportunity in the past. I made my mark in coaching and in business. For the past 16 years, I've lived the "dream life" I always talked about in A.L. Williams. Other business ventures, worldwide travel with Angela and our family, many wonderful new friends – these special things add richness and reward. Now, as I play out my fourth quarter, I intend to spend the rest of my days teaching, mentoring and motivating others.

I've always said, "In the big leagues, you don't win with tricks and gimmicks." Do you know what the "big leagues" are? Your life. And you only get one shot at it.

We are only here for a flicker. So many people seem to think they've got endless days and years to do something. Well, that's wrong. Life goes by so fast. Making lots of money will never ultimately make you happy. Not down deep where it counts.

Doing something meaningful for others, with all your heart, will.

That is destiny. Believe me, it's worth the price.

Co-Author's Note

May 17, 2006

A lovely day in May 2001 – I pulled up to The Hill for my first meeting with Art Williams. Our purpose: discuss the possibility of writing an A.L. Williams history book. Yvonne Tyson had recommended me for the project. As I got out of the car, I felt both nervous and excited. But before I walked up the back step, I took a second to gaze at the magnificent house and grounds... and to remember.

I'd started with A.L. Williams in February 1989 as the publications writer for Angela Williams' Partners Organization, working just down the street in Monroe. I worked out of that office for 18 months, before joining the Publications staff at the home office in Duluth. Often I had occasion to come to The Hill, playing hostess with the Partners' office staff to hundreds of Partners from all over the country, who arrived by the busload for Monday morning tours. Those Partners loved visiting Art and Angela's antebellum home. Their boundless enthusiasm for all things A.L. Williams infected me.

A young writer not long out of college, I'd worked for other companies, but this one was different. The people, the stories, the energy, the purpose, the staff, trips, meetings. The sheer volume of work. I'd never seen anything like any of it. *A real job*. I loved it. The best part – *the people*. "Average and ordinary" families from all over North America doing amazing things on a daily basis – building teams, changing their lives and communities, sharing their experiences with passion on television, in person, in print. Total action, all so positive, so good. The A.L. Williams way of thinking and doing changed me. I spent nearly eight years as a senior writer at the company, then "retired" to my own home office and produced freelance work for one of the company's top sales leaders, Larry Weidel, as well as other clients.

But now, twelve years after my start with A.L. Williams, I found myself back again at this special place... to meet Art. Would he look the same, be the same? After a warm hug and exchange of pleasantries, Art launched into his ideas for creating a book about the history of A.L. Williams. Yep, I thought, he's a bit grayer around the edges maybe, but still the same 'ol feisty Art Williams. *Good*.

Two hours later, still talking. Or rather, Art talked, I listened. About that time, the back door flew open. In swept Angela, smiling and happy, just as I remembered her. "Well?" she asked quizzically. "Has he totally worn you out yet?" How well she knows her husband!

And so began our journey of writing down, for the sake of history, the amazing story of A.L. Williams.

This project? A privilege... but not easy. The daunting task of endless hours of doing interviews, transcribing interviews, researching dozens of old documents and piecing together events that happened 20 and 30 years ago, felt overwhelming at times.

An unexpected pregnancy threw a curve into our production timeline. The addition of a third son into my family's busy household made for an interesting writing schedule. Suddenly I was birthing both a baby and a book! *Whoa*.

But, you know what? It was all good. Both births came out great, although (of course) the book proved to be a far lengthier process. The total conviction that this book had to be written overshadowed the ups and downs, worries and challenges of writing and research. This all-American story with its David vs. Goliath theme and colorful cast of thousands... *Destined to come to life on paper.* I never doubted that for a second.

HOW-TO'S

Many, many decisions shaped this project, but the biggest one involved format: How would we tell the story? I suggested first-person narrative. "People will want to hear from you," I told Art. "This is your memoir of what it took to build A.L. Williams. It should be told in your voice." Art agreed.

And that is what you now hold – Art's story of how it all happened. It is not Boe's story, or Bob Miller's story, or even Angela's story. It is Art's, and Art's alone. And that is as it should be.

Also, we made the decision to include an account of Art's early years in Cairo and coaching. While this time period is typically unremarkable for most biography subjects, I felt that, in contrast, Art's early experiences formed the foundation for the rest of the story. It is in Cairo where Art meets Coach Taylor, where he spends impressionable years with this tremendous leader and friend, learning how to do the single most important thing that influenced his career: *motivate people to achieve.*

Art effectively adhered Coach Taylor's wisdom and inspire-ability to his own charisma and leadership skills. The result produced a company – not of employees and managers – but of leaders, coaches, players, new recruits, veterans, even cheerleaders. He took the dull business of life insurance and turned it into a game. Suddenly, selling and recruiting became fun, competitive, doable and rewarding. After all, it is a rare person who has never played any kind of game. People attracted to A.L. Williams didn't give a hoot about the subtleties of a six-month business plan, but they absolutely grasped the notion of putting on a "term-ite uniform" and going "kneecap to kneecap" against those "trash value" guys in the "wrong-colored jerseys." Building a business now made sense. Life insurance would never be the same.

That Art, as a coach, turned the arena of life insurance into a football field is a fundamental fact the reader must "get" in order to fully comprehend the success of A.L. Williams. What Art learned in Cairo from Coach Taylor, he has carried with him his entire life. To his credit, he has never really changed.

THANK-YOU'S

About midway through the project, Art asked Bob Miller to sit in on our many book discussions. Bob quickly made himself indispensable to both Art and me. His ability to recall events with accuracy, his vast attic stash of old ALW materials, his unbridled enthusiasm for the project and its completion... absolutely invaluable.

Bob, you are truly one of the world's Great Encouragers. Your support, wisdom and problem solving ability kept us all on track. Thank you, Bob, from the bottom of my heart, for all your time, knowledge, help and hope. You made everything better.

Thank you, too, to Danny Murray and Virginia Carter who willingly dug out old company materials and documents for my perusal. Thanks to the many A.L. Williams leaders who took the time to share their memories over the phone and in person. What a joy and privilege to hear your stories.

A huge thanks goes to Mitch Slayton who used his boundless energy and expertise to help get this behemoth printed. You made that part fun, Mitch.

Thank you, too, to Charles McNair, who masterfully edited every page.

Thanks and much love goes to my parents, Ken and Janice Kassel, my biggest fans for 43 years. I'm so grateful for your support, love, kindness and the many opportunities you provided me in life, including supporting me through journalism school at Iowa State University.

Special thanks goes to my mother-in-law, Louise Hutto, who happily and helpfully took care of a blissfully busy toddler, so I could finish writing. Your efforts are appreciated beyond measure.

Heartfelt thanks to my husband, Joey, who helped in countless ways. Thank you for your patience, love and faithfulness. I couldn't have done this without you. And to my three sons, Nathan, Andrew and Samuel, who endured some crankiness and not a few hasty meals.

You four guys motivated me to do my best. I love you.

Thanks, too, to my pastor and his wife, Doug and Cheryl McIntosh, and my church family, Cornerstone Bible Church in Lilburn – your prayers sustained me.

And finally, I want to thank Art Williams. Without him, there would be no A.L. Williams, no story to tell. Art, what would the world be like today if you hadn't listened to that clarion call in your heart to "correct an injustice" and launch a crusade. Thankfully, you not only listened, you acted. What an original.

Thank you both, Art and Angela, for believing in me enough to write your story. The more time passes, the more I stand in awe of all you have accomplished, and the thousands of lives you have helped. You've given so much to so many. So thankful to have played this small role in helping you.

– KKH

Company Timeline

1964 –Art graduates with Bachelor's degree in Physical Education from Mississippi State University; takes assistant football coach position at Thomasville High School

1966 – Takes head football coach position, Appling County High School, Baxley, Georgia; receives 1st Georgia High School "Coach of the Year" award

1967 –Head football coach and athletic director, Kendrick High School, Columbus, Georgia; cousin Ted Harrison introduces Art to "Buy Term and Invest the Difference" concept

1968 –Gets insurance license, starts part-time with ITT Financial Services

1969 –Kendrick team wins AAA region championship; Art receives 2nd Georgia High School "Coach of the Year" award; earns Masters degree in School Administration from Auburn University

1970 –Goes full-time with ITT Financial Services; moves to Atlanta

1973 – Promoted to Regional Vice President with Waddell & Reed (six states); last place region

1974 – 1st place region in 8 months

1976 – Signs up Financial Assurance (with handshake agreement) as product company for new agency

1977 – "Financial Asssurance"

February 10 – Founds A.L. Williams & Associates with 85 team members, Financial Assurance as underwriter

December 13-17 – First A.L. Williams Convention at Grand Hotel in Point Clear, AL; Randall Walker promoted first RVP in ALW; year ends with 8 offices in three states (Georgia, Florida, Alabama)

1978 – "National Home Life"

April –ALW signs contract with National Home Life Insurance Company

August – Bill Orender moves to Texas as first expansion RVP

December – Second A.L. Williams Convention in Point Clear; Bob Miller promoted as 11th RVP

1979 – "PennCorp"

January – Atlanta Data Systems (ADS) opens with 2 employees in 500 sq. ft. office

July – FTC releases 455-page Staff Report on Life Insurance Cost Disclosure, exposing cash value life insurance as poor investment

August – Art DeMoss dies

September – Art and Stanley Beyer sign $100-million general agency agreement with PennCorp Financial Services; MILICO becomes new product company; state of Mississippi declares two-week "cease & desist" against A.L. Williams

October – Bob Buisson named first SVP

December – Third A.L. Williams convention at Sea Island; first spouse meeting launches Partners organization; sales force numbers 4,000 licensed reps

1980 – "Greatest Growth Year"

February – 125 RVPs

March 1 – MILICO opens regional office in Tucker; processes 2,500 apps in first month

April – Rome incentive trip

June – New record: 4,000 apps in one month; North Carolina launches replacement and pyramid investigations into ALW; in-house print shop opens

July – In-house publication department and distribution center open at home office

August – ALW convention in Montreal with 88 RVPs; persistency blow-up with PennCorp; Opportunity magazine introduced

November – New record: 2,000 apps in one month!

December – Dallas RVP meeting; second persistency blow-up with PennCorp; Bob Miller and Bobby Buisson named in-house NSDs; year ends with 115 RVPs

1981 – "Crossroads"

February – New Mod-11 product rolls out; Penn Corp signs 10-year contract with A.L. Williams

March – First American National Corporation (later renamed The A.L. Williams Corporation) established

April – Incentive trip to San Francisco; top RVPs travel on to Hawaii

August – José Rivera, Puerto Rico, 1st RVP outside of continental U.S.

October – Insurance consumerist Arthur Milton endorses ALW; record-breaking 18,000 apps; 200 RVPs

November – FANS opens for business; Arthur Milton speaks to Atlanta-area RVPs

1982 – "Going Public"

January – Congress announces expanded IRA legislation; January RVP meeting introduces new NSD position

February – Company celebrates 5th anniversary!

March – 1st ALWC stock offering announced; life apps surge to 21,500 in one month

April – Art announces first field NSD, Hubert Humphrey; new company logo introduced at Atlanta RVP meeting

May – ALW leaders begin 14-city "Super Seminar" tour across country

June – First A.L. Williams convention to Boca Raton Resort & Club; Wall of Fame portraits introduced

July – Record month: $1.3 billion in new business!

August – SVP "Rendezvous on the Rhine" trip; first field office computers installed

September – PennCorp signs merger with American Can

December – ALWC stock sells over the counter on NASDAQ; largest selfunderwritten stock offering in business history; four NSD promotions (Ronnie Barnes, Bob Turley, Larry Weidel Rusty Crossland)

1983 – "Big Time"

January – PennCorp merges with American Can; PennCorp extends contract with ALW to year 2000

February – 6th Anniversary

March – Saturday Evening Post runs cover story on A.L. Williams; 87,000 reprints distributed via salesforce

April – ALWC experiences first stock split (5 for 2); Hubert Humphrey becomes first agent paid $100,000 in one month

May – Roll-out of new UltimaTerm product series; first ALWC stockholders meeting

June – New record: $2.01 billion life insurance in force; MILICO opens multi-million-dollar data center; National Underwriter ranks MILICO as 64th in insurance in force, up from 103rd

July – FANS ranks first place nationally in sales of Fidelity Destiny mutual funds

August – Second company convention at Boca; Art unveils Common Sense; 16 million copies eventually sold; second ALWC stock split (5 for 4); top 80 producers tour England and Scotland

September – UltimaTerm price comparison brochure released; FANS opens discount brokerage

October – Record month: $3.7 billion in life insurance placed in force!

December – Art launches "I want Pru Bad" campaign; Treacy Beyer joins MILICO in Atlanta; four more NSD promotions (Bob Safford, Mike Tuttle, Neal Askew, Kip Ridley)

1984 – "National Champs"

    February – 7th Anniversary

    June – Art & Angela meet President Reagan in Washington, D.C.

    July – Halfway mark: Production already matches 1983 total

    October – Art introduces Pushing Up People; FANS' sales force totals 10,508 reps, produces record 154,242 sales

    November – Record month: $6 billion in new business!

    December – A.L. Williams beats Pru! Becomes #1 producer individual life insurance in industry! 1,200 couples celebrate in Boca for largest company convention to date; sales force now 80,000 licensed reps

    1984 - NSD promotions: Bill Anderton, Virginia Cartter, Bill Orender, Ed Randle, Dick Walker, Randall Walker, Doug Hartman, Mike Sharpe, Rich Thawley, Lloyd Tomer, Bill Whittle

1985 – "Momentum"

    January – 13-city international tour for second major stock offering

    February – 8th Anniversary; Common Sense commended in Congressional Record

    March – Official year-end 1984 numbers released; A.L. Williams #1 in life insurance placed in force; company celebrates again

    June – 4,000 A.L. Williams leaders enjoy reward trip to Acapulco; First Partners Open House (with 500 Partners)

    August – Top producers travel to Germany and Austria; ball at famous Hofburg palace in Vienna celebrates ALW success

    September – The A.L. Williams Way introduced at Las Vegas convention; ground-breaking ceremonies for new ALW International HQ in Duluth

    October – First wave of ALW Reps and home office personnel move to Canada to begin first ALW international expansion effort

    November – Milestone: ALW puts $100 billion new business on books (cumulative from March 1, 1980)

    December – FANS grows to 3rd largest securities sales force in industry with 14,400 registered agents

1986 – "Common Sense"

    February – 9th Anniversary; Canada sales force officially launches in Ontario

    March – Common Sense Term 20-year level product introduced; official year-end '85 numbers released: A.L. Williams #1 in life insurance placed in force for second consecutive year, beating #2 and #3 companies combined

    April – Art announces plans to form ALW-TV at press conference at the Waldorf-Astoria in New York; first broadcast airs via 500 satellites around the country

May – New York Times runs positive profile on A.L. Williams

July – Time magazine publishes positive ALW article

October – Art hosts Victory '86 rally for President Reagan in Atlanta; coincides with SVP meeting in Atlanta Civic Center

1987 – "New Era"

February – 10th Anniversary; original RVPs join Art for ALW-TV commemoration; Art makes famous "Do It" speech at Religious Broadcasters Convention in Washington, D.C.

March – #1 again! National Champions for 3rd consecutive year (1984, 1985, 1986)

April – Milestone: $200 billion life insurance in force since 1980! New Orleans convention celebrates "10 Years of Greatness"; Gerry Tsai renames American Can "Primerica"; Hubert Humphrey becomes first million-dollar earner

April – FANS introduces Common Sense Trust family of mutual funds, produces $225 million in first four months

July – Art & Boe launch 10-city "Super Seminar" tour

October – Stock market "crashes;" FANS continues upward trend

December – Canadian sales force becomes #1 producer of individual life insurance in Canada, after two years in business

1988 – "Dynasty"

January – 10-city "Super Seminar" tour begins in San Francisco

February – 11th Anniversary

March – Year-end '87 numbers show ALW #1 for the 4th consecutive year; company breaks own record by $10 billion

June – Annual convention in Boca; Art & Boe meet Sandy Weill

July – ALW posts welcomes sign for Democratic National Convention in Atlanta

August – ALW and Coca-Cola host reception at Republican National Convention in New Orleans

August – All You Can Do Is All You Can Do book hits newsstands; stays on New York Times' bestseller list 14 weeks

November – A.L. Williams Corporation (public company) becomes majority-owned by Primerica

1989 – "Dynasty"

February – 12th Anniversary; ALWC begins trading on New York Stock Exchange

March – A.L. Williams #1 5th consecutive year

April – Las Vegas "Magic is Back" convention hosts 20,000 term-ites

June – A.L. Williams-Primerica merger announced

August – ALW puts biggest month ever on books with 107,000 apps; California judge dismisses "misrepresentation" case fueled by competitors

October – Partners Open House at Atlanta Civic Center (5,000 Partners)

November – ALW Corporation and Agency merger completed, bringing entire ALW organization into Primerica family

December – New company logo introduced at Palm Springs NSD meeting; sales force numbers 225,000 licensed agents

1990 – "A Hard Good-bye"

February – 13th Anniversary

March – Milestone: $300 billion life insurance in force sincce 1980; year-end '89 numbers: $93.4 billion in new business; A.L. Williams #1 6th consecutive year

March – 40,000 ALW leaders pack New Orleans Superdome for largest ALW convention ever

May/June/July/August – Company spends $10 million on ALW Builder reward trips to San Francisco, Hawaii, Boca, Bermuda, England & Scotland

July – Art steps down as president of A.L. Williams Past to Present – "Legacy"

1990 – A.L. Williams #1 producer for 7th consecutive year – 1984, 1985, 1986, 1987, 1988, 1989, 1990

1991 – Name change to Primerica Financial Services

2000 – John Addison & Rick Williams become co-CEOs of PFS; international expansion into Spain

2003 – International expansion into England

2004 – PFS produced $91.4 billion in new business, all countries

Glossary

Terms & Abbreviations

ADS – Atlanta Data Systems

ALW – A.L. Williams; NYSE trading symbol

ALWC – A.L. Williams Corporation; NASDAQ trading symbol

ALWLIC – A.L. Williams Life Insurance Company

ALU – Association of Life Underwriters (often preceded by a state name)

App – life insurance policy application

ART – Annual Renewable Term

CIC – Continental Investment Corporation

CST – Common Sense Term (20-year level term product)

CST – Common Sense Trust (FANS family of mutual funds)

DL – District Leader

DM – Division Manager

FAI – Financial Assurance Inc.

FANC – First American National Corporation

FANS – First American National Securities

FSS – Fast Start School

FTC – Federal Trade Commission

GA – General Agent

IRA – Individual Retirement Account

ITT – International Telephone & Telegraph Company

MILICO – Massachusetts Indemnity Life Insurance Company

Mod-11 – Modified 11-year term product

Mod-15 – Modified 15-year term product

NALU – National Association of Life Underwriters

NASD – National Association of Securities Dealers

NASDAQ – National Association of Securities Dealers Automated Quotation

NHL – National Home Life

NSD – National Sales Director

NYSE – New York Stock Exchange

PFS – Primerica Financial Services (formerly A.L. Williams)

Rep – Representative (licensed agent)

RM – Regional Manager

RVP – Regional Vice President

SEC – Securities Exchange Commission

SNSD – Senior National Sales Director

SVP – Senior Vice President

W&R – Waddell & Reed

1989 Top ALW Earners*

Snapshot of Success: How the A.L. Williams Opportunity Changed Lives

Bob & Marion Buisson
Former occupation/annual income:
School teacher & coach/$6,000
Joined 1972
1989 ALW income: $2,892,000

Hubert & Norma Humphrey
Former occupation/annual income:
Railroad conductor/$18,000
Joined 1978
1989 ALW income: $2,820,000

Bob Safford
Former occupation/annual income:
Insurance executive/$155,000
Joined 1978
1989 ALW income: $2,280,000

Ronnie Barnes
Former occupation/annual income:
School teacher/$12,500
Joined 1978
1989 ALW income: $2,250,000

Bob & Carolyn Turley
Former occupation/annual income:
Professional baseball player/$150,000
Joined 1974
1989 ALW income: $2,146,000

Mike & Marna Sharpe
Former occupation/annual income:
Sales/$25,000
Joined 1980
1989 ALW income: $2,144,000

Larry & Renee Weidel
Former occupation/annual income:
Contractor/$20,000
Joined 1975
1989 ALW income: $1,866,000

Doug & Berti Hartman
Former occupation/annual income:
Business Owner/$30,000
Joined 1979
1989 ALW income: $1,758,000

Rusty Crossland
Former occupation/annual income:
School teacher & coach/$20,000
Joined 1972
1989 ALW income: $1,518,000

Mike & Stephanie Tuttle
Former occupation/annual income:
Campus Crusade for Christ/$1,000
Joined 1979
1989 ALW income: $1,484,000

Kip & Carole Ridley
Former occupation/annual income:
Computer sales/$40,000
Joined 1978
1989 ALW income: $1,188,000

Bill & Dannie Anderton
Former occupation/annual income:
Truck leasing executive/$105,000
Joined 1978
1989 ALW income: $1,148,000

Virginia Carter
Former occupation/annual income:
Insurance sales/$14,000
Joined 1972
1989 ALW income: $1,112,000

Neal & Nita Askew
Former occupation/annual income:
Police sergeant/$26,000
Joined 1980
1989 ALW income: $1,096,000

Bob & Jane Miller
Former occupation/annual income:
School teacher & coach/$14,500
Joined 1974
1989 ALW income: $1,006,000

Dennis & Patti Schechter
Former occupation/annual income:
Insurance sales/$200,000
Joined 1981
1989 ALW income: $945,000

Dick & Beth Walker
Former occupation/annual income:
Banker/$14,400
Joined 1979
1989 ALW income: $933,000

Bill & Carol Orender
Former occupation/annual income:
Salesman/$12,000
Joined 1974
1989 ALW income: $865,000

Bill & Leslie Whittle
Former occupation/annual income:
School teacher & coach/$15,000
Joined 1980
1989 ALW income: $772,000

Ed & Barbara Randle
Former occupation/annual income:
Insurance sales/$30,000
Joined 1978
1989 ALW income:: $765,000

Randall & Mary Walker
Former occupation/annual income:
Farmer/$6,300
Joined 1972
1989 ALW income: $706,000

Hector & Jann LaMarque
Former occupation/annual income:
Jewelry sales/$55,000
Joined 1984
1989 ALW income: $690,000

Ken & Kendy Parent
Former occupation/annual income:
Insulation sales/$40,000
Joined 1983
1989 ALW income: $551,000

Tim & Margaret Harper
Former occupation/annual income:
Financial services/$35,000
Joined 1979
1989 ALW income: $523,000

Greg & Sharon Fitzpatrick
Former occupation/annual income:
School teacher & coach/$12,000
Joined 1975
1989 ALW income: $423,000

Jimmy Meyer
Former occupation/annual income:
Newspaper pressman/$18,000
Joined 1984
1989 ALW income: $414,000

Myrna Lema
Former occupation/annual income:
Insurance sales/$18,000
Joined 1981
1989 ALW income: $413,000

Randy & Marcy Godfrey
Former occupation/annual income:
Manager/$30,000
Joined 1980
1989 ALW income: $391,000

John & Angela Lennon
Former occupation/annual income:
Insurance & real estate/$40,000
Joined 1980
1989 ALW income: $389,000

Bill & Cindy Olive
Former occupation/annual income:
Business owner/$52,000
Joined 1979
1989 ALW income: $385,000

Frances & Lee Avrett
Former occupation/annual income:
Greenhouse nursery/$18,000
Joined 1981
1989 ALW income: $376,000

John & Gloria Roig
Former occupation/annual income:
School teacher & coach/$15,000
Joined 1977
1989 ALW income: $369,000

Jeff & Debbie Miles
Former occupation/annual income:
Building contractor/$18,000
Joined 1980
1989 ALW income: $353,000

Richard & Carol Falcone
Former occupation/annual income:
Contractor & carpenter/$30,000
Joined 1982
1989 ALW income: $323,000

Mike & Darlene Wooten
Former occupation/annual income:
Construction/$31,000
Joined 1983
1989 ALW income: $266,000

Wallace & Gillia Murphy
Former occupation/annual income:
Respiratory therapist/$21,000
Joined 1981
1989 ALW income: $262,000

David & Terry Francis
Former occupation/annual income:
Attorney/$150,000
Joined 1986
1989 ALW income: $259,000

David & Jill Landrum
Former occupation/annual income:
Student & health spa manager/$10,000
Joined 1979
1989 ALW income: $254,000

Kevin & Judy Coelho
Former occupation/annual income:
Guidance counselor/$40,000
Joined 1987
1989 ALW income: $222,000

Cheryl Bartlett

Former occupation/annual income:

Program director for disabled children/$36,000

Joined 1983

1989 ALW income: $155,000

Brenda & Henry Sharp

Former occupation/annual income:

Senior home economist/$23,000

Joined 1982

1989 ALW income: $137,000

*All above information excerpted from the brochure, Great Things Can Happen to You, distributed at the New Orleans RVP Convention in March 1990.

Author's Note

I read mostly biographies. Books about Churchill, Reagan, Lincoln, General Patton, General Lee, Coach Bryant, Coach Lombardi – those are my favorites. I also enjoyed Seabiscuit – the saga of a little racehorse nobody thought could win… except the people who loved him and trained him. Seabiscuit did the impossible. He beat all the "fancy" horses. He earned his place in history. There's just something about a story like that I like.

Maybe because it reminds me of A.L. Williams.

It might be hard to believe, but this is a book I did not want to write. I put it off for twelve years. During that time, many of my A.L. Williams family, and my own family (especially some of my grandbabies), asked me to write the story of A.L. Williams. Finally, I agreed. It took nearly five years to produce what you now hold. The journey of reliving old memories, recalling events, putting down thoughts… Sometimes it became difficult… and emotional. But now, as I look back on this trip… well, it was worth it. I'm thrilled with how it came out.

Some very important people helped make this story possible. First of all, I want to thank God for giving me the opportunity to lead a great company like A.L. Williams. Without Him, none of it would've happened.

I want to thank the A.L. Williams people – leaders in the field, home office staff, everybody. Together, we made history.

I want to thank my wife, Angela, our two children, Art and April, their spouses, and the grandbabies. Through every hill and valley, you've all loved me, just as I am. Not a simple thing to do. You all mean the world to me.

I want to thank Bob Miller for his involvement and total support of this project. Bob, you are a true friend. You saw it through to the end.

And finally, I want to thank Karen Hutto. There's not another writer in the world I would've wanted to write this book. From Day One, I knew she loved A.L. Williams. I knew she loved the story… and I knew she had the heart to capture it. Karen, I love the work you did. I'm so proud of you.

The A.L. Williams story now rests on paper. For my family. For A.L. Williams. For generations to come. I'm so thankful. My prayer is that this story will inspire you, the reader, to find your cause, your crusade. And when you do, I hope you'll face down the impossible odds and just go "do it."

Coach

Made in the USA
Middletown, DE
07 December 2019